COUNSELOR

BOOKS BY THEODORE C. SORENSEN

Why I Am a Democrat (1996)

"Let the Word Go Forth" (editor; 1988)

A Widening Atlantic? Domestic Change and
Foreign Policy (coauthor; 1986)

A Different Kind of Presidency: A Proposal for
Breaking the Political Deadlock (1984)

Watchmen in the Night:
Presidential Accountability After Watergate (1975)

The Kennedy Legacy (1969)

Kennedy (1965)

Decision-Making in the White House (1963)

COUNSELOR

A Life at the Edge of History

Ted Sorensen

HARPER LUXE

An Imprint of HarperCollinsPublishers

FOR MY GRANDCHILDREN

Rory, Hannah, Olaf, Lincoln, Trey, Sophia —
so they can know what Grandpa Ted
tried to do for their world.

————————

FIRST HARPERLUXE EDITION

HarperLuxe™ is a trademark of HarperCollins Publishers

Library of Congress Cataloging-in-Publication Data is available upon request.

ISBN: 978-0-06-156274-7

08 09 10 11 12 ID/RRD 10 9 8 7 6 5 4 3 2

SAY NOT THE STRUGGLE NAUGHT AVAILETH

Say not the struggle naught availeth,
The labour and the wounds are vain,
The enemy faints not, nor faileth,
And as things have been, things remain;

For while the tired waves, vainly breaking
Seem here no painful inch to gain,
Far back, through creeks and inlets making,
Comes silent, flooding in, the main.

And not by eastern windows only,
When daylight comes, comes in the light,
In front the sun climbs slow, how slowly,
But westward, look, the land is bright.

—ARTHUR HUGH CLOUGH (1819–1861)

[Written in 1849, from *The Poems and Prose Remains of Arthur Hugh Clough* (1869)]

Contents

Author's Note

Special thanks to Adam Frankel, a graduate of Princeton University and the London School of Economics, who served as my chief assistant and close collaborator—almost literally as my eyes—on this book for more than six years. His loyalty and dedication made the book possible—and his outstanding research, organizational, and editing skills strengthened it in innumerable ways.

As his friend and admirer, I am confident that Adam's many talents will take him far.

TED SORENSEN

Preface

I wrote this book for three reasons.

First, when I wrote *Kennedy,* my 1965 memoir on my eleven years with John F. Kennedy, the pain of his assassination in Dallas still seared my mind; Lyndon Johnson was still president; Robert F. Kennedy was still in politics; Jacqueline Kennedy was still in mourning; and I did not want to offend any of them. The passage of time has made a broader, more candid perspective possible.

Second, a historian recently told me that the history community knows a great deal about Kennedy's impact on our nation and world, and something about the impact of my ideas and ideals on Kennedy, but little or nothing about where my ideas and ideals originated. He added: "You have an obligation to history to tell us." It reminded me of the 1962 magazine headline: "Ted Sorensen: Administration Mystery Man." Perhaps this book can help clear up any remaining mystery. No doubt my story will be weighed in time with many other bits and pieces of information—that is what history is all about.

Third, disillusioned American citizens today are filled with cynicism and mistrust about presidential politics; most young people today assume that all modern presidents have deceived or disappointed the American people. Perhaps it is worth reminding them that it is *possible* to have a president who is honest, idealistic, and devoted to the best values of this country. It happened at least once—I was there. In fact, the sorry spectacle of today's national political leadership, so deplorably different from that of JFK, spurred me on while writing this book, rekindling my memory and reinvigorating my conscience.

Yet, as I wrote, I increasingly recognized several major obstacles: (1) the hazards of memory, inevitably influenced by selectivity and hindsight (I was too busy and discreet in both my Senate and White House days to keep a diary); (2) the habit of modesty (this book has required more use of the first-person pronoun than I have ever been comfortable with, but I remember the wisdom of that quintessential American philosopher, baseball great Jerome "Dizzy" Dean: "If you done it, it ain't braggin'"); (3) the obligations of loyalty, which for me outweigh all pressures to cast prudence, privacy, discretion, and the secrets of others aside; and, finally, (4) the limits, both of time and space, requiring me to avoid redundancy and the temptation to meander into every detour and byway. I did not feel footnotes were necessary or appropriate, particularly since the book is intended for lay readers of all ages and not merely for scholars.

After my stroke in 2001, I expressed doubt that, with my eyesight and energy diminished, I would be able to undertake this book. A friend—and gifted writer—advised me: "Just tell stories." I have always liked telling stories, and have lots of stories to tell. Historian David McCullough has worried that "we are losing the national memory of America's story, forgetting who we are and what it's taken to come this far." This book is simply and primarily a collection of one man's memories. It may not fully satisfy either serious historians or sensation seekers. But I hope it will help recall not just my own story, but an inspiring chapter in America's story.

TED SORENSEN
NEW YORK CITY, 2007

Prologue

One morning in the late 1980s, as the cold war ground to a halt, a distinguished Russian lawyer and former Soviet official, Feodor Burlatski, upon entering my New York City law office, remarked: "You and I have corresponded." He being a total stranger, I expressed doubt. But he persisted: "Didn't you help draft Kennedy's letters to Khrushchev during the Cuban missile crisis?" I smiled. "Well," he continued, "I helped draft Khrushchev's letters to Kennedy." Probably an exaggeration on his part; many others on Khrushchev's staff likely had primary responsibility.

But, in fact, no moment in my life has ever placed more pressure upon me, or ultimately given me greater satisfaction, than the moment late in the afternoon of Saturday, October 27, 1962, when the President of the United States, John F. Kennedy, asked me to draft, with guidance from his brother, Attorney General Robert F.

Kennedy, a letter for the president's signature to Soviet Council of Ministers Chairman Nikita Khrushchev.

It was the most fateful message I would ever draft. I was thirty-four years old.

October 27 was the twelfth day of what historians have called "the most dangerous thirteen days in the history of mankind," the time of the first (and technically only) hostile confrontation between two nuclear superpowers, each possessing the capacity, if not the intent, to incinerate the other—and as a by-product the entire Earth; a crisis precipitated by Khrushchev's swift and reckless decision to emplace in Cuba, ninety miles from our shores, under cloak of deception, a chain of nine bases for more than thirty medium- and intermediate-range nuclear missiles capable of reaching, striking, and destroying tens, even hundreds, of millions of people in the United States and Western Hemisphere.

The president—only forty-five years old—had dispatched his thirty-six-year-old attorney general and me to prepare this letter at the end of an intense debate among his principal advisors, who constituted the Executive Committee of the National Security Council or "ExComm," which, while RFK and I sat in my office drafting, was still assembled in the Cabinet Room down the hall, meeting with the president and awaiting our handiwork. Earlier that afternoon, RFK and I had joined

Llewellyn Thompson, our country's foremost Soviet expert and a former U.S. ambassador to Moscow who knew Khrushchev, in urging ExComm and the president to send one letter responding not to each of the two letters received from Khrushchev in the previous twenty-four hours, but only to his first, received on the evening of Friday, October 26. That letter had seemed to convey in part a hopeful tone and, even if obscured, at least the seeds of a potential formula for disengagement. We urged the president to ignore the second letter, which had arrived that same Saturday, October 27, conveying a much stiffer tone, including a demand that the United States on its own (knowing full well that we could not quickly do so) undertake the immediate removal of NATO nuclear missiles situated in Turkey on Soviet borders, in exchange for removal by Khrushchev of his missiles from Cuba. A quarter century later, Kennedy's secretary of state, Dean Rusk, wrote me a letter stating that Thompson "was the one who originally came up with the idea of ignoring the second message from Khrushchev . . . and responding to the first message—a point which had been discussed with Bobby Kennedy before the meeting in which Bobby Kennedy made that suggestion."

With the help of taped transcripts, I recall that our discussion that Saturday afternoon ended roughly as follows:

Me: "It may be possible to take elements of his first letter as part of ours."

RFK: "I think we just say: You made an offer, we accept the offer."

Me: "If we could take our letter and introduce some of the elements of his letter . . . that might do it."

RFK: "Why do we bother you with it, Mr. President? Why don't you let us work this out?"

JFK: "I think we ought to move. There's no question of bothering me. I just think we're going to have to decide which letter we send."

RFK: "Why don't we try to work it out for you without you being there to pick it apart?" [Laughter]

Me: "Actually, I think Bobby's formula is a good one. It doesn't sound like an ultimatum if we say: 'we are accepting your offer of your letter last night, and therefore there's no need to talk about these other things' [meaning the NATO missiles in Turkey]."

General Maxwell Taylor: "The Joint Chiefs' recommendation is that the big [U.S.] air strike . . . be executed no later than Monday morning . . . to be followed by invasion seven days later."

RFK: "Well, that was a surprise."

JFK: "That's the next place to go, but let's get this letter to Khrushchev . . ."

The president gave that assignment to RFK and me, urging speed and consultation with UN Ambassador Adlai Stevenson in New York, and noting his intention to woo world opinion by making our letter public, provided it was not too bellicose. RFK and I then left the Cabinet Room to begin drafting in my office down the hall.

I felt the weight of the world on my shoulders. If our response letter failed to satisfy Khrushchev, or for some reason served only to antagonize him, then his next step was wholly unpredictable, and almost certainly unimaginable. Equally unpredictable was whether President Kennedy would be able to restrain the U.S. military and the more hawkish members of the ExComm, who felt that only a bombing assault on Cuba and the Soviet missile sites, followed by an invasion "to take Cuba away from Castro," as they put it, could assure the destruction of all the Soviet missiles and protect America's long-range security interests and survival.

Although I had no diplomatic training and little international experience, I anxiously undertook my grave letter-drafting task, with no instruction from the president on what to write, but secure in the knowledge that I had the personal confidence of the president whom I had then served for almost ten years, as well his mandate to find a peaceful solution to this ghastly crisis. If the letter I was drafting under Bobby's vigilant gaze was deemed harsh or insulting by Khrushchev, then we could expect a worst-case scenario. The grim intelligence summary delivered by the CIA at the commencement of that day's ExComm meeting reported that work on the Soviet missile sites in Cuba had been completed, that the nuclear warheads for the missiles were presumably stored somewhere nearby on the island waiting to be loaded, and that the missiles were now ready to be fired. If, on the other hand, our letter struck the rest of the Western alliance and the world as too weak, meek, or submissive, I knew it was doubtful that even our strongest allies would long continue to have much confidence in America's willingness to take military risks for the survival of freedom in Europe. Our precious alliances, essential to our collective security, depended upon those other countries continuing to hold that confidence in us.

By this time, two drafts of a proposed U.S. response had been prepared by the Department of State and the U.S. Mission to the United Nations for circulation within ExComm; but, after long debate, neither had been approved. The frustrated ExComm's inability to decide how and to which Khrushchev letter we should respond was understandable. Whether Khrushchev's intent in swiftly sneaking missiles of that power and range into Cuba was nuclear war or nuclear blackmail, we could not know; but we did know that nothing we had tried had yet succeeded in persuading him to remove them— not pressure from UN Secretary-General U Thant or world opinion, not our military blockade of Cuba or warnings. There was no reason to believe that another letter from JFK would help, and every reason to believe that we were on the brink of nuclear war.

As I worked on the draft, I could hear a divided crowd of protesters continuing to shout in Lafayette Park, across Pennsylvania Avenue from the White House, one group of peace lovers carrying signs warning the president not to precipitate mankind's final war, the others angry patriots urging the president to lead the Western alliance's military forces against this imminent Communist threat. That afternoon I would have thought crazy anyone who told me that within a few decades I would not only make repeated business trips to Moscow, but would also meet in reflective eye-opening "reunions" in the United States, Russia, and Cuba with other former officials from all three governments—including my Russian friend Burlatski—who had personally participated in this historically unique crisis.

Undoubtedly weighing on the president, as he considered his choices, and not forgotten by either his brother or me, was the painful memory of his earlier Cuban crisis at the very start of his term, April 1961, at Cuba's Bay of Pigs. There he tarnished both America's reputation and his own by approving the misbegotten and defeated invasion by Cuban exile forces secretly trained by the CIA. Robert Kennedy and I, who were not among the advisors on that fiasco, had been asked by the president to participate thereafter in National Security Council meetings. Both of us were determined that he achieve a more successful result in Cuba this time. A failed outcome at the Bay of Pigs had meant a political black eye for the president; but failure on that October afternoon eighteen months later could have far graver consequences.

In the words of the old spiritual, on that Saturday Kennedy and Khrushchev literally "held the whole world in their hands."

This was not the first letter I had drafted to Khrushchev. For nearly a year before the Cuban missile crisis, I had helped draft JFK's private back-channel letters to the Soviet chairman, who had initiated a secret personal correspondence after a friendly Thanksgiving visit by his journalist son-in-law to the Kennedys at Hyannis Port in 1961. When the first letter arrived—delivered to RFK through a Washington KGB operative, Georgi Bolshakov—the U.S. State Department, nervous about being intentionally bypassed along with the Soviet Ministry of Foreign Affairs, was deeply worried by the letter's personal, irregular tone. "Mr. President," said Undersecretary of State George Ball, normally calm and sagacious, in a hastily convened White House session: "Your decision as to who drafts your reply [i.e., the Department of State or the White House] may be the single most important decision you will make as President!" "Oh," said JFK, with a smile and nod to me, "we get one of those over here every week."

Under the president's supervision, I helped draft that first reply and many others. I also served, one Saturday morning, when neither RFK nor press secretary Pierre Salinger was available, as the designated courier, melodramatically meeting Bolshakov for a prearranged chat on a Washington street corner, during which he surreptitiously slipped to me from under his arm his copy of that day's *Washington Post*, within which was concealed a sealed envelope from the Soviet chairman.

When the attorney general and I sat down to draft the president's reply to Khrushchev, we studied his letter of the previous day and reflected upon the earlier

ExComm discussion. Khrushchev's letter bristled with warnings, threats ("you will be subject to every bit of such destruction as you inflict upon others") and repeated denials that he had placed any offensive weapons in Cuba; but it also contained genuine calls for a peaceful solution and some vague hints of what that solution might encompass—hints so vague that Defense Secretary Robert McNamara had remarked:

> Hell, that's no offer! There's not a damn thing in it that's an offer. . . . He didn't propose to take the missiles out. . . . 12 pages of fluff. That's no contract. You couldn't sign that and say we know what we signed.

My approach to drafting a response was borrowed from an old Lincoln High School debate class technique of taking the other side's presentation and interpreting it as supporting your own objectives. My draft letter called for a "permanent" solution (his did not) "along the lines suggested in your letter . . . *as I read it* . . . The key elements seem generally acceptable *as I understand them*. . . ." Those weasel words were partly a bluff, as I carefully tried to be positive.

In essence, Khrushchev was willing to "assure" the United States that no Soviet ships were *then* carrying or would carry any offensive weapons into Cuba while UN-sponsored negotiations were being conducted, thereby enabling, he argued, the United States not only to halt its blockade ("high seas piracy") but also to pledge that we would never invade Cuba, and would restrain others from doing so. Only then would there no longer be any need for Soviet nuclear missiles to remain in Cuba. He never said explicitly that the Soviets would take out of Cuba those weapons that were already there, only that "the question of the armaments would disappear" *after* such a no-invasion pledge had been made by the United States.

In my much shorter response, we described his letter as "offering" a Soviet withdrawal from Cuba of all Soviet weapons "capable of offensive use." That wording not only included the IL–28 bombers we had discovered in addition to the missiles, but also circumvented his clever semantic ploy of insisting that the weapons he had placed in Cuba, whatever their ominous capability, were "intended" by him for "defensive" use and therefore were not "offensive." My letter also described this "offer" of Soviet withdrawal as being made in exchange for a *subsequent* U.S. withdrawal of the blockade and pledge not to invade Cuba. It ignored his "assurance" that the ships then steaming toward Cuba did not carry weapons, and his assurance that the issue of the "specialists" in Cuba would "look different" to him after our pledge not to invade. Instead, we made clear that the weapons already in Cuba had to be "dismantled" (RFK's suggested wording), crated, and returned home to the USSR *under UN inspection* (which his letter had not mentioned) or other public verification, accompanied by a new pledge from him that no such offensive weapons would *ever be reintroduced into Cuba.* (His letter had not contained that either.) The necessary U.S. actions and pledges were, under our draft, to be undertaken only *after* "the establishment of adequate U.N. arrangements" to assure the immediate and permanent implementation of the Soviet pledges. In subtly switching the time sequences envisioned by his letter, I was trying to emphasize that, in the last analysis, the net result was the same in both his letter and our response.

Our letter made no specific reference to his second letter's demand regarding Turkish bases, stating instead that the Cuban crisis was the greatest danger and priority, and that the early settlement of that crisis, along the lines envisioned, "easing world tensions, would enable us to look at any general arrangements regarding other armaments as requested in your second letter."

In short, while calling for peace and praising his call for the same, we in fact conceded nothing of substance. We were willing to lift our temporary blockade, which had been initially established only because of the Soviet missiles that would now be withdrawn. After their withdrawal, we would pledge not to invade Cuba—an invasion that the United States (or at the very least its president) had no intention of launching. The additional oral assurance secretly conveyed that evening by RFK in his session with Soviet ambassador Anatoly Dobrynin, to remove subsequently the missiles in Turkey, simply gave us time to work with NATO and the Turks in replacing that particular deterrent—antiquated, first-generation, unreliable, and provocatively visible weapons on the Soviet border—with far more powerful, reliable, and concealed Polaris nuclear submarines under the Mediterranean.

It was a giant gamble on our part. Khrushchev had recklessly gambled that he could secretly rush nuclear missiles into Cuba without Kennedy noticing or responding. He lost. We gambled that we could brazenly induce Khrushchev to accept our position as consistent with his proposal for a settlement. We succeeded. But one of the reasons for our success—the fact that we "accepted" Khrushchev's proposed exchange of moves, in a form and sequence that he never proposed—has not previously been disclosed.

On Sunday, October 28, the world stepped back from the very brink of destruction, and has never come that close again. I am proud that my letter helped contribute to that conclusion. But it was utter madness that the world ever came that close to annihilation. That morning, after he returned from Mass, the president and I stood talking in his secretary's office outside the Cabinet Room where the ExComm had excitedly assembled for its presumably final meeting. As we talked, one of his ablest, most trusted aides, Carl Kaysen, walked up and interjected: "Now, Mr. President, you can settle the India-China border dispute," which had broken out a week earlier in what we had feared might be part of a coordinated global crisis. "No," said the president, smiling, "I don't think either one of them will want to hear from me on that." "But, Mr. President," protested Carl, "today you're more than ten feet tall!" "Oh," said the president, "that will last about a couple of weeks."

In July 2007 *Time* magazine called John F. Kennedy a "timeless icon" whom "national polls over the past 20 years have consistently placed in the top three of greatest American presidents . . . a prudent warrior for peace, a man who despised war and sought above all to avoid nuclear conflict, a wily pragmatist . . . Kennedy's example will help you better understand not only his world but our own."

PART I
Lincoln, Nebraska, 1928–1951

Chapter 1

Roots

I was born in Lincoln, Nebraska, on the morning of May 8, 1928, Harry Truman's forty-fourth birthday. Harry took no notice of my arrival, being a busy county judge in Missouri at the time. More than twenty years later, I would make my way to Washington, D.C., where my first employer was the federal government over which he presided.

I was born in a Catholic hospital, where my Jewish mother, Annis Chaikin Sorensen, valued the loving care of the nuns on the hospital staff. My father, Christian A. Sorensen ("C.A."), an insurgent Republican making his first run for public office that year, wrote to the head of America's "Hoover Booster Clubs": "Our family was increased this morning by another son. I am going to have a Republican club of my own." A journalist friend, referring to my birth as well as my father's campaign, wrote him from Ohio: "That, properly press-agented, ought to be good for a few thousand extra votes."

There was no christening or baptism rite in the Unitarian Church which my parents attended. I was named at birth Theodore Chaikin Sorensen. Theodore Roosevelt, decades earlier, had led the progressive wing of the Republican Party to which my father belonged. When I was three years old I received a letter from Theodore Roosevelt Jr., the result of a chance encounter between him and my father; it noted that he and I had both been named for the same great man. "From the commotion that the letter caused in the Sorensen household," C.A. wrote back, "[little Ted] knew that something unusual had happened which some way or other involved him."

My mother, a pacifist who did not approve of Teddy Roosevelt's resort to military means for semi-imperialist objectives, always insisted that I was named not for the hero of San Juan Hill, but for the Greek words meaning "gift from God." An early feminist, she also insisted that her children receive her maiden name in addition to our father's last name—and the five of us were Chaikin Sorensen ever since; two names sufficiently unusual that we all became accustomed to misspellings. Books, newspapers, and magazines continue to do so; the *New York Times* has misspelled my name more than a hundred times in headlines and articles over the past fifty years. My mother's successor as editor of the *University Journal*, noting upon her departure that "Annis Chaiken resigned to become Mrs. C. A. Sorenson," misspelled both her maiden and her married name in the same sentence.

Throughout my life, I have reflected on my good luck; but never was I more fortunate than on the day of my birth. Among the hundreds of thousands of babies born that day, I won what my fellow Nebraskan Warren Buffett has called the "great genetic lottery." My friend Khododad Farmanfarmaian was born that same day on the opposite side of the world, in Persia. He was ultimately forced to flee for his life from his native country, hidden in a Kurdish hay wagon. I was born into a country protected by the rule of law.

I was raised by parents who were healthy, intelligent, college educated—and determined to see their children be the same. I was also fortunate to have been born in Nebraska. The city of Lincoln in my youth was small, lovely, and quaint; full of parks, stone churches, low buildings, small shops, and shaded streets. Although I heard rumors in grade school from older boys about an establishment called "Ma Kelly's," Lincoln was a wholesome place in which to grow up, the kind of small-town environment now seemingly gone forever. It was a city "in the middle of everywhere," as one Nebraska roadside sign proclaims. That message was confirmed for me as a small boy on a drive through central Nebraska with my parents, when we came upon a sign with two arrows, one pointing east, reading "New York World's Fair, 1,454 miles," and the other pointing west, reading "San Francisco World's Fair, 1,454 miles."

Even after I moved to Washington, D.C., and thereafter traveled the world over, from Fujairah to Bujumbura, from Skopje to Singapore, I always cherished the city of my birth—the safe, peaceful, predictable environment that nurtured my childhood and laid the foundation of my life and career. Of all the cities in which I have lived—Lincoln, Washington, Boston, and New York—the air, water, and politics were always cleaner in Lincoln.

I have occasionally wondered: Can a political career be affected by the name of one's hometown? Hope? Independence? What I do know is that growing up in a city named for Abraham Lincoln, whose stately statue stood by the state capitol in front of a wall on which his Gettysburg Address was inscribed, intensified my interest in the man, his life, and his speeches—speeches I have been quoting ever since.

Nebraska remains in my heart the wonderful home that shaped so much of my youthful outlook. In those halcyon days, Nebraskans spoke plainly, dressed plainly, and opposed elites and sophisticates of any kind. They were mostly middle class with middle-of-the-road views, isolationists increasingly interested in stable overseas markets for Nebraska crops, churchgoers who supported traditional church-state separation (except for school prayer), community-minded pragmatists and businessmen who were skeptical of the far right as well as the far left, and opposed to big spending by politicians. They did not like politicians of either party who showed too little concern about truly big issues but hypocritically expressed too much concern over trivial issues.

Yet Nebraska produced a host of political leaders with the courage to challenge conventional thinking— from the fiery political iconoclast and religious conservative William Jennings Bryan, to the civil rights leader Malcolm X, to Herbert Brownell and J. Lee Rankin of the Eisenhower Justice Department, who helped put courageous pro–civil rights judges on federal courts in the South.

But the best known Nebraskan of all was not in politics—the late Johnny Carson. Johnny and I attended the University of Nebraska in the 1940s, where he was known campus-wide for his magic and ventriloquism acts. My brother Tom thought Johnny the brightest prospect in the Beginning Journalism class Tom taught. As graduation neared, Tom suggested that Johnny come work for him at the local radio station where Tom was news director. "Gee thanks, Mr. Sorensen," Johnny replied, "but I thought I would try Hollywood." "Hollywood?" Tom retorted in disbelief. "I'm talking about $55 a week!"

Nebraska has always been a proud state. Nebraskans have long resented those Easterners who, unaware of its charms, dismiss Nebraska as a boring "fly-over state." After I moved East, I soon wearied of hearing what a long, flat, unchanging drive it was from its eastern to western borders. That's all right; Easterners will learn.

As a Danish Russian Jewish Unitarian, I am surely a member of the smallest minority among the many small minorities that made this country great. My paternal grandfather, Jens Christian Sorensen, was born in Nykobing, Denmark, in 1866 to Mette Marie and Soren Pedersen, who was also unofficially known as Soren Post, apparently because he supplemented his North Sea fishing and farming income by some kind of postal work. Soren's ancestry could be traced, through church and other records, to my great-great-great-great-grandfather Peder Christensen, who in 1683 married Anne Sorensdatter and went to live on a farm in Byergby on Mors Island, a small by-product of the Ice Age in the middle of a sizable lake in the Jutland sector that occupies most of western Denmark.

The several generations that followed, all on Mors Island, were farmers and fishermen, including Nielsens, Knudsens, Christensens, Larsens, and Pedersens, with an occasional teacher, parish clerk, church singer, and schoolmaster. For generations, it was a highly religious family. One ancestor on my grandmother's side went to northwest China as a missionary of the Scandinavian Alliance. One of my grandfather's grandfathers may have lived for a time in Schleswig-Holstein, which for years was claimed by both Denmark and Germany. He reportedly fought in the German army against the French, and, after his capture and return, married the daughter of a local German baron before returning to Mors, the only hint of royalty in my lineage. The only hint of scandal was the rumor that Great-Grandfather might have been a love child sired when his father was in His Majesty's military service in German territory.

When grandfather Jens Christian was fourteen, he and four younger siblings accompanied my great-grandparents to America, sailing on the S.S. *Habsburg* from Bremen, and docking in New York harbor on May 28, 1880. They were among eight hundred passengers crowded into steerage. By the time he set sail with his family from Mors Island in 1880, Jens Christian, although the fifth born, was the oldest of Mette's five surviving children, his four older siblings having died young from smallpox, diphtheria, scarlet fever, and tuberculosis.

After arriving in the United States, they made their way to Nebraska. Reportedly Jens's father was attracted by the inexpensive land being distributed by the Union Pacific Railroad to encourage settlement, and thus customers, in the under-populated new state. Several years later, young Jens moved to Cheyenne, Wyoming, to work as a section hand on the Union Pacific, then as a construction worker on the state capitol, then as a hospital orderly, along the way anglicizing his name to James. In 1889 he married a fellow immigrant from Jutland, Ane Madsen, the young cook and seamstress at his boarding-house, who had come to the United States with her step-father and two siblings one year earlier at age nineteen. Ane was the grandmother I knew, loved, and often visited when I was very small. Her own great-grandfather, it was said, had an ear for music and a love for poetry.

When Soren brought his wife and children to America in 1880, it was the first departure of my ancestors from Mors after nearly two hundred years. Early in our association, Senator John F. Kennedy sent me a letter from Scandinavia, noting the beauty of the land and expressing puzzlement as to "why any Scandinavians emigrated."

When my daughter, Juliet, and I visited Mors in 2003, I tried to guess the reason for Soren's departure. The people were friendly. In Soren's day they were not subjected to religious or political suppression, and they tilled a fertile soil. But Soren apparently had the Viking spirit of adventure to try a new world where he had heard that productive land was plentiful and available without the headaches of absentee landlords. He wanted more room in which his children could grow, and he had a zest in his blood for new opportunity.

Juliet and I were welcomed and feted by the colorful mayor and hospitable inhabitants of Mors, and we were served, as a special treat, the island's traditional delicacy, fried eels. Then I realized why Soren had left. My hosts only smiled when I hailed their special treat as "different!" Jutlanders are famous for understatement, which I try to explain to my friends when I respond to their funniest jokes with "not bad."

After their marriage, my grandparents moved back to Nebraska in 1889 to find farmland in the north-central part of the state, under President Abraham Lincoln's

Homestead Act of 1862. Grandfather Jens went back to work for the Union Pacific Railroad to earn a living, while Grandmother stayed on the homestead to fulfill the residency requirements. Grandmother, who came from an educated family, helped teach neighbor women to read and write, while Jens attended a nearby school to complete his own education. When it was too dark to continue work in the fields, the neighbors banded together for conversation and reading by the light of a kerosene lamp. Family members and neighbors took turns reading biblical verses and discussing their meaning.

Jens and Ane first lived in a dugout, which was little more than a cave cut into the south side of a hill, with logs, branches, bushes, straw, and sometimes tar paper or odd shingles for a combination roof and outside wall. Winter on the Nebraska prairie was tough, even for Scandinavians accustomed to the cold. As soon as possible, the dugout was replaced by a sod house built of stacked layers of uniformly cut turf, sometimes called prairie bricks or Nebraska marble, which had been baked in the intense summer heat and frozen in the bitter winter cold. There is some uncertainty, not unlike that surrounding those politicians of the nineteenth century who claimed to have been, but may not have been, born in log cabins, as to whether my father, Christian Sorensen, was born the following year in the dugout or the sod house, the latter having a more politically en-nobling ring.

Either way, it was a barren and rugged existence. There was no electricity, and drinking water had to be carried in buckets from the well to the home. The area had little or no medical care; three of Ane's babies were stillborn, buried beside a border of iris not far from their dwelling. Ten children survived, of whom my father was the oldest. The crops, on which my grandparents depended to eke out a living from the land, could be wiped out by drought, flood, hail, and blizzard, as well as by legions of grasshoppers and sky-blackening dust storms. Even growing up in Lincoln almost half a century later, I experienced the phenomenon of grasshoppers descending en masse on our lawn and dust storms darkening the sky, covering lawns and homes, seeping into the cracks of windows and cupboards. Woody Guthrie, the prairie troubadour, wrote a ballad about one particularly severe dust storm in April 1935, shortly before my seventh birthday: "It fell across our city like a curtain of black rolled down, we thought it was our judgement, we thought it was our doom . . ."

Half a century earlier, Grandfather Jens survived it all to become the proud possessor of an official Notice of Grant of Land, signed by the president of the United States, Grover Cleveland. In time the federal government under President Franklin D. Roosevelt provided a rural electrification program for America's farmers, revolutionizing their lives, bringing them electrified water pumps, lights, washing machines, radios, later television and a host of other appliances. In Nebraska, that revolution was sparked by my father (and, in Texas, by Lyndon Johnson).

The courageous families who settled Nebraska were poor immigrant farmers who braved the hazardous crossings of first the Atlantic and then half the country to reach the loneliness of the prairie, a fertile but desolate land. Those strong and determined enough to leave home and family, and endure the unknown, were a bold, hardy group.

Two years after Soren brought Jens to America, my mother's father, a scholarly Russian Jew named Pincus Chafkin, set out with his wife, Sterne (later Stella) Smehoff, from the town of Chernigov in the Ukraine, then Russia (and part of the Pale), where they had been born, raised, and married. He was thirty-eight years old; she was eight years younger. Surrounded by orchards, considered the heart of old Ukraine, Chernigov, "the Princely City," was, on the surface, not an unpleasant place to live. But, in the late nineteenth century, throughout the Russian Empire, the Jewish population was terrorized by brutal pogroms, some fueled by the czar himself, resulting in the immigration of more than one million Jews to the United States between 1870 and 1900. Pincus and Stella were among them.

Somehow they made their way by train to Liverpool, where they set sail on the S.S. *Italy* for America, arriving in New York on July 10, 1882. In those pre–Ellis Island days, they were processed through Castle Garden, a fort off the southernmost tip of Manhattan. It had been a difficult and unpleasant voyage in steerage, where a ticket cost roughly $25 per person. Before boarding they were required to take an antiseptic bath, to have their few bags fumigated, and to be examined by steamship company doctors. The trip by sea required well over a month of rough water, too rough for most passengers to stand on deck, but the deck was still preferable to the reported prevalence of stench, lice, fistfights, gambling, and theft in steerage.

On board the S.S. *Italy* with the Chafkins were Germans, Irish, English, Swedes, and Russians, the largest ethnic group—probably most of them fellow Jews. Few of these Russian Jewish émigrés went to Nebraska. But Stella and Pincus, who had listed himself on the ship's manifest as a laborer and his only language as Jewish—almost surely Yiddish—followed the path of friends and wound up in Omaha. There the scholarly, if impractical, Pincus Chafkin, later anglicized as Peter Chaikin, may have owned and operated, but more likely supervised, a secondhand store. He, Stella, and their son, and two younger daughters (the younger of whom would become my mother) lived above the store, in a poor home in a poor neighborhood. A tragic roll of seven siblings died young. My mother once told us she had only two dresses as a girl, one on her back and the other in the wash, and that her sister had married at fifteen to "get away."

By the time of the 1900 census, eighteen years after Pincus and Stella arrived at Castle Garden, both parents and all three children were reported able to read and write English. But it is not clear to me that Pincus was home in 1900 to answer the census taker's questions. Apparently more scholar than laborer, he had reportedly decided to leave behind his impoverished family in Omaha and take a trip around the world. His hope, he alleged, was to visit his two equally adventurous brothers, who had somehow traveled many years earlier from Chernigov seeking their fortunes in Madagascar and India. This whole tale sounded most unlikely to me until friends uncovered records in India of a "Vladimir Hafkin," described as a "European Jew from the Ukraine" who had arrived in Calcutta in 1860, and was heroically involved in helping to combat the plague in that city in 1893, performing the same service for Bombay in 1896. Later, the Plague Treatment Center in Bombay was named the Hafkin Institute. Imagine, my Jewish great-uncle was an early Mother Teresa! But Stella was not impressed by her husband's travel adventures; when he returned to Omaha years later, he found that she had obtained Nebraska's first Jewish religious divorce (a get).

My own travel adventures took me to Chernigov in 1967 with my three young sons—Eric, Steve, and Phil. We found no relatives, but were generously hosted by the local Communist officials. Unfortunately, my memory of that visit is somewhat dimmed by the fact that they not only hosted us but repeatedly toasted my mother, each of my boys, relations between our two countries, and every other dignitary or subject worthy of toasting. I had assumed this was the oft-rumored Communist trick of getting visiting Americans too intoxicated to think clearly, leading them into compromising and well-photographed situations; but no. I soon found that my hosts were even more inebriated than I. That was the one and only experience with alcoholic intoxication in my sheltered life. But it was the least I could do in memory of Pincus and Stella.

Chapter 2

Mother

In 1905 Annis Chaikin left Omaha, where she had been born and raised, to work her way through the University of Nebraska in Lincoln as a maid—a practice not uncommon in those days when few scholarships were available to women. Her employer, the activist dean of women, Edna MacDowell Barkley, became a mentor, whom my mother would honor more than three decades later with a "Peace Mural" on campus.

She no doubt felt a thrill when she arrived at the university that fall, not yet seventeen, having passed entrance exams that were said to be as demanding as those of Yale and Harvard—a point of pride to Nebraskans, as was the university itself. It all must have looked to young Annis Chaikin much as the author Willa Cather had described it about a dozen years earlier:

. . . everything looked big. The University was big. The seniors were big. The professors were big. . . . [But] the young scholars had a kind of fire, a really burning ambition and devotion . . . to do for their state and community the work of several generations in one short lifetime.

In 1908, not yet twenty, Annis received her undergraduate degree in classics, with honors in Greek and Latin, and went on to earn a master's degree in both subjects the following year. Many years later, in an editorial she wrote for the *University Journal*, she described a college coed—without acknowledging that it might be autobiographical—"the girl who has courage enough to exchange her home and friendly circle . . . for the uncertainty of earning her way through the University by doing housework in some citified family . . . and will in turn go forth with better and higher values of life than had she never ventured from home."

Seeking both a job and still more education—and equipped with a graduate degree of little interest to Nebraska's public schools—Annis applied either to teach or to study at one of the great universities of the East, but failed, possibly because of her gender or religion. Undeterred, she decided that social work—open to women, and consistent with her idealism—was the right avenue for her, and promptly enrolled in a social service course at the New York School of Social Work, in a city where she knew no one.

Though wholly new to New York, she soon began work in 1911 for the Ladies Committee of the New York Jewish Protectory and Aid Society, later called the Jewish Board of Guardians. The judges of the New York Children's Court had urged the society to provide some assistance for the increasing number of delinquent Jewish girls appearing in that court. Miss Chaikin was hired as a probation officer and liaison with the court, overseeing the girls, many from low-income immigrant families not so different from her own. Soon her role was formalized as the first executive director of the Jewish Big Sisters Society. Many years later she would tell me with amusement of the very proper and prominent Ladies Committee member who, upon being informed that one particular girl needed special attention because she had been an "inmate" in what was then euphemistically known as a "disorderly house," asked Annis why there was any urgent need for intervention in the case, adding that many women, including herself, "were not good housekeepers."

Annie, as she became known in New York, was, according to one report, "always ready to tell everyone she went to school out in Nebraska." One coworker wrote to her: "You had such fresh stimulating views . . . typically western in your delightful disregard of convention, precedent and authority." Fifty years later, a New York businessman told me how he had, as a young man, admired this spirited redhead from faraway Nebraska.

In New York City, my mother came to know noted pacifists, feminists, intellectuals, and liberals, including Jane Addams, Rabbi Stephen Wise, social work leaders, and radical muckrakers. Finally, in 1916, upon learning that her mother was ill, she returned to Nebraska and to the University of Nebraska at the invitation of its Alumni Society, whose board unanimously selected her to be its executive secretary and editor of its *University Journal*. It was said that the job's "purely detailed and clerical duties . . . did not appeal as strongly to her creative energy and strong personality, [but] she had the 'big vision'. . . . There was character and personality in her writing. Her style was excellent and her sentences clear."

At the university, where she was known not only for the clarity of her sentences but also for her involvement in antiwar and women's suffrage movements, influenced no doubt by Dean Barkley, she heard about the young lawyer alum, C. A. Sorensen, who had sailed on Henry Ford's "Peace Ship." In a letter, she asked him to compose an article on that experience for the *Journal*.

Having never encountered the name Annis, C.A. began his letter of acceptance with the words: "Dear Mr. Chaikin."

Not too long thereafter, Annis was caught up and potentially targeted in the anti-German hysteria that World War I injected into American discourse in general and into Nebraska in particular. It all began when a hastily organized State Council of Defense closed German newspapers, banned German books from libraries and German studies from colleges, and induced the state legislature to criminalize the teaching of German before the eighth grade in Nebraska schools, even in private German Lutheran Church schools. The council also harassed the State Non-Partisan League for its radical and unpatriotic positions until my father came to its defense. He sued the council and succeeded in obtaining its agreement not to interfere with league meetings, after the league agreed to hire only Nebraskans as organizers and to withdraw a controversial pamphlet on war aims.

But the Nebraska State Council of Defense was unyielding. In a public summary of its activities on July 10, 1917, it singled out the university as a problem, urging the Board of Regents to deal with it immediately. The regents responded by issuing a summons to alumni secretary Annis Chaikin and others, stating that she had been reported to have been "very excusive regarding the IWW" (a radical organization), and that she had been observed speaking cordially with the antiwar dean of the graduate school.

Annis prudently decided that, for the first time in her life, she needed to consult a lawyer. She thought young C. A. Sorensen might be sympathetic. Ultimately, the dean and two other professors were fired for having "destroyed their usefulness to the Institution"; but C.A. succeeded in having the flimsy charges against Miss Chaikin dismissed. Soon they were working together on women's suffrage for Nebraska, on world peace, limits on child labor, and other causes.

After several years of collaboration and courtship, C.A. and Annis surprised almost all their friends on the weekend of July 9, 1921, by suddenly eloping to Kansas City, Missouri, to be married in a civil ceremony, unaccompanied by anyone, possibly because they suspected their respective families might not approve. It must have been true love; it was also a repudiation of their roots. As children, we did not understand that there was anything particularly unique or significant about a Christian-Jewish marriage, or that interreligious marriages had not been common in those days, particularly in Nebraska, and particularly among Jewish women. Even today, a rabbi told me, it is easier for him to perform a marriage for a gay couple than a mixed religious marriage, where the woman is Jewish. To whatever extent intermarriage takes courage and determination today, it took far more in 1921.

But the newlyweds were not as different as their backgrounds might suggest. True, they represented two very distinct streams of the many that entered the Nebraska immigration pool during the late nineteenth century. My father was a country boy from rural Nebraska, descended from devoutly conservative Danish Christians. My mother was a city girl from Omaha, descended from devoutly conservative Russian Jews. But both were highly educated, highly principled liberal intellectuals, with, in the words of my mother's coworker, a "delightful disregard of convention." Both were more concerned with helping others than enriching themselves. One of my father's friends, who had earlier met Annis, wrote her after the ceremony: "I dream great things for you. You can put great ideas in concrete form and get them into life." That must be what attracted my father—though I am certain that her long red hair and hazel eyes helped.

Having blossomed in New York, Annis apparently had doubts about whether she wanted to live the rest of her life as a housewife in Nebraska, giving up a writing career. Not many women intent on marriage and family sought graduate degrees in Greek and Latin in those days. She had no fear of remaining single, once telling my sister: "Ruth, the only old maids I know are men." She even acknowledged in a letter to a friend that she had previously been "permanently wedded to single blessedness . . . But when the time came to leave Lincoln—I had had enough of Main Street—I found there was someone I did not want to leave behind." In the same letter, she described her new husband:

Abe [C.A.] is a real doer, a leader, and one of Nebraska's sanest liberals, born with a love for politics . . . the fact that he spent the first 16 years of his life on a farm gives him a love for and understanding of the farmer. He believes in the soil as a great purifier of the human spirit. He'd rather tramp ten miles on ploughed ground than dance the fox trot half the night.

Less than a year after her marriage, she wrote with a touch of whimsy to a friend: "Here I am, a full-fledged housekeeper-dishwasher, with dustpan and all . . . Fortunately we both like the simple life. If I offer him bread, milk and honey, he is content. So you see, I am hardly a full-fledged housekeeper." But over time, raising a family became very important to her. "I feel the dignity as well as the weight of my position" as a mother, she wrote to an old friend in 1933, after the birth of her fifth child. "What opportunities seeing life a mother has, it unfolds in all directions—from our oldest boy," referring to Robert, then ten, "who wishes I could play duets with him, to my five year old [me] who chides me for not laughing more—he has a very hearty and contagious laugh."

However many difficult adjustments she faced in her new status, religion was not one of them. Since college, my father had been a Unitarian. Both Unitarians and Jews believe that human beings represent the one true God here on earth, and that good works by man are sanctifying God's name. The local Reform Jewish rabbi in Lincoln, a friend of the family, once joked that the similarities between Reform Judaism and Unitarianism would make it logical for the two religious groups to join as "Jewnitarian." Given those broad similarities, my mother did not object to her children being raised in the Unitarian Church. She and C.A. agreed in advance to decide for themselves what holidays and religious principles and practices they would observe in their new home. They exchanged ideas about creating their own religious standards, at least for their own family.

The decision to embrace Unitarianism was made easier for them by the fact that each had been disillusioned by their respective religious upbringings. It happened to my father as a fifteen-year-old boy, when a country preacher hailed the death from disease of his beloved four-month-old sister, Esther, as a cause for rejoicing in heaven. My mother, a strong feminist, resented Orthodox Judaism's restrictions on women. Thereafter, to the best of my knowledge, she was not observant, and never attended services in a synagogue. In the last years of her life, she took comfort in occasional Seders with friends. But, even then, the contrasting currents of her faith were evident in a letter to me: "Enjoyed Passover Seder at home of Norman Krivosha and next day Sunday Easter dinner at Eleanor Hinman's . . ." Upon my return from Chernigov in 1967, I gave her an ornately carved Russian box filled with Chernigov soil, which she displayed on her mantelpiece as a cherished keepsake. But not even her final days brought a full return to the religion of her birth or a request for the services of a rabbi.

Nor did my father return to the religion of his youth. His youngest sister, a born-again Christian fundamentalist missionary, came, with a similarly devout sister, to see him on his deathbed. The wish being father to the thought, they interpreted an involuntary nod, induced by his illness, as an assent to their religious pronouncements. "It's so wonderful" they exclaimed, without sensitivity to my mother, "Chris said he accepted Jesus!" Mother tactfully decided not to make them unhappy by challenging that conclusion.

Under Jewish law, my siblings and I, as children of a Jewish mother, were (and are) Jews. We were not raised as Jews. We didn't think of ourselves as Jewish. I doubt that we were known or regarded as Jews by our friends or their parents, but I have no way of knowing. Some of our friends, whose parents could afford it, enjoyed swimming and social activities at the local country club not far from our home. We assumed our nonmembership was a matter of money. Only later did I learn that the club excluded Jews in those days, ironically lifting the ban during the Depression only for those wealthy Jews whose membership dues the club urgently needed. But, in Lincoln, even when live Jews were admitted to the golf course, dead Jews were still barred from many of the local cemeteries.

While raising five children, my mother still found time to pursue other interests and goals, helping move the women's suffrage movement into the Nebraska League of Women Voters, serving as editor of its monthly statewide journal, the *Intelligent Voter*, editing the local league's newsletter for many years, and leading its effort to get more women into political office. Somehow she also found time to help organize my father's political campaigns—all five of them—temporarily shifting her registration from Democratic to Republican as long as he was running for office as a Republican, then shifting to independent. "Lincoln," she wrote in a letter late in her life, "is too Republican for me to enjoy a campaign." When she wasn't working on these or other causes, she was always reading, most often serious works by Lincoln Steffens, Ida Tarbell, and the Dutch philosopher Baruch Spinoza, or novels by Pearl Buck and Mari Sandoz, continuing to read while nursing each new baby as we came along, writing a fan letter to one author: "I like the association of a worthwhile book with the beginning of a baby's life."

Suddenly, mysteriously, it all changed. That beautiful mind, so precisely attuned to both maternal and civic responsibilities, so energetically full of both caring and intellectual instincts, careened off the tracks, like some fine timepiece racing inexplicably out of control. It began slowly, we later realized—small isolated incidents of aberrational speech or behavior, at first seemingly innocuous—but it ultimately became a prolonged nightmare for us all. No one knew what to do, not my father, not our family doctor, not the specialists whom my father called, not my mother's friends, and clearly not Mother herself.

With that gradual, unrecognized onset of her mental

illness, I cannot fix a single date in my mind. It may have begun in 1943 when I was fifteen, and learned while away at summer camp that hospitalization prevented her from coming to the family's first wedding, my oldest brother Robert's in the western part of the state, a wedding that she apparently had strongly opposed. No one in the family or among the medical consultants knew whether her condition would last a month, a year, or a lifetime, whether it had been triggered by the onset of menopause, by years of suppressed tension as an intellectual would-be writer trapped in the role of traditional housekeeper for a family of seven, with money scarce and her husband frequently away on long business and campaign trips, or by years of worry as an antiwar mother whose sons faced the prospect of dangerous military service, or as a Jew hearing ghastly reports of Hitler's systematic extermination of her people, including those in the Ukraine starting in 1941. Had her parents never left Chernigov, what would have been their fate and hers by 1943?

Despite the physical inertia often accompanying depression, she seemed strong and fit, and no physical cause could be detected. Because she was almost forty years old at my birth, she had always seemed old to me; but today, from the perspective of my own advanced years, I am dismayed to realize how young she was, still in her early fifties, at the time this demon seized her brain and would not let go, robbing her of so much for so long.

The medical profession knew little or nothing then about chemical imbalances in the brain. In those days people talked about a "nervous breakdown," without defining the term, explaining the cause, or finding a cure. Today she would almost surely be termed bipolar or manic-depressive, and treated with lithium and newer drugs. More than sixty years ago, there was no reliable diagnosis or treatment. My father ruled out lobotomy, the most barbaric of the remedies then used. I do know that she was subjected to electric shock treatment, which may or may not have prolonged the periods of remission, but seemed to me to impair her energy, memory, and morale without preventing the next episode. My father pleaded with her doctors for medications, but they had none. Gradually, various treatments emerged, each with its own harsh side effects—but no cures.

At first these spells seemed monthly, as if related to the female hormonal cycle; but in time the length of both the episodes and the remissions varied, sometimes bringing us relief and hope for months, occasionally years, only to see those hopes crushed. When I was sixteen, away for the summer at a high school debate institute, I corresponded with my father about whether her condition made it advisable for me to find another living arrangement for my senior year in high school. "I was unaware that her condition was that serious," I wrote. "Is it really necessary for me not to be in Lincoln?" No such alternative arrangement for me came to pass; but the mere discussion was another illustration of the strange and sad dimensions of my family life, of which I said nothing to outsiders, but which gave me a less rose-colored view of the world.

All we children knew was that, at times, a totally different person, almost a stranger, lived in our house, neglecting herself and her family, with sudden, violent mood swings followed by uncharacteristic lethargy. In horror, we listened to her weird and incomprehensible statements, sometimes in a stream of consciousness, one word or sentence leading to another, often by use of puns or wordplay, all totally unlike her in character. Sometimes she would wander around the house or even the neighborhood in her nightgown, babbling nonsense. Occasionally residents of other neighborhoods would call us to come and fetch her. Strangers or even acquaintances, not knowing of the illness underlying her odd or heated answers in casual conversation, would insist: "No, that's not true . . . not right . . . that's crazy," and walk away angry or baffled. We learned to avoid confronting, even correcting her. Fortunately we did not have to worry about her safety because there were no weapons in the house. As always, some neighbors were kind, bringing casseroles to us for dinner, while some children were unknowingly cruel, mischievously running up onto our porch to press the doorbell in hopes of provoking a tirade at which they could run off and laugh. We gave up inviting friends to play at home during the bad spells.

Still children ourselves, we learned not to be angry, even if we were sometimes embarrassed, and to keep our troubles and trials to ourselves. We learned quite a lot. If it can be said that anything good came from this ordeal—as it so often does—it was good for us to learn so much so early. We learned compassion for those who are miserable, whatever the cause. We learned to distinguish between the minor irritants and imperfections of life, which need not disturb us, and truly major problems such as the one we endured for all those years. We learned to joke in order to submerge our own despair. We learned when it was useless to reason, much less argue, with her. We learned that in this world bad things can happen and that life is full of tragedies as well as joys. We learned, finally, to take responsibility early in life, to manage, to cope. Without our brilliant, caring mother taking quite the same interest and involvement in our studies, work, and personal lives, we made more decisions on our own. We matured quickly. We all threw ourselves into our studies and early jobs. We all married young.

For my father, visibly tormented by this drastic change in the woman he loved, the suffering must have been the greatest. But in his strong, selfless manner, even though frustrated by his inability to solve this problem, he stood by her with the quiet patience of a saint and the determined courage of a soldier, managing the household and raising the children almost on his own, weathering it all with his "usual philosophical calm and courage," as I wrote him. Fortunately my sister could help with the cooking, at which C.A. had no great skill. My brother Tom and I, who shared an upstairs bedroom, once agreed that we could tell upon awakening in the morning whether Mother had been hospitalized during the night by the smell wafting upstairs of my father scorching eggs.

But there was no laughing one night when my mother was so out of control that my father, fearful that her condition might produce still more tragic consequences, called the doctor, who sent an ambulance; the horrifying scene is permanently burned in my memory, of my mother, still physically strong enough to wrestle loudly with the young ambulance attendants who were attempting to force her onto a gurney, while the doctor attempted to inject a sedative into her hip, a scene that caused my little sister and brother to burst into tears and run upstairs to escape the sight.

This is the first time I have written or spoken about this part of my life, and it is difficult to do so for two reasons. First, it is difficult because those painful experiences horrified us all. Even as reasonably intelligent teenagers, with the resilience that children in most families instinctively seem to have in those situations, it was difficult to accept her loss of mental control. No matter how often one reminds oneself that "She cannot help it," "She does not mean it," "It is not her fault," encounters with persistent aggression, agitation, irritability, shouting, and accusations from one's own mother become difficult for a young person to bear with equanimity, much less recount to outsiders.

Second, it is difficult because I find myself, even though I now know better, unavoidably feeling the sense of shame and stigma that mental illness brought to our family back then, leaving me with a feeling even now that I am wrongly exposing or embarrassing my mother by telling others of her illness, somehow violating my deep sense of loving loyalty to her. No, it was not a path she chose, but our plight and hers were made more difficult by the fact that she could not or would not discuss it with us. Occasionally she implicitly acknowledged that something had gone wrong, but never specified what she was enduring or whether she even understood it. Once, when temporarily institutionalized, with her family persuaded by the doctors not to visit or contact her, she wrote in a hospital-supplied diary of her bewilderment as to why she had been confined. For this once most supremely rational of women, these episodes of irrationality must have been as hard to accept as they were for us.

Even at her sickest, my mother's love of family prevailed. She never struck her children or husband, and took good care of him in his last days in 1959. He remained completely devoted to her in a mutually caring union, during which I never heard either of them utter an angry or resentful word about the other. It is sad to reflect that their best times together had lasted barely more than twenty years, followed by seventeen years with intermittent anguish before his death. But, had my father ever been asked whether it was all worth it, I am certain he would have replied in his customary way: "You bet!"

Similarly, even as her recurring bouts of illness persisted, my mother continued to take great pride in all her children and their careers. In my White House days, when friends would say: "Aren't you proud of your son?"

she would always reply: "Which son do you mean? I'm
proud of all my children." We were all proud of her,
and are proud today that the University of Nebraska
has both an Annis Chaikin Sorensen Award for Distinguished Teaching in the Humanities, established by her
family, and an Annis Chaikin Sorensen Student Fund,
established by the Kennedy family to honor her upon
her death—appropriate salutes to a brilliant mind.

Chapter 3

Father

Fully acknowledging the important ways in which my mother shaped my character and intellect, I still believe that most of the skills that I brought to my later life and career were learned from my father, C. A. Sorensen. My grandfather gave each of his sons, upon that lad's reaching age ten, the right to select his own middle name. As a result, I have Sorensen uncles named William McKinley, John Wesley, James Monroe, George Washington, and Clarence Woodrow. My father, named Christian for Danish kings, chose Abraham to honor his political hero, the sixteenth president, upon whom this new "honest Abe" hoped to model his own life.

As a young college student, though often called Chris by his family and Abe by his friends, he began signing himself "C. A. Sorensen." During my first ten years, we children called him "Daddy." But, in 1938, our home and life became filled with talk and leaflets about "C. A. Sorensen" who was campaigning for State Supreme Court chief justice. One evening late in the campaign, dinner table conversation turned to the possibility, outrageous as it seemed, that he might lose. Listening was my youngest brother, Phil, who was just five. He suddenly asked: "Does that mean he won't be 'C.A.' anymore?" We all laughed and assured Phil that Daddy would remain C.A., and we used that name thereafter.

Born and raised in a sod house (we think), the oldest of ten children, C.A. spent his childhood working on his father's farm, where he learned a lot about hard labor plowing corn and tending livestock. In his high school days, standing on top of adjoining haystacks, he and a friend would pretend to be U.S. senators, arguing about the tariff and other issues of the day. Meanwhile, he was saving money for college by doing janitorial work, clerking in a store, and caring for mules on a nearby farm. After working his way through Loup City High School, he took two summers of higher education at Wesleyan College outside Lincoln, which he financed by shoveling coal.

Young C.A. then pleased his devout parents by enrolling closer to home at Grand Island Baptist College;

his brief time there would change the direction of his life—and his children's—forever. As a twenty-one-year-old sophomore, on the evening of Friday, February 17, 1912, he represented the college in the Nebraska State Oratory Contest. He wrote and delivered a provocative speech entitled "The Dead Hand of the Past," decrying the "popular belief" that "things are sacred because they are old." He called on his audience to question the traditions of their ancestors.

Eyebrows were raised when he applied this theme not merely to government, politics, and economics, but also to religion itself. The "essence of religious life," he said, "is the duty of man to man." To lead a religious life, he proclaimed, a person need not observe illogical and irrational religious customs, merely because those customs are traditional. Leading a religious life means showing kindness and generosity to others, upholding the brotherhood of man.

He illustrated his message with a Sam Foss poem, about the trail of an aimlessly wandering calf, "The Calf Path," which concludes:

> For men are prone to go it blind
> Along the calfways of the mind
> And work away from sun to sun,
> To do as other men have done.

The response to his speech was explosive. The local *Grand Island Independent* headlined: "Protest; Pastors of Several Churches Deprecate Oration of College Student." The newspaper reported outrage that a student from a Christian college was permitted to voice such beliefs. The college president reassured the clergymen that "an able but headstrong young man deliberately disregarded the college authorities." For his speech, young C.A. received both a top prize in the Nebraska State Oratory Contest and dismissal from Grand Island Baptist College.

Not long after his dismissal, he received an astonishing letter from a total stranger, Walter Locke, the associate editor of the *Nebraska State Journal*, Lincoln's principal newspaper. Locke informed C.A. that he had read about his expulsion from Grand Island, and that C.A. belonged in two places, both in Lincoln—the University of Nebraska and the Unitarian Church. Having some influence in both institutions, Locke offered to assist with his admission, and invited C.A., while he was getting settled, to reside with the Locke family.

The Lincoln Unitarian minister, Dr. Arthur L. Weatherly, soon reinforced that invitation with the offer of a scholarship to cover young C.A.'s university tuition. C.A. accepted those extraordinary offers.

At the university, he served as editor of the campus

newspaper and was a champion debater, even writing a letter to a prominent Boston lawyer, Louis D. Brandeis, seeking that future Supreme Court justice's help on an upcoming debate question: "Should corporations engaged in interstate commerce be required to take out federal charters?" While he was at it, young C.A. asked sweeping questions about federal incorporation. Brandeis's courteous reply referred the young debater to his earlier Senate testimony on the subject.

C.A.'s most passionate cause was keeping America out of a war in which he believed it had no stake. He was an active member of both the Nebraska Peace Society and the Emergency Peace Federation to Keep America Out of War. In 1913, the year he received his undergraduate degree, C.A. led a campaign to block the construction of an armory in Nebraska City.

In 1915, at the invitation of the pacifist Unitarian minister Dr. Weatherly, C.A., then a law student, accompanied peace activists on the "Peace Ship" chartered by the industrialist and inventor Henry Ford, to sail to the capitals of European neutrals and urge those governments to stay out of the war and to establish a peace conference. The would-be peacemakers traveled to Norway, Sweden, Denmark, and other countries, holding mass meetings with supporters. Ridiculed by the press, which called it the "Flivver Ship" carrying "a bunch of nuts," the Ford Peace Ship carried sixty-seven "delegates," thirty-six students, and twenty-eight journalists.

Many years later I learned that on board, C.A. met another young religious antiwar activist, Lella Secor, three years his senior. Both were smitten; their friendship and correspondence continued for several years after the voyage. Lella's diary and letters were published many decades later by her granddaughter, who visited me in my New York law office to tell me about her book. I saw a whole new side of my father, as a surprisingly sentimental young man, who wrote:

> *Your supreme unselfishness and your gentleness and kindness of heart make a visit with you the finding of a wonderful oasis . . . I wish that HG Wells would perfect his time machine and have it on a reverse lever . . . Would that I might again sit with you on the top deck!*

After graduating from law school in 1916, C.A. drafted and achieved the passage of a partial women's suffrage law on behalf of the Nebraska Women's Suffrage Association, then acted as the association's lawyer in battling those trying to suspend its adoption. He also continued his antiwar activities. Having voted in 1916 to reelect the Democratic president, Woodrow Wilson, on the grounds that "He kept us out of war," he said when Wilson changed his mind a few months later, "I could not so quickly change mine."

In early 1917, not yet twenty-seven years of age (five years younger than I would be when I first set foot in the White House), he was selected by a mass church-sponsored meeting in Washington, D.C., to be one of a delegation of three to call upon President Wilson to urge that America stay out of the war. Mrs. Oswald Garrison Villard, wife of the editor of the *Nation*, was one of the other two. "For twenty minutes," C.A. recalled twenty years later in a letter to Senator George Norris, "I poured all of my soul into a plea that our country should stay out . . . I spoke not only of the inevitable death and suffering . . . but of some of the economic effects which were bound to follow."

As some of his brothers enlisted in the army, young C.A. was undecided about whether to do the same, finally choosing to await his notice of induction. He later acknowledged: "The death of a friend of mine on the battle-front made me feel a coward staying at home." C.A.'s notice arrived in late October 1918, but the global influenza epidemic postponed his induction; and the November 11 Armistice made it moot; he had already sold his law office furniture and traveled to mid-state to say good-bye to his parents. With the war over, he resumed a private law practice in Lincoln and his devotion to public affairs.

Reflecting later on those times, he felt torn, C.A. said, between his "world peace convictions" and his hopes for a political career. In considering the impact on his career, he was prescient. Ten years later, as a candidate for attorney general, he was denounced by the state commander of the American Legion, J. B. Cain, who said C.A. had "consistently avoided military service."

C.A. responded that he had complied with all U.S. Army regulations and procedures, and that one week more of delay of the Armistice would have guaranteed his final, formal induction, thereby entitling him to become a member of the Legion "and a patriot in regular standing," able to wave the flag and march with all the "super-patriots" who were attacking him. His old mentor Walter Locke spoke up: "If the rest of us put our patriotism into action as Mr. Sorensen has always done, there would be no fear for our future."

My father came to believe that the best path for making an important contribution to society was through elective office. But like George Norris—whose Senate campaign he would manage in 1924—he had little regard for the "regular" leaders of either major political party. The Republicans, he felt, had abandoned the principles of Lincoln and Teddy Roosevelt, and were captives of corporate interests like the cement, power, railroad, and other trusts. The Nebraska Democratic organization, he wrote Norris, is "nothing but a patronage machine operating under a sign: 'To the victor belongs the spoils.'" Initially C.A. and his fellow "insurgents," like Norris and the La Follettes of Wisconsin, hoped to integrate their nonpartisan third-party movement into the Republican Party to move that party in a more progressive direction, but they later became increasingly independent, supporting FDR and Democratic Party programs.

It was in this context that my father decided in 1928, the year I was born, to become one of many candidates for the Republican Party' s nomination for the office of state attorney general. The Tobias, Nebraska, *Times* editorialized: "He represents genuine Abraham Lincoln Republicanism." A sufficient number of Nebraskans agreed.

My father was a bold and innovative attorney general. A June 23, 1929, *New York Times* article reported:

"Everyone in Nebraska these days is talking about the state's young Attorney General, Christian Abraham Sorensen," who had become "the sensational darling of the out-state voters . . . A man of great political sagacity and audacity . . . So the political wiseacres are now saying, 'Watch Sorensen'" . . . the possible successor to the halos of William Jennings Bryan and George W. Norris as a commoner and friend of the people.

It was an era when progressives felt that state governments, adopting reforms that were often blocked at the national level, could be "laboratories of democracy" in the words of U.S. Supreme Court Justice Brandeis, my father's earlier correspondent, before whom C.A. as attorney general argued two cases. As a reformer, C.A. had strong convictions. "Straddling by candidates on important issues ought to be punishable by political oblivion," he declared. "A candidate who trims himself to fit the notions of every group will soon whittle himself down to nothing." But he was a stickler for law enforcement, and said that a state does not perform its first function for its citizens if it allows rats and vultures in human form to prey upon its citizens. Because he had worked closely with Nebraska churches in the antiwar movement and with women's organizations on the suffrage movement, where his efforts were opposed by beer and vice interests who hoped never to see women vote, it is not surprising that he became an anti-vice crusader and a champion of the Women's Christian Temperance Union. Though generally supportive of Roosevelt's efforts to revive the economy, C.A. ridiculed, as "a reckless campaign statement," FDR's promise in 1932 to justify the restoration of the sale of beer by a new tax of five cents per quart to balance the budget: "Every man, woman and child in the United States," C.A. said, "would have to drink 240 quarts of beer per year in order to raise the necessary money . . . what a solution to offer a discouraged and stricken nation!" Antigambling provisions were the law, Prohibition was the law; and no citizen can choose to obey only those laws in which he believes. He felt that "every law should be enforced . . . laws against corruption in high places as well as laws against chicken stealing."

In Omaha, where illegal activities gave the city the label "a small Al Capone Chicago," C.A. was widely despised throughout his four years as attorney general. His investigations and prosecutions, publicly naming names, resulted in a number of police raids. None of this pleased Tom Dennison, who controlled the Omaha underworld, the police department, and much of the city government, with a political machine matching his formidable vice machine. When informed that an unpopular ban on racetrack gambling had caused a mob in Omaha to burn him in effigy, C.A. replied, with his usual calm: "I am quite willing to be burned in reality, if it is necessary to do my duty."

Confronted with death threats, my father was advised by the police to buy a gun, which he once showed me in his office desk drawer. The atmosphere grew more tense when an Omaha businessman, Harry Lapidus, the father-in-law of an assistant attorney general, was murdered by unknown assailants. Some suspected hired gangsters from Kansas City, where Dennison had unsavory friends.

Finally, C.A. interested the U.S. Justice Department in investigating the Omaha underworld; and ultimately a federal grand jury indicted Dennison, eight of his associates, and "The Omaha Liquor Syndicate" for, among other things, conspiracy to violate the national Prohibition Act, bootlegging, the protection racket, the fixing of juries, hijackings, and political influence over the police department. It was the end of Tom Dennison.

The Sorensen children knew little of this. We only knew that our father suddenly moved his card and board games with us from the front porch back into the living room , lest some of his anti-vice supporters disapprove. We liked the popular radio show *Gangbusters*, but did not realize that our mild-mannered daddy was one of them.

In 1930, when he ran for reelection, the regular

Republicans joined the Democrats in seeking to oust him and his fellow "insurgent Republicans," especially Senator George W. Norris. As a result, two nationally noted trials ensued:

Case one: On July 5, 1930, hoping to confuse the voters, a grocer in Broken Bow, Nebraska, "coincidentally" named George W. Norris, filed for the Republican senatorial nomination in the August 12 primary. The obvious intent was to split the Norris vote, thereby electing the "regular" Republican candidate, W. M. Stebbins. A legal wrangle followed in which Attorney General Sorensen said that the grocer Norris filing had missed the statutory deadline and should be rejected. The Republican secretary of state nevertheless accepted it, and Chairman Gerald Nye of the U.S. Senate Elections Committee in Washington decided to investigate. The growing controversy caused the last-minute withdrawal from the race of an Omaha dentist named Sorensen who had been recruited to file for attorney general as part of a similar plan.

The truth finally emerged when an anonymous caller suggested to my father that the secretary of Republican chieftain Victor Seymour be placed on the witness stand under oath. It turned out that Grocer Norris's filing fee had been paid by the regular Republicans, who had induced him to run and given him a substantial amount of cash for his campaign. Both Grocer Norris and Seymour were tried, convicted, and sent to federal prison for perjury. In a typically Nebraskan sequel, Seymour's son and C. A. Sorensen's children, more than a decade later, became close friends, with no awareness on our part of this history.

Case two: On August 11, 1930, the evening before the Republican primary, Richard Wood, the regular Republican candidate for the State Railway Commission, went on KFAB radio in Omaha to read a prepared campaign speech on behalf of Senator Norris's "regular" Republican opponent, Mr. Stebbins. The principal target of the speech turned out to be not Norris but C. A. Sorensen. Referring to my father, Mr. Wood read: "He took an oath before God and man that he would uphold the law. His promises to man are for naught, and his oath to God is a sacrilege, for he is a non-believer, an irreligious libertine, a madman and a fool, one of the Judas Iscariots of our state and party."

The next day, threatened with a Sorensen lawsuit over these and other falsehoods, KFAB offered its "apologies for any unwitting offense" that this speaker might have given; Mr. Wood followed with his own halfhearted apology. Not impressed by these insincere regrets, or by KFAB's offer to provide him with air time *after* the primary to say that he was not a libertine, madman, or fool, C.A. sued both Wood and KFAB for $100,000 in damages for defamation. The state district court decided that the falsehoods had been spoken, not published, and therefore constituted slander, not libel; that slander required proof of damages; that Sorensen, having won renomination handily, could not prove he was damaged; and that the jury could therefore award him only a symbolic $1 against Wood, who had merely spoken the defamatory words, and that KFAB, having said nothing, was not liable at all.

At the suggestion of a University of Nebraska law professor, C.A. changed his lawsuit to one of libel, arguing that the radio station had in effect "published" the defamation with the same consequences as if it had been printed in a newspaper, resulting in such widespread circulation of the defamation that it was impossible to verify how extensive the damages were. On appeal, the Nebraska Supreme Court supported Sorensen, stating: "a radio licensee has no privilege to join and assist in the *publication of a libel*," the first case in the nation to decide this question of law.

Because the case appeared in my law school textbook, I knew I would be called upon in class to report on it, and I asked my father what had followed the verdict. The radio station had appealed the decision to the U.S. Supreme Court; but the National Association of Broadcasters (NAB) rushed out to Omaha from Washington to demand withdrawal of the appeal, lest the U.S. Supreme Court uphold the Nebraska decision, thereby applying nationwide a doctrine that thus far applied only to one state. KFAB dropped the appeal and reached a modest monetary settlement with my father. The NAB made certain that both statutory and regulatory changes immunized future broadcasters in that situation.

I am particularly proud of my father for two other bold positions he took as attorney general. First, he vigorously dissented when a majority of the state Committee on Pardons and Paroles, on which he served, denied the commutation of the death penalty for a young drifter from a troubled background who, in Attorney General Sorensen's words, "inflamed by alcohol and lust," had murdered the farmer who employed him as well as the farmer's wife and daughter, whom he also raped. C.A.'s dissent on the death penalty was eloquent:

Capital punishment tends to make the state . . . imitate the murderer. . . . The time for society to protect itself against criminals is before they are made. . . . The schoolhouse rather than the electric chair is the symbol of the kind of civilization I want to see in America.

Today the annual award established by Nebraskans Against the Death Penalty is named for C. A. Sorensen.

A second controversial decision centered on the question of race. Although he had met W. E. B. DuBois, my father had little experience with this issue; the progressive and populist movements with which he had been associated did not emphasize civil rights. Yet C.A. went on to serve on the board of the Lincoln Urban League, to challenge the constitutionality of segregation in Lincoln's movie theaters, and to denounce an antiquated state statute that held Indians and blacks "incompetent to testify" in court, thereby lumping them with those of unsound mind. A concrete issue confronted him as attorney general in 1931 when the chairman of the Legal Redress Committee of the Omaha NAACP asked his view of an Omaha café with a sign in its front window reading: "No Colored Patronage Solicited."

C.A.'s reply was clear and direct:

Such a sign is a violation of law, a denial of "full and equal enjoyment of the accommodations, advantages, facilities and privileges" of the restaurant which the law requires. The sign for all practical purposes means "stay out." It tells the colored people of Omaha that they are not wanted in that particular eating place. . . .

C.A.'s most lasting legacies in Nebraska, however, concern not the issues of race or capital punishment, but nonpartisanship and public electric power. The culmination of the Norris-Sorensen effort to streamline and depoliticize government in Nebraska was a constitutional amendment converting the traditional two-house partisan legislature into a nonpartisan one-house or unicameral legislature. It remains the only one in the United States. Norris and C.A. believed that voters could not hold their representatives accountable so long as the representatives in one house could blame the other house for delaying, changing, or defeating legislation, or so long as secret conference committees between the two houses, supposedly limited to adjusting differences in wording, could delay, defeat, or amend beyond recognition legislation previously passed by both houses. My father explained to me that, at the time, the state legislature concerned itself primarily with questions of highways, bridges, and infrastructure on which there was no particular Republican or Democratic position.

C.A.'s election as attorney general was also viewed as a victory for the cause of low-cost publicly owned electric power for the people of Nebraska, particularly those in rural areas. Within months of his first election in 1928, a conference on municipal ownership of electric power was held in Lincoln. The movement spread to the farms; rural public power districts were established. The Nebraska Association of Rural Public Power Districts was formed, with C.A. as its first president. Many times, as a boy, I heard my father speak to farm audiences when a regional electric switch was about to be activated. Meanwhile, in Washington, Senator Norris pushed the Roosevelt administration to establish a Rural Electrification Administration. There were rumors in 1948 that Republican nominee Thomas E. Dewey, confident of defeating Truman for the presidency, had prepared a tentative list of appointees, including C.A. as rural electrification administrator.

As a child, I also visited the Nebraska state capitol building; "Daddy's Capitol," we called it. While waiting for our father to complete his day's duties, my two older brothers and I played hide-and-seek in its massive halls. We were thrilled to stand on its highest balconies, beneath the mighty statue of *The Sower*, gazing out on the city and the plains that spread beyond. But his career in elected office did not last. In 1932, when he unsuccessfully sought a third term, the Roosevelt Democratic landslide ousted all Republicans, regular and irregular. Two years later, he agreed to carry the insurgent Republican banner in the Republican gubernatorial primary, but was defeated. In 1938 he was a candidate for the post of chief justice of the Nebraska

State Supreme Court. He won the primary but lost the election. It was his last campaign. By 1940, then over fifty, having been on the statewide ballot in Nebraska five times between 1928 and 1940, he promised my mother that he would never run for office again.

Central to my father's career was Nebraska's greatest statesman, George W. Norris. In his days of glory, I was too young to talk with him, and in his later years he was too old to talk with me. But I knew his story well. The man whom FDR once called "the gentle perfect knight of American ideals" was elected as a congressman in 1902, becoming famous for his efforts in 1910 to depose the House "Czar," Republican speaker Joseph Cannon. In 1918 he was elected to the U.S. Senate, a race in which young C. A. Sorensen organized Farmers for Norris, only one year after Norris had opposed U.S. entry into World War I, an episode I successfully persuaded JFK to include in *Profiles in Courage*. Norris finally lost his seat in the Senate in 1942, when he was eighty-one years old, only after being persuaded to run at that advanced age by FDR and his allies, who were hoping to keep the Nebraska Senate seat in friendly hands. To my father, Norris's loss was a sad commentary on popular government.

My father was as devoted and loyal to Senator Norris, almost thirty years his senior, as I was to JFK. Norris's only opportunity to reciprocate my father's loyalty and support came near the end of his final term when U.S. federal district judge Munger, based in Lincoln, decided to resign. My father's friends immediately recommended him for that position. Senator Norris promptly urged the nomination upon President Roosevelt, who was even more indebted to Senator Norris than the senator was to my father. The president wrote a cryptic note to his attorney general, Francis Biddle:

Sen. Norris says . . . Abe Sorenson Lab. Repub . . . from Lincoln. Voted for Norris and me . . . Try to get [Jim] Lawrence [a Nebraska power broker, whom my father knew] to O.K. Get him on a list of acceptables.

F.D.R.

In ways that I could not know or understand at age thirteen, it was unofficially rumored that the post was "a done deal." The appointment seemed so certain that the *Martindale Hubbell Law Directory* for 1942, about to go to print and in need of filling a blank, listed C. A. Sorensen as federal judge for Lincoln.

But the date for Judge Munger's resignation came and went, the seat was vacant, and no name was sent to the Senate. Speculation over the appointment was deemed by the press in early August 1941 to be "the most popular pastime in Nebraska legal and political circles." The *Colfax County Call* reported that "stand-pat Republicans don't like Sorensen because he belongs to the progressive group. Democrats don't like him because he doesn't adhere to strict party lines as set up by them." Democratic national committeeman J. C. Quigley succeeded in bringing Eugene B. Casey, one of President Roosevelt's assistants, to secret meetings in Nebraska with Democratic leaders. Casey's Lincoln meeting, at the Cornhusker Hotel, was decisive. The key attendees included a little-known Omaha businessman, O. Fletcher "Red" Neal, a successful insurance executive, who had lost a fortune when hog prices fell during the 1920s farm depression. Mr. Neal had a murky past that apparently engendered a long-standing grudge against C.A. The story involved Neal taking the rap for others when stolen cars were found in his commercial garage in Auburn, Nebraska, but avoiding confinement by serving his time as chauffeur for a corrupt Democratic state prison warden.

Also in the hotel room was a liberal Democrat who, unbeknownst to the other participants, reported on the meeting in a long letter to Senator Norris at the latter's vacation home in the Wisconsin woods. He described Neal as "the real dictator of patronage distribution in

Nebraska, the head of the Omaha organization without title, who handles all the campaign funds. It was Mr. Neal who sealed the fate of Mr. Sorensen, who had offended him in many ways during his term as attorney general, when he took sundry pokes at the Omaha underworld, and was especially ungracious to Mr. Neal." At the conference, Mr. Neal put his foot down firmly: "This Sorensen will never be a federal judge or anything else . . . This is a personal matter."

Word of these discussions alarmed C.A.'s friends and Nebraska liberals, who began sending letters to the White House objecting to the substitution of a leading conservative Catholic lawyer for C.A. President Roosevelt was uncomfortable antagonizing Norris and cautious about the warning that he had appointed too many Catholics in a Protestant state. In a memorandum to Attorney General Biddle, dated December 30, 1941, little more than three weeks after the Japanese bombing of Pearl Harbor, the president wrote:

In the matter of this Nebraska vacancy, I get two stories: A, that in a state which is 90% Protestant, a large majority of my appointees have been Catholics. B, that this is not true. Will you get me the correct figures?

Biddle replied that, although many of the top federal positions had gone to Catholics, "it would appear that a majority of your appointments have not been Catholic." By mid-January, John W. Delehant, the Catholic Democrat urged by Democratic Party leaders, had been nominated, with Norris's acquiescence. Within weeks, C.A. had faded from the picture. As so often happens in politics, he did not know who or what hit him.

The episode has ironic echoes in my own life. In 1941–1942, my first hero, my father, was denied the high federal position to which he aspired (federal judge) at least in part because he was *not* a Catholic; nearly twenty years later, my second hero, John F. Kennedy, came close to being denied the high federal position to which he aspired (the presidency) in large part because he *was* a Catholic.

Two years after I joined JFK's Senate staff, my father wrote to me, "Sitting out here in the middle of the United States, Senator Kennedy impresses me as a real statesman and a political leader with a great future." To my profound regret, my two mentors met only once, when the senator and I rode from a Democratic Party appearance in Omaha to a university appearance in Lincoln in the family car in May 1957. My father's health had already begun to decline, and there was little conversation in the car that day. That was sad, because they had so much in common. Neither placed politics above principles; both were men of great wisdom and calm in a crisis; neither complained about his own pain or disappointments. Both died before I had learned all they had to teach me.

All his life, my father worked too hard, spent too many hours at the office, exercised too little, and ate too much, due in part to a sweet tooth I share. He aged prematurely with cancer, ulcers, arteriosclerosis, and diabetes. For years he stoically injected himself with an insulin syringe daily as I watched, cringing. But he remained calm about his galaxy of illnesses, never losing that impish spirit. "How are you doing?" I asked, as we took a final walk around the block on one of my last visits to him in Lincoln. "Pretty good," he whispered, "considering the alternative." He died in 1959, at age sixty-nine, after several sad years of physical and mental deterioration. He did not live long enough to visit me in my White House office, a few doors down from the president.

At my father's funeral, the Unitarian minister eulogized:

Because the public man spoke as a bold, thunderous crusader or Old Testament prophet on public issues, some people never knew the humorous, gentle, almost sweet person underneath. Despite many provocations, he never struck at his opponents with personal hatred or abuse . . . Perhaps someday the conviction and courage of his life will be resurrected from dusty archives by some historian to be a fitting testimony to the man. . . .

Today, I am that historian.

Chapter 4

Childhood and Siblings

Although the Great Depression dominated the 1930s, and World War II the early 1940s, the harsh realities of that outside world rarely intruded on our life in Lincoln. Occasionally during the thirties, unemployed farmhands and factory workers, migrating from town to town, could be seen near the railroad tracks. Some knocked on our front door asking for food or money. My mother almost always gave each one a paid chore in the backyard and a sandwich on the back steps. On a drive near the city, she explained to me that the fenced-in area, in which I could see aged men or hungry families milling about, was the "County Poor Farm," that era's predecessor to the New Deal's federal welfare and social security programs.

We heard about the voices of extremism, Father Coughlin, Francis Townsend, Huey Long, Gerald L. K. Smith, the Ku Klux Klan. The country's political system seemed in danger of falling apart. As war threatened to erupt in Europe, Daddy had to reassure my little sister, Ruthie, that it would not reach us. Just in case, she wrote a letter to President Roosevelt: "Please keep us out of war. My brother [Robert] is almost 16 and I don't want him to leave."

The real center of the Sorensen kids' universe was neither the battlefront in Europe nor Washington, D.C., but 2451 Park Avenue, Lincoln, Nebraska, our home throughout my childhood, a modest two-story stucco house. We had an Edison to play Sousa marches and Victor Herbert operettas, and a radio in the living room on which to hear comedians like Jack Benny, dramas on *Lux Radio Theater*, and music on the *Telephone Hour*. In my earliest days, we had an icebox, soon replaced by a small refrigerator. Pool and Ping-Pong tables in the basement were used frequently. Judging from old snapshots, our backyard had once been an Eden of flowers and shrubs, but that had been transformed by years of bike riding, ball games, horseshoes, amateur circuses, and dust storms into a multipurpose dirt playground, complete with swing and sandbox, a frequent gathering spot for kids on the block.

Little more than two years after my parents married in 1921, and five weeks prior to mother's thirty-fifth birthday, she gave birth to her first child, Robert, producing four more over the next ten years. She turned forty the year I was born, and forty-five the year my youngest sibling, Phil, was born. Despite the uniformity of our heritage and upbringing, each of us pursued different interests. I was never as interested in the financial world as my older brother Tom, my best friend and confidant; nor was I ever as devoted to scholarly pursuits as my oldest brother, Robert; despite my many trips, I never pursued or enjoyed world travel as much as my sister, Ruth, who was always more family-minded than the rest of us. Nor was I ever as successful in sports or in seeking elective office as was my brother Phil, whose reply as lieutenant governor of Nebraska to a persistent reporter, asking him about his plans to run for governor, still brings a smile to my face: "I have no plans to seek any office beyond my present stepping-stone."

By age eight, I had concluded that my parents gave certain privileges to my two elder brothers on the grounds that they were big enough to enjoy them fully, and certain other privileges to my younger brother and sister on the grounds that they were little enough to deserve special treatment. I thereupon solemnly announced to my parents that I had calculated that I was "the biggest of the littlest and the littlest of the biggest," and therefore entitled to both sets of privileges.

In the Sorensen home, Mother was the lioness, fiercely protective of her cubs. Her strong principles applied to her child rearing, permitting no toy soldiers or toy guns of any kind, except water pistols and cap guns on the Fourth of July, preferring instead to give us toys like Erector sets, a hectograph, and picture puzzles that encouraged creativity. To her, uniforms—even Boy Scout uniforms—meant uniformity, conformity, and obedience, not traits she wanted to cultivate in us; but her pride in my music outweighed her initial disapproval of my uniform in the high school marching band.

On her fiftieth birthday in 1938, when I was ten, I composed a poem in her honor:

> This poem is about my mother,
> When I was sick in bed,
> She would bring me up my food,
> Which was usually milk and bread.
> She would try very hard to keep me well
> Against sickness she put up a fight,
> And when I had a large fever
> She would stay up late at night
> My mother is now 50 years old,

And has lived 10 of those years with me,
And I hope I'll support her for the rest of my life
I hope that's the way it will be.

My father was the big-shouldered bear who, for all his serious reserve, had a twinkle in his eye and a soft spot in his heart. Before the birth of my two younger siblings, he wrote my mother:

> *Because I am not the demonstrative kind, I fear you have little conception of my great love for these three brown-eyed boys of ours. Were the occasion to arise, I would not hesitate an instant to give my life for . . . any one of them.*

Daddy tried to spend evenings and weekends with us, but often had to work Saturdays. I remember crying one day as a teenager when he left on a business trip because he would not let me carry his suitcase to the bus stop for him. My own first poem in a lifetime of doggerel was about his busy schedule: "I always know when it is Christmas, because that's when Daddy stays home from his business." (There remains some dispute whether brother Phil or I penned this.)

My father's frequent practice of taking me along on some of his long car trips to meetings around the state created a special bond. I learned a lot, not only from listening to him talk about life, politics, and law as he drove, but also from gazing out the front-seat window at rural Nebraska, a plain but shimmering landscape with colorfully named towns like Big Springs, Elkhorn, Seldom, Red Cloud, Broken Bow, Table Rock, and Wahoo. The highway usually took us along small-town main streets, past retired farmers chatting on a bench in front of the general store, wearing feed company caps and overalls, watching the traffic go by. I could see majestic barns; hear meadowlarks perched on roadside fences; wonder aloud about the optical illusion of rain pools ahead on dry concrete highways; and simply take in the vastness of the open skies, the neatly cultivated fields, and the sheer grandeur of the Nebraska horizons and sunsets.

On one trip to Omaha, when I was only eight, Daddy took me to a hotel where he had a meeting, leaving me in the lobby with a copy of the local newspaper, so that I could read the comics. After an hour or two, I was walking about restlessly, with the newspaper under my arm, when a stranger, mistaking me for a newsboy, asked to buy it. I explained it was "my daddy's paper." He asked me my daddy's name, and then sat down for a talk. Only when I learned several days later that the *Omaha World-Herald* was reporting that "C. A. Sorensen's son Teddy wants to grow up to be a fireman" did

I realize that the man was a journalist. It is not a coincidence that it was the last time in my life that I had a confidence violated by a member of the press.

Another trip with my father, about eight or nine years later, led to one of the most successful speeches of my life. In the lobby of a small-town hotel, the clerk informed me that the local high school was about to host my own Lincoln High in an evening basketball game. I attended the game, sat next to one of the local school's prettier cheerleaders, escorted her to a late movie after the game, took her home after the movie, and kissed her good night on her front porch, despite her warning about a passing car. As I was blithely walking back to the hotel, that same car pulled up and I was suddenly surrounded by a tough gang of local boys, whose leader informed me that, for my having "messed" with his girl, I was about to be beaten within an inch of my life.

My response began, as all good speeches should, with the basic facts—that I had no designs on the young lady, had not previously been informed of his exclusive rights, had not violated them in any serious manner, and was from far away where I was about to return as soon as I could get back to my father's hotel, leaving the young man, his young lady, and their lovely town forever, with my very best wishes for their every happiness. As

I spoke, edging my way northward in the direction of the hotel, the angry boyfriend and his gang stood there, dumbfounded by my blessing. Picking up speed, I discovered that I was not being followed, and made my way quickly and safely back to the hotel. I saw no need to tell my father of my adventure.

Like most of the people we knew growing up, our family was neither rich nor poor. By the time I reached my teens, I had a vague impression that my father's income might have been somewhere around ten to fifteen thousand dollars a year. Our house was large enough—barely—for a family of seven. My father was always as plainly dressed as he was plainspoken. We rode in the same Ford sedan year after year. Many items—including the piano that Mother insisted all five children learn to play—were acquired secondhand. I acquired my parents' Great Depression frugality. Some years later, in a letter welcoming Eric, my firstborn son, into the world, C.A. joked: "As to your father, well, he is learned in the law; and he is thrifty—he never uses a three cent envelope for a letter when a penny postcard will do." When I was still very young, one of my father's friends promised my older brothers and me $20 each if we would not smoke or drink before age twenty-one. That sounded like a lot of money, so I—and I alone—kept that pledge.

Much later I learned that Joseph P. Kennedy's sons were each promised $1,000 by their father if they met the same test. Somehow I doubt they all passed.

It was a simple and largely contented life. My father had seen enough hard times on the farm, and my mother had seen enough real poverty in New York City, that neither took relative comfort for granted. Even with his modest income, Daddy sent money to his parents, to my mother's mother, and to some of his less fortunate siblings. I once accidentally came across a sad letter from my grandfather to C.A., pleading for additional funds because the price of his crops during the Depression had fallen so low.

We could afford to take a brief vacation by car almost every year until the war—to lakes in nearby Iowa; cottages in the Colorado Rockies; once to the World's Fair in Chicago. Occasionally we made weekend trips to visit Grandmother Sorensen in the tiny Nebraska town of Dannebrog (Danish flag). Saturday afternoons, I would take long walks by myself, learning the delights of solitude, sometimes ranging past the city limits, past the state penitentiary, past the Catholic orphan asylum, along the railroad tracks, where hoboes exchanged food, blows, and get-rich schemes. At night, before falling asleep, I heard the whistle of the Rock Island Railroad as it passed a mile from our neighborhood, and wondered where it was heading and who was on board and why. My knowledge of other countries was limited to my stamp collection. The largest and most colorful stamps—from far-off places like Cameroon and Guatemala—seemed the most intriguing, but I did not know enough about the wonders of the world even to dream about them, much less aspire to see them.

I met a Southern Baptist belle one summer when I attended a high school debate institute at Northwestern University. I exchanged lengthy letters with her every day, and looked forward to a reunion in her Dallas home over the Christmas holidays. Such a trip and such a relationship both being firsts for me, I prepared for my father a formal five-page "debate brief" stating the "affirmative case" as to why I should be permitted to make this trip. My brief must have worked, because I made the trip, hitchhiking both ways, sleeping one night in a ditch when no cars appeared. The visit was a delight; but soon thereafter, the correspondence dwindled, and then halted on her end, without explanation. After some months, a letter from her parents informed me that this lovely, intelligent girl had committed suicide. I was stunned. It was an early, horrifying lesson of the unpredictability of life.

In our teens, all the Sorensen boys held jobs. Mine included knocking on strange doors and trying to interest the lady of the house in subscribing to *Collier's, American,* or the *Women's Home Companion,* a job that required—if I were to emulate Robert's success—both more persistence and more charm than I could muster. I also served as a runner on a florist's delivery truck, taking the designated bouquet from the truck to the specified address, ringing the doorbell, and being met inevitably with squeals of delight by whatever pretty young girl answered. My mother encouraged me to apply at age fourteen, the earliest legal working age, for a job in the local department store, where I ended up as a dishwasher in the coffee shop. At last, a job for which I had some experience!

My most memorable job, for which I recruited my young neighbor John to join me, oozed macho appeal—readying the municipal tennis courts after winter months of neglect and overgrowth. Stripped to the waist, we pulled up by the roots the massive weeds that were as tall as we were, used hand sickles on the remaining grass, and achieved in our first long day both sufficient reduction in the brush to make the next day's scheduled mowing look wholly possible, and sufficient overexposure to the sun and muscle strain to make rising from our beds the next day wholly impossible.

. . .

Camp Strader, a YMCA camp twenty-six miles southwest of Lincoln, on the Blue River, played an important part in my early life. Beginning at age eight, I was
there for at least ten days each summer, except my first
stay, which was cut short by homesickness and poison
ivy. My homesickness vanished in subsequent years as I
became friends with other campers. My swimming improved each year until I became a lifeguard and swimming instructor. Unfortunately, my poison ivy often
recurred. A local tradesman, looking at my blistered
legs, advised that I apply horse manure, leave it on, and
let it dry out and harden, adding that when it finally fell
off, I would find the poison ivy rash gone. Convinced I
would also find my friends gone, I decided to stay with
more conventional treatments.

Artemas W. Browne ("Brownie") was the camp
director. I served for two summers as assistant camp
director and program director, and considered him
a mentor. I learned a lot from Brownie. On one occasion, an abusive young assistant counselor-in-training,
who had been imposed upon the camp by his influential mother, so bitterly resented my disciplining him one
evening, while Brownie was in Lincoln, that he angrily
left camp in the middle of the night, leaving behind a

letter addressed to me with the foulest language I had ever encountered. When Brownie returned, his ears apparently burned by the young man's indignant mother, he demanded an explanation. Upon receiving both the explanation and the letter, he merely nodded and said, "I think we'll just turn this over to his mother."

A far more harrowing experience at camp brought me my first brush with death, shortly after I turned seventeen in 1945. I reported it all in a letter to my father:

> *You came very close to having one less son in the Sorensen family. We had the worst flood out here . . . The river is fast and high. A few days ago, when the river suddenly rose, several young counselors and a kitchen hand were in town at a movie, and could not [cross the Blue River to] come back until yesterday. I took one of the large "Indian war canoes" across to pick them up with their luggage. By paddling hard and keeping the bow of the boat pointed upstream, I was able to keep it under control, get across to the dock on the other side, and load them in, pleading with them to climb in carefully with their luggage and to paddle in unison with all their might. They were all frightened, inasmuch as the river—not far below the docks on each side where we cross—flows . . . over*

*a dam. . . . As you may also recall, an emergency
cable is strung across the river for any lost boatman
to seize should he find himself drifting down
toward the dam against his will. In yesterday's
crossing, when the current—despite my attempted
navigation—swept us back and the canoe struck a
submerged tree right beneath the cable, several of
the boys [young counselors] panicked and stood up
to grab the cable, causing the boat to capsize, spilling
into the river the rest of its contents—including the
luggage, one counselor, Larry, too short to reach
the cable, Bobby, our equally short 13-year old
kitchen boy, and me. When I came up for air, I shed
my shoes and jeans, started swimming upstream
as strongly as I could, saw the canoe rushing
downstream past me, spotted Larry swimming for
the camp dock ahead of me, and finally managed to
swim far enough to lunge for Larry's leg after he had
grabbed a low-hanging branch on the camp side, just
in time for me to turn around and see, in addition to
four frightened yelling counselors still clinging to the
cable, little Bobby thrusting up one skinny arm in
vain or farewell as he was swept over the dam, as the
parents who had driven these boys back to camp that
morning stood on the side above the dam hysterically
screaming.*

Our camp director, Brownie, gathered us under the flagpole to calm us down, put us to work clearing camp of the layers of mud that the flood had deposited, and informed us that after lunch we would drive around the back way into town to see a relaxing movie, and that he had been notified that there would be an inquest the next day. The police and fire departments had already made a comprehensive search of the riverbanks without finding any trace of Bobby, and said their next step was to drag the river bottom. Only the splintered pieces of the canoe, which had been dashed at the bottom of the dam on its concrete apron, had turned up. We had to assume that Bobby had been smashed into splinters as well.

My letter ended there, as I had no more time to write; but the story did not end there. An "inquest," I wondered. I had been responsible for that canoe full of younger boys. Was I going to be led off in manacles?

I will never forget our incredulity, astonishment, and tears of relief three hours later when a downstream miller telephoned to say that a little boy had apparently been washed ashore on a small mid-river sand island, about a mile from the camp, and was calling for help. It was Bobby. The fire department, which had spent hours looking for him, was called to rescue him. Aside from swallowing a lot of water, he was unharmed. All was well. He was light enough to have been tossed free of the dam's concrete apron, and tough enough to have struggled to the surface, grabbed and held on to a fragment of the canoe until he was swept close enough to the island to see it, swim to it, stagger ashore, and fall into an exhausted sleep. His parents were each called again, this time to convey the wonderful news that Bobby had miraculously survived being swept over the dam.

Chapter 5

Education

Whatever capacity I developed as a writer was nurtured in an articulate family. My father was an outstanding speaker and trial lawyer. My mother was a professional editor and writer. My brothers and sister were all debaters. It all began at the family dining table.

My mother taught me tongue twisters to improve enunciation and played word games with us. My father, precise in his use of the English language, insisted that his children follow his high standard. Whenever any of us at the dinner table related an event that we had "never experienced before," he would always ask, "Before when?" He taught us the importance of clear, direct speech.

Our house was always overflowing with reading material, with bookcases, magazine racks, and small tables covered with newspapers and magazines of every kind: the *Saturday Evening Post, Life, Look, Harper's, Atlantic Monthly,* the *Saturday Review of Literature, Omnibook* (in which I devoured condensed versions of current best-sellers), and the monthly *Reader's Digest.* As a boy, I read everything I could get my hands on. Our set of encyclopedias consisted of several massive volumes on the bottom shelf of the living room bookcase. An individual volume was too heavy for me to lift. I would pull one out and sprawl on the floor on my stomach and elbows, looking up facts of history, geography, and biographies of the famous.

Every Saturday morning, our mother took us to the children's section in the Lincoln Public Library, carrying a bushel basket into which each of us added the books of our choice, bringing them back the following Saturday in the same basket to be replaced with our next selections. *Treasure Island, Tom Sawyer, Aesop's Fables, Caddie Woodlawn, Call of the Wild,* and the works of Dickens, Sandburg, Swift, Lewis Carroll, and others fascinated me. The first books I could read featured stories about the animal kingdom by Thornton Burgess, then I moved on to fairy tales, in time *The Wonderful Wizard of Oz* and all the rest of that series (the Harry Potter series of my day). The Hans Christian Andersen and Grimm Brothers works, to say nothing of Frank Capra's films, reinforced my idealistic belief that justice and true love could prevail against wicked kings, witches, and politicians.

In high school, I read about Cyrano, Othello, and other dedicated heroes. My interest and even my literary style were inspired by the speeches of Jefferson, Lincoln, Churchill, and Franklin Roosevelt. In college, I enjoyed Robert Sherwood's *Roosevelt and Hopkins*, about the remarkable relationship between a progressive president from the aristocratic East and his trusted, nerdish liberal aide from the Midwest. I read my parents' antiwar books—Remarque's *All Quiet on the Western Front* and Harrison's *Generals Die in Bed*. I read about famous lawyers like Clarence Darrow and orators like Robert G. Ingersoll. I discovered from reading newspapers that events in the real world were more dramatic than novels, more comical than the comics, and more thrilling than mysteries.

Although I rarely left the Midwest I was carried afar, on the wings of words, to Persia and Paris, to Cathay and Capri, over the Silk Road and the Spice Route, to the Tower of London, the Tower of Babel, and beyond to the Land of Oz, never imagining that in the second half of my life I would travel to every corner of the globe, to meet with prime ministers, princes, and potentates.

As an author, my first book was a compilation of my poems written in elementary and junior high schools. With one exception, each poem was short, one to three verses. They included: "Books," "Armistice Day" (already antiwar), "Pirates Had Me" (lively fiction), and "Dishes" (putting a cheerful face on my regular chore). Eerily, the only two-page poem in this work, titled "The Hero," is about a heroic young man named Jack who bravely tried to save me and our fellow passengers and pilot from a fiery plane crash, but fell dead before he could finish the job.

My public speaking career did not get off to a promising start. When I was in first grade, my mother organized a home recital in which I was to recite from memory "The Gingham Dog and the Calico Cat." I had barely begun when I saw my brother Tom smirking from the front row of chairs arranged in our living room. I broke into uncontrollable giggles, and ran from the room. I had better luck as a counselor one summer at Camp Mishawaka near Grand Rapids, Minnesota, when a violent storm blew down the camp's flagpole, lifeguard tower, several trees, and the one and only electric power line, leaving me with the job of telling a story to 130 boys huddled in a darkened mess hall to keep them safe, quiet, and calm during the storm. I no longer remember what story I told, but I was touched to learn from a recent letter that at least one of those campers still remembers that dramatic night roughly sixty years ago.

I could not have received a better education than I received from Sheridan Elementary School, Irving Junior High School, and Lincoln High. My parents were attentive but relaxed about my intellectual choices, with one exception—my mother insisted that all of her children study Latin, and years of it. My responsibilities as president of the Lincoln High writers' club and editor of its literary magazine, the *Scribe*, also helped to develop my writing skills. My self-portrait in the *Scribe*'s thumbnail description of contributors read "interested in sports. . . . has an antipathy for hypocrites. Ted considers Senator Norris the greatest living statesman."

The clarity, quality, and color of my writing also improved as a result of my experience as a high school debater. Before a competition, I would draft an outline, organizing my arguments and materials around that outline in a comprehensive yet concise way. Then I would compile relevant quotations from distinguished Americans and other experts, copying those quotations onto three-by-five index cards, and using them where they seemed most relevant. To give credit where credit is due, to the extent that my help in 1960 might have contributed to JFK's successful debate against Richard Nixon, my high school debate coach, Florence Jenkins, who taught me much of what I knew about public speaking and debating, deserves at least a footnote in the history of that election.

Drama also drew my attention in high school. But I had no illusion that theater was a possible preparation for my career. Or was it? To build friendships in politics, to further congressional relations from the White House, to advance diplomacy in international capitals, all occasionally required some acting skills.

The grand finale of my high school speaking career was my commencement address in St. Paul's Methodist Church to my 386 fellow seniors and their parents and friends on June 2, 1945. Grandiloquently titled "It's Our America Now," my speech referred not only to our nation's "high ideals," but also to "corruption and bribery, war and internal strife, discrimination and crime."

> It's all being tossed in our laps. What are we going to do with it? Some believe we will only make matters worse, believe us to be silly irresponsibles who care nothing about our nation. They only think of the boys and girls pouring out of dances and drug-

stores with their painted cars and jive talk . . . But we'll prove that they're wrong . . . Underneath our happy-go-lucky aspects, there are deep feelings and thoughts, a desire to serve our country, a wish to prove our worth. Now the time has come. . . . We should prove our worth by improving our country. [I liked that line so much that I repeated it immediately.] It's our America now.

It may not have soared, but I was seventeen.

Despite its location in the heart of the American agricultural belt, Lincoln in 1928 liked to call itself "the Hartford of the West" because of the many insurance companies that chose to locate their headquarters there. More important for me was the fact that three institutions of higher learning were located in the city, including my beloved alma mater, the University of Nebraska. In our household, it was always assumed that each of us would attend the University of Nebraska, as our parents had. The tuition and bills for a Nebraska resident during my first year totaled $150; and I had a merit scholar stipend that covered most of that. Fred Ballard, a local playwright friend of my mother, told her that I should go to his alma mater, Harvard, and that he would make inquiries on my behalf, which he did without success. Perhaps just as well. Even at the University of Nebraska, I seemed a fish out of water, a seventeen-year-old freshman who did not drink, smoke, or even (with any skill) dance.

To accommodate older veterans returning from World War II, the University of Nebraska and its College of Law had adopted a combined curriculum. Under that system, two years of undergraduate liberal arts studies made a student eligible for four years of law school, awarding the standard law degree after six years at the university. Because I was anxious to get into the real world by following my father's footsteps into the legal profession, I made the mistake of applying under this combined system. During my first year at the university, I reminded my faculty advisor, in an accidental campus encounter, that the liberal arts catalogue contained several courses on constitutional history, tax accounting, and other topics that might relate to my future legal career; and I asked whether I should not switch into those courses. "No," he said, pointing to the law college one block away, "they will make a plumber out of you soon enough." I switched no courses. By not recognizing the wisdom of his remark, I missed out on additional courses in literature, history, and economics that I later wished I had taken.

Not expecting to be a speechwriter, I took no university course in the principles of classical rhetoric, declamation, or even English composition. But I learned a lot from two wise university debate coaches and speech instructors, Dr. Leroy T. Laase and Dr. Donald Olsen, and from my participation in one debate and oratory contest after another. I also learned a lot when one of my debate partners and I were trounced by a visiting British team with superior capacity for witty riposte and extemporaneous rebuttals.

The center of my campus life was the University YMCA, not for religious reasons but because my brother Tom and I became close friends with its dynamic, liberal executive secretary, the tall, chubby, bespectacled, warmhearted, witty Gordon Lippitt, a fierce Ping-Pong player and an ordained Methodist minister. Gordon was linked to the Christian student social activism movement, and teamed with Ruth Shinn, the equally effective leader of the university YWCA. Together they introduced their members to liberal activism, particularly on behalf of minority rights and workers' rights, and to New York's left-wing newspaper *PM*, to which my brother Robert became a subscriber.

I grew more interested in international affairs when the university's extraordinary chancellor, Dr. R. A. Gustavson, having been active in UNESCO, started a "model" UNESCO conference on campus, with me as moderator. Chancellor Gustavson's contacts enabled us to secure outstanding keynote speakers, including the noted author, poet, and diplomat Archibald McLeish, and the brilliant statesman who later became one of my lifelong heroes, Ralph Bunche, a Nobel Peace Prize winner and civil rights leader who was a principal draftsman of the United Nations Charter. A quiet and unassuming man, Bunche paid me the honor of visiting my small student apartment before returning to New York.

Law school—particularly the first year—was hard work, but I enjoyed it, especially the freshman course in constitutional law taught by the Dickensian bull-necked law school dean, Frederick K. Beutel, whose thunderous denunciations of unprepared or tongue-tied students terrorized us all. Whenever a student replied to the dean that he was unprepared to report on the assigned case, the "Red Dean," as conservative state legislators called him, would shake his massive jowls and loudly mutter, "How unfortunate! How unfortunate!" while scribbling in the class roll next to that pitiable student's name several words that we sensed were truly unfortunate. The following year, after I had worked with the dean on liberal causes and studied under him in a much gentler second-year class, I assumed that age or illness had diminished his thunder, only to discover, when I passed by that year's freshman constitutional law class, and heard his denunciatory roar, that his gruff and imperious conduct during our freshman year had been largely an act for our benefit.

I served as editor in chief of the law review, requiring both editorial and writing responsibilities. My father had held that post thirty years earlier. One of my own law review articles was the basis for an article published in the March 1951 issue of the *Progressive*, to which my parents had long subscribed. The article, "Can't Teachers Be Citizens Too?" deplored the tendency of local governments and school boards to treat teachers not as professionals, but as hired hands who were forbidden to participate as candidates or activists in local elections, particularly those involving educational issues, adding that the Lincoln chapter of Americans for Democratic Action had prevented the passage of a similar resolution by the Lincoln school board.

I also made several lifelong friends in law school, including Omaha's Lee White, one of my future deputies in the Senate and the White House. Lee, who has written his own memoirs, tells me that we first met when I told a professor that the facts in the case he had described reflected the "Queen Mary syndrome." When the professor demanded an explanation, says Lee, I related the story of the New Yorker who told his wife that, while at the Hudson Pier during his lunch hour, he had leaned against the *Queen Mary* to light a cigarette and it had gone out to sea, a mistaken identification of cause and effect.

I treasured growing up in Lincoln; but, like my siblings, I felt restless. Little more than one year after my family gathered for a celebratory picnic in Lincoln's Pioneers Park upon my graduation from law school, an item in the *Lincoln Evening Journal* said it all: "The mailbox at the C. A. Sorensen home has an international flavor. Letters from five children keep Mr. and Mrs. Sorensen pretty well informed on the world's events." Ruth had just been admitted to Johns Hopkins University Graduate School of Advanced International Studies and left after graduation with her husband, Derek Singer, for Bolivia to work with CARE, an international nonprofit organization. Robert was doing research for government projects, which soon took him to Munich for Radio Free Europe. Tom, a newspaperman, was in the Lebanese Republic in Southwest Syria with the State Department Information Service (whether he worked for another agency was not discussed in public), and Phil went to Japan with the Coast Guard after serving in the ROTC, where he claimed he wore mismatched socks with his spiffy uniform as a silent protest against militarism. "We had five children so we could see some of them often as we grew older," my father told a reporter. "Now they're all on different continents." I was their only child still in the United States, having moved to Washington to find a job.

After his military service, my brother Phil returned to Lincoln, graduated with honors from the University of Nebraska College of Law, clerked for a federal judge, and entered the private practice of law. In one of his most remarkable cases, Phil obtained the release from a state mental institution of an illegally committed white Nebraska coed, whose only act of alleged insanity was to disclose to her wrathful father her intention to marry a black student. Long after he invoked the full force of the law to free the young woman, Phil's representation of her was later the basis of a smear campaign in rural Nebraska when he successfully ran for the office of lieutenant governor.

Chapter 6

Conscience

Political Activism

I had no interest in politics until I was four years old. That year, my father introduced his three little sons from the platform at a county fair in southeastern Nebraska where he was making a campaign appearance. Afterward we were taken to the local dairy cooperative and treated to all the ice cream we wanted. I decided then and there that politics was pretty good.

Four years later, on October 10, 1936, President Franklin D. Roosevelt, as part of his first reelection campaign, delivered a speech at Omaha's Union Station, where he spoke from the rear platform of his train. My father drove me to Omaha and put me on his shoulders at the edge of the crowd so I could have my first glimpse of an American president. I also remember the cold and dark November night before Election Day that November when I witnessed up the block on Sheridan Boulevard, an old-fashioned torch-light parade of boisterous Democrats singing "Happy Days Are Here Again," the Roosevelt campaign song. My whole family backed Roosevelt, except my thirteen-year-old brother Robert, who supported Alf Landon. But, not surprisingly, considering my father's nonpartisanship, we were not raised as partisans. Asked decades later whether we were brought up as "Republicans, Democrats or what," my brother Tom replied, "or what."

During the next election year, 1938, I had my first real political experience. I returned from summer camp to find that my father had launched a campaign for the nonpartisan post of chief justice of the Nebraska State Supreme Court, a multicandidate race in which he faced an uphill fight. When my father reserved time on a statewide radio hookup to present his case on the Sunday evening before the primary, he discovered that one of his opponents had purchased the following block of time, letting my father build an audience for him. At home, our family gathered around the radio, heard my father's statement, and noted that it had been cut short. The remainder of his purchased time was filled with the worst, shrillest semi-operatic music we had ever heard. We promptly turned off our radio. No doubt a loud sound reverberated statewide as other radios were clicked off before my father's hapless opponent could begin his allotted time. When my oldest brother, Robert, returned home with Daddy from the studio, he smilingly reported that he had been sitting in the waiting room with Daddy's opponent when the "musical interlude" began, and saw the other candidate's face fall. Dirty tricks did not originate with Nixon.

My proudest campaign assignment in the general election that November—in which C.A. was one of two nominees—was to stand in front of my elementary school, a designated polling place, handing out to voters palm cards containing my father's name, picture, and slogan. I dutifully planted a yard sign—a full-scale replica of the palm card—in the lawn at the beginning of the sidewalk that traversed the hill to the school. With each card I added a wistful oral injunction: "Please vote for my father." Basking in the glow of what seemed to my untutored ears the warm responses of passersby, I was astonished and angered to see a well-dressed couple turn into the sidewalk at the bottom of the hill and yank my yard sign out of the ground and discard it. I was even more astonished to see, when they passed me and rejected my card, that the perpetrator of this outrage was none other than my father's opponent. He won, became a distinguished chief justice and a family friend.

Our interest in politics was not limited to campaigns. We subscribed to the *Nation*, the *New Republic*, and the *Progressive*, all liberal magazines. A portrait of President Roosevelt held the place of honor in our living room, accompanied in later days by a framed copy of the "Four Freedoms" proclamation. Tom frequently confided in me at bedtime his secret master plan to climb the political ladder, starting with a race to become a trustee of the local sanitation district, then move from there to the local school board, from there to state legislator, to mayor, to congressman, to United States senator, possibly even to the White House. Many years later, when I actually had an office in the White House, he told an interviewer: "If you had taken a secret ballot of the five of us in 1940, when Ted was 12, we would not have picked him as the one most likely to become Special Counsel to the President. . . . I told him he'd have to stop spending all his time cutting out the baseball pictures from the back of the Grape-Nuts packages if he was ever going to get anywhere." Only to such a keenly political family could I have seemed uninterested in politics.

But Tom had a point. To me, most politicians seemed dull compared to sports stars and bold aviators like

Charles Lindbergh or Amelia Earhart. That changed in 1944, when our Northwestern University summer debate institute adjourned one evening to hear the radio broadcast of FDR's famous Teamsters Union speech, in which he ridiculed the Republicans for attacking his little dog Fala, whose Scotch blood, said FDR, resented Republican complaints that a U.S. naval vessel had been used to transport him. Roosevelt's artful combination of humor, eloquence, and political zingers was eye-opening. Soon I was listening to recordings of great orations while my classmates were listening to pop music.

My growing interest in politics was reinforced in high school. Under a program designed to give students experience in possible fields of future endeavor, I was a temporary assistant to a senior member of the state legislature, who kindly went through the motions of asking me to prepare a memorandum on a pending bill. Too shy to walk onto the legislative chamber floor to hand my analysis to him, I nervously hung around the entrance until an officious sergeant-at-arms asked: "Can I help you, sonny?" With all the indignation a high school senior could silently muster, I thought: *Sonny? Someday I'll be back.*

In those early years, my siblings and I were involved in more than one local campaign. One night Robert and

I learned of a potential scandal involving our candidate's opponent. What to do with it? We had no standing or credibility with the local press, no access to favored journalists. We decided to take this potentially explosive (we thought) information to the candidate's more experienced campaign manager, Mr. A. V. Dowling. It was late at night. He came to the door in his robe and pajamas, and listened to our presentation. When we expressed our concern that there was no one who could get this to the press, he replied with a question: "How about A. V. 'Dirty' Dowling?"

At the age of fourteen, I caught my only glimpse of the statesman whom I had described as my political hero in every high school survey on that question, and whose picture would grace the wall of my White House office two decades later. When an aged and weary Senator George W. Norris returned to the state to make one last try for reelection, my father brought the entire family to help swell the crowd at the state fairgrounds, and my sister, Ruth, posed on Norris's lap for the news photographers.

The other statesman whose name was known to every Nebraska child, even though his heyday was decades earlier, was William Jennings Bryan. I regard three true Bryan stories in my repertoire as delightfully illustrative of basic political truths:

✦ No Political Party Is Monolithic. After Bryan's first surprise presidential nomination, the more conservative Democratic Senator David Hill of New York, when asked by reporters if he could support his party's nominee, replied carefully: "I am a Democrat still—very still."

✦ All Politics Is Local. When the Bryan family was in Lincoln awaiting the outcome of one November presidential balloting, his daughter Ruth—later a distinguished American diplomat—impatiently went outdoors to jump rope and was asked, by the journalists gathered around her, if she had any early reports on that day's election tallies, she replied: "I don't know about the rest of the country, but we're doing all right here on D Street."

✦ Once a Governor, Always a Governor. When I was very small, a hand-in-hand stroll with my father in downtown Lincoln was interrupted by a brief conversation with a man whom he addressed as "Governor." Afterward, when I asked who that was, he replied: "Charlie Bryan," the brother of William Jennings Bryan, often called the Great Commoner. Even at that age, I knew enough politics to protest: "He's not governor." "But he once was," my father explained, "so he is called that forever."

My Unitarianism

Paraphrasing Will Rogers on politics, I can truly say: I am not a member of any organized religion—I am a Unitarian. The term "Unitarian" arose initially to distinguish its adherents from those other Christians who believed in the Holy Trinity, a concept introduced into Christianity many centuries after the death of Jesus. To honor the compassionate teachings and courageous life of Jesus, Unitarians do not find it necessary to attribute divine intervention to the circumstances of his birth or death. Jesus was a "son of God," Unitarians believe, in the sense that all human beings are children of God, that there is a spark of divinity in all of us. We look upon him as a great teacher, not a miracle worker, saluting him as a messenger of peace, decency, and wisdom. As I wrote in my youth, "I believe in a God of the Universe, of love, truth, goodness, and humility."

It would both simplify and shorten this narrative if I could reprint here the official Unitarian creed. But there is none. Uniquely, Unitarians maintain a unity of spirit with a diversity of convictions. We don't believe that our church is the only true religion or the only path to heaven or God. One of the fundamental principles that binds us together is our ability to believe differently, with each individual Unitarian thinking for himself. In the words of Morris Cohen, one of my favorite philosophers when I was a teenager: "There may be more wisdom and courage as well as more faith in honest doubt than in most of the present creeds." The invocation of honest doubt has been useful to me all my life. By nature, Unitarians are doubters, looking for evidence, too modest to believe that they can define God, calling themselves humanists rather than atheists.

Personally, I have known too many sincere religious believers, who have led constructively good lives, to adopt a defiant, confrontational attitude by labeling myself an "atheist," however much my personal invocations of God as a natural force beyond ordinary proof and prediction may differ from others. I cannot deny that much happens in this world that we cannot understand, including some patterns that could reflect some greater power than we will ever know. Even truth and reason—my two bywords—sometimes raise questions for which there are no clear answers.

But while Unitarians observe no binding doctrines and therefore have no apostasy or heresy, surely this does not mean that we have no faith. I have faith—in humanity, in the family, in democracy, in justice, and in morality. I have faith in universal values—not all of which come solely from Christian denominations or leaders.

I have encountered many people who are Unitarians

but do not know it (much like the character in a Molière play thrilled to discover he had been "speaking prose" all his life). In Unitarianism's early days in this country, it was said, more in jest than in truth, that Unitarians stood for three basic principles: "the fatherhood of God, the brotherhood of man, and the neighborhood of Boston." In Lincoln, the old brick Unitarian church that I attended proclaimed that it stood for "the ennoblement of man and world brotherhood." Some might say that's not enough; but I say it's not very different from original Christianity. Like the Good Samaritan, of whom Jesus spoke, Unitarians have a love for the least, the last, and the lost, a belief in integrating faith with works. It is a religion of universalism and humanity, not one of fire and brimstone. Most Unitarians are political liberals; Forrest Church, the Unitarian minister who officiated at my daughter's wedding, entitled one of his books *God and Other Famous Liberals*.

During my earliest years, religion was not discussed in our home. My father would sometimes sing the old evangelical hymns of his youth, but more out of sentiment than spirituality. He privately noted later that "as a pale-faced, overly-serious lad, I accepted the teachings of the New Testament as literally true." Some of his campaign speeches routinely invoked God, causing one letter writer to chide C.A.: "I agree with you except where you bring in the Bible stuff. Every rascal, horse thief and Wall Street banker is for the Bible."

A self-proclaimed "realist idealist," he once wrote me a letter explaining his "idealistic philosophy, or religion, if you want to call it that":

> *The future of the universe has not been written in any book; it is in the blood and brains of the stumbling human race. We human beings are on our own; nothing has been irrevocably settled. The job is ours. So I offer you a philosophy of an unfinished world where there still remains the adventure of building it as we want it, a glorious opportunity for youth to help write and act in the drama of earth's story to be . . . We are thus, all of us, the small and the big, builders of the universe for all time.*

In my childhood, Christmas was our favorite time of year, a family—not a religious—holiday. On Christmas Eve, our practice was to drive past those Lincoln residences that had won prizes for the most elaborate outdoor decorations. Icicles, not angels, decorated our living room Christmas tree. We sang Christmas carols, but had no idea what "our dear savior's birth" referred to.

Along with my siblings and classmates, I recited the Lord's Prayer in class—in fact, I recited two different versions, never being certain whether I needed to be forgiven my sins or my trespasses—but I attached no deep religious feeling to that recitation. When my brother Phil was born, Daddy asked his devout sister Grace to come look after us; and she insisted that we all learn and recite at bedtime the familiar child's prayer: "Now I lay me down to sleep . . ." That did not last long after her departure. She made a more lasting impression when she played softball with us in the backyard.

This wholly secular life changed suddenly when mother summoned us from the backyard one day when I was eleven or twelve years old and announced that we could no longer attend our church's Sunday school parties if we did not at least try out Sunday school. Thereafter we attended the All Souls Unitarian Church every Sunday morning, and the three youngest—Phil, Ruth, and I—would go to Sunday school. This interfered with my neighborhood softball and touch football games; but gradually we adjusted, and became a part of the church community, making many new friends, including Dr. Weatherly, the aging minister who had helped bring my father to Lincoln from Grand Island College and had taken him on the Ford Peace Ship.

The Reverend Dr. Weatherly was succeeded by Carl Storm, a dynamic young minister from New England, who preached every Sunday a brilliant and informative sermon about Unitarianism, other religions, and their place in our country and world. I learned a lot from those sermons—about life and liberalism and the difference between idealism and fanaticism. He could expose hypocrisy in both public and religious matters more incisively than anyone I have heard or read since. His sermons drew me to regular church attendance in my teens. Unitarianism became a major influence on my life. Between my years in elementary school and my departure for Washington at age twenty-three, All Souls Church became a social and intellectual as well as religious center, second in influence only to my parents and siblings. I even considered, briefly, a career as a Unitarian minister. My Unitarianism was shaken only in my last year of high school when my Dallas girlfriend filled me with doctrine from her Southern Baptist upbringing. While that lasted, my wise father patiently discussed my new spiritual leanings with me, offering only a few questions, but no objections.

On Sunday, May 16, 1948, at the age of twenty, I delivered a sermon to the entire congregation titled "Do Unitarian Youth Get Religion?" a question occasionally raised by Unitarians within the church as well as by outside critics. My "Youth Sunday" sermon answered that question by first acknowledging the variety of views and practices in our denomination. I drew from my father's philosophy, quoting a poem by Edward Markham: "Here on the common human way is all the stuff to build a heaven." In those postwar days, I called for a "plan of . . . global reconstruction consistent with the human capacity to meet human needs in a human way, a concern for human values and progress." It was the only sermon I would deliver before the age of forty, except for one on civil rights to the Lincoln African Methodist Church while I was still in high school. Re-reading my Unitarian youth sermon now, almost sixty years later, I stand by my conclusion that Unitarians of all ages do in fact "get enough religion."

My Unitarian Church and the Catholic Church, into which John F. Kennedy was born, stand at opposite ends of the religious spectrum on matters of absolute faith, unchanging doctrine, church-state relations, rituals, symbols, and the obedience of the faithful to a church hierarchy. Thus it is ironic that the two of us collaborated so well for so long on reducing the obstacle that his Catholic faith posed to his hopes for becoming president of the United States. In 1960, when JFK became the Democratic nominee for president, his religion was the single largest negative in his path. Yet by 1963 the president of the Unitarian Universalist Association of North America acknowledged that, despite the Catholic position on church-state separation, he had come to value highly JFK's "devotion to democracy, peace and freedom" and "his liberalism, reason, and courage."

JFK's most notable speech on the subject was his comprehensive address as nominee to the Houston Ministers' Association in September 1960. En route to Texas on his campaign plane, as we worked side by side on the final draft of that speech, he laughingly asked whether my years of involvement in this issue on his behalf, my contacts with Catholic clergymen and reading of papal encyclicals, had influenced me: "Is any of my Catholicism rubbing off on you?" "No," I replied, "but I think some of my Unitarianism is rubbing off on you." Many of the speeches that I drafted reflect Unitarian principles.

It is not a coincidence that Unitarians were mentioned by name in that speech to the Protestant ministers in Houston, or that one of JFK's principal assistants on the New York Liberal Party speech several days later was Arthur Schlesinger Jr., another Unitarian.

Draft Registration

More than a decade earlier, as I approached draft age near the end of World War II, I confronted a personal dilemma. The nonviolent philosophy of both the Unitarian Church and my upbringing led me to oppose war, but Hitler's attempted world domination and Japan's attack on Pearl Harbor required a national effort with which nearly every American family wished to cooperate. Ours was no exception. My father promised to pay me $300 for every month I was in the army as an inducement to enlist. In his view, the rise of fascism and totalitarianism threatened the principles of democracy that he had always championed. I did not know enough then about his past to realize how sharply these later views differed from the positions he had taken as a young man opposed not only to war but also to military training.

On August 16, 1945, when I was seventeen, I wrote to my father from my YMCA camp:

> Until yesterday, I had the fullest intentions of enlisting in the Navy at the end of summer . . . This was for your sake as much as anything. But yesterday the situation changed in every aspect. It was V-J Day [Victory in Japan, following May's victory in Europe and thereby totally ending the war]. The United States and her allies are completely victorious against all enemies. No more fighting men are needed. . . .

On August 17, my father replied:

Now that the war is over, I also see no need of your enlisting. . . . I doubt if the draft law will be in effect when you become 18. If it is, then of course you can and will go with the other boys . . .

In the year that followed my letter, I met, fell in love with, and was deeply influenced by Camilla Palmer, who had been raised a Quaker and was a strong believer in pacifism. We would later be married in a Quaker wedding ceremony at All Souls Unitarian Church on September 8, 1949. The two of us served as staff members in a Boone, Iowa, summer institute sponsored by the American Friends Service Committee, an organization devoted to the causes of peace and nonviolence.

When I turned eighteen in 1946, I found many of my friends going in different directions on this issue. Some regarded mere draft registration as a violation of their pacifist principles, and preferred to go to jail. Some hid or moved to Canada. Some vowed to register as noncombatants, but changed their minds when the time came. Some sought total exemption on whatever grounds they could find.

I chose none of those courses. I was willing—indeed, hoping—to serve in my country's armed forces, whether as an ambulance driver, or medic, or in some other form of noncombatant service. It was for this reason that I applied for noncombatant service as a conscientious objector.

My "Statement of Position," which I filed with my local draft board in Lincoln, began by acknowledging my choice of a path "which will not relieve me of the difficulties and dangers of service" or the criticism "of many," a path chosen because

> *I am a Unitarian . . . [and I was] taught that every man is my brother, every man has within him the spark of the divine, every man bears this relationship to the totality called God. Thus it is I could kill no man. . . . So it is I am what is called a pacifist—what Jesus called a peace maker. . . .*

That statement was filed with my draft board the year following the end of World War II; peace reigned, and no serious prospect of another shooting war appeared on the horizon. I was eighteen years old.

Because by law conscientious objector status required a religious base, my statement also included a mixture of familiar Unitarian positions from my family's church, traditional Quaker positions from my fiancée's faith, and expressions taken from the literature on nonviolence distributed by the student Christian movement.

I quoted Justice Musmanno at the Nuremburg Trials, U.S. Supreme Court Justice William O. Douglas, and Justice Oliver Wendell Holmes. I quoted Gandhi and Unitarian philosophers; I cited my father's activities as well as my mother's—all in a long, passionate five-page statement. It succeeded.

Later I reported my position and action in a letter to my sister, who shared my views, telling her that I could not join those acquaintances who were refusing to register at all, and that I had instead registered as a conscientious objector for noncombatant service:

> It's a tough position, since I can be condemned by the conservatives and militarists (hard on one's political future and law career), and yet also by some "more extreme" pacifists who believe in nonregistration. I understand their viewpoint, but do not so believe myself. . . .

Several years later, when I first arrived in Washington, before I met Senator John F. Kennedy, I made inquiries about joining the army's Judge Advocate General's Corps as a reserve attorney, stating: "my desire to serve in a role where I might contribute most, and where my own training and background will be most utilized . . . as a lawyer." The army promptly replied that its regulations denied eligibility for appointment in the Officers' Reserve Corps to "persons who are conscientious objectors" without an "abandonment of such beliefs and principles."

When I went to work for JFK, I believe he neither knew nor cared what my draft status was, although he may have later concluded (after an attack on my status by Senator Barry Goldwater) that he had to be cautious about including me in meetings or publicity on potential military crises. Obviously JFK, a World War II combat hero in the Pacific, was neither a pacifist nor a conscientious objector. Perhaps I should not say "obviously," inasmuch as General Eisenhower himself, according to his son John, became deeply convinced, as the result of his World War II experience, of the inherent wastefulness and cruelty of war. Over the years those military leaders whom I came to know best and admire most—General Maxwell Taylor during my White House days, Admiral Elmo Zumwalt in later years, and General Wesley Clark in still more recent years—were all more consistently against the use of combat troops as a means of solving international disputes than were politicians who had never experienced firsthand the horrors of war.

In 1961 my draft registration of more than a decade

earlier as a conscientious objector was resurrected when Walter Trohan, the conservative Washington bureau chief for the even more conservative *Chicago Tribune*, discovered that my mother was a "dedicated feminist who was accused of pacifist and radical sympathies in World War I" and that I had "escaped military service as a conscientious objector and Korean war service as a father."

This prompted Senator Barry Goldwater to say on the Senate floor: "It often requires more courage to seek this classification [conscientious objector] than to serve [in the armed forces]. However, I can't help but wonder at the thoughts of the fathers and mothers of American boys who right now are being called up for active military service when they learn that one of the President's closest advisors is an objector because of conscience."

Letters to President Kennedy from the general public included some echoing the Goldwater position. Fortunately the longtime director of the Selective Service System in Nebraska, Guy Henninger, a retired army major general, issued a supportive statement shortly after Goldwater's remarks, saying he had reviewed my draft record and found it

very regular . . . I noticed where some member of Congress said Sorensen avoided military service by claiming to be a conscientious objector. This 1AO classification does not avoid military service. A person with that qualification goes into uniform the same as anyone else and serves in a branch such as the Medical Corps.

He added that if all draft registrants had been as scrupulous as I had been about notifying my draft board of all changes of address, family status, and otherwise, the system would work much more smoothly.

In response to this public controversy, I summarized the facts in a September 28, 1961, memorandum to the president:

> At the age of 20 [sic], when engaged to a Quaker girl and impressed by the humanistic-pacifistic tendencies of my own parents, church and associates in that post-war era, I registered in the draft for non-combatant service (not non-hazardous service). I did not register as one opposed to any military service; but for non-combatant status which did not affect one's liability or likelihood of being called. . . . [Some years later I was] called for a physical, and reclassified 4F because of a tumor operation. Since then I have been classified 3A (married with children).

While hoping for the best, let us prepare for the worst. Goldwater and the Tribune may yet discover that my mother's parents came from Russia, that I have a cousin named for Eugene Debs, and that I have belonged to such obviously suspect organizations as the Native Sons and Daughters of Nebraska, the Nebraska Bar Association, Group Health and the YMCA.

Two years after leaving the White House, I was asked in a letter from a young stranger for advice on how a conscientious objector declaration on his part would affect his hopes for a career in public service. I replied: "this decision may hazard your career in public service, but it is only the first of many acts of courage which you may risk, if you are to be loyal to your conscience on matters of principle." That much I could advise him.

Interest in Civil Rights

Civil rights was the issue on which I was most active during my youth. This may seem odd for a boy growing up in Nebraska, a rural state that never had a large black population outside its only big city, Omaha. When my great-grandfather Soren settled in the state, census figures showed only fifteen black residents in Lincoln. As black settlers increasingly migrated from the South, there were growing racial tensions, even a riot.

Racism was a mystery to me. I did not understand how good churchgoing Nebraskans could knowingly exclude, insult, and injure fellow citizens simply because of the color of their skin. It was through the YMCA, which, in my youth, still set aside Tuesday evenings for "Negro Night," that I first socialized with blacks, including the Lincoln director of the National Urban League, Clyde Malone, on whose board my father served. While I was still in high school, Mr. Malone asked me to write a monthly column for the Urban League newspaper, the *Voice*, distributed to all members of the small, segregated black community in Lincoln. My *Voice* columns included a blast at the Lincoln City Council for its inaction on a housing project needed to relieve overcrowding for blacks, who had encountered fierce resistance to their attempts to move into traditionally white neighborhoods. Through the YMCA I also became familiar with both the Student Christian Movement and a religiously oriented peace organization, the Fellowship of Reconciliation and its Committee on Racial Equality (CORE), which later played an important role in the civil rights movement.

Upon hearing a report during my sophomore year in high school of a reprehensible slight against my young black coeditor of the school's literary magazine, I became angry at the hypocrisy of so many respectable white citizens. Applying some discipline to my own bad habits, I stopped using phrases then current among my peers—like "that's mighty white of you." I even urged a girlfriend to stand up at her college sorority's national convention and denounce its whites-only membership clause.

The injustice of it all became a recurring theme in my student orations. Instead of my involvement in the civil rights movement leading me to speak on the subject, my speeches led me to become involved in the movement. In view of the American Legion's ill will toward my father in his first race for attorney general, it was ironic that my highest honors in oratory came when I prevailed in the annual high school oratory contest sponsored by the Legion's Americanism Commission. My speech emphasized the proper interpretation of the Bill of Rights. "It is hard to be a Jew in Nazi Germany today," I said. "But is it not also hard to be a Negro in democratic America?"

Asked, while still in high school, to deliver a sermon to an all-black church, I entitled it "There's a Great Day Coming!" Deploring the fact that in Lincoln, "a city named for the Great Emancipator," "Negroes could buy or rent land freely only in an area restricted to 30 square blocks, and for higher prices" . . . "Look for your rights as Americans," I said, "but do not expect too much in a hurry, for this is a tangled question dating back to the beginnings of mankind. . . ." In later years, I regret to say, I would also show some initial caution.

The high school orations for which I twice won prizes were both attacks on race discrimination. In one, entitled "The Story of an American Failure," I told of the highly decorated Nisei (Japanese-American) war hero Ben Kuroki, who was subject to blatant racial discrimination upon his return to Nebraska from World War II combat. I may have been inspired by two Nisei university coeds I knew, whose families had been unjustly relocated after Pearl Harbor, a result of FDR's single greatest mistake.

My principal opportunity to take action, not merely make speeches on this subject, came when a biracial group of friends formed the Lincoln Social Action Council, and asked me to serve as chairman. It was a stirring experience. SAC members wanted action and they took it—direct action, like interracial sit-ins, which instantly and symbolically, if only temporarily, desegregated private establishments. We sought integration at the municipal swimming pool, restaurants, roller-skating rink, and student dormitories at the university. We even pressed the university to end the segregated athletic team policies of the Big Six Athletic Conference, as it ultimately did.

One night our little organization formed an interracial group of young couples to visit a roadhouse outside town known for barring blacks. On an evening when Duke Ellington and his band were playing, we assumed that the club's management would not bar black patrons; and we vowed to talk to the Duke himself if it happened. We were admitted without difficulty; and only later did it occur to me that the Duke might have had a clause in his contract specifying that there was to be no segregation enforced at any of the establishments at which he was performing.

Through the Social Action Council I led an effort to seek the enactment by the Nebraska State Legislature of a State Fair Employment Practices law, modeled after the national Fair Employment Practices Commission established by FDR during World War II. I cannot recall why I was selected to lead that effort. But I threw myself into it, speaking, lobbying, organizing letter-writing campaigns, strategizing with the bill's sponsor from Omaha and its few other legislative supporters, even testifying before the legislative committee holding hearings on the bill.

I was chagrined as well as surprised when the self-designated "chairman" of the Nebraska Communist Party appeared at the legislative hearing in support of the bill, knowing that his appearance could only hurt our cause in the legislature, and that he represented very few voters other than himself. Nor did it help when the head of the Associated Industries of Nebraska declared our bill to be "Communist" legislation and me to be a Communist, despite the fact that his two sons had been our neighbors and playmates for years. My colleagues and I were treated more gently if not more favorably by the head of Lincoln's largest factory, when he piously said of us in his statehouse testimony: "Forgive them, for they know not what they do . . . After my son fought in this war, you couldn't force me to hire a Jap." (I believe his factory may have later been acquired by a Japanese company.)

The committee killed the bill in a secret vote in 1947. We revived it in 1951, the year we received support from the new Omaha Urban League field secretary, Whitney Young, who, fifteen years later as head of the National Urban League, would work closely with me in the White House. We said the effort would never die. It did not. According to a *Lincoln Journal Star* survey decades later, "Things began to change in the 1960s and racial blinders were gradually removed from hiring practices, laws and attitudes," due at least in part to our efforts twenty years earlier. I was also pleased to read a recent analysis concluding that the Fair Employment Practice Act approved by the Nebraska State Legislature in 1965 differed little from the bill that I helped draft and promote in 1947–1951.

My parents were aware of all these activities. In fact, they inspired them. My mother, who had felt the sting of religious prejudice, had written in a 1916 editorial in the *University Journal* that "the pioneer spirit and the brotherhood of man are inseparable doctrines—the spirit of the broad prairies, that a man is a man regardless of race or color or creed." Yet, as they saw me grow increasingly involved in the battle for civil rights, they said nothing, though I heard later that my father disapproved of a law review article I had written proposing that the Nebraska legislature reexamine our state's statute on miscegenation. When informed by Nebraska Senator Hugh Butler's office in Washington that my sister had been among those demonstrators arrested in the District of Columbia in a 1950 sit-in to desegregate a Washington restaurant chain, C.A. reacted with neither anger nor righteousness, but a simple "That's Ruth," and sent her bail money.

Not long after I arrived in Washington and began my career as a lowly government attorney, some unauthorized moonlighting that I undertook in 1952 as a private pro bono lawyer afforded me the privilege and honor of playing a small role in the landmark school desegregation case before the U.S. Supreme Court, *Brown v. Board of Education of Topeka*. Consolidated with that Kansas case were four other Fourteenth Amendment challenges to segregated school systems, including that of the District of Columbia. In the latter case, *Bolling v. Sharpe*, eighteen civic organizations joined together in sponsoring an amicus brief arguing that the high court had an obligation to consider not only the judicial and legislative history of school segregation, but also the fact that "community experience" provided no basis for the defendants' argument that school desegregation would lead to widespread defiance and disruption.

The lead counsel of one of those eighteen organizations, the American Jewish Congress Commission on Law and Social Action, asked me to lend a hand after I explained that my government attorney duties at the time focused on a program concerning the establishment by Congress of integrated public schools on military bases nationwide—their integration, I noted, having proceeded largely without incident. To the best of my recollection, my only contribution to the brief, in addition to some minor editorial suggestions, was a short description of these schools. For that small contribution, the brief's main authors insisted that my name be listed with theirs as one of four lawyers signing the document.

Evolving Liberalism

Liberal idealism was imparted to me as part of my genetic composition. Our parents taught us by example to improve the world for all mankind. We took this lesson to heart. At the same time I was helping to organize the Lincoln Social Action Council, my siblings and I were among those organizing a Lincoln branch of Americans for Democratic Action (ADA), the national group of non-Communist liberals devoted to advancing the progressive movement in the United States; my brother Robert's wife, Marge, had worked in Chicago for an ADA affiliate. Organizing the ADA in Lincoln, I told friends, was like organizing the Anti-Defamation League in Cairo. At a Nebraska dinner honoring me in 2003, the former longtime governor of Nebraska, Frank B. Morrison, paying a lengthy tribute to my family in his speech, added: "Early in my political career, I was advised by a friend: 'Better stay away from those Sorensens—they are a little pinko.'"

Untrue. But I suppose our family did stand out in

those years, when FDR's successful farm programs were making many once-radical poor farmers more prosperous, giving them a stake in the status quo, and turning them into conservative Republicans. As the state became more conservative, the Sorensens were becoming Democrats, unwilling to remain in the political limbo of independents who were unable to take a side in major battles and less able to influence them. By the time I received word in 1948 that former Minnesota governor Harold Stassen, a Republican presidential hopeful, was interested in hiring a young law student to help in the Nebraska primary, I felt too little identification with his party to be tempted by the feeler. Upon reaching the age of twenty-two in 1950, I registered as a Democrat. Two years later, my political heritage experiencing a resurgence, I reregistered as "nonpartisan." Sometime thereafter, probably after I joined JFK's staff, I changed my registration back to Democrat.

I was hardly a revolutionary; the only law student demonstration in which I took part was a march on the capitol to demand more parking spaces. But in 1951, at the time of my first federal civil service background investigation, the FBI's sources—all presumably law school faculty or students—described me as "a militant liberal . . . Idealistic and in some respects perhaps impractical, based on the fact that the applicant recently wrote several law firms throughout the United States, indicating . . . that he would not be interested in employment unless these law firms followed the principles" of Americans for Democratic Action. "However," the report continued, "source believes applicant will outgrow his expression of immaturity and develop into an excellent lawyer." Another source said, "Sorensen's philosophy might be summed up by stating that Sorensen wants to be dead sure that this government will give the average fellow a break." "An idealist in the matters of world government and civil rights." "Very liberal in political philosophies." Still another did "not believe that either the applicant or his wife would be race conscious, inasmuch as they have friends of all races visiting them at their apartment." One complained that, as editor in chief of the law review, I would never listen to any ideas for an article in the Law Review unless the article dealt with civil liberties.

My favorite response to the FBI interrogator was given (I assume) by one of my conservative law school classmates: "Ted is a real liberal; but he's a loyal American." I will settle for that. I am still a loyal American, and I am still a real liberal.

PART II
Washington, D.C., 1951–1964

Chapter 7

Move to Washington, D.C.

As law school graduation neared, most of my class-mates were planning to stay in Nebraska. A few of the bolder ones went to Chicago, Kansas City, or California; but few chose to go East. I could not stay, despite my fondness for the state. I loved Lincoln, its serenity, its greenery, and its friendly people. But I always sensed that I had a larger purpose; I aspired to something I knew I would not find in Lincoln.

At law school, I had found myself increasingly attracted to public law, including administrative, international, and constitutional law. My interest in Washington was piqued by two D.C. lawyers who visited Lincoln during my final year in law school. One was on a recruiting trip for a firm handling Federal Communications Commission (FCC) work. The other was Stanley Gewirtz, a partner in a D.C. law firm and chairman of the Washington chapter of Americans for Democratic Action, in Lincoln to visit one of the few ADA outposts between Chicago and Los Angeles. During our brief conversations, both lawyers encouraged me to apply to their firms, which I did. I also wrote to the American Civil Liberties Union, the Anti-Defamation League of B'nai B'rith, and the American Friends Service Committee.

As editor in chief of the law review, and tied for first in my class, I had high expectations, but the initial responses to my job inquiries were discouraging. One of my professors wrote a friend on the U.S. Supreme Court, who replied that his clerkships for the next year were already filled. Dean Beutel wrote the distinguished Washington law firm of Arnold and Porter, but was told that it was a small firm with no vacancies or plans for expansion. I heard nothing from the two firms whose traveling partners had encouraged me to apply. With no advance notice to my wife or parents, I decided to go to Washington to pursue my job search in person.

When I informed my father of my plan, he did not try to talk me out of it. He had, I believe, quietly hoped and assumed that upon graduation, I would join him in his office. But that was not something I seriously considered. It was his practice, not mine, and I wanted to develop my own career. I also felt that the kind of legal work I might be able to find in Washington would offer me a greater opportunity for public service than any I would find in Nebraska. I wanted to make a difference.

On July 1, 1951, I left Lincoln. It may have been a headstrong, impulsive decision, I reflected, as I settled into my seat on the train to Chicago, where the next day I would change trains. I knew no one in Washington. My father knew no one there well enough to make any introductions or appointments on my behalf. I had only one marketable skill, and no license to practice it in the District of Columbia. With the exception of my youthful hitchhiking excursion to Dallas, I had never left the Midwest. Yet here I was, aboard an eastbound train, leaving behind everyone I cared about, even my wife, Camilla, who would join me in Washington a short time later.

Looking back, I have often wondered whether the fact that I came from the Middle West was an advantage, not the disadvantage that most people, including me, might have assumed. I understood the typical American because of my own middle-class Midwestern roots. But all I could think about, on that train ride, was the immense gamble I was taking.

I arrived in Washington's Union Station on the evening of July 3, having traveled farther by train than ever before in my life. I picture myself stepping off that train, greenhorn that I was: I had never drunk a cup of coffee, set foot in a bar, written a check, or owned a car. Clutching my father's battered suitcase, I took my first taxi ride, to the YMCA, where I had heard that inexpensive rooms were usually available. In those days, Pennsylvania Avenue was not closed to traffic; and I was thrilled when we drove by the White House with its front porch chandelier lit. I gazed at it with awe. That night, too excited to sleep, I lay on my narrow bed in a small YMCA room in the center of a strange and noisy city, feeling full of both uncertainty and wonder about what was to come, already missing my family.

In those years, Washington was not wholly attractive to an idealistic twenty-three-year-old newcomer from the Midwest. Senator Joseph McCarthy was tarnishing the city, country, and Senate with his reckless accusations. His association with the Republican Party was a major reason for my growing preference for the Democratic Party, although the Democrats had their own witch-hunter, the conservative senator from Nevada, Pat McCarran. Walking past the White House one day, I found the sidewalk crowded with pickets opposing the execution of Julius and Ethel Rosenberg, sentenced to death on charges of atomic espionage.

The occupant of that White House, President Truman, was under constant investigation, facing attacks from within his own Democratic Party. I admired President Truman's Midwestern liberalism, although I deplored his sweeping loyalty program for federal government employees. (At the request of one of my sister's friends from Nebraska, I provided free legal advice on that loyalty program to a young Japanese-American civil servant.) Upon becoming slightly acquainted years later, President Truman and I would discover that we shared not only a birthday, but also a White House secretary, Toi Bachelder, who came to the White House with FDR in 1933, and worked with me thirty years later.

The day after I arrived in Washington was the Fourth of July, a fact I had not considered in my hasty departure from Lincoln. No offices were open. My career was stalled for a day. That evening, at the suggestion of the desk clerk at the YMCA, I attended a National Symphony concert and fireworks display on the Washington Mall, along with a hundred thousand other spectators. Sitting on the lawn, surrounded by more people than inhabited the entire city of Lincoln, I felt totally alone.

The next day, trying to find Stan Gewirtz's law office on Jefferson Place, I discovered that every Washingtonian I encountered thought he knew where Jefferson Place was, but in fact did not—confusing it with

Jefferson Street, Jefferson Avenue, and Jefferson Drive. On a very hot, steamy Washington day, having neither the money nor the inclination to indulge in another taxi ride—in Lincoln, it had always seemed to me, only millionaires and drunks took taxis—I walked to each of these many Jefferson roadways until I finally arrived at the law firm, where I found Stan Gewirtz was not in his office. A kind partner told me they had no need for another lawyer and no plans for expansion, but he generously made some telephone inquiries for me.

As I continued my search on foot for several days, almost all the lawyers to whom I was introduced, whether in government or private practice, gave me encouragement and hope, but no job, each promising to call another office on my behalf, as they sent me off on another weary journey.

Finally, having submitted applications to a number of government agencies, I was hired by the Federal Security Administration (FSA). As I happily reported to my father by mail:

> Jack Tate [whom I had met in the course of my
> job search] of the State Department, who'd formerly
> been General Counsel for FSA, sent me there
> with his recommendation . . . The FSA building
> is new and beautiful and air conditioned, with its

own lunchroom and cafeteria, and as an agency
is generally very progressive and alert. Physical
facilities, office, desk, telephone, steno services, all
better than elsewhere. The man whose office I'll
share is very able and friendly, and asked me out to
dinner five minutes after he met me the first day I
walked in. I'm very happy about the whole situation
and anxious to begin tomorrow.

Less than two weeks after my arrival in Washington, I had a job. Camilla joined me, and we found a place to live.

In those early cold war days of loyalty tests and "pinko" suspicions, I was obligated to explain to curious friends and family that this agency was concerned not with national security but social security. It would soon become the Department of Health, Education, and Welfare, and later the Department of Health and Human Services. My first supervisor, a gentle career government attorney named Donald V. Bennett, taught me about both bureaucracy and government legal practice. My first lesson came when I asked to take leave the day after Thanksgiving, when my parents would be visiting, perhaps exchanging it for a full workday on some other holiday. Mr. Bennett firmly informed me that bureaucracy did not operate that way.

I supported myself, Camilla, and our firstborn son, Eric, on my initial government salary of $3,285 a year. "Seems pretty good to me," I wrote my father. "Don't tell 'em I'm not worth it, because it's not too much these days in this town." Among the family and friends visiting us in those days were my brother Tom and his wife, Mary, who asked me at a family reunion many years later: "Was that not horsemeat you occasionally served us?" I admitted it was. We were poor.

In the next several years, school and jobs brought three of my four siblings and other friends to Washington, most staying with us in our little house, now crowded after the birth of two more beautiful sons, Steve and Phil. Camilla was a full-time mother. For the first time in my life, I was making life decisions on my own. Visits to Lincoln became rare, as did visits from my parents, as their health deteriorated.

During my lunch hour at FSA, I would sometimes walk up Capitol Hill to watch the Senate in session or to drop in on a committee hearing. Much of what I saw disillusioned me about the intellectual and moral quality of our elected representatives in both parties. Observing politics firsthand showed me more of its flaws than I had ever recognized in Nebraska—more hypocrites than heroes, more sinners than saints. Neither my shy personality nor my idealism seemed suited to a political career. In time I came to see politics as the arena in which both an ambitious young idealist can realize his highest ambitions and a greedy demagogue can exercise his worst traits.

I enjoyed my work with FSA, but I knew my days were numbered. I told Stanley Gewirtz that, if Congress lopped even a tiny sum off the agency's appropriation, my job would vanish. He asked whether I would be interested in a job with Congress. Despite my reservations about the institution, I was excited at the chance to work there, and instantly said yes.

Some weeks later, he called to ask if I knew anything about the Railroad Retirement System, inasmuch as a joint temporary committee of the two houses of Congress had been established to study that system's relationship with Social Security. Like a true lawyer, after quickly searching my mind and coming up with nothing, I replied that in two weeks I would be an expert. He promised to recommend me to the staff director, Robert Wallace, who simultaneously held the job of legislative assistant to Senator Paul H. Douglas of Illinois, the new joint committee's chairman. Shortly thereafter, I received an offer.

The Joint Senate House Committee on Railroad Retirement was charged with producing a report entitled "Retirement Policies and the Railroad Retirement

System," and I was assigned to research and write part two of the report, which discussed the challenges facing American society in supporting its growing number of senior citizens. I surveyed experts throughout the government, and particularly enjoyed becoming acquainted with one of the original New Dealers in the Social Security Administration, Wilbur Cohen, who was a fount of facts and figures on the economic importance and problems of aging.

Within a few weeks I wrote my father reporting, "My new job is excellent so far . . . I've spent most of my efforts in meetings with the various governmental agencies and private parties concerned to determine their role and their suggestions of issues for our study . . . I try not to let on how completely ignorant of it all I'd been, and have read up on the issues as much as possible." A week later, he replied: "Congratulations Ted on the fine position that you have gotten. It would seem to me that you have one of the most interesting jobs in Washington." I doubt that, but that brief committee assignment had at last given me a direct tie to national issues.

Chapter 8

Joining Senator Kennedy

A s the expiration of the joint committee's term approached at the end of 1952, with part two of the report scheduled for publication on January 7, 1953, I had to begin my job search all over again. Dwight D. Eisenhower had been elected president in November, and immediately requested a freeze on executive branch employment. My hopes of returning to the executive branch—either to the Federal Security Agency or to one of the other agencies that had offered me a job the previous year—were dashed. So I turned my sights toward Congress.

The joint committee staff director, Bob Wallace, assured me that he and committee chairman Douglas would contact other Senate offices, including those newly elected senators who might have staff vacancies.

Bob wrote his counterparts in several Senate offices, including those of two Republicans, the liberal maverick Wayne Morse from Oregon and the moderate Republican from New Jersey, H. Alexander Smith. He also sent copies of the same form letter to three newly elected Democratic senators who had previously served as members of the House and had worked with Douglas: Mike Mansfield of Montana, Henry "Scoop" Jackson of Washington, and John F. Kennedy of Massachusetts.

The letter that Bob sent, shortly after the November 1952 election, was overly kind to me in its description and recommendations, referring to my

> ability to write in clear understandable language, to master any legislative problem . . . pleasant to work with, self-confident, but modest, an extremely happy medium . . . a sincere liberal, but not the kind that always carries a chip on his shoulder . . . among my very top choices.

He noted that I had written for the *Progressive* magazine, founded by former Senator La Follette. He said that he and I had worked together writing speeches for the Democratic National Committee in 1952, which I do not recall. Convinced that, at twenty-four, my youth was my biggest handicap for any serious job, Bob changed my résumé, which he attached to his letter, to read "age 25," explaining to me: "If you are well over twenty-four, we could put down twenty-five and that would be pretty close." We never learned whether that little stretch made a difference.

Meanwhile, I was exploring other possibilities. One exchange of letters, reflecting a job inquiry I had made the previous year, resulted in an invitation to meet the leaders of a new civil liberties organization formed in response to the machinations of Senator Joseph McCarthy and others. In a letter to my prospective employers, I raised a number of questions about the organization, specifically asking whether they were convinced, as I was, that one "cannot work with Communists to achieve civil liberties . . . I am convinced that such cooperation inevitably destroys the very objective sought, as well as the usefulness of the organization." In the end my philosophical reservations were irrelevant; I terminated these discussions for a more mundane reason: Camilla and I signed a two-year lease in the Washington area, and could not easily move to New Jersey, where the job was based.

In late 1952 I also had an interview with the head of a new office studying federal pension plans, who had concluded that my experience with both the Joint Committee on Railroad Retirement and the Federal Security

Agency would make me ideal for his staff. The interview went well until he inquired what I had done before I joined the Federal Security Agency. I replied, "I was in law school." "When did you graduate from law school?" he asked. "June 1951," I replied. He practically leaped from his chair, his voice rising: "June 1951?! June 1951?!" I did not get that job.

With my other options dwindling, I increasingly placed my hope in Bob Wallace's connections. When Senator Morse's administrative assistant expressed interest to Bob, I was excited. I admired Morse, an independent Republican in the Norris tradition. But Morse decided that the position should go to a lawyer from Oregon. I do not recall hearing anything from Mike Mansfield, but I soon received word that the two other new senators were interested: Henry "Scoop" Jackson and John F. Kennedy.

Because both Jackson and Kennedy, as members of the House, had worked with Bob Wallace, and had admired Senator Douglas, Bob's recommendation carried weight. For years thereafter, I retained my great respect and admiration for Senator Douglas, and I told all those who asked how I came to meet Kennedy that Senator Paul Douglas had recommended me. In fact, Douglas had been campaigning and lecturing during most of my time with the joint committee staff, and thus had met me only briefly. Later, when my work with Kennedy drew attention, Douglas asked Bob Wallace whether he had in fact recommended me, and Wallace reminded him that he had, and in fact had himself sent a letter to Senator Kennedy.

My initial meetings with both Jackson and Kennedy in early January 1953 were pleasant but brief. Kennedy had not yet moved into his new Senate office, and his House office, at the time of our interview there, was being vacated. In the midst of transition confusion, with two staffs milling about, the young senator-elect moved two chairs into the hall, outside the office's front door, where we perched and spoke for little more than five minutes. In that brief exchange, I was struck by this unpretentious, even ordinary man with his extraordinary background, a wealthy family, a Harvard education, and a heroic war record. He did not try to impress me with his importance; he just seemed like a good guy. I do not recall the specifics of that initial conversation, other than his need for a lawyer who could draft legislation, and he noted that he was considering hiring the House of Representatives legislative counsel, whom he knew. But the meeting went well, as did my meeting with Jackson, and both offered me jobs.

Once again I had to make a quick decision. I consulted my two mentors, Wallace and Gewirtz. Both thought

Jackson was clearly the better choice. He had enjoyed a brilliant career in the House, they said, and had an unlimited future. They thought he was the more serious legislator, who would get things done in the traditional progressive mold of the upper Northwest, while Kennedy's commitment to civil liberties, New Deal spending, church-state separation, and civil rights was uncertain; and his closeness to his famously conservative father gave them pause. Kennedy, they both implied, was a wealthy dilettante with a poor attendance record in the House (due to illness and foreign travel, I later learned). They also noted that he had voted for the no-third-term constitutional amendment, viewed by most liberals as a retrospective censure of FDR, for his liberal views and physical weakness at Yalta. JFK later justified that vote to me on the grounds that two terms in the world's most difficult and demanding office are certain to deplete any occupant's physical, intellectual, and political resources. I still remember Stan Gewirtz insisting that Senator Kennedy would not hire anyone his father wouldn't hire, and that, with one exception, Ambassador Kennedy had hired only Irish Catholics.

On a chart that Wallace and I had earlier prepared to measure the extent to which the new Senate was more liberal than the old, we rated Jackson, the new senator from Washington state, a clear liberal, but the new occupant of the Massachusetts seat as only marginally more liberal than his predecessor, the moderate Republican Henry Cabot Lodge. Nevertheless, in my initial brief interviews with both senators, Kennedy had made a more favorable impression upon me; and I was consequently in a quandary.

With the impertinence of youth, I requested a second interview with each of them, essentially asking each new senator what he was hiring me to do, what my main tasks would be. I also voiced to Kennedy my concern about reports that he was soft on Senator Joe McCarthy and his witch-hunting tactics, about which my siblings and I felt strongly. JFK must have thought I was a bit odd, as well as headstrong and presumptuous, a new job applicant asking questions about his political positions. But he did not resent it, calmly explaining that McCarthy was a friend of his father and family, as well as enormously popular among the Irish Catholics of Massachusetts. Although he did not agree with McCarthy's tactics or find merit in all his accusations, he did think it likely that sinologist Owen Lattimore, a professor at Johns Hopkins University, had some sympathy with the Chinese Communists.

Satisfied with that answer, I asked him how he envisioned my role. He noted his campaign's concerns for the long-term economic slump in New England, which had lost most of its textile and shoe industries to the South; its fisheries were in danger as well; and there was no new industry to replace them. He planned to send me to Boston to meet with Professor Seymour Harris of the Harvard economics department; with Alfred Neal of the Federal Reserve Bank; Bill Belanger of the Massachusetts AFL-CIO; and the Boston business columnist John Harriman. Then, Senator Kennedy said, "I want you to prepare for me a legislative program for the revival of the New England economy." Pretty tall corn for a young lawyer from Nebraska who knew little about economics and nothing about New England. It was a challenge I could not resist, and I was impressed by the ease with which he rattled off these issues and identified the experts to be consulted.

I then put the same role question to Senator Jackson. He replied that Senator Douglas had said I was the smartest lawyer he ever met (likely relying on the Wallace letter) and that he needed someone like that to get his name in the newspapers. He also liked my Scandinavian name, which his Seattle constituents would welcome. Even a greenhorn like me had no trouble deciding which of those two job opportunities was more interesting. The next day I called Senator Kennedy to accept his offer to be his number two legislative assistant for a trial period of one year.

I never told JFK about the Jackson offer. The two men remained friends and Democratic Party allies for many years. Both were initially considered cold war liberals, but their ideological views soon diverged. As Kennedy's opposition to war became increasingly clear, Jackson became a hard-liner. After Kennedy's death, Jackson supported the Vietnam War and called early protesters appeasers. He basically opposed arms control negotiations with the Soviet Union. He fought to increase federal spending on unnecessary or untested weapons systems, many of which were built in his home state. To his Senate office, committee staffs, and presidential campaign team of 1972, Jackson attracted William Kristol, Alan Keyes, Richard Perle, Eliot Abrams, Douglas Feith, and other hawkish conservatives, some of whom would later be the chief architects of the Iraq war. Had I accepted his offer in 1953, would I have been a cheerful part of that neoconservative team? Would I have succeeded in helping elect Jackson president? I doubt it.

Why did I choose JFK over Jackson, who had been described to me as the more liberal senator with the brighter future of the two? I have adapted the words of Robert Frost to my own crossroads: Two roads diverged in the Old Senate Office Building, and I took the one less recommended, and that has made all the difference. The truth is more prosaic: I wanted a good job. I chose Kennedy over Jackson, not with any expectation, hope, or even thought that he would become president, but because his description of my immediate role and assignment was far more challenging, exciting, and promising than the role Jackson contemplated for me.

The more difficult question is why JFK chose me, despite all our apparent differences—differences that journalists and biographers have never tired of noting. I was "an unlikely choice," wrote historian Robert Dallek. "Poles apart in background and personal style," wrote the conservative Victor Lasky. William Lee Miller, a friend from Lincoln, wrote of me in the *Reporter Magazine*:

> His background was strikingly different from that of his boss . . . Sorensen was not only very young and new to Washington; he was also not a Harvard man or an Easterner or a Catholic or an Irishman or a hereditary Democrat or a political middler or culturally sophisticated or rich or an aristocrat or an urbanite or an intellectual dilettante or widely traveled or weak on civil liberties or a master of the Ivy League's casual style or anything of a playboy. He was instead . . . somewhere near the opposite of all of them.

All true, but JFK hired me anyway. That says a lot more about him than me. What other senator would have hired an unknown liberal from an unranked college with no serious political experience or connections, when there were probably dozens of Harvard graduates eager for the job?

Why did he hire me, and then keep me for eleven years? I am immodest enough to hope that in later years JFK might have answered that question in the same way that Franklin Roosevelt answered Wendell Wilkie, when the latter asked him on a visit to the Oval Office why he kept Harry Hopkins so close, a man many people in the New Deal distrusted or resented, and who was—in background and nature—very different from FDR. "Some day you may well be sitting here where I am now as President of the United States," FDR reportedly replied to his 1940 reelection opponent, "and when you are, you'll be looking at that door over there, and knowing that practically everybody who walks through it wants something out of you—you'll learn what a lonely job this is, and you'll discover the need for somebody . . . who asks for nothing except to serve you."

Chapter 9

Relationship with JFK

From January 1953, when I first reported for work in room 362 of the Old Senate Office Building, until the day late in November 1963 that I ran onto the south lawn of the White House to hand the president some papers as he walked toward the helicopter that would take him on the first leg of his trip to Dallas, I remember John F. Kennedy clearly. I remember him clearly despite the idolaters who have almost buried the memory of the real man under a Camelot myth too heroic to be human, despite the exaggerated attention and speculation, some malicious, some merely mindless, focused on allegations about his private life, and despite the revisionist detractors whose hindsight distortions of his life and record have not lessened his hold on America's affectionate memory.

I do not remember everything about him, because I never knew everything about him. No one did. Different parts of his life, work, and thoughts were seen by many people—but no one saw it all. He sometimes obscured his motives and almost always shielded his emotions. Too little of what he said privately was written down; all too little was written with his own hand or recorded in his own voice. Hindsight, grief, and wishful thinking no doubt make somewhat selective the recall of even those of us who knew him well. But what I do remember, I remember clearly—not as a professional historian or as a detached observer, but as a friend who misses him still.

John F. Kennedy was a natural leader. When he walked into a room, he became its center. When he spoke, people stopped and listened. When he grinned, even on television, viewers smiled back at him. He was much the same man in private as he was in public. It was no act—the secret of his magic appeal was that he had no magic at all. But he did have charisma. Historians still write about it. Charisma is often largely in the eye of the beholder, and that was particularly true in Kennedy's case. It had to be experienced to be believed. It wasn't only his looks or his words; it was a special lightness of manner, the irony, the teasing, the self-effacement, the patient "letting things be." Although he could be steely and stern when frustrated, he never lost his temper. When times were bad, he knew they would get better— when they were good, he knew they could get worse.

JFK presented a strong, cool image, but was very human, capable of tears. He wept publicly when his and Jackie's son, Patrick, was born in August 1963 and lived only a short time. They had joyfully anticipated the arrival of their third child. Dr. Janet Travell related to me in a 1965 letter how the president and his wife had asked Dr. Travell to take over Jackie's care and keep her pregnancy private as long as possible. Dr. Travell and the attending physician were the only outsiders who knew, Dr. Travell wrote me, adding, "It was like a James Bond thriller how we managed until after Easter in Palm Beach," to keep it quiet.

Like my father, JFK was almost always calm. He once told me at length about a dramatic but comic episode, at a moment of deadly atmospheric quiet when the eye of an early 1950s hurricane passed over the family home on Cape Cod, and the chauffeur and butler—each suspecting the other of trifling with his wife—pursued each other with knives and golf clubs, upstairs, downstairs, all about the house, while JFK, otherwise alone in the house, sat calmly reading under a blanket on the front deck.

On my initial overnight stay in Hyannis Port I was most impressed by the fact that the Kennedys had a movie theater in their basement. Later opportunities to swim in family pools or off family ocean beaches in Palm Beach and Hyannis Port reinforced my awareness of our very different backgrounds.

During my first year in JFK's Senate office, when dropping me off after work to catch my bus home, he confessed that he had never ridden one in his life. Ah, the deprivations of the rich! Eight years later, when I donned my first ever white tie and tails for an elegant dinner at Versailles Palace, hosted in 1961 by Charles de Gaulle, as I came along the receiving line JFK whispered in my ear a mischievous question about what time I would need to return the outfit to the rental shop.

He never pretended that he was middle-class. I enjoyed the tale of his 1946 Boston appearance in his first campaign at a Democratic meeting in which many other local candidates were introduced ahead of him— each described by the chairman as "a young fellow who came up the hard way." Finally, when JFK was ushered to the podium, he began his speech by declaring: "I seem to be the only person here who did not come up the hard way."

Yet this millionaire Ivy Leaguer was not a snob. He loved sports, pop music, and movies; he had suffered injury and endured family tragedy; he had a wonderful sense of humor and a deep love of family. In the early Senate years, we occasionally walked over to Union Station for lunch. It was, he said, the only place in town serving genuine New England clam chowder and oyster stew. He possessed a realistic sense of himself, his limitations, and his shortcomings, and a rare quality among politicians—humility. Even as he welcomed his two younger brothers to Washington, he scoffed at the media notion that the Kennedy family would someday lend itself to so un-American a concept as a "Camelot dynasty," scoffing particularly at one writer's speculation that the three brothers might successively occupy the presidency through 1984, with the mantle then passing to their sons.

Was John F. Kennedy an intellectual? He read and wrote books, and was at home in discussions of American history, foreign policy, the presidency, and arcane issues of government and public policy. He enjoyed talking with intelligent women as much as intelligent men, including the brilliant author and Republican diplomat Clare Boothe Luce, of whom he later told me: "She's bitter because now all her power is derived from a man"—her husband, Henry. Compared to some of his predecessors and successors in the Oval Office, he was an intellectual giant. The poet Robert Frost, citing the new president's Irish and Harvard backgrounds, advised him "not to let the Harvard in you get too important." He didn't, but neither would he let it be suppressed. As a longtime political observer, I have noted that some highly educated politicians in Washington have thought that political success required them to conceal their intellects with coarse humor, slang, or bad grammar. Not JFK, who sprinkled erudite references in everyday conversation. Once, as senator, pulling his car up in front of a downtown Washington travel agency, he ignored the official "No Parking" sign, with a winking allusion to Shakespeare: "This is what Hamlet means by the 'insolence of office.'"

Early on, two facts about his health were clear to me. First, like many middle-aged men, he suffered from a bad back. He was convinced that his World War II injuries in the Pacific had done further damage, and that the initial military hospital surgery on his back had increased the likelihood of pain without solving the problem. But it now seems more likely that his back problem was congenital, not due to either Harvard football or PT-109.

The other basic fact about John F. Kennedy's health was that he suffered from an adrenal insufficiency, the medical equivalent of Addison's disease. Early in his Senate days, he told me that he was vulnerable to high fevers and that he needed to go to bed when those fevers occurred. This occasionally meant the cancellation of speaking engagements, a telephone call I never enjoyed making, and even more occasionally my substituting for him—which I did enjoy.

Either malady—the bad back or the adrenal insufficiency—was a major problem by itself. The combination was worse. The operation to relieve his back pain in 1954 was dangerous, and twice delayed because of the additional risks posed both by the adrenal insufficiency and by the suppression of his immune system resulting from the steroids still used to treat that insufficiency. But he told me he was determined to have the operation to avoid spending the rest of his life on crutches. It was only a limited success.

Afterward he talked with me about the brighter side of hospital life—the cheering mail from friends and strangers, the constant attention from pretty nurses, the ample time to read, think, and write that would never have been available in his normal routine, and an increased empathy for those countless Americans of every age and class who are confined to their beds, whether at home or in a hospital.

In the late 1950s when we traveled the country together, I would ask each hotel to provide him with a hard mattress or bed board. When that failed, sometimes we moved his mattress onto the floor of his hotel room.

On the political circuit, I assumed that his practice of eating in his hotel room before a Democratic Party luncheon or dinner was intended to avoid the bad food and constant interruptions that characterized his time at the head table; but I now realize, after reading an analysis of his medical file, that his many stomach, intestinal, and digestive problems (of which I was largely unaware at that time) simply required a more selective diet.

In the White House, he continued to be treated by Dr. Janet Travell, whom—despite the doubts of the medical establishment—he trusted for her expertise and loyalty. It was Dr. Travell who recommended the rocking chair that became a Kennedy trademark. It helped his back. I was uncomfortable about a doctor of questionable reputation visiting the White House, Max Jacobson, known as "Dr. Feelgood" for his reportedly dubious prescriptions; but, upon inquiry, I was informed that he was treating Jackie, not the president.

In retrospect, it is amazing that, in all those years, he never complained about his ailments. Occasionally he winced when his back was stiff or pained as he eased himself into or out of the bathtub, or picked up a heavy briefcase or one of his children. In 1961, after aggravating his back as president when planting a tree during a Canadian ceremony, he became far more careful. He even had his right shoulder checked before he threw out the first ball on opening day of Major League Baseball, and held a secret practice session behind the White House. The transcript of his vigorous participation in the 1961 Vienna summit meeting makes clear that neither his aching back—which flared up on that trip—nor any other health problems impaired his performance as president. The only complaint I remember, during the presidency, came when he worried that the steroids prescribed for his adrenal insufficiency, combined with the necessarily more sedentary existence in the White House following his long, physically rugged campaign, were increasing the fat in his face and belly.

At all times, he kept his sense of humor and perspective, and could joke about his medical problems, never becoming irritable with me or my colleagues. After one of the most exciting and exhausting days of his life—in West Berlin in June 1963—he told me about the medical theory of the body's "fight or flight syndrome" in response to the kind of stress produced by enormous danger or challenge. Since early times, he said, the body has responded to challenge by pumping more adrenaline, a very good thing for someone normally suffering an adrenal insufficiency, and in JFK's case, making him more high-spirited and healthy than ever.

Early in our relationship, JFK and I discovered that we both saw plenty of humor in the world and hypocrisy in politics, and that we enjoyed kidding each other and laughing at ourselves. There was not a day in all the years that I worked with him that he did not relish witty exchanges and self-deprecating jibes. His sense of humor helped insulate him from excessive self-importance, helped him weather setbacks while in office, and helped him place both gains and losses in perspective. He was an outwardly humorous but inwardly serious man, in contrast with so many other American politicians who are essentially humorless, superficial, and frivolous in their thinking while going to great lengths to appear serious.

Humor was always part of his public speeches, but neither he nor I fully appreciated its value in speeches until the 1958 Gridiron Dinner, the annual Washington gathering in which journalists and politicians entertain one another with skits and gags, including an opportunity for one speaker from each major political party to show how funny he could be. After being afforded that opportunity in 1958, JFK agonized over it for weeks: "Why did I accept this? If the speech is a success, so what, I'm funny, that won't help a national campaign; but if I flop, it's all over town." With help from veteran Gridiron participants—attorney Clark Clifford and journalists Fletcher Knebel and Marquis Childs—we gathered to review and vote on more than one hundred suggestions I had compiled. JFK's father, who also had a good sense of humor, joined that jury, which sat for hours. JFK and I then worked and reworked a draft speech, until the big night arrived.

Having been tipped off that his speech would follow a skit portraying him as a free-spending candidate singing "Just Send the Bill to Daddy" to the tune of "My Heart Belongs to Daddy," JFK opened his remarks: "I just received the following message from my generous daddy: 'Dear Jack—Don't buy one vote more than is necessary—I'm damned if I'll pay for a landslide.'" The room exploded with laughter. Within a week, the remark was being quoted and praised all over Washington, and within a month all over the country. It defused the father's money issue that Eleanor Roosevelt and others had raised against him, and it proved that the senator could laugh at himself. Although Clark Clifford in his memoirs gave me credit for originating the joke, I stole it from Will Rogers.

Throughout his remarks that night, JFK gently needled everything and everyone, including his own political prospects, his religious problem ("my personal envoy to the Vatican will open negotiations for that trans-Atlantic tunnel immediately"), and his own party ("split right down the middle—more unity than we've had in 20 years"). And those are the funniest lines—maybe you had to be there.

It was a reassuring revelation to both JFK and me that he could make people laugh loudly, not merely listen with amusement. Thereafter he wanted jokes on current events and politics at practically every stop as we continued to crisscross the fifty states. Winning laughs became as enjoyable and almost as important as winning support. It helped politically too, with audiences skeptical of a young Harvard-educated intellectual; they liked him instantly and paid more attention.

Many of his best opening lines were repeated in town after town. As his demand expanded, I had to increase my supply, mining Will Rogers, Mark Twain, Finley Peter Dunne, and other old sources, as well as receiving contributions occasionally from comedian Mort Sahl and Kennedy brother-in-law Peter Lawford. In a letter to JFK while he was traveling abroad, I wrote from Washington : "I am refurbishing my supply of jokes for your use, but refuse to try them by letter or telephone where their true effect might be lost."

By the time of the 1960 presidential campaign, I had an enormous folder entitled "Humor File" that traveled around the country with my luggage. We avoided the tasteless, the cruel, and the obscure. We had one rule: If someone might be offended, cut it out. We learned this in his first year when he used a joke I had suggested as an opening line to a Washington hotel audience: "The cabdriver bringing me here did such a good job, I was going to give him a big tip and tell him to 'vote Democratic'—then I remembered the advice of Senator Green [reportedly a stingy millionaire] and gave the driver a small tip, and told him to 'vote Republican.'" Angry letters poured in from formerly supportive cabdrivers in Boston. Even his mother was not amused.

Few could realize, then or now, that beneath the glitter of his life and office, beneath the cool exterior of the ambitious politician, was a good and decent man with a conscience that told him what was right and a heart that cared about the well-being of those around him. During the early Senate years, when I was confined to bed with the flu, I was surprised when he drove up to our house, rang the bell, greeted my wife, and came upstairs to talk with me. On another occasion, when my lower back muscles went into spasm, he offered a long list of advice: Lift and carry nothing heavy; apply wet heat or hot pads; avoid soft mattresses and lengthy periods of standing. When I seemed not to be either improving or taking his advice, he demanded to know why. I assured him that I would follow his directions "as soon as a medical expert on bad backs gives me that advice"; he replied, "Let me tell you, on the basis of fourteen years' experience, that there is no such thing." But soon thereafter he arranged for me to visit Dr. Travell, in New York.

Perhaps because of the closeness of his own family, he was always kind to mine, inviting me and my wife, Camilla, to his wedding to Jackie on September 12, 1953, in Newport, Rhode Island. Unfortunately, the trip was too expensive for us, and we did not go. The following year he arranged for us to fly to New York, stay at his father's Park Avenue apartment, and see the hit Broadway musical *My Fair Lady*. When my father died in Nebraska in 1959, JFK made a donation to the University of Nebraska student loan fund that we had established in my father's name. He understood the importance to me of my three sons, my commitment to attend their Little

League and football games, and their Saturday visits to the White House, where they would be remembered years later by the head usher for playing hide-and-seek in the West Wing lobby.

When I showed the president a note my son Eric had written to him on a Saturday visit ("Dear Mr. President: I like the White House. It is a neat place. You have nice people here. I would like to live in it someday"), the president wrote in the margin before returning it: "So do I. Sorry, Eric, you'll have to wait your turn." On January 19, 1961, the day before his inauguration, as he rested and prepared at the Georgetown home of his friend Bill Walton, the president-elect graciously welcomed me with my siblings, sons, and little nephews and nieces, who were listed on his official schedule right after the chairman of the Joint Chiefs of Staff and just before the new head of the Federal Aviation Agency.

On a few occasions we discussed my personal life. When I apologized to him because a story about my legal separation from Camilla appeared in the *Washington Star*, he smilingly replied that it was nothing compared to the foibles of other White House staff members he had discovered in reviewing their FBI files. When my years of work-related absences and consequent inattention to my family finally led to a formal, wrenching divorce, the president apologized to me, saying he felt responsible—I assumed he meant for the long hours his tasks required of me. But I told him the fault was wholly mine.

After my divorce, perhaps in an effort to improve my social life, he suggested I would look better wearing contact lenses instead of my old-fashioned horn-rimmed glasses. He was right, but I made no change. In 1961, after he asked me to fly to Paris and sample French intellectual opinion in advance of his own arrival to see de Gaulle, he asked whether I would be taking a girlfriend with me. When I replied with an astonished negative, he nodded with a grin: "No, you're right, that would be like taking a cow to cow country."

But he also respected my privacy. Late one night I slipped away from a boring social function at the White House to attend a private party, attended by my friend Gloria Steinem. I accidentally gashed my brow, and had to summon the assistant White House physician in the middle of the night. No doubt he reported his first aid mission to the president; but when I reported for work the next morning with my forehead bandaged and no explanation, JFK did not ask for one.

Needless to say, JFK was a wonderful boss. We never argued, quarreled, shouted, or swore at each other. He never bawled me out. He never asked me to lie to anyone. He never misled or lied to me. In the early days, he did not treat me as the green kid that I was. He never asked me to write or do anything inconsistent with my principles, never asked me to write up or support any principle or proposal in which I did not believe—not surprising, inasmuch as we shared the same beliefs and values.

In both the Senate and the White House, his staff loved him. One happy demonstration of our affection was the surprise party we gave him for his forty-sixth birthday in May 1963, complete with a cake, toasts, and humorous fake telegrams and presents, including water wings supposedly sent from the World War II Japanese destroyer commander who had sunk his PT boat, and a pair of boxing gloves from his pugnacious political bête noire, Governor George C. Wallace of Alabama.

When mistakes occurred, whether in his campaign or in his presidency, he never blamed me or anyone else on his staff, or disavowed me or others when under political or journalistic pressure. To the contrary, he always defended and protected us. When a speech of his on which I had worked went well, or a political task I had undertaken for him succeeded, he often telephoned me the next day with profuse thanks.

There were occasions, of course, when he found fault

with my work. One year, when he was on vacation from the Senate, I sent, in his name, a telegraphed message to a state Democratic Party dinner praising the local Democratic candidate for the U.S. Senate, thereby irritating the Republican incumbent, who complained to him on the Senate floor. He in turn complained to me. He did not like disparaging people, and particularly did not want me doing it to a colleague in his name.

Another lapse of judgment on my part incurred his understandable displeasure when I asked the pilot of the private plane we were chartering for a cross-country campaign trip to stop for me in New York, where I was on assignment, before picking him up in Cape Cod, thereby causing him to fall behind schedule.

On a more widely publicized occasion during his presidency, we were each vacationing with our respective families on Cape Cod on the weekend that the threat of a national rail strike caused him to cut short his visit. He had to wait for me at the Air Force One landing strip, long enough to permit the local newspaper to capture his impatient discomfort in a humorous series of photographs, showing him repeatedly checking his watch and walking restlessly outside the plane, until I finally arrived.

Unlike many in politics, he understood the importance of loyalty down as well as up. During my first year in the White House, 1961, I was invited to represent the president at ceremonies honoring the centennial of George Norris's birth in McCook, Nebraska, Norris's home base in the western part of the state. I took the opportunity to deplore statistics showing the continuing exodus of young families from the state, linking those statistics to the consequences of Nebraska's limited tax base for public school finance. My intention was to speak out in the blunt, provocative, and progressive tradition of Norris and my father. I warned Nebraskans that, without proper funding for public schools, the state could ultimately become "old [and] outmoded, a place to come from or a place to die."

Hundreds of letters poured into my White House office. Only a few were positive. One couple from Kearney expressed the hope that my "frank appraisal . . . will rock a few people out of their lethargy." Another gratifying letter came from Senator Norris's son-in-law and longtime assistant, John P. Robertson: "You've said things that needed to be said . . ." But the state Republican national committeewoman reflected the tone of most of the letters when she demanded in a press statement that I apologize, adding, "If Ted Sorensen ever comes home again, even to die, it will be too soon."

Yet, when all this spilled into the national press, the president greeted me with the comment: "That's what happens when you permit a speechwriter to go out on his own!" When I apologized for any embarrassment I had caused him, he laughed it off: "I don't mind. They can criticize *you* all they want!"

Unlike most of his presidential successors, he was superb at handling criticism. When Nobel laureate Dr. Linus C. Pauling of Cal Tech, with his wife, joined a 1962 picket line outside the White House protesting the resumption of nuclear testing by Kennedy, the president responded by inviting the Paulings to a large dinner at the White House, where he and Jackie joked with Pauling about his giving the president such a hard time.

On another occasion, when thousands of students from across the country began a two-day demonstration for peace outside the White House on a bitterly cold day, the president sent two members of his kitchen staff out with hot coffee. The marching students dropped out of line in small groups to be served. Several demonstrators were even invited inside to meet with me and other aides. Another group tried to demonstrate in front of the Soviet embassy, but were turned away by the police.

His calm acceptance of criticism was rooted in a breezy confidence that he would succeed in every challenge. Jackie told me that when she had jokingly told his brother Teddy at a family dinner that, upon JFK's

retirement, Teddy would need to yield his Massachusetts Senate seat back to him, Jack cautioned her afterward, "Don't tease Teddy about that. It makes him
uncomfortable, and the Senate seat is very important
to him. Don't worry about what I'll do after the White
House. The future will take care of itself." His confidence reassured me of my own future, and I never worried about it, or imagined a future without him.

His only notable weakness as a boss was his reluctance—indeed, his inability—to fire anyone. Instead,
he promoted them. During the Cuban missile crisis, the
chief of naval operations inexcusably argued with both
the secretary of defense and the president on how passive or aggressive the blockade should be. He became
ambassador to Portugal. An early occupant of a sensitive defense post within the executive offices, though
highly recommended by political sponsors to whom
JFK felt indebted, proved to be a square peg in that
round hole. The president appointed him to the federal
bench.

I first discovered this Kennedy shortcoming back in
the Senate when JFK told me that Evelyn Lincoln—the
most loyal, devoted, hardworking, and totally trustwor-
thy member of his team—did not have the intellectual
capacity to handle his increasingly important telephone
calls and correspondence, that he had tried firing her,

but that she kept showing up at her desk every day anyway; and would I please try? I had no more success than he. JFK kept her on, took her to the White House, and continued to value her loyalty.

Throughout our years together, there was a dichotomy in our relationship. I was totally involved in the substantive side of his life, and totally uninvolved in the social and personal side. Except for a few formal banquets, we never dined together during the White House years. The times we were together socially over the eleven years we worked together were few enough that I can remember each one. In Boston, he took me along to two informal gatherings with friends, one addressed by his Senate colleague Leverett Saltonstall, and the other by the distinguished Boston author Edwin O'Connor. In Washington, he once took me along to a meeting of the Massachusetts Business Council, advising me to tell anyone who asked that I was from "West Hyannis Port, Massachusetts. No one at the dinner will be from there." I'm not sure there was any such place. On New Year's Eve during the 1960–1961 transition, when I was staying in a Palm Beach hotel with my three boys, he arranged for me to be invited to a glittering Palm Beach social bash, from which I slipped away early to be with my sons. Big, noisy parties were not my style.

There was another reason I was not part of his social circle: Coming from a different background, with few social skills, I never felt entirely comfortable with the cool crowd with whom he enjoyed partying, laughing, drinking, and gossiping. Nor did many of them conceal their lack of enthusiasm for a young, serious-minded, abstemious intellectual from the Midwest with a shy manner and horn-rimmed glasses. Their thinly veiled patronizing bothered me in the early days; but I never wanted to be JFK's drinking buddy; I wanted to be his trusted advisor. I felt lucky to have that role. Ultimately, only his brother Robert had more access and was consulted more often.

For eleven years I loved him, respected him, and believed in him, and I still do.

Chapter 10

My Perspective on JFK's Personal Life

It has never been a secret that John F. Kennedy was attracted to beautiful women and they to him. On the campaign trail, I observed that JFK was unfailingly deferential and respectful to all women, particularly older women, and unfailingly flirtatious with all young women, particularly pretty, single women. His trim, youthful appearance, dazzling smile, handsome face, boyish charm, gentle teasing manner—combined with his wealth, glamour, fame, and potential political power—attracted women.

Like his father before him, JFK did not resist these temptations when they became available. To paraphrase E. B. White, "He awoke every morning torn between a desire to improve the world and a desire to enjoy it." Perhaps he was, more than I knew, a fatalist about the consequences of his poor health, and had therefore concluded that his life would be short and he should make the most of it, both in his service to the world and in his personal enjoyment of it. Abraham Lincoln is reported by historians to have said: "Folks who have no vices have very few virtues." JFK had many virtues, and would probably have been a less interesting man if he had had no vices.

Once he became a popular national figure, enough men claimed to have served on his little PT boat with him to have staffed a battleship, enough voters told pollsters after his narrow election victory that they had voted for him to have given him a landslide; and after his death, enough women claimed to have gone to bed with him to have left him time and energy for little else.

Some of the more prurient reports about JFK as well as other presidents reportedly came from members of the Secret Service. How reliable is the word of a Secret Service agent willing to sell a story in violation of his obligation of secrecy? In the White House, we said of those federal officials who leaked confidential decisions to the press: "Those who know don't talk; those who talk don't know."

Yet those claims of promiscuity have been regurgitated in the literature by some reputable writers and historians, and many who were not, while some Kennedy biographers chose in their books to ignore vastly more important aspects of his life in public service.

As the late James A. Wechsler pointed out in his *New York Post* column, the recollections of Judith Campbell Exner, the most notorious claimant of Kennedy's misconduct, were "steadily refreshed as her agent solicited more money . . . resolved not to let her story be topped by other women who, based on reality or fantasy, are prepared to tell all." The more women who claimed such a role, the less newsworthy and less credible their retroactive revelations became. It was easy to sell sensational allegations when no one was alive to disprove them.

Unfortunately, in both Washington and New York, speculation, rumor, and humor about the alleged peccadilloes of presidents and lesser politicians, and their private lives, loves, mistresses, and mistakes, have long circulated freely without any need of evidence. Even in the absence of hard facts, there is no presumption of innocence. Constant repetition is deemed enough to generate widespread belief and acceptance that some of it must be true.

In JFK's case, some of it is.

His personal life is not a subject I have previously discussed over these last forty-plus years; not in my earlier books, interviews, or writings on his career. My reason is simple: I had no firsthand knowledge. I realize that this has not stopped dozens of other authors who have written on the subject with an implied claim to knowledge—authors who have not hesitated to castigate JFK solely on the basis of hearsay, rumor, gossip, and innuendo. Moreover, at the time of my early books and interviews, his widow was still alive; and I felt his private life was no one else's business.

I did not lie. I did not assert that he was an abstemious man who maintained a monastic life. But I wanted my first major book, *Kennedy*, published in 1965, to be a serious work based upon a compilation of facts about his presidency. I did not rely in that book on the claims and accounts of other individuals and the media on any subject. I was able to discuss the man, his beliefs, his accomplishments, and his leadership without prying into private matters, which the general public had no urgent need or legitimate right to know. The greatest Kennedy historian of them all, Arthur Schlesinger Jr., said on this subject: "Questions which no one has a right to ask are not entitled to a truthful answer."

Since my book *Kennedy*, much has changed in this country. Our politics and press have been dumbed down, stripping those who hold or seek public office of their private lives to such an extent that many sensible good men and women decline to seek office or serve. Both writers and readers have tended to focus on the superficial and salacious over the substantive. Their allegations have provided ammunition for conservative critics of JFK who conclude that he did not respect women, even though many of these self-proclaimed champions of women have for years opposed—as he never did—equal education and employment opportunities for women and their emancipation from the burden of unwanted pregnancies. Nor did JFK ever lecture members of the press, public, or Congress on the importance of high moral standards and marital fidelity, unlike those worthies of the religious and political right who have been exposed as hypocrites for not hesitating to violate the standards they were preaching to others.

Now, amid all the allegations and fabrications, enough hard facts have emerged and been documented to make a complete denial or absolute defense on my part foolish. At this stage, it does not honor JFK for me to attempt to cover up the truth. All my life, the principle of loyalty has been important. But sometimes blind loyalty is trumped by overriding principles of truth and decency. On balance, I believe the truth—taking this chapter and book as a whole—serves his memory well, better than books by those who have largely ignored all the good he did, disparaging or dismissing his greatness as a leader solely because of his one personal weakness.

Although I am willing now to acknowledge, as illustrative, a number of incidents and conversations we shared, anyone who hopes that this book will set forth names, details, or intimate secrets that have never previously appeared in print will be disappointed.

During my first year in his office, the bachelor senator once asked me to wait for a telephone call he was expecting that evening while he was engaged on the Senate floor, and to convey his apologies and explanations to the caller. I was glad to do so. The caller turned out to be a young actress, then relatively unknown, Audrey Hepburn, who asked if I was related to the Danish architect Sorensen. At the time, I wondered what sort of relationship they had, but I never asked or learned.

After 1956 I was vaguely aware of a few flings and fancies along the campaign trail. Once, by the hotel pool during a stop in Nevada, a woman approached me, seemingly aware of my relationship with JFK, although I had not the slightest idea who she was. It was not until many years later when I saw her face on TV that I realized it was Judith Exner. If, as subsequently reported,

Ms. Exner had links with organized crime, then JFK, as a potential presidential candidate, was not exercising due caution in his private life.

Early in our cross-country tour, the weather required both a change of planes and an overnight delay in Chicago, where we took rooms in the airport inn, asking our Washington office to communicate with our impatient hosts out West. Imagine our chagrin when we learned that our host was privately reporting that JFK had not arrived "because he was shacked up in a Chicago motel with some broad named Sorensen." I laughed. He did not, sensing that it was another false rumor to be fed along the political grapevine.

Over the years I attended various emergency meetings on potentially embarrassing family matters, but I can flatly state that none involved either JFK's sex life or any threat to his marriage. I seriously doubt that any such revelations, much less any lawsuits, were ever threatened during his years in office or even in his lifetime. Once, during JFK's quest for the presidency, his father not only warned him against any sexual misconduct that could derail his political success, but also threatened to appoint me as guardian of his morals on the road. JFK reported this to me, adding with a chuckle: "I did not tell him that would be like putting the fox in charge of the chicken coop." I protested that I had not done anything to deserve that appellation.

During the presidency, in one of our preparation sessions for a press conference, I told him that a media outlet was reporting the possibility that he had had an earlier marriage in Florida. He laughed. "I know the husband is often the last to know," he said, "but not about whether he was married!"

After our 1963 motorcades through Germany and Ireland in 1963, he told me, in an exuberant, boastful mood, of the difference he claimed to have perceived in the shouts or whispers of admiring young ladies on the sidewalks as his motorcade passed. "God love you," he believed the Irish lasses were saying, far less earthy than what he suggested the German girls were communicating.

I never met Marilyn Monroe, and do not know whether she and JFK ever had a romantic relationship. However, when investigative reporter Seymour Hersh showed me decades later an incriminating letter to her supposedly signed by the president, I told him that I knew JFK well enough to be absolutely certain that he would never have been stupid or reckless enough to write, much less sign, such a letter, and that it was a forgery. When Hersh insisted that the signature had been authenticated by experts, I replied: "Then it is a very good forgery." A forgery it was, and the forger went to prison.

Former secretary of state Dean Rusk, when asked by a writer what he had observed of JFK's personal life, replied stiffly: "Sir, I was his policy advisor, not his nurscmaid." I could have given the same answer. Despite his father's suggestion, I was never asked to monitor his personal life. Nor did I ever arrange a date for him, although I would not be shocked to learn that Dave Powers, JFK's longtime friend and special assistant, or others may have.

After we were in the White House, it was a subject I never discussed with him or any member of his family. He never asked me to lie to the press or to his wife, and he knew that I would not talk to others about his personal life. On the whole, he was discreet about the women whom he saw, and discreet as well, to the point of being secretive, about time and place.

I knew briefly a few of those who I assumed to have shared his bed. They were intelligent conversationalists as well as lively, sophisticated, beautiful, and humorous. One woman, who I guessed might have had a relationship with the president, and whom I had met at the home of a mutual friend, was briefly hospitalized in Washington, and later told an interviewer that she was surprised to receive visits in the hospital from me, adding: "I think he was interested in me as a woman, but I sort of wondered if he was concerned that I might be saying something about JFK." In fact, she was one of three friends whom I visited on that particular ward one month, thinking I was doing a good deed. I was not there either to woo or silence her, and the president knew nothing of my visits. No good deed goes unpunished.

In a 1980 speech on JFK at the National Portrait Gallery in Washington, I included the following:

Not all his hours were spent at work. He liked parties . . . and lively companions. He sought fun and laughter. He made no pretense of being free from sin or imperfection. But he never permitted the pursuit of private pleasure to interfere with public duty.

My words went unnoticed. But when a mutual friend sent a copy of the speech to his widow, Jackie praised this paragraph as an accurate description that she accepted, adding, in reference to the portrait as a whole:

I was so moved. I think it is the only true portrait of him that has ever been done. No one has ever so understood and so expressed all the facets of that

unforgettable, elusive man. . . . There was a portrait
of you too, Ted, in your speech, though you probably
weren't aware of that. I felt your emotion. . . .
It would not have been possible for him to be all he
was if you had not been there too.

A copy of the entire speech was also sent to John Jr., then nineteen, whom a mutual friend described to me as a young man who had "shown an increasing curiosity to know who his father really was."

How much Jackie knew or suspected before his death, I do not know. Nor do I know whether she would have responded to her husband's womanizing with the same philosophical acceptance as Lady Bird Johnson, who reportedly said, "Everybody in the country loves Lyndon, and half the country are women." I do believe JFK loved his wife dearly, enough to take pains not to confront, humiliate, hurt, or anger her with public misconduct. Any confession, apology, or request for forgiveness that JFK could have offered, had he been so inclined, was owed not to the American public but to his wife; and we are unlikely ever to know whether that occurred even in a private moment that neither had any incentive to disclose. After all these years, it is unpleasant for me to acknowledge even these limited observations of his philandering. He did not ask me to judge him in his lifetime, nor would my doing so have done any good. I was in no position to do so, having made a painful mess of my own marriage to my college sweetheart. It is still not my role to judge him.

I did not see him then, and do not now, as flawless. I admired him as a good man, and still do. Those who think that I would defend or rationalize his carefree misconduct and broken marriage vows do not know me any better than those who think I might condemn his presidency for these flaws. It was self-indulgent. It does not reflect well on his attitude toward his public office, the sacred trust. It was wrong, and he knew it was wrong, which is why he went to great lengths to keep it hidden. I know he had a conscience, and there must have been times when his conscience tortured him. In every other aspect of his life, he was honest and truthful, especially in his job. His mistakes do not make his accomplishments less admirable; but they were still mistakes.

"Mistakes were made," that familiar passive phrase used by so many spokesmen for other presidents, to depersonalize errors and offenses of all kinds, will not suffice in this case. The familiar refrain, "Everyone's human, everyone does it," is also an inadequate defense. Not everyone does it—perhaps a majority of American adults, according to surveys, but not on the same scale or with the same stakes at risk. Nor is Kennedy's inability to resist all temptation excused by the behavior of other heads of state. (There were rumors in my days in Washington that the U.S. State Department or CIA supplied prostitutes upon request to certain visiting dignitaries.)

Nor can I excuse JFK's behavior by saying that he was under a lot of pressure and tension. He should have known that ultimately the inevitable disclosure of his misconduct could diminish the moral force and credibility of all the good he was doing, the standards he was setting, and the lessons he was teaching.

Nonetheless, I know of no occasion where his private life interfered with the fulfillment of his public duties. Even hijinks in the White House swimming pool, long alleged, were perhaps inappropriate but not illegal. There is no requirement in law or logic that solid, thoughtful public officials who make intelligent policy decisions must always be equally solid and thoughtful in their personal lives and private decisions. The qualities of the ideal husband and the ideal president are not the same. National polls continue to show JFK held in the highest esteem, by historians as well as the American public, who have a way of putting issues in the proper perspective over the long run.

Was JFK a moral leader? An American president, commander in chief of the world's greatest military power, who during his presidency *did not* send one combat troop division abroad or drop one bomb, who used his presidency to break down the barriers to religious and racial equality and harmony in this country and to reach out to the victims of poverty and repression, who encouraged Americans to serve their communities and to love their neighbors regardless of the color of their skin, who waged war not on smaller nations but on poverty and illiteracy and mental illness in his own country, and who restored the appeal of politics for the young and sent Peace Corps volunteers overseas to work with the poor and untrained in other countries—was in my book a moral president, regardless of his private misconduct. Public officials should be judged primarily not by their puritanism in private, but by their public deeds and public service, by their principles and policies.

Chapter 11

My Evolving Role on JFK's Senate Staff

I began my eight Senate years in one tiny windowless corner of JFK's three-room suite 362 in the Old Senate Office Building. Listed as research assistant, I was hired on a temporary one-year trial basis, subordinate to the senator's legislative assistant, Langdon P. Marvin Jr. Briefly JFK's roommate at Harvard, Langdon was the son of a prominent New York lawyer; FDR was his godfather and his father's law partner. Unfortunately for the senator, but fortunately for me, his old friend Langdon proved to be totally obsessed with one minor issue— the airmail subsidy paid to Pan American Airlines. In a short time, the senator resolved the problem by gently suggesting to Langdon that he spend full time on this subject in a little office in the Library of Congress; I was promoted to legislative assistant.

One new responsibility as a result of my promotion was the handling of all legislative mail from Massachusetts constituents, some of it thoughtful, some grateful, some frivolous, some threatening or just plain weird; some of it required congratulations, proclamations, and exercises in cautious public relations. Most letters simply requested a statement of his position on pending legislative issues, or set forth the writer's views approving, opposing, or objecting to JFK's position on a variety of issues. I responded, mostly with preapproved form letters.

In late 1953, when my friend and University of Nebraska law classmate Lee White was considering joining our staff, I wrote to him, describing our office:

> There is no problem with respect to the transfer
> of your annual sick leave inasmuch as we don't have
> any such thing; just as we have no overtime, regular
> hours, desk space or any of the other attractions
> one normally expects for a new job. Actually, I have
> been more worried about whether you would be
> disappointed in the subordination of the legal mind to
> the political, and in the great multitude of non-legal
> tasks which we perform here . . . At any rate, I enjoy

this job more all the time, including the non-legal
portion. At present, I am terrifically swamped with
a long list of major projects—articles to be written,
statements to be drafted, speeches to be written, etc.

Lee joined us, and in time I cheerfully passed the legislative mail chore along to my fellow Nebraskan.

The staff was small, headed by chief of staff and administrative assistant Ted Reardon, who had served in that same capacity during JFK's six years as a congressman. The senator's personal secretary, Evelyn Lincoln, was joined by one or two other secretaries and a small staff of young women from various parts of Massachusetts who reflected the state's diverse ethnic population. In Washington conversations, I discovered, almost everyone was identified with a hyphen—an Irish-American, Italian-American, or Greek-American, ethnic labels which were new to me. I had never considered the fact that my father was Danish-American, or my mother a Russian-American, or that my father's devoted secretary, Mabel Angelo, was apparently Italian-American.

My starting salary on JFK's Senate staff was just over $8,000 a year; four months later, I received an increase of about 5 percent. It may have been an automatic Senate-wide cost-of-living adjustment, but JFK made it sound special with an accompanying letter: "As your work has been outstanding since you started with us, I am increasing your salary . . ."

My first major task in the Senate was outlined by the senator in our second and decisive interview—the formulation of a legislative program for the economic revival of New England. After months of study and consultation with experts, I drafted, and the senator delivered on the Senate floor, three long, dense speeches, each approximately two hours in length, with approximately forty recommendations for legislative or executive action.

The speeches—his first major statements on the Senate floor—were delivered over three days in May 1953, barely four months after he took office. They detailed the economic plight of Massachusetts and the New England region and the effects of these conditions on workers, families, communities, and industries in the hard-hit area once saluted as "the nation's toolbox." The Senate floor was not crowded late in the day when he spoke; but several of his friends, mostly liberal Democrats like Paul Douglas, Hubert Humphrey, and Herbert Lehman, stayed in their seats, listening with attention and occasionally asking pertinent, friendly questions.

Senator Kennedy and I were nervous about this debut; but supportive newspaper editorials and columns from throughout New England began to pour in. Invoking the national interest, he had stressed that New

England's problems were shared by other regions that had surplus labor, and that his proposed solutions would benefit the country as a whole. He had spoken on many of these same issues as a congressman and a senatorial candidate, but this time he added more facts and figures. The three speeches, with supplements, were combined into one reprint that we titled and distributed as "The New England Economic Report."

One of his recommendations called for the organization of the New England congressional delegation into a unified bloc that could compete with the more powerful regional organizations of Southern and Western legislators. The proposal met with immediate favor from his New England colleagues, and a twelve-member New England Senators Conference was organized, with me as its executive secretary, the only nonsenator attending their periodic meetings and preparing the agenda.

Over time, I came to know which senators in both parties were all talk and which had substance, who was worth listening to and who had a first-rate staff. Among the other New England senators whom I came to know, I especially enjoyed my relationship with the courtly senator from Connecticut, Prescott Bush, whose son and grandson would later be U.S. presidents. Lister Hill of Alabama was among the non–New England senators I admired most. He sat on the temporary joint committee on which I served in 1951, could quote stirring poetry and oratory without notes, and once told me that his Senate colleagues paid attention when JFK rose to speak because they knew he had done his homework. I also admired Phil Hart of Michigan, and Wayne Morse and Dick Neuberger, both of Oregon.

Early in his first Senate term, while awaiting an opportunity to speak, JFK sat next to one of his older and crustier colleagues, whom he asked what changes the senior senator had seen over the years. The veteran senator replied, "New members did not speak much in those days." (I am certain JFK told me that the senior senator was Carl Hayden of Arizona; but Jackie, having been told the same story, believed that it was Walter George of Georgia. Whoever it was, JFK was more amused than chastened in retelling the story.)

I also had the pleasure of meeting and working with talented federal career servants—I never called them bureaucrats—and with legislative aides throughout the Senate—all congenial and hardworking, many of them veterans of several years on Capitol Hill. Many left eventually for better-paying positions with Washington's major lobbying firms.

I found most of the lobbyists who called on me useful and informative. I was scrupulous to a point of eccentricity about not accepting favors, ranging from a guest ticket to a Democratic fund-raiser, to a ticket to a sports event, to an expensive Christmas present actually thrust upon me by a lobbyist in a sidewalk encounter during the three months of presidential transition—a gift that I returned that afternoon by mail. I found those lobbyists who were hired guns on a dozen different issues and organizations to be the least effective, and those who offered me dinners or gifts generally not as persuasive as those who promised valuable information—such as those promoting the St. Lawrence Seaway.

When I had been with him barely eighteen months, JFK took me to Boston, where he decided to oppose quietly the Democratic Party's nominee for the Senate against Leverett Saltonstall, JFK's Republican Senate colleague, in the 1954 election. He instructed me to stay in his bachelor apartment, supply Saltonstall's staff with campaign material on those issues concerning the New England economy on which Saltonstall and Kennedy had collaborated, and help to formulate and monitor statements by the Saltonstall campaign on the Republican senator's collaboration with the state's most popular Democrat. This was the circumstance for Kennedy's oft-quoted remark that, even as a loyal Democrat, "sometimes party asks too much." Saltonstall's opponent, in Kennedy's view, was an empty suit, an ambitious politician in the worst sense of that term. When the two appeared on television together, just before Kennedy went into the hospital, the Democratic senatorial nominee, Foster Furcolo of Springfield, said to him: "The main thing is, take care of your back." Kennedy told me afterward that he did not believe one word of that sentence was sincere.

When the 1954 legislative session ended, and JFK had decided that back surgery was the only certain relief from his severe, recurring pain, I was left in charge of all legislative work while he was in the hospital and recuperating, a total of seven months. During that time, I responded in his name to constituents, political inquiries, even scheduling invitations, and did what I could to make certain that his responsibilities were fulfilled and his name favorably promoted. From the time he left the hospital, he expected me to exercise my judgment on both policy and political issues. In this sense, I was, during this period, not unlike Louis Howe looking after Franklin Roosevelt's career during the latter's long recovery from polio. It was a lot of responsibility for a twenty-six-year-old who had not yet been in JFK's office two full years. Ted Reardon was always helpful.

As he came to know my abilities and to trust me, JFK dispatched me on a variety of missions—to ask a conservative Republican senator from the West to cosponsor a Kennedy bill; to see the Harvard Press about the possibility of publishing his "New England Economic

Report" as a book; to see a renowned theater producer and director about the possibility of converting *Profiles in Courage* into a Broadway show or television documentary; to meetings of the two Senate committees to which he was originally assigned: labor—public welfare, and government operations.

I summed it all up in a letter to my father in the spring of 1956:

> *Life here continues at its usually hectic pace. My work at the office varies 100% from week to week. One week it may be a commencement address . . . another week it may be a legislative matter . . . and another week, politics. I am writing this on a plane back to Washington after a quick trip to Massachusetts and Connecticut to see some people on "political business," including a stop in Hartford to see Governor Abe Ribicoff and his state Democratic Chairman. Next week I may be working on an article—and so it goes. It is the most interesting, challenging, exciting, wonderful job in the world—with plenty of drawbacks and an indeterminable future—but for a wonderful, responsible guy whom I deeply respect and admire, and with whom I get along excellently. His greatest years are still ahead of him. . . .*

Chapter 12

Speechwriting

During my eleven years with JFK, my most important national contributions—advising him on civil rights, on the decision to go to the moon, and especially on the Cuban missile crisis—did not center on speechwriting. In the more than four decades that have passed since his death, neither my activities as a lawyer nor those in international affairs have made much use of my speechwriting experience. Yet I have little doubt that, when my time comes, my obituary in the *New York Times* (misspelling my last name once again) will be captioned: "Theodore Sorenson, Kennedy Speechwriter." I accept the inevitability of that description, and upon reflection do not object. After all, many of Kennedy's speeches have been listed among the best in the twentieth century.

JFK never pretended, as senator, candidate, or president, that he had time to draft personally every word of every speech he was required to make virtually every week and ultimately virtually every day. Many historians have it wrong. He did not dictate first drafts for me to polish. Our collaboration was not a secret; nor was it without historical precedent. During the Renaissance, many of history's most famous artists would employ apprentices, who began with such lowly tasks as sweeping out the shop and grinding pigments, while practicing drawing under the master's supervision, at first sketching the less demanding portions of the master's proposed scene and then gradually expanding the scope of their contribution by imitating the style of the master, ultimately assisting him in the execution of the final work of art. For eleven years, I was an apprentice. John F. Kennedy was my mentor. The debate among journalists and historians over who wrote a particular passage or speech wrongly puts the emphasis on the student, not the teacher.

The Brownlow Report, which in the 1930s first recommended professionally staffing the White House, urged administrative assistants with "a passion for anonymity." Presidential speechwriters in particular, I believe, should have that passion, lest they diminish their principals' stature by receiving, accepting, or seeking credit for his speech's ideas and proposals. I did my best to maintain an even stronger position on speeches, and until now have largely tried to minimize my role. My reticence was the result of an implicit promise that I vowed never to break, not an order or even a request from him. I note that many a modern political speech-writer's role becomes public almost as soon as the speech is delivered, often through an indiscreet disclosure or publicity grab by the writer.

Some observers express pity for a speechwriter who sees his principal receive all the credit for a magnificent statement, or conversely they express admiration for the speechwriter's selfless loyalty for not claiming credit. Both in the Senate and in the White House, I have felt differently. As a young man raised by his parents to help improve society, I could hardly have asked for a more psychologically rewarding opportunity than to be in a position to help a dynamic leader, whose values I shared, reshape our country and planet at a time when I had no power to do so. No one was interested in my views. My reward was the thrill and satisfaction I invariably felt when first a United States senator, and later the presi-dent of the United States, delivered important words that I had contributed.

Whatever success I achieved as a speechwriter for Kennedy arose from knowing the man so well—from the years we spent working, traveling, and talking together, as close friends and collaborators who communicated constantly at a time when I regarded his election and stature as my principal professional goals. That success could not later be replicated with someone else with whom I did not have that same relationship.

During the intensive four years of pre–1960 convention travel and speaking, I attended, with rare exception, every speech he delivered, noting what succeeded with the audience, what words or phrases were unclear to listeners, taking mental notes for the next draft. By the time our postconvention travels began in September 1960, I had worked with him on so many speeches, long and short, important and routine, and spent so much time traveling and talking with him about every issue, that I knew what he wanted to say and how he wanted to say it on virtually every topic, and probably could not determine then—and certainly cannot now—which words in a final draft had originally been his and which were mine.

Kennedy's 1960 opponent, Richard Nixon, told an interviewer in 1962:

You need a mind like Sorensen's around you that's clicking and clicking all the time. You can get a beautifully tooled speech; but at best just one sentence of it will make the difference . . . It takes an intellectual to come up with the phrase that may penetrate . . . Sorensen . . . is tough, cold, not carried away by emotion; and he has the rare gift of being an intellectual who can completely sublimate his style to another individual; and in his case, it's the right combination. Sorensen is analytical and unemotional, so is Kennedy. There hasn't been such a combination of speechwriter and President since Raymond Moley and Franklin D. Roosevelt . . . A public figure shouldn't be just a puppet who echoes his speechmaker. The ideas should be his, the opinions his, the words his. . . .

In fact, Kennedy did deeply believe everything I helped write for him, because my writing came from my knowledge of his beliefs.

In the White House I also had an advantage that many subsequent presidential speechwriters have not had—participating in the principal's policy decisions. I could listen to the arguments presented to him, assess which facts most impressed him in the Oval Office or Cabinet Room, hear the formulation of his conclusions, and then walk a few steps to my own office to put into words what I had just observed.

Other speechwriters for other presidents have written

about fierce turf battles in the White House over phrases intended to commit the president to one or another side of an internal ideological struggle, all part of the clearance process through which each speech draft journeys on its way to the president. I was fortunate to face no clearance process and no ideological struggle. In another White House, the domestic policy advisor would rewrite the speech; in the Kennedy White House, my previous eight years with the senator qualified me to be the domestic policy advisor. In some White Houses, speechwriters have to cope with senior staff members slipping in their own pet issues; in the Kennedy White House, I *was* the senior staff member. When a presidential speechwriter knows his draft will be considered by his principal word for word—and very often used word for word—he approaches the drafting chore with special care and pride in his craft, even though that more painstaking approach means harder work and longer hours. I approached my writing with special care, because I knew it would be heard and read all over the country, perhaps all over the world. That realization first dawned on me when JFK's first major speech after announcing his candidacy for president was reprinted in full in the *New York Times*. That had never happened to us before.

As a general rule, my drafts were reviewed only by JFK. His edits often modified my language, but rarely if ever the substance of the policies that speech was to convey. Occasionally, in the White House, he would delete a whole paragraph, page, or sentence. Even more occasionally, if I still liked the language, I would try to use it again in a subsequent speech. Sometimes JFK would spot this, and laughingly delete it again. But sometimes I succeeded.

There was no need for me to ask Larry O'Brien, JFK's longtime friend and campaign director, later special assistant to the president, to check my draft references to pending legislation on which I had worked; but I laughed at a cartoon that portrayed an O'Brien-like aide reviewing a draft speech with a speechwriter who I thought resembled me: "It's a good speech—just a couple of points that need obfuscation." Every speechwriter should hang a copy of that cartoon on his wall.

Our collaborative writing process was not wholly free from error. In my first year when JFK asked me to draft, for his submission to the Harvard alumni magazine, an essay on the role of the university's famed Widener Library, I wrote of "thoughts upon gazing at the Library while walking across the Harvard campus," only to learn later that he had lacked time to proofread my draft. Every Harvard graduate—including the author of a sarcastic letter to the editor in the magazine's next issue—knows that in Harvard the campus is called the "Yard."

On another occasion, rushing to put together, on the eve of the 1960 Democratic National Convention, a nationally televised speech in response to former President Truman's attack on JFK as not being "ready" for the presidency, we used in closing an Abraham Lincoln quotation suggested by a distinguished and reliable historian, James McGregor Burns. The quote perfectly met our needs to finish that speech with dramatic emphasis, but we heard later that no other historian could find any trace of Lincoln ever having spoken the words that we attributed to him.

Similarly, some of the ancient Chinese proverbs that JFK liked to cite could not be verified by my Chinese friends as even modern proverbs. But he continued invoking "ancient" sayings like "Failure is an orphan, but success has a hundred fathers," and "A journey of a thousand miles begins with a single step."

Not every American can write a presidential speech, but many think they can. Over the years, unsolicited drafts poured in; some were even thrust upon me by strangers on the street. Each word in a presidential speech must be weighed with special care for its possible multiple meanings and consequences, particularly in foreign affairs, where the president's word alone can be deemed national policy. In addition, every agency in government and every special interest group in the country believes that, if only the president would make a speech on its particular cause, that cause would succeed; I was deluged by those requests as well.

My assignment to help JFK draft his speeches—in addition to other writing—was first given to me early in 1954, after I had completed roughly one year in his United States Senate office. It was a role I could not fully shed for the next nearly ten years, no matter how demanding my other duties and emergency tasks in his campaign and presidency became. More than once, I tried to delegate to others the chief speechwriting obligation, but couldn't find a suitable full-time replacement acceptable to my boss. "I know you wish you could get out of writing so many speeches," JFK once said to me on the presidential campaign trail. "I wish I could get out of giving so many. But that's the situation we're both in for the present." During the campaign Dick Goodwin helped; we worked both separately and in the same room on speeches. From time to time, others contributed, including both Arthur Schlesinger Jr. and Harris Wofford, later a distinguished U.S. senator. During the postconvention campaign in 1960, John Bartlow Martin and Joe Kraft ably fulfilled the unique role of "speech advance" that Martin had pioneered in the Stevenson campaigns. They would travel with or ahead of the campaign plane, sometimes on a rotating or leapfrogging basis, to each future Kennedy stop, collecting local information, opinion, color, and commentary, and then draft introductions, notes, conclusions, and themes for the final speeches to be delivered by the candidate. We almost always made good use of their material.

Unfortunately, we were less able to make use of the material submitted by the high-powered team of gifted writers back at campaign headquarters in Washington, led by Harvard professor (and later solicitor general) Archibald Cox, a brilliant public servant with a genial personality who blamed me, sometimes heatedly, for his team's material not appearing in the candidate's speeches. It was one of the few elements of discord in the campaign, and JFK insisted that I accommodate Archie. I very much wanted to do so. But Archie was many miles away, out of touch with the ever-changing tempo of the campaign.

I have often told practitioners of the profession not to let journalists, historians, or political colleagues dismiss them as merely speechwriters, as if their role were nothing more than slinging sound bites together. Alexander Hamilton and John Jay, I remind them, worked on speeches for George Washington. So did Thomas Jefferson. William Seward helped Lincoln on his first inaugural. Mark Twain worked on the memoirs of President Grant. The best presidential speechwriter in American history was Abraham Lincoln, who wrote his own. Other men and women of distinction and accomplishment have drafted other works for other distinguished leaders who were too preoccupied with other responsibilities to find time for that task.

More than fifty years ago, when I began working on Senator JFK's speeches and other writings, I did not know that forty years earlier my father, as a student at the University of Nebraska and editor in chief of its student newspaper, the *Daily Nebraskan*, had prepared for its staff a style book with rules and recommendations not unlike my own, including "do not spin it, boil it." With his sense of humor and commitment to proper usage, my father might have enjoyed a less serious list of rules that I have occasionally cited: Avoid clichés like the plague . . . Try not to ever split an infinitive . . . Make sure that every pronoun agrees with their antecedent, and I've told you a million times, don't exaggerate!

My chief qualification for speechwriting was a love of the English language as a beautiful instrument of precision. Despite learning to type in eighth grade, I have always preferred to write by hand. I wrote my first drafts of Kennedy's speeches in longhand on long, yellow legal pads, editing as I went along, with more arrows, deletions, insertions, circles, and directions in the margin than most stenographers could follow. I almost literally thought through my pen, sometimes not certain of my position on a nuanced issue until I had written it.

I am not a fast writer; I am a painstaking writer, careful with my prose and often pausing at length to choose the right word and the right order of words. My handwriting, no more illegible than JFK's, suffered from my always having too little time to write carefully. For me, writing required—and still requires—as much quiet uninterrupted time as possible, as much immersion in the subject as possible, drawing from—and surrounded by—my notes and research papers, divided into piles reflecting each subject in my outline.

In general, JFK and I agreed, a typical speech need not last more than twenty or twenty-five minutes, even less depending on the setting, schedule, wishes of the host, or occasion, and depending as well on whether time is to be left for questions. Woodrow Wilson is said to have asked those inviting him to address a trade association convention how long they wanted him to speak, adding that a ten-minute speech would take him a week to prepare, a five-minute speech ten days to prepare, but, for an hour or longer speech he was "ready right now."

Even a major political speech should not be too aggressively partisan, with slashing attacks on an opponent. Its tone should be positive, inspirational, hopeful, and forward-looking—not an endless litany of negative complaints about past misdeeds or the status quo. Without being a laundry list of detailed specifics, a good political speech should contain one or more (not more than three, unless it's the State of the Union) constructive, realistic proposals to solve those current problems most troubling the country. No politician can please every audience with his speech—the key is to please yourself, making sure you are satisfied with the quality of the effort.

One elementary rule for a speechwriter: If you are carrying the speech text, stay close to the speaker. On a trip to Knoxville, where Senator JFK was to discuss the Tennessee Valley Authority (TVA), he and I were directed to ride in separate cars from the airport. My driver, heading for the hotel where the senator was to speak at lunch (we thought), became separated from the others. We turned on the radio; to my shock and dismay, I heard that JFK had just arrived at a site overlooking a new TVA dam. I heard him being introduced to give his speech, the only copy of which I still had in my coat pocket. My, what that man knew about the TVA!

Speech presentation is also important. I attempted, halfway through JFK's first year as president, to improve the television production of his major speeches, suggesting a reduced temperature in the Oval Office to avoid scenes of his wiping his brow; sharper lighting; better and closer camera work; hiring a full-time television consultant/producer/director; and continued improvement in his delivery, which was by then slower, with more pauses for effect and more emphasis on underlined words. I did not share his later opinion that too many television appearances would bore the public, though I acknowledged the common sense of his concern that the public temperature could not long be kept at a high crisis level. (He was relieved to learn from Arthur Schlesinger that FDR had actually conducted relatively few fireside chats.)

Over the past fifty years, I developed a style of speechwriting that can be boiled down to six basic rules.

LESS IS ALMOST ALWAYS BETTER THAN MORE.

Make it as simple and direct as the Ten Commandments; as simple as J. P. Morgan's alleged response to the youngster who asked him the secret to the stock market: "It fluctuates." Some politicians mistakenly believe that the art of political speaking is to stretch as few thoughts as possible into as many words as possible—JFK and I believed exactly the opposite. I've always treasured the wisdom of William Strunk Jr. and E. B. White's classic book, *Elements of Style*. Among its watchwords: "Omit unnecessary words." My favorite rule, because it illustrates itself.

I like two examples: Winston Churchill's opening line in his radio address after the fall of France in June 1940: "The news from France is very bad." Not one unclear or unnecessary word. And the second, a sign for a fish store window: "Fresh Fish for Sale Here Today." The only necessary word on that sign is "fish."

CHOOSE EACH WORD AS A PRECISION TOOL.

Care and prudence in selecting the right word and sequence of words, important in every speech, were even more important in helping draft the president's letters to Soviet Chairman Khrushchev during the Cuban missile crisis. In his foreign policy speeches, JFK stayed out of the terminology trap, the common tendency to label groups with names that put them beyond the pale of negotiation, such as "Communist," or "enemy," or "evil." He often used metaphors, especially nautical metaphors, which he knew better than I. But he did not resort to casual reliance on the war metaphor—never declaring a war on cancer, a war on crime. I do not recall whether he, RFK, or LBJ first described the new antipoverty program for 1964 as a "war on poverty."

ORGANIZE THE TEXT TO SIMPLIFY, CLARIFY, EMPHAS!ZE.

A speech should flow from an outline in logical order. Number points, when appropriate; each numbered paragraph can start with the same few words. There should be a tightly organized, coherent, and consistent theme— a rule reinforced by Churchill's criticism of an opponent's speech, "That pudding has no theme." Coherence and consistency suffer when there are too many writers working on one speech. Many people can contribute suggestions and corrections, but only one can truly write it.

USE VARIETY AND LITERARY DEVICES TO REINFORCE MEMORABILITY, NOT CONFUSE OR DISTRACT.

Alliteration and repetition can help make a speech memorable—as can the "reversible raincoat," another technique occasionally used by JFK and me, but often parodied. Academic analysts called this chiasmus, a new word to me, but an ancient literary device. "Let us never negotiate out of fear, but let us never fear to negotiate." "Bring the absolute power to destroy other nations under the absolute control of all nations" (from JFK's inaugural).

Another device I employed—and since childhood enjoyed—was rhyming. Partly as a result of seeing Burma

Shave signs along the Nebraskan roadside on our early family travels, I always liked to hear and read poetry, all kinds, from childhood verse by Mother Goose to limericks and doggerel. As a speechwriter, I felt that words that roughly rhymed were more easily remembered and more clearly communicated: "Let every nation know . . . that we shall oppose any foe."

In each case, the test is not to ask how it reads but to ask how it sounds.

A personal experience is more credible evidence and more likely to be remembered by the hearer. The right quotation from the right person can help. Do not covet thy neighbor's entire speech; but do not feel ashamed to improve upon some ancient statesman's good line, or apply it in a different context, alluding to the source or citing him by name. Just as there are no new jokes in the world, there are very few epigrams, phrases, or even speech ideas that are entirely new. Almost every line of almost every great speech can be said to bear some resemblance or relationship, however tenuous, to something someone else, somewhere else, said at some earlier time.

In early 1960 my campaign colleague, friend, and early mentor, Bob Wallace, told me that a speech draft of mine was "little more than a collection of some *Bartlett's*

Famous Quotations." I resented it—mostly because he was right. But JFK gave the speech with little change, and his college audience loved it.

Kennedy liked to embellish his speeches with quotations from the widest possible variety of sources: Hemingway, Shaw, Aristotle, Socrates, Pericles, Demosthenes, Solon, and Pindar. One American politician asked me whether Kennedy's frequent invocation of ancient Greek philosophers and culture represented an effort on his part to woo the Greek-American vote in Massachusetts or nationally. Apparently that politician did not share JFK's passion for history. I was told that, when LBJ received a speech draft containing a quotation from Socrates, he scratched out the philosopher's name and replaced it with "my granddaddy."

Ironically, JFK is sometimes quoted by speakers attributing to him lines that he had quoted from others. When working in my first Kennedy year on New England economic problems, I noticed that the regional chamber of commerce, the New England Council, had a thoughtful slogan: "A rising tide lifts all the boats." JFK borrowed it often. Now the line is frequently quoted by others who attribute it to him. (During the George W. Bush pro-wealth era, one critic described the Bush motto as "a rising tide lifts all the yachts.")

Another example is "Some men see things as they are and say, 'Why?' I dream of things that never were and say, 'Why not?'" That maxim is now attributed to Robert Kennedy, who got it from JFK, who had also borrowed it.

Some political commentators said that Kennedy's 1960 campaign speeches may have "erred on the side of overestimating the literacy and intelligence of the American people." Possibly; but Kennedy won, proving that both he and the American people were a lot smarter than some political commentators.

EMPLOY ELEVATED BUT NOT GRANDIOSE LANGUAGE.

To paraphrase Browning, "A nation's reach should exceed its grasp, or what's a president for." A president who elevates the sights of his countrymen above and beyond the limits of their daily chores, a president who offers hope to the world's deprived and dispossessed, a president whose words enable the young dreamers of his country to feel that someone is listening who cares— such a president is bound to antagonize some and ultimately disillusion others, but he nevertheless fulfills as he speaks an essential role of national leadership consistent with the Founders' vision of this country as a beacon to the world.

JFK and I tried to elevate and yet simplify his speeches; not to patronize his audiences, but to keep his sentences short, his words understandable, and his organizational structure and ideas clear. He used straightforward declarations, not "maybe" or "perhaps," setting forth lucid, well-reasoned concepts of where we were headed as a nation and what we had to do as a people. His speeches were dignified but in the vernacular, never so esoteric that they could not be easily and quickly comprehended by the average listener.

A policy speech is not a statute, which needs to specify every detail in legally precise and comprehensive terms— nor should it be, if it is to be both enjoyed and understood by all its listeners. I was gratified to read a statement from one of my White House colleagues: "Ted Sorensen can use words that everybody can understand—intellectuals, milkmen, diplomats, politicians."

SUBSTANTIVE IDEAS ARE THE MOST IMPORTANT PART OF ANY SPEECH.

A great speech is great because of the strong ideas conveyed, the principles, the values, the decisions. If the ideas are great, the speech will be great, even if the words are pedestrian; but if the words are soaring, beautiful, eloquent, it is still not a great speech if the ideas are flat, empty, or mean-spirited.

Those politicians who have tried in the last forty years to emulate Kennedy's success on the speaker's platform forget that his best speeches moved people not because of the grandeur of his phrases, which can largely be imitated by any White House wordsmith, but because of the grandeur of his ideas. He who pens the final draft has an opportunity to shape the final version of those ideas. I once joked at a staff gathering that the old saying—"Give me the making of the songs of a nation, and I care not who makes its laws"—could be amended by substituting "speeches" for "songs."

I approached each speech draft as if it might someday appear under Kennedy's name in a collection of the world's great speeches; that may have been immodest and presumptuous, but it motivated me to use elegant prose and the King's English. JFK and I shared an appreciation for great oratory. Early in his Senate career, I gave him for Christmas a *Treasury of the World's Great Speeches*. He devoured it, often citing passages to me for possible inclusion in his own speeches or *Profiles in Courage*. I borrowed the book back and used it as my own standard reference. Many years later, he would reciprocate by selecting as a Christmas present for me a beautiful leather-bound edition of all presidential inaugural addresses. He did not live to give it to me; but I was deeply moved by his widow's inscription in

December 1963: "For Ted, Jack was going to give you this for Christmas—Please accept it now from me—with all my love and devotion always—for all the devotion you gave Jack."

Yet, after all is said and little is done, a speech—even an elevated, eloquent speech—is still just a speech. Saying so doesn't make it so. A speech can stir men's minds by describing what is; sometimes it can stir their hearts by describing what should be; but rarely can a speech by itself change their fate by determining or changing what will be. It does not have the power of law. It seeks to persuade people to change their views, but it may represent only the view of the speaker or his powerless speechwriter. Rare is the speaker who has the power to make others listen, and, if they listen, to act, and if they act, to do so in the manner he advocates.

Nevertheless, I do not dismiss the potential of the right speech on the right topic delivered by the right speaker in the right way at the right moment. It can ignite a fire, change men's minds, open their eyes, alter their votes, bring hope to their lives, and, in all these ways, change the world. I know. I saw it happen.

Chapter 13

My Role in
Profiles in Courage

When I started working with JFK in January 1953, we agreed that my duties would include assistance on the writing of articles and other publications, much as Senator Paul Douglas's assistants did for him; and that I would be compensated, separately from my Senate salary, for these literary efforts, receiving at least one-half of any fees or royalties he received for such publications—again the Douglas practice. (In fact, I had received from Senator Douglas, in December 1952, the month before I started work for Kennedy, a check for $25 representing one-half of a fee Douglas had received from the *New Republic* for an article I had helped write.) At a modest level, this literary collaboration arrangement worked well for JFK and me during those initial years. I worked on articles for a wide variety of publications—including *Vogue*, *Life*, *Look*, the *New York Times Sunday Magazine*, the *Kiwanis* magazine, the *General Electric Defense Quarterly*, the *Bulletin of Atomic Scientists*, and the *National Parent-Teacher*. One article was for the *Progressive*, which had published my law student piece on teachers' rights several years earlier. The subjects of these articles were also diverse: politics, education, social security, minimum wage, labor rackets, lobbying, the arts, disarmament, college loyalty oaths, and the New England economy. Often I drafted these articles in a first-person voice, as if—if relevant—I were a Catholic, a New Englander, a foreign policy expert, or a young politician recovering from illness.

So many articles by a young senator represented a new approach to climbing the national political ladder. Douglas, Morse, and other academics-turned-politicians whose intellectual standards JFK admired, also wrote articles. But, in Kennedy's case, articles on serious subjects like foreign and domestic policy presented not only his views but an image of intensive progressive thought, nationally disseminating his personal philosophy and helping balance the flood of superficial articles about his good looks and his romance with Jackie.

After he had been in the Senate for less than a year, JFK called me into his office and said he wanted my help researching and writing a magazine article on the history of senatorial courage. He showed me a passage, in Herbert Agar's *The Price of Union*, that described the political punishment risked and received by John Quincy Adams as a senator from Massachusetts, when he opposed all the important economic interest groups in New England by supporting the embargo that President Jefferson had placed on trade with Great Britain in retaliation for British attacks on American merchant ships. JFK told me his idea of an article exploring the willingness of elected officials to defy the pressure of powerful interest groups, or the protests of concerned constituents, to stand up for what those officials conscientiously believed to be in the national interest.

It may have been during his 1954 hospitalization for back surgery, confronted with the possibility of early death or crippling illness, that he decided to make more of his life, to become more serious about his career than he had been as a congressman, even to think seriously about running for higher office.

Later, while he was convalescing in Palm Beach from his surgery, with ample time on his hands, he decided to expand the senatorial courage article into a full-length book. He had shown the draft article to his brother-in-law Michael Canfield, hoping that it might interest *Harper's* magazine. Michael's father, Cass Canfield, Harper and Row publisher, suggested a full book, requiring at least sixty thousand words. JFK enthusiastically telephoned me about the possibility. We had earlier worked together on a twelve-hundred-word piece for the *New York Times Sunday Magazine* on an unrelated subject; and when I told him the book would require the equivalent of fifty such articles, he paused for a moment, but said he wanted to proceed.

Soon thereafter, in December 1954, I started sending books, memos, and research materials to him in Florida for the project. When he ultimately returned to his Senate office in June 1955, he brought back three cartons of books, which we had called—until we returned them— "the Library of Congress Palm Beach Annex." Library of Congress staff members for years referred to me as the fellow who borrowed more books than anyone else on Capitol Hill. To help JFK on the book, I flew to Palm Beach, accompanied by my secretary from his Senate office, in March and again in May, staying ten days to two weeks on each visit. While in Washington, I received from Florida almost daily instructions and requests by letter and telephone—books to send, memoranda to draft, sources to check, materials to assemble, and Dictaphone drafts or revisions of early chapters. After JFK returned to the Senate, our collaboration continued in his office and home.

After I persuaded him to include Nebraska's Senator Norris, I was delighted to learn that my father had old 1924–1930 correspondence from Norris as well as newspaper clippings. In one of several letters to my father about the book, I noted:

> We have decided to expand the Norris chapter to include his support of Al Smith in 1928. As I recall, you headed the Norris for President organization that year (taking time out only to preside over the birth of your favorite son). I wonder if your files might contain some materials relating to Norris' support of Smith . . . as usual, we're in a terrible rush for this.

I can only hope that my father understood and forgave my impertinence.

JFK worked particularly hard and long on the first and last chapters, setting the tone and philosophy of the book. I did a first draft of most chapters, which he revised both with a pen and through dictation. He decided, for reasons of senatorial courtesy, not to identify in his opening chapter the name of the fellow senator who acknowledged to him one day during a roll call vote that he voted with the special interests on every issue, hoping that, by election, all of them added together would constitute nearly a majority that would remember him favorably while the other members of the public would never know about it, much less remember his vote against their welfare.

I see no reason for anonymity now: It was his close friend, the late Senator George Smathers of Florida. Maybe Smathers was joking when he said that; maybe not.

Some charge that the book was written as a part of JFK's drive for the presidency. But in late 1953 and 1954, when the original draft article was conceived and the book begun, he was not yet a prospect even for the vice presidency. Others have charged that the book was written to atone for his avoidance of the 1954 McCarthy censure motion while he was in the hospital. But there was no such censure vote pending in the Senate when the book's theme was conceived the previous year. Whether he ever linked the two in his mind, he never said and I do not know.

Shortly before he commenced what became virtually a four-year quest for the Democratic presidential nomination, *Profiles in Courage* was published on January 1, 1956, and became an instant best-seller and financial success. It was bought by more than two million American readers and by magazines, book clubs, reprint publishers, foreign publishers, television producers, and others, with all of whom he asked me to negotiate. Clearly one-half of his earnings from all the direct, indirect, or prospective *Profiles* royalties would total far in excess of anything either of us had ever contemplated, much less expected, when that fifty-fifty royalty-sharing understanding had been reached a few years earlier. He had no financial need to renegotiate or reconsider that long-standing agreement. I had not worked on the book for monetary reasons, nor had he. I made no financial requests, and imposed no conditions. He had publicly acknowledged in his introduction to the book my extensive role in its composition. In May 1957 he unexpectedly and generously offered, and I happily accepted, a sum to be spread over several years, that I regarded as more than fair.

I never learned what prompted that move. If his father's advisors, who drafted the new agreement, thought it was necessary to prevent me from leaving his service prior to the next presidential election, or from publicly demanding one-half of the book's direct and indirect proceeds, they were wholly mistaken. There was never any possibility of my doing either. The agreement diminished any interest I might otherwise have had in public recognition of my role. As I wrote to JFK at the time: "Because of our agreement concerning my work and pay for such publications (which agreement has . . . been extremely helpful to me), I am unwilling to push this point concerning recognition of my participation."

The letter of agreement was binding on our respective heirs, should either of us die before the agreement's expiration—something I never considered at age twenty-nine, though he did at age forty. I kept the agreement confidential until now, lest it fuel speculative exaggeration of my role in the writing of the book. I knew the man and the facts well enough to know that his generosity resulted not from a sense of guilt, but from his innate sense of fairness. By January 1961, when we entered the White House, his total net earnings from *Profiles* had not yet reached a level twice as high as the sum he had promised to me, but he requested no adjustment. Another reminder of how lucky I was.

The book, a global success, also won a Pulitzer Prize. Both the prize and JFK's reported presidential ambitions inevitably fueled speculation on the book's authorship. The opening shot was fired on Mike Wallace's ABC television show on Saturday night, December 7, 1957. Drew Pearson, the nationally syndicated political muckraker and columnist, was a guest on the Wallace show, partly because of his column two months earlier attacking JFK's father for supposedly "spending a fortune on a publicity machine . . . on a public relations advance buildup." It was in this context that Mr. Pearson "blurted out" (his expression) his indignation that JFK had "won a Pulitzer Prize on a book which was ghostwritten for him . . . the book, *Profiles in Courage* was written for Senator Kennedy by somebody else and he has never acknowledged the fact." Mr. Wallace asked who; Mr. Pearson replied that he didn't recall at the moment. In response to a subsequent telephone inquiry by ABC, we later learned, he had identified me as the author, claiming I had provided not merely the assistance described and acknowledged by Senator Kennedy in the front of the volume but that I had actually written the book.

JFK called me at home the next day, Sunday, December 8, uncharacteristically angry: "We might as well quit if we let this stand. This challenges my ability to write the book, my honesty in signing it, and my integrity in accepting the Pulitzer Prize." His father was even more upset, urging JFK to hire Washington attorney Clark Clifford to sue Pearson, ABC, and Mike Wallace. Clifford, in reply, warned that a lawsuit would drag on for years, giving the accusation even more publicity, and that a request for a retraction would be more prudent. Clifford also reviewed JFK's book files and handwritten notes, concluding to his own satisfaction that the book was in fact JFK's.

After the initial allegation, JFK also invited Pearson to come review his Dictaphone tapes and those same handwritten notes. At a long conference with ABC officials in New York City, he showed them sample pages from the book, his notes, and an affidavit from me:

> I wish to state under oath that these charges are wholly untrue. I am not the author of *Profiles in Courage*. I did not write the book for Senator Kennedy, and I have not at any time to any person declared myself to be the author. I have never written any book of any kind . . . I undertook at his direction and under his supervision to assist him in the assembly and preparation of research and other materials on which much of the book is based . . . [as] very generously acknowledged by the Senator in the Preface. The author is Senator Kennedy, who originally conceived its theme, selected its characters, determined its contents, and wrote and rewrote each of its chapters. The research, suggestions and other

materials received by him in the course of writing the book from me and the others listed in the Preface were all considered by the Senator, along with his own material, in part rejected by him and in part drawn upon by him in his work. To assert that any one of us who supplied such materials "wrote the book" for the Senator is clearly unwarranted and in error.

That affidavit was accurately, if carefully, worded. I took my oath seriously. The ABC executives finally agreed that JFK was the author of *Profiles*, but then leveled another charge—that I had privately boasted or indirectly hinted that I had written much of the book (a charge that, I regret to say, may have been—it was all too long ago to remember—partly true). "Perhaps," said an ABC executive to JFK, as I waited in another room, "Sorensen made the statement when drinking." "He doesn't drink," said JFK. "Perhaps he said it when he was mad at you." "He's never been mad at me," replied Kennedy.

The Kennedys were anxious to have the retraction and apology included in the next Mike Wallace show the following Sunday; and it was. On December 14, a statement by ABC's vice president in charge of television was read:

This company has inquired into the charge made by Mr. Pearson and has satisfied itself that such charge is unfounded and that the book in question was written by Senator Kennedy. We deeply regret this error and feel it does a grave injustice to a distinguished public servant and author, to the excellent book he wrote, and to the prize he was awarded. We extend our sincere apologies to Senator Kennedy, his publishers, and the Pulitzer Prize Committee.

On February 16, 1958, Drew Pearson's column referred to a sermon by Norman Thomas (ironically, the father of Evan Thomas, the editor of *Profiles in Courage*) stating that "it's easy to write profiles in courage about men who are dead—what we need is profiles in courage among men who are living." To this, Pearson added: "Author of *Profiles in Courage* is Senator Jack Kennedy of Massachusetts." That ended most of the controversy, and JFK dropped Pearson a handwritten note: "Dear Drew: I appreciate your comment on the book Sunday—it clarifies the record and I am grateful. I hope to see you soon."

Rumors about the book's authorship persisted. Conservative and intellectually challenged Republican senator Homer Capehart of Indiana, while debating Kennedy on another issue on the Senate floor, tried to score points and unsettle his Democratic colleague by inserting into his remarks the question, "Who really wrote that book?" Kennedy deftly replied: "Well, there's one thing certain. I'm confident that no one has prepared for you the remarks that you are delivering now."

I was not the only one alleged to have "ghosted" the book. Arthur Krock, an old Kennedy family friend and *New York Times* columnist, was also said to be the author. So was the Library of Congress staffer who found hundreds of items of research for us. Neither of them did any of the writing. Jules David, Jackie's Georgetown professor, who submitted several helpful monographs, and James Landis in Joseph Kennedy's office, who did a research report on Webster, were also each alleged to be the real author. Both made useful contributions, but neither was responsible for the finished product.

The charge, which still lingers, was and is nonsense about a brilliant Harvard graduate who had written two books before *Profiles*; one, *Why England Slept*, had been a Book-of-the-Month Club best-seller. He was a man whose sense of history was demonstrated time and again as senator, and as president. He retained on his presidential staff a resident historian, and he continued to read and quote history not only in his speeches to the public but in his private advice to his staff.

As I said under oath, the book's concept was his, and the selection of stories was his. He immersed himself in the book's research, provided its philosophy, wrote or rewrote each of its chapters, chose its title, and provided constant directions and corrections to those of us supplying him with raw material; yet JFK generously thanked in the book "my research associate, Theodore C. Sorensen, for his invaluable assistance in the assembly and preparation of the material upon which this book is based."

Looking back on the issue more than fifty years later, perhaps I can answer the skeptics' question of authorship by asking my own question: Is the author the person who did much of the research and helped choose the words in many of its sentences, or is the author the person who decided the substance, structure, and theme of the book; read and revised each draft; inspired, constructed, and improved the work? Like JFK's speeches, *Profiles in Courage* was a collaboration, and not a particularly unusual one, inasmuch as our method of collaboration on the book was similar to the method we used on his speeches. But to answer the speculation of my would-be defenders—I never felt—not for a moment—that I was wrongfully denied part of the credit, much less a share in the Pulitzer Prize. In fact, it is because the book was so deep a collaboration and because I was so intimately involved at each stage that I know exactly where the credit ultimately lies—with JFK.

Throughout JFK's subsequent presidential campaign, whenever his unrecorded position on the censure of Joe McCarthy was recalled, it was often accompanied by the sardonic quip that he should "show less profile and more courage." In JFK's entire political career, no issue more clearly presented him with an extraordinarily difficult test of his own personal political courage, in the terms described by his book, than the question of censuring Senator McCarthy, who was strongly admired by many of Kennedy's fellow Catholics, by a substantial number of his Massachusetts constituents, and by his family. JFK's brother Bob worked for one of McCarthy's Senate subcommittees. His sister Eunice and her husband, Sarge Shriver, were good friends of McCarthy, who may have had a romantic interest in Eunice before her marriage. Other family members, including Bobby's wife, Ethel, were close to McCarthy's wife, Jean. But lined up on the other side against McCarthy were most members of Kennedy's party. Even some moderate and conservative Democratic senators neither trusted nor respected the Wisconsin demagogue. They disliked his methods and regarded him as a source of political poison in a democracy, and an embarrassment to the Senate. "One day," Senator Lister Hill of Alabama told me as we stood talking at the back of the Senate in 1953, long before any censure was discussed, "we are going to have to face the issue of what to do about that man. Then the roll will be called on all of us."

When the roll was first called in July 1954, JFK knew that, if he voted with his fellow Democrats and anti-McCarthy Republicans on a motion to censure McCarthy, he would be defying many in his home state and family; but if he voted against such a motion, he would be denounced by the leading members of his party, by the leading liberals and intellectuals in the country and his alma mater, by the leaders of the Senate, and by the major national newspapers. He would even have trouble with both his conscience and his young legislative assistant. Whichever way he voted, he faced trouble.

In July 1954, after he attended a meeting with other liberal Democratic senators, I prepared for him at his request a speech in support of censure. He intended to vote accordingly, when the matter came to the Senate floor on the evening of July 31. He liked the strategy I urged of censuring McCarthy primarily on legal and senatorial grounds; and he put the finishing touches on my draft, which read in part:

There are difficulties in explaining the deep-rooted feelings which motivate one on such an issue where so many emotions run high. I am not insensitive to the fact that my constituents perhaps contain a greater proportion of devotees on each side of this matter than the constituency of any other Senator. The zeal with which these citizens view this issue emphasizes their sincere concern for exposing the Communist threat in this country and for combating Communism without adopting its methods . . . This censure motion, like those previously adopted by the Senate, is more concerned with the dignity and honor of this body than with the personal characteristics of any individual Senator. . . . It is for these reasons . . . that I shall vote to censure the junior senator from Wisconsin.

This speech also included an apt quotation on a Senate censure in a previous generation delivered by Nebraska's Senator Norris: "We owe it to the country to take that action, or see ourselves stand condemned in the eyes of respectable people."

It was a mild, cautious speech in favor of censure, but it was still a speech in favor of censure. However, he never had an opportunity to deliver it or to cast the vote it foretold. The Senate decided that evening that no such vote should be taken without a special committee investigation and hearing. By the time that committee report was delivered and debated, JFK was in the hospital, effectively incommunicado (or at least with me). I had no contact with him and no instructions. Under Senate rules, I could have registered with the Secretary of the Senate on his behalf an "announcement" or "pair" in favor of censure, in effect casting the vote of a juror who had not been present at the trial, who had not read the report or heard the debate. As a cautious lawyer, I decided not to record him or even try to obtain through any family member at his bedside his approval or disapproval of that course. Having been out of touch with him for months, and having received no guidance on this particular issue, I made no decision. I was a relatively new twenty-six-year-old legislative assistant, who feared the wrath of the senator's brother and father more than the senator's, had I followed my own instincts and announced his position as pro-censure. I did not know what to do. I suspected—correctly, I still believe—that there was no point in my trying to reach him on an issue he wanted to duck.

Kennedy was the only member of the Senate whose position was unrecorded. Over time, he increasingly made it clear that he had in general supported censure and would have spoken and voted for it had he been given the opportunity. Eventually the issue faded away. In time, many of the party's liberals and Harvard intellectuals forgave him for this one major mistake; but others, including Eleanor Roosevelt, did not forgive him for years. Later, writer Patrick Anderson would state: "It remains the supreme irony of Sorensen's career that he, the devotee of civil liberties, *made the decision* on the McCarthy vote that did most to raise liberal doubts about Kennedy in the years ahead." True, but at the time I cravenly rationalized my not casting the vote of an "absent juror" on civil liberties grounds.

I would have been much happier had I received instructions from that hospital bed to announce or pair him in favor of censure. McCarthy was a moral issue. JFK, gravely ill, did not voluntarily absent himself; but neither did he take any steps to make his position public and clear; and I have no doubt that political safety as well as family harmony was a major reason. He did not ask me to take the blame. Nor did he later express any criticism or disagreement with my decision not to have him paired or announced. My guess is that, if he had truly wanted to reach me from the hospital, he could have. I was—and remain—disappointed by his inaction, even though I recognize the political and personal realities behind it. JFK showed no courage on that vote. Neither did I.

This one failure should not obscure his many acts of political courage. Almost a year before his June 1963 reversal of his party's and the country's refusal to mandate equal opportunity for blacks, a reversal he knew might cost him reelection, he stated at his July 23, 1962, press conference, when asked about a Gallup Poll showing a drop in presidential popularity from 79 percent to 69 percent, JFK replied: ". . . if I were still 79 percent after a very intense Congressional session, I would feel I had not met my responsibilities. . . . As I make my views clearer, some people increasingly are not going to approve of me. So I dropped to 69 percent, and will probably drop some more."

Years ago, the John F. Kennedy Foundation established a Profiles in Courage Award to honor those in public life today "who stand on principle . . . which often exacts a high price for acts of conscience . . . amid the clamor of polls and consultants." I truly believe that, with one sad exception, John F. Kennedy was a "Profile in Courage." But that one exception still hurts, and I cannot in good conscience defend either his failure to reach me, or my failure to record him in favor of censure.

Chapter 14

A Catholic Candidate
for President?

S trange as it seems today, the chief obstacle to John F. Kennedy's nomination and election as president of the United States in 1960 was based not on doubts about his age or experience, or his controversial family, or his voting record in the United States Senate, or even his health. It was based largely on his Roman Catholic faith. This opposition fell into four categories:

First, the bigots, located mostly but not exclusively in Southern and rural America, who were unwilling to listen to facts or reason, and who deeply believed and had widely disseminated their passionate hatred and vicious untruths about the Catholic Church, and all its popes, priests, and parishioners.

Second, the liberal intellectuals, who were influential in the Democratic Party and in universities in the North and the South, and both fearful and suspicious of the American Catholic hierarchy's obtaining more political power. They opposed the church's positions on church-state relations, particularly its requests for public funds for parochial schools and its attempts to influence public policy on private family concerns ranging from contraception to divorce.

Third, anxious Democrats, tired of losing, who were convinced that any Catholic nominee would be overwhelmingly defeated, citing the crushing defeat suffered by Al Smith in 1928—a defeat that had traumatized Democratic Catholics as well as Protestants. When they looked at Kennedy, they saw Smith.

Fourth, many Catholics themselves, including some Democratic Party leaders, who were nervous for selfish reasons about the prospects of the religious issue being raised in a campaign. Some felt it was too soon for a Catholic to seek the presidency, and still others thought Kennedy was not a sufficiently strong, doctrinaire Catholic. Kennedy publicly disagreed with the church hierarchy on many public policies, was alone among the presidential hopefuls in opposing a 1960 bill that would have authorized public funds for nonpublic schools, and also opposed the U.S. government recognizing the

Vatican as a state by appointing a U.S. ambassador. On the most sensitive issue of all, he opposed any attempt to reduce U.S. foreign aid to nations using public funds for birth control.

In the most ironic twist of my years with Kennedy, I was placed in charge of studying and combating this issue, despite or possibly because of the fact that I was a lifelong Unitarian. My ability to understand those religious and political liberals who were afraid of the Catholic hierarchy—and to reassure them about JFK's independent views—was founded on an adolescence in which such fears were voiced frequently in my church, even in my family. I had long been a strong supporter of the separation of church and state. When I first started in Kennedy's office I knew so little about Catholicism (other than the distortions I had heard as a child) that, on Ash Wednesday, I was puzzled by the number of Kennedy office secretaries who arrived with smudges on their foreheads. Kennedy's assigning the issue to a Unitarian may have seemed an odd choice; but I was able to increase his understanding of at least the more reasoned opposition to him on religious grounds, and simultaneously increase the understanding of many of those more reasoned opponents that he was a different kind of Catholic from those they feared.

My role in the religious issue began in late 1955 with

a news item, buried deep in a news story on the Democratic Party, listing JFK as a possible running mate for Adlai Stevenson in the event that Adlai was renominated for president in 1956. Following the publication of that story, two journalists—Theodore H. White of *Collier's* and Fletcher Knebel of *Look*—in separate, unrelated visits to Kennedy in his Senate office, conveyed the same message—namely that he was on the short list of the Stevenson camp for the vice presidential position, but it was still unclear to the decision makers whether a Catholic running mate would hurt or help the ticket. (I suspected their message may have been a plant by the Stevenson forces to help win Massachusetts.) Kennedy told Knebel he wanted to examine the question. Knebel, sympathetic, contemplated an article, "Can a Catholic Be Elected Vice President?" JFK hypothesized that the Catholic votes attracted to the ticket by a Catholic running mate might offset the handicaps, and asked me whether that hypothesis could be documented.

My response was to research and analyze the possible electoral benefits of a Catholic running mate for a Democratic presidential nominee, focusing on the number and importance of Catholic voters in each of the then forty-eight states. To the best of my recollection, this particular focus represented my own initiative.

By the spring of 1956, I had produced a seventeen-page memorandum, with several tables of data and a dozen pages of analysis, setting forth the size and significance of the Catholic voting population in the fourteen most pivotal states. Previously Democratic, those fourteen states in the North and West had been lost by Stevenson to Eisenhower in 1952, giving Republicans their first presidential victory in twenty-four years. Citing polls, election returns, and political science analyses, I pointed out that, without the traditional Irish-American, Italian-American, and other Democratic Catholic voters in those states, the Democrats would have lost the presidential elections of 1940, 1944, and 1948; that Stevenson (a divorced intellectual liberal) had run significantly behind Catholic Democratic candidates for the Senate and the House in those states in 1952; that Catholics had shifted in large numbers from the Democratic column to vote for Eisenhower (against Stevenson) in 1952; and that, if those traditionally Democratic voters could be recaptured by means of a Catholic running mate for Stevenson, those states, combined with the then solidly Democratic South, could provide Stevenson with a majority of electoral votes. For good measure, I threw in a new analysis of the Al Smith defeat in 1928, demonstrating that it was a Republican year regardless of whom the Democrats nominated, a year for "drys" favoring Prohibition, and that, of the states that Smith lost, only four in the South had been previously solidly Democratic.

In a "Special Appendix," no doubt added with Kennedy's potential competitors for the vice presidential nomination in mind, I demonstrated that recapturing the Catholic vote was more important to the Democratic ticket in 1956 than either the Southern/border vote or the farm vote. Another appendix listed additional states, beyond the fourteen, with sizable proportions of Catholic voters, stating that I had excluded them from my analysis either because they were not among the key swing states, or because their Republicanism was too strong to claim them among the possible states that a Catholic vice presidential nominee could bring back to the party. Including them, I wrote, would be dismissed as speculative—as if the entire memorandum were not speculative in assuming that there was such a thing as a Catholic vote.

Although JFK was not a declared candidate for vice president, he felt that such a memorandum on the Catholic vote coming from his Senate office would be disregarded as self-serving. To protect his plausible deniability, we arranged for it to be circulated by Connecticut state chairman John Bailey, the only politician of national stature then clearly in the Kennedy camp. Bailey was himself a Catholic. There was no Protestant politician of equal stature supporting Kennedy for vice president at that time, or we might have asked if we could attribute the memorandum to him. The group to which the memorandum was distributed included fifty or more prominent Democrats who I calculated might have a voice in selecting Stevenson's running mate and other actual or potential delegates and party leaders.

The memorandum, by cross-analyzing election returns and national opinion surveys broken down by religion, Catholic population figures, and polling data proved to be sufficiently persuasive to gain the attention and favorable reaction of hundreds of delegates to the 1956 convention, helping to make possible the senator's surprising showing in the race for the vice presidency that launched his long quest for the presidency.

I was excited to get a call one day from Stevenson campaign manager Jim Finnegan, who introduced himself on the telephone as though we were old friends and asked me to "send over a dozen copies of that survey." Playing dumb, I asked, "What survey?" He replied: "You know, about the Catholic vote." I sent it to him.

That memorandum ironically took the exact opposite position that JFK would take as a presidential candidate four years later, when he argued that there was no such thing as a "Catholic vote," and that no one should vote for him or against him on the basis of his religion.

In 1960, even though Kennedy tried to downplay

the religious issue, the press publicized it, and analyzed presidential primary returns from the first primary, in Wisconsin, almost solely on the basis of the religious faith of the voters pro and con. His religion was clearly hurting him with many voters, despite a claim by Arthur Schlesinger that, if JFK had been just another wealthy Protestant senator who went to Harvard, no one would have paid any attention to him, and that his Catholicism, by making him more controversial, brought his candidacy added interest and attention. Arthur should have read our hate mail to get a better feel for some of that attention. Others claimed that Kennedy's candidacy created the issue, that by even replying to bigoted attacks he was running on the religious issue in the West Virginia primary, and that by answering questions he was fanning the controversy. He was urged to accept the vice presidential nomination to avoid a dangerous controversy, to which he replied, "Oh I see, Catholics to the back of the bus."

I made several trips to West Virginia to talk to both political and religious liberals on this subject, and to answer questions and charges about Kennedy's religion. Earlier, JFK had dispatched me to visit his friend Bishop John Wright in Pittsburgh to discuss how Kennedy's evolving position on church-state issues could be squared with his Catholicism.

I was also involved in several frontal attacks on the problem, the first occurring when the senator, during the West Virginia primary, asked me to explore with the Senate chaplain, the Reverend Mr. Harris, whether he would be willing to issue a public statement deploring religious bigotry and prejudice in presidential politics. The chaplain had earlier assured JFK that he would be happy to speak out on that issue at the appropriate time. No doubt remembering that he also worked for presidential hopefuls Vice President Nixon and Majority Leader Johnson, to say nothing of Senators Humphrey and Symington, the reverend declined my request. I then took it upon myself to obtain such a statement from other nationally known Protestant leaders, and succeeded far beyond my hopes. I made it clear that I was not asking them to endorse JFK in West Virginia or in the national convention or election, much less to say that those who opposed him were bigots. My goal was a joint statement that religion should not be an issue, that candidates should be voted up or down on their merits. I also made clear that Kennedy would not disappoint them on church-state separation issues.

I began by soliciting Woodrow Wilson's grandson and look-alike, the Very Reverend Francis B. Sayre Jr., dean of the Washington Cathedral, and next, my boyhood friend's father, the Reverend Arthur L. Miller, moderator of the United Presbyterian Church in the United States. I also arranged a confidential meeting in the Oyster Bar of New York's Grand Central Station with Bishop G. Bromley Oxnam, who was not only bishop of the Methodist Church in Washington but a leader of the Protestants and Other Americans United for the Separation of Church and State, one of the principal groups hostile to the Catholic Church hierarchy and its views on public policy. My initial successes with those three led me to Dr. Eugene Carson Blake, the stated clerk of the United Presbyterian Church in the United States, and the Reverend Edwin P. Dahlberg, minister of Delmar Baptist Church, in St. Louis, Missouri, and president of the National Council of Churches of Christ. With that base and assistance, additional signatures were gathered.

The group letter, highly publicized and circulated in West Virginia and throughout the country, was addressed to their "fellow pastors in Christ." It did not mention any candidate by name, but noted that one presidential candidate had been "attacked (and by some, supported) merely because he is a Roman Catholic. We find this profoundly disturbing. . . . To classify any candidate in this way threatens the mutual forbearance and the hard-won tolerance upon which rests our democratic government and the broad unity of our people."

As I recall, I had little or no hand in wording that letter. I could not have drafted one with the credibility that these good churchmen lent to it. The letter was published on May 3, 1960, shortly before West Virginians voted.

Through my work with these church leaders, I also gained the friendship and assistance of a wise and wonderful man, James Wine, an expert on interfaith matters who had worked for the National Council of Churches. After the convention Wine was hired by campaign manager RFK to head an office in the Kennedy campaign handling this subject. I was happy to leave the issue in his hands. Prior to Wine's arrival, I occasionally sought or received advice from my friend and fellow Kennedy Senate office staff member Ralph Dungan, a devout Catholic, who often thought I was unnecessarily positioning JFK in opposition to the traditional church view on matters of public policy. But JFK wanted to be strong in dissociating himself from centuries of Vatican doctrine inconsistent with the Jefferson-Madison principle of separating church and state.

When the senator was invited to speak to the American Society of Newspaper Editors on April 21, 1960, I had a hand in the speech. It was his first full-length, comprehensive treatment of the issue:

I want no votes solely on account of my religion. Any voter, Catholic or otherwise, who feels another candidate would be a superior President, should support that candidate. . . . There is only one legitimate question [to me]: Would you, as President, of the United States, be responsive in any way to ecclesiastical pressures or obligations that might . . . influence or interfere with your conduct of that office? I answer that "no."

The April speech received far less attention and acclaim than his address in a far more dramatic session to the Houston Ministerial Association as the Democratic nominee in September. The Houston speech was JFK at his best, forcefully, frankly stating:

what kind of America I believe in . . . where the separation of church and state is absolute, where no Catholic prelate would tell the President—should he be a Catholic—how to act, and no Protestant minister would tell his parishioners for whom to vote; where no church or church school is granted any public funds or political preference; and where no man is denied public office merely because his religion differs from the President who might appoint him or from the people who might elect him.

As I worked on that draft, Mike Feldman called me late at night, with an answer to my question about whether any Catholics had died at the Alamo. There was no way of confirming whether the list of fallen fighters with Irish and Hispanic-sounding last names were actually Catholics, Mike told me, because there was no religious test. "That's it!" I said to him. "That's the line I want!" It appeared in the speech: "At the Alamo, side by side with Bowie and Crockett died Fuentes and McCafferty and Bailey, Badillo and Carey—but no one knows whether they were Catholic or not. For there was no religious test there."

I thought the religious issue had been buried twice, first by Kennedy's victory in Protestant West Virginia, and again by Kennedy's forthright answer to all such questions in his appearance before the Houston ministers. I was wrong. The issue persisted.

Leading Protestant clergymen opposed to Kennedy held a "Conference of Citizens for Religious Freedom" in September 1960. The tone at their daylong meeting was set by the group's spokesman, the Reverend Norman Vincent Peale, who said, "the election of a Catholic President would change America." "I would like to think he was complimenting me," said Kennedy, "but I'm not sure he was." Adlai Stevenson, campaigning for JFK across the country, had the best comment: "I have always found the gospel of Paul appealing, but I find the gospel of Peale appalling."

Despite all the furor, Kennedy was right to give the American people credit for enough brains and fairness not to be dominated by the bigots in their midst. He confirmed their confidence by conducting an administration free of any bias toward the Catholic Church or any other religion. He recommended no aid for religious schools, channeled no funds to faith-based programs, created no breaches in the wall between church and state, sent no ambassador to the Vatican, and was not unduly influenced by any clergyman from Catholic or other denominations. The country moved on.

Was Kennedy a "good Catholic"? Senator Eugene McCarthy of Minnesota, in 1960, eight years before he considered seeking the Democratic presidential nomination against Lyndon Johnson, reportedly quipped that he should be the nominee in 1960 because he was "taller, older, more liberal and more Catholic than Kennedy." Maybe. Personally, I had no reason to question the sincerity of Kennedy's religious observances, including his attendance at Mass every Sunday, even when I occasionally wondered whether there might have been an element of political necessity as well as personal piety motivating him. As to the balance between the two, no one but JFK could know, and he never said.

He often discussed his private thoughts with me, but he never mentioned any explicit hope or fear of an afterlife, or his innermost thoughts on man's relation to God. He routinely salted his speeches with references to God, as my father had done; but this was, I believe, for both of them more a matter of political convention than religiosity. In his inaugural address, he limited his references to God to three, one in a customary opening, one regarding the true source of human rights, and one to close. Noting these and other religious references, Arthur Schlesinger asked my brother Tom: "If you Sorensens are Unitarians, what are all these quotations from the Bible doing in the speech drafts?" It is true that biblical quotations appeared throughout many of his speeches and my drafts. He and I may each have interpreted them in different ways, in our own minds giving a different power to those passages, while also satisfying his diverse audiences who also differed in their interpretation of Scripture and their individual concepts of the divine.

During the Kennedy presidency, I met secretly more than once at JFK's direction with Catholic bishop Philip Hannan at the Washington Chancery. In one meeting we discussed a proposed amendment to pending legislation providing aid to both public and parochial schools. The issue was only a distant cloud on the horizon, but the president wanted no storm on this subject. Neither the bishop nor I offered instruction to him or to each other. In a confidential memorandum to the president of April 12, 1961, I reported that, given the sensitivity of the issue, "there was to be no mention or indication that the Administration had played any role or taken any position on this amendment or strategy." At day's end, I added an oral footnote—that the bishop and I had gotten along splendidly, and that I first heard from him the joke about the new pope's supposed prediction about the possibility of married priests: "In my lifetime no, but in my children's?"

In the spring of 1962, at the president's request, I visited Justice William O. Douglas to seek a "heads up" from him on whether a heated revival of the 1960 religious issue was about to burst on us. Any White House visit to the United States Supreme Court is understandably sensitive, and mine was doubly so—first, because the Warren Court was already controversial for its courageous and wise opinions on racial desegregation and criminal justice; and second, because the subject under discussion, the public school prayer case, involved religion, always touchy, and particularly so for the country's first Catholic president. But JFK wanted to be supportive of the Court and to continue his cautious course on religious issues without inflaming the religious conservatives who had so bitterly opposed his election. He also wanted my private visit to remain private—so much so that years later, at RFK's request, I deleted from my book *Kennedy* a brief reference to the visit.

When JFK was asked, at a June 27, 1962, presidential news conference, about the potentially adverse effects of the Supreme Court decision on prescribed public school prayers, his superb reply was disarmingly simple compared to the complex evasions adopted by so many politicians on controversial issues. It was not an answer that I had scripted or suggested in advance, though it perfectly expressed my views. He said simply, "We have in this case a very easy remedy . . . We can pray a good deal more at home."

Church-state separation does not mean—nor did JFK and I favor—totally excluding or disregarding the moral issues involved in public controversies. Our country is not so rich in intellectual and inspirational leadership, or so certain of its course in the world, that it can afford the suppression or repression of any thoughtful view or voice, and that includes the views and voices of our clergy. As I write this today, the chief violator of church-state separation is not the Catholic Church, despite the hierarchy's increasing efforts to reverse judicial and legislative permission for abortion and to prevent stem cell research; it is Protestant conservatives and their president. In 1960, their predecessors, in their pulpits and vicious pamphlets, warned that the election of Kennedy raised three threats to the American way: the threat that the beliefs of one religious faith would be favored or imposed over others; the threat that a public official's personal religious convictions might take priority in his public policy decisions over his constitutional obligations; and the threat that religious leaders would politically instruct their congregants on how to vote or decide, including those congregants who held public office. Today's religious and political conservatives, ironically in their zeal to tear down the wall between church and state which has served both church and state so well for so long in this country, are themselves fulfilling all three of the prophecies of doom that their forebears had falsely inveighed against John Kennedy.

Chapter 15

Senator Kennedy's Quest
for the Presidency

Of my eleven years with John Kennedy, the largest block of time—from the end of the 1956 national Democratic convention until Election Day 1960—was spent helping him become president. In retrospect, it's almost hard to believe he was actually elected. When he started his quest, most experts considered his chances somewhere between poor and pitiful.

To a significant extent, the prospects were poor for any Democrat; but his prospects, of all the Democrats, seemed especially bad. No Catholic had ever been elected president. No one that young had ever been elected president. No sitting member of Congress had been elected president since 1920. Every poll that year—of House members, Senators, state chairmen, and the nation's newspaper editors (most of whom were pro-Republican)—predicted that someone other than Kennedy would be elected president. The leaders of his party opposed him. Senate leader Lyndon Johnson and liberal Democratic leader Hubert Humphrey, along with previous Democratic nominee Adlai Stevenson, were likely to be candidates themselves; House speaker Sam Rayburn, former President Harry Truman, and conservative Democratic leader Richard Russell all opposed his nomination, disliking Kennedy's religion or his brother or his father or his family's wealth. The national committee chairman was for Stevenson; the majority leader in the House, John McCormack, was a suspicious rival in Massachusetts politics. Large parts of the Democratic coalition were against Kennedy: Farmers and labor were for Humphrey, as were urban areas and minorities; the South was for Johnson; Jewish voters were for Stevenson, as were the liberals and intellectuals. Senate Democrats generally dismissed JFK as an independent-minded newcomer who was not a member of the party establishment. His only political base for national office was tiny New England, where Catholic city leaders opposed his running for fear of inflaming the religious issue. Even his best friends advised him, "It's too soon."

The opposition of Eleanor Roosevelt, one of the most respected and influential people in the party and country, particularly hurt his prospects. "Mrs. R," as she was called, distrusted Kennedy's father, whom she considered a conservative isolationist, in part because of his breach with FDR twenty years earlier; she thought he was trying to buy the White House for his son in order to gain influence for himself. Nor did Mrs. R think JFK was sufficiently liberal or as intellectual as her favorite, Stevenson, pointing to Kennedy's absenteeism on McCarthy. She used her widely syndicated newspaper column to deplore the Kennedy candidacy.

For years, JFK had approached her cautiously, usually through emissaries, as if she were a proud and fierce lioness, knowing that one resounding slap of her great paw could end not only his hopes to win her over but his presidential prospects for all time. He hoped, even if he could not win her support, at least to neutralize her strong opposition. In the end, Mrs. R grudgingly supported him only after Stevenson withdrew. Even after JFK was elected and invited her to his inauguration, she chose to sit in the audience with other politicians rather than on the platform.

In the midst of all this opposition, the political pundits in Washington, who talked mostly to one another, to the professional campaign consultants, to party leaders and large donors, were convinced that JFK had no chance. But the real campaign for the nomination, JFK and I knew, was not being decided in Washington. It was at the grass roots, where JFK had been traveling, speaking, working, and winning supporters for years among prospective delegates. His electability would be settled not by the experts, but by the electorate.

Why did he run for president? In conversations with me, he scoffed at the speculative magazine articles he characterized as psychological gobbledygook, suggesting that he was running because of his older brother's death or his father's ambition. Instead, he ran because he was frustrated by his limited ability, as one of one hundred senators, to accomplish real change. The presidency, he felt, was the one position where he could contribute the most to our country.

When I met him in 1953, he expressed to me no interest in the presidency, although my Senate secretary, Gloria Sitrin, would later recall: "I think Ted Sorensen expected big things [of the senator, when he] said to me 'Stick with me and we'll go places.'" When JFK and I first discussed the possibility—roughly a year into his first Senate term—he was more pessimistic and skeptical than I. Later, when he gave it more serious consideration, he was convinced that his youth and inexperience would be his single greatest obstacle. I predicted (correctly, as it turned out) that religion would be a larger obstacle, and that his youth could be converted into an asset. I felt people would respond to the kind of fresh leadership his young approach offered. Repeatedly, in the years that followed, his young countenance caused some of his opponents, both at home and abroad, to underestimate his toughness, experience, and wisdom.

It was not until late in the spring of 1959 that he surprised me in his hotel room in Indiana, as we prepared to go down to still another political dinner, by saying: "I've decided to go for it, I now think we can make it." "What are you talking about?" I answered. "I always thought we could make it, I thought that's what we've been doing out here all these years. I thought you had made that decision long ago."

The quest for the presidency actually began back in the winter of 1955–1956 when JFK learned that he was a possible prospect to be the vice presidential running mate of the likely nominee, Adlai Stevenson, in the 1956 presidential election. The senator did not really want to be vice president, he told me. It was a dull job in those days, uninvolved in policy formulation and decision making. Nor did he want to be running mate on a losing ticket. But, he added, "This year, it's the only game in town." Nor, as I reflect on it, would he have made a particularly good vice president at a time when loyalty and silence were the job's principal qualifications. Kennedy knew how to be loyal, but he was ambitious, restless, energetic, and full of ideas that he had no reluctance to voice.

Some writers have credited me with persuading JFK to seek the vice presidential nomination over the senator's own ambivalence and his father's strong opposition. There is some truth to this. As I told JFK, I believed that the nomination, to say nothing of the vice presidency itself, could be a first step to overcome the religious obstacle to his becoming president. Once he came into actual consideration for the vice presidential nomination, I conducted or coordinated virtually all the related activity, including writing and circulating the "Bailey Memorandum," although such activities were relatively few and he remained free to disown them.

In the spring of 1956 I wrote my father: "Our only planned vacation as a family this year consists of two weeks at a Virginia State Park, with a cabin on a lake around the first of September. This might hopefully be changed if the Senator is nominated at Chicago . . . At this point, I am counting on neither the nomination nor the vacation, but have planned for the latter and am working for the former."

Around the same time, as his special envoy to liberals, hoping to reduce their opposition to JFK's nomination, I flew to Cape Cod for my first visit with Arthur Schlesinger Jr., a close Stevenson advisor, at his vacation home at Wellfleet. When our meeting ended, he kindly offered to drive me back to the airport, but ran out of gas en route—which I never let him forget. We got along well that day, as we did in the more than fifty years during which we collaborated until his death at age ninety in 2007.

When Massachusetts Democratic State Committee chairman William "Onions" Burke declared that Massachusetts would not support Stevenson at the 1956 convention, JFK regarded the statement as a challenge to his leadership of the state party and a threat to his chances of being Stevenson's running mate. He enlisted me and all his closest allies in Massachusetts politics in an effort to unseat Burke, lavishing attention on each member of the state committee, a body that he had previously ignored; I was designated unofficial liaison with the committee's more liberal members, though I had no standing or experience in Massachusetts politics.

As I had hoped, the 1956 Democratic convention in Chicago turned out to be a national showcase for the young Massachusetts senator, who a year earlier had been little known across the country. He was chosen to narrate a film about the Democratic Party when Ed Muskie of Maine, the original choice as a rising star, turned that assignment down. JFK was also chosen by the Stevenson camp to place Adlai's name in nomination for the presidency, which he did with a stirring speech.

Though I never drank coffee I was hyped-up on caffeine and sugar during my stay; too busy for meals, I found myself relying more and more on the free Coca-Colas dispensed in Convention Hall.

Stevenson surprised the convention by throwing the vice presidential nomination open to selection by the floor for his own reasons—partly indecision on making a choice among the candidates pressing him for second place on the ticket and perhaps partly because he thought it an exciting, democratic move that would win favor in the convention and the country. The senator jokingly said to me: "What do we do next? This is your baby." "Oh no," I replied. "It's only my baby if you lose. If you win, you will be known as the greatest political strategist in convention history."

Once the vice presidential balloting began, watching the televised proceedings with JFK in his room at the Stockyards Inn behind Convention Hall, we could see that the unprecedented contest might soon come down to Kennedy versus Estes Kefauver, with Humphrey following Senator Albert Gore Sr. and others in dropping out. Kennedy then dispatched me to ask Humphrey—or his campaign manager and fellow Minnesota senator, Eugene McCarthy—for support. I had not the slightest notion of how to find Humphrey, but by chance encountered McCarthy on a stairway and put the question to him. He replied that the Humphrey campaign had nothing for Kennedy, "only Protestants and farmers," later telling the press with disdain that Kennedy had "sent some kid" to see him. In the end, Kefauver captured the vice presidential nomination, with a generous concession speech from Kennedy. But most important, that convention was a success for JFK. He had almost accidentally tested whether he could build a national following; and the answer was a clear yes.

When the senator returned from his postconvention vacation in Europe to his home not far from mine in McLean, Virginia, I took over a briefcase filled with speaking invitations that had poured in from all over the country. I placed on his dining room table those I thought were of serious interest, arranging them by geography and date, trying to form a rough speaking schedule for the next several months, arranging them also in terms of priority and category—including political gatherings, universities, and civic organizations. After a long night working out a tentative schedule, he casually uttered seven fateful words: "You may as well come with me."

Soon we were traveling across the country, while he pursued what every expert considered to be his impossible dream. For the next four years, we traveled together to all fifty states, most of them more than once, initially just the two of us. For Christmas that year, 1956, I gave him a blank map of the United States, with each state shaded or colored by (my) hand according to a code indicating what percentage of that state's 1956 convention delegation had supported him for vice president. He pored over that little map often in the next few years, and it became a guide to our early strategy and travel priorities in his quest for the presidency. Before he became an official candidate for the 1960 presidential nomination, audiences were more open. People look at a speaker differently when they know he is asking for their votes, not merely conveying his views. Broadcasters, campaign regulators, and competing candidates also look at a politician differently once he has formally announced. After his sweeping reelection to the Senate in 1958, it became obvious to his hosts at every stop that he had his eye on the 1960 nomination, making it still easier to generate new speaking invitations. The smaller states were flattered by his attention; the larger states were pleased to have him speak at their annual fund-raising dinners. But still, he made no announcement until he was fully ready to go in January 1960.

The constant travels and collaboration deepened our personal relationship. We found in those long plane rides that we enjoyed each other's company, joking, talking politics, and planning his future. We became not only employer and employee, mentor and student, but friends. I stopped addressing him as "Senator," instead calling him "Jack," about two years before I started calling him "Mr. President." We came to know each other's strengths, weaknesses, hopes, and dreams. In time I was able to read his face, his thoughts, his moods. I came to know his questions almost before he asked them. I could finish his sentences. I knew his position and vote on virtually every issue in the Senate, and what he had said in public speeches and private comments on every topic. When I was asked the senator's position on almost any subject and could not answer, it usually meant he had not yet made up his mind.

We must have seemed an unlikely pair as we traveled across the country, spending long flights with our faces buried in newspapers, memos, and books; he occasionally taking a drink or in his hotel a cigar, I doing neither. His pregnant wife, Jackie, was not able to accompany us on most trips; but, when she did, she was an enormous attraction on the platform. When he invited his sister Eunice to join us on one trip, she felt less honored upon discovering that she was expected to help carry the luggage for two men with bad backs. My wife, Camilla, made one trip with us, Dave Powers helped on some trips; and near the end of the first three years, JFK's brother-in-law Steve Smith, then playing an active role in campaign organization and management, traveled with us as well. But, until JFK became the official party nominee in the summer of 1960, there was no traveling staff, no entourage of any significant size, just the two of us.

Before we got off the plane at each stop, I briefed the senator on who would welcome us. In addition to writing speeches, I did a lot of listening—listening to local politicians, to reporters on the bus, to voters at the edge of crowds, conveying to them his empathy, conveying to him their opinions. When we got back into the plane, I offered him an evaluation of the speech and the crowd reaction. "You were in much better form tonight than last night" was an acceptable way of telling him that his previous night's delivery was poor, repetitive, or disorganized. When we said good-bye to almost every Irish-American mayor, party leader, or legislator we met around the country, JFK would turn to me and say—depending on whether our host had been warmhearted or cold, compassionate or conservative—"Now, that's our type Irish."

To reach small towns not served by major airlines,

private planes were an unavoidable part of political campaigning. Most politicians can tell stories of scary plane travels. Prior to my journeys with JFK, at least two sitting senators had been killed in small plane crashes. When I was chartering a plane for one of his trips, I urged the pilot to pay no attention to my boss's pressuring him to fly at any time he thought the weather made it inadvisable. "Listen," he acidly replied, "there is only one life on this plane that's important to me!" I felt reassured. When a small single-engine plane, taking us from Idaho to Nevada, turned upside down as we approached the landing strip in Reno, JFK and I exchanged glances that silently asked: "Is this the end?" We did not criticize the pilot, especially since he was a county chairman in Idaho, who later explained that in his fatigue he forgot to come in for a landing against the wind instead of with it.

On another small plane flight from Massachusetts to Maine, during which I was instructed to hold tight the loosely latched back door, the pilot acknowledged that he had never landed on this particular airstrip before, and asked JFK, sitting in the copilot's seat, to peer out his window on the right looking for any sign of it while the pilot looked out to the left. In Alaska, we landed on a bay (in a seaplane, thankfully!), in Iowa in a cornfield.

Until his father gave him a private plane, named *The*

Caroline after the senator's baby daughter, I sometimes made these travel arrangements, including hotel reservations, occasionally ordering breakfast. Once, in an emergency, I even drove a car in a short motorcade from his hotel to the local TV station, a disconcerting job, with other cars cutting in and out and pedestrians venturing too near. We were just two guys traveling across the country together, and travel details were part of my chores, which I did not find demeaning. Occasionally we shared a two-room hotel suite, neither of us wanting to share a bedroom. That occurred once unavoidably when a university president hospitably offered us the twin beds in his guest room. JFK accepted, not wanting to appear ungrateful. It turned out that he was a noisy sleeper who kept me awake.

While he was building nationwide recognition for his ideas, vigor, and leadership abilities, I was building card files listing potential supporters. It was more than a list of names and addresses. I attempted to add to the files notes on which people were most influential in each state, their attitudes toward JFK, and the issues that mattered most to them. I also made certain that they received Christmas cards, personal notes, some even phone calls, from JFK, gradually building a "Christmas card list" of thirty thousand influential Democrats across the country, reported by the *New York Times* to be the most extensive political index "in the hands of any Democrat." It was estimated that by October 1959, JFK and I had met more than half of all the potential delegates to the 1960 convention.

State by state, our quest continued. I remember the key players, from the Northeast, Congressman Frank Coffin in Maine and Mayor Bernie Boutin in New Hampshire; to the Northwest, Ancil Payne in Washington and Congresswoman Edith Green in Oregon; to the Deep South, Governor Fritz Hollings in South Carolina, Bob Troutman in Georgia, Congressman Frank Smith in Mississippi, and Ed Reid in Alabama. Referencing Graham Greene's then-current novel, *Our Man in Havana*, we gave the nickname "Havana" to our first and principal supporter in West Virginia, a businessman named Bob McDonough. Other early supporters, from the little-known George McGovern in South Dakota to Congressman Stuart Udall in Arizona, to the devoted Teno Roncalio in Wyoming, I remember them all—those blocks on whom the campaign was built—Millie Jeffrey in Michigan, Jack Beaty in New Mexico, John Lord in North Dakota, Woody Bean in Texas. In Louisiana, Edmund Reggie, decades later well known as the father of Ted Kennedy's wonderful wife, Victoria. In my home state of Nebraska, Jim Green; JFK's PT boat mate Cecil

Sanders in Kentucky, my sister's friend John Bystrom in Minnesota, Joe Smith in Arkansas, Governor Pat Lucey in Wisconsin. These names and more were the beginnings of a national campaign, tireless men and women who were largely unknown, unrecognized, unreported, and after it was all over, largely unrewarded. They helped change America. The fact that I still remember their names fifty years later is an indication of their importance to our effort.

Those early trips were a way to test the presidential waters for 1960, to make friends and contacts while ascertaining whether a young, inexperienced Catholic senator would have any serious chance as a presidential candidate. We discovered that there was no true national party, only a coalition of forty-eight (later fifty) state parties. JFK set out to win them over, state by state, building grassroots support, starting in smaller states, and encircling the big cities until we were ready to tackle them. One historian friend compared our strategy both to Mao's encircling the cities of China until they fell, and to an English prime minister's "rotten borough" strategy of building early support in those depopulated areas that had overly long retained their original right of representation in Parliament. There was some similarity. Many of our forays were to remote states of the

West and Midwest where his candidacy could make solid gains without alerting the national party and press barons to mount a "stop Kennedy" movement.

He became better known, but it took time. On some of those early trips I heard him introduced variously as Senator John B. Kennedy, Senator Joseph Kennedy, Senator Wagner, Senator John Fitzgerald, and the junior senator from Wisconsin. Everywhere we went, local citizens filled our arms and suitcases with local products, including in that first year alone two bushel baskets full of Louisiana yams, two boxes of Mex-Tex candy, four pieces of Arizona Indian pottery, outsized keys to a dozen cities, a large framed scroll making him a Marshal West of the Pecos, and a sombrero clearly large enough to camp under had our plane ever been forced down in the Texas desert. One day, before we had professional help in scheduling, we had a breakfast meeting in Dallas, followed by a dinner meeting in Philadelphia, and later traveled from Washington, D.C., to Richmond, Virginia, by way of New Orleans. Our tour of New England, we joked, consisted of Vermont, New Hampshire, Connecticut, and Nevada.

In New York, I was treated to a barbershop shave and haircut—my first such combined luxury—by a local supporter. I was sunburned in Alaska—having fallen asleep under a sunlamp. In Tucson, where we were to spend a weekend, the harried local Democratic chairman found himself a Protestant in the middle of competing pressures from the two leading Catholic churches in town, each of whom wanted JFK to attend its Sunday Mass. He compared himself to the legendary courtesan who, upon exiting the English king's palace in the royal coach and finding herself pelted with stones by townspeople assuming she was the king's despised daughter, cried out: "Stop it, you fools—I am not the popish princess, I am the Protestant whore."

The most influential Democrat in one state was a woman older than both JFK and I, who, JFK claimed, looked upon me with some affection. It amused him to claim that I could tie up that delegation if I would "romance" the lady. I was willing to do almost anything for his success, but not that.

A campaigner must "be prepared," Kennedy told an off-the-record press dinner in Boston following his 1956 travels, "to eat chicken patties, chicken Creole, chicken gumbo, chicken a la king, and chicken casserole." As a previously sheltered Nebraskan, I learned to eat all kinds of new foods, including lobster tails in Maine, with instructions from Ed Muskie. But at a Hawaiian luau, I drew the line at eating the eyes of some sea creature. When JFK and I sat down for breakfast with Governor Coleman of Mississippi after a speech to the state's Young

Democrats, friend and practical joker Bobby Troutman telephoned to advise us not to lose the South by putting syrup on grits.

Occasionally during those early travels, I would offer the senator unsolicited political and personal advice. In one highly publicized instance in Lincoln, Nebraska, when our car drew up to the site of his next speech, I jabbed the senator heartily in the ribs and said, according to a local journalist, "Presidential candidates do not chew gum." On rare occasions when his voice gave out, I would give the speech in his place, delivering not only the speech I had helped prepare, but also the jokes. Once, a *Wall Street Journal* reporter, upon checking, discovered that I had been "reading" Kennedy's speech from blank pages.

In a 1957 letter to my father, I reported with excitement that JFK and I, when visiting his sister Pat and her husband, actor Peter Lawford, in California, had gone to a party at film star Gary Cooper's home, where I met some of the most glamorous popular movie stars of the time. One of them, Van Johnson, struck up a long, friendly conversation with me, but I did not recognize him, and at the end of the conversation asked his name. When I reported this to Jack, Peter, and Pat during the car ride back, they advised me, "Actors hate that." I also wrote my father that, for a Hollywood party, I had

worn a tuxedo for the second time in my life, the first
having been an elegant press dinner in Boston the previous fall. I did not tell my father that it was there in
California that JFK persuaded me to try a rum daiquiri
before dinner, at age twenty-eight my first "hard" alcoholic drink. Journalists in Washington once exchanged
stories about both politicians and reporters coming to
meetings in my office at cocktail hour or receptions in
my home and finding to their dismay that no liquor was
served.

Those four years filled me with an indelible sense of
the magnificent diversity of this country, its topogra-
phy, and its people as well as its politics and problems.
Both JFK and I learned volumes about America—the
number of sizable cities in Ohio, the politically and
religiously conservative stretch between Pittsburgh
and Philadelphia, the vastness of Texas, the variety of
Southern accents, ranging from Charlestonese to Louisiana Cajun, the rival political fiefdoms in northern and
southern California. When our initial travels ended,
JFK and I compiled some of our more humorous and
colorful adventures in an unpublished piece, with hi-
larious illustrations by Jackie.

Both the senator and I did our best to keep up with
his Senate office duties as our travels increased. His 1958
reelection campaign for the Senate required my residing

and working in Massachusetts for a few months. To the extent that federal law and congressional rules at that time prohibited staff from participating in partisan political functions without taking official leave, I can only hope the statute of limitations protects me, although I truthfully maintained at the time that advising the senator on policy and assisting him with his speeches still described my job—in all parts of the country.

Occasionally the senator made cash campaign contributions—in amounts too small to require reporting under the law at that time—to friendly candidates for Congress who he thought might support him for president, using me as his courier. He had no way of knowing whether I was following the custom of Massachusetts cash couriers of keeping a small percentage of each contribution for themselves. I never did. But my cash courier role became problematic the night I absentmindedly left a roll of small bills in a telephone booth. He was unhappy about my error, but not suspicious.

Some of the missions on which he sent me were to woo, ascertain the intentions of—or, if necessary, discourage—important state Democratic leaders who were potential supporters or competitors: Governor Meyner of New Jersey, former Governor Bowles of Connecticut, governors Loveless of Iowa, Docking of Kansas, and Edmondson of Oklahoma. I was also sent to woo

the Democratic National Committee members at the
Western States Democratic Conference in Denver in
May 1959. I met on his behalf with one Republican governor, the liberal Mark Hatfield of Oregon, asking him
for changes in the pending Oregon presidential primary
law. On my birthday in May 1960, the senator sent me
to see Governor Williams in Michigan and persuade the
Michigan delegation to support JFK for president.

As we built the foundations of his 1960 campaign,
JFK authorized me to travel occasionally on my own
to relate to local Democratic leaders and journalists
his position on key issues in states including Michigan,
Nevada, Idaho, and Washington. My remarks to local
Democratic leaders at each stop were basically good-
natured advice to get on the bandwagon now while
there's still room. That would be followed by a question
and answer session, in which I often planted in advance
the toughest questions—such as those about religion,
Joe McCarthy, and Eleanor Roosevelt—to make certain
they were covered. Frequently I was asked privately by
one or more local politicians after such sessions: "What's
in it for me? I would make a good United States Attorney
or state campaign organizer." I simply replied that when
Kennedy was elected, he would "need people all over
the country whom he can trust in important positions."
I was even approached by one U.S. senator's wife sug-

gesting that her husband would make a good vice president. I assured her that I thought very highly of him.

By the spring of 1959, our informal trips had begun to grow into a formal campaign. On April 1 JFK convened at his father's Palm Beach residence what I called "The Summit." The meeting included his father; his brother Robert (brother Ted was honeymooning); our new pollster Lou Harris; brother-in-law Steve Smith; Bob Wallace, whom I had recruited the previous month; and Larry O'Brien and Kenny O'Donnell, both Kennedy family political advisors in the past. Sitting in a circle of chairs on the beach, facing the ocean, JFK and I presented state-by-state summaries of where we had been, whom we had contacted, and what we saw as his prospects. I also had prepared notes on the two possible Republican nominees, Richard Nixon and Nelson Rockefeller, analyzing their respective strengths and weaknesses, and presented the following categories of other Democratic presidential possibilities: those from the South and the West, and the "dark horses"; memos on the approaches taken by FDR in 1932 and Truman in 1948; and a plan of organization making RFK the de facto campaign manager, permitting the candidate to concentrate on making speeches, top-level statements, and senior campaign appointments. When the matter of financial requirements was raised, Ambassador Kennedy, the crusty patriarch, said, "We've come this far, we're not going to let money stand in our way, whatever it takes, even if it requires every dime I have." RFK piped up: "Wait a minute now—there are others in the family."

By the time we held a second, similar but larger meeting in Hyannis Port on October 28, 1959, our two-man campaign had become a highly organized army. For that meeting, I prepared a memorandum setting forth Kennedy's potential strength on the first and subsequent convention ballots in each state, and a shorter "fact book" to be used by Kennedy organizers and advocates, with pages on Kennedy's voting record on civil rights, civil liberties, labor, and agriculture, and a discussion of his age, the religious issue, and other major pieces of advocacy or information for potential supporters around the country. Most political strategy meetings, I find, produce little more than an exchange of political gossip, humor, boasts, praise, and denunciation of others. But that October 1959 meeting produced a remarkable number of firm decisions regarding campaign planning.

After he formally announced his candidacy on January 2, 1960, both JFK and I recognized that I lacked the stature, skill, and time to continue doing all that I had tried to do in those exploratory years. "Damn it,

Ted," the senator said, "when a half-dozen important things come up here, I don't want you in New Mexico or someplace." So at his request, I prepared a memorandum dividing my job into five separate positions, suggesting which jobs I might retain—speeches, ideas, messages—and which might go to others, to RFK as the actual campaign manager, and to brother-in-law Steve Smith as the headquarters coordinator and fundraiser. Bobby and Steve largely took over the political strategizing and operations in which I had been involved during the three years of cross-country travel. I became responsible only for drafting JFK's speeches and major statements. I was initially reluctant to give up some of my tasks, but felt better when informed by a historian friend that Louis Howe in 1932 had similarly given up the political management of FDR's campaign and contented himself with his roles as speechwriter and confidant.

During those four years following the 1956 convention, a series of individuals joined and left the informal, makeshift campaign, or rose and fell in the candidate's favor; but the 1960 campaign team had no major shakeup and no warring factions. Through all the ups and downs, the core team remained intact: I was still on the plane, with writing help from a young man I had recently hired, Dick Goodwin; Mike Feldman, whom

I had hired in 1957 as my chief assistant in the Senate, was still coordinating research back in Washington; Pierre Salinger was still on the press bus; Kenny O'Donnell still managed logistics and advance; Larry O'Brien oversaw political contacts, strategy, and organization; and RFK managed the entire campaign.

It's amazing how young we all were. As 1960 began, the candidate was forty-two; his brother, the campaign manager, was thirty-three; I was thirty-one, absurdly young and inexperienced for many of the roles JFK asked me to fill; Dick Goodwin was twenty-nine; Kenny O'Donnell, thirty-six; Salinger, thirty-five. No wonder one opposing campaign manager sarcastically referred to us as "The Children's Crusade," referring to the supposed thirteenth-century attempt to "liberate" the Holy Land by an army of children from Europe. Our youth also prompted the veteran hard-boiled congressman and Democratic boss of the Bronx, Charlie Buckley, to admonish JFK's father: "Why doesn't Jack get rid of all these kids like Sorensen and hire some experienced campaign consultants?" "Hell," replied the Ambassador (as we all called Joseph P. Kennedy), "the only experience they have is losing!" We kids had no national campaign experience but we were a band of believers, completely committed to our candidate.

In the months before the 1960 convention, at RFK's

instruction, I traveled to states that the candidate could not personally cover again. In one of these, Minnesota, I attended the state Democratic-Farmer-Labor Party convention in hopes of finding a few friends and delegates for Kennedy after Minnesota's Hubert Humphrey dropped out. Minnesota Governor Freeman asked me to meet him at his home after the event. I sat shivering on his front steps for some time before he and his gracious wife returned. She prepared hot chocolate, and Orville and I talked late into the night, his willingness to talk no doubt encouraged by the possibility of being Kennedy's vice presidential choice. He would have been a good one, but he made a great secretary of agriculture, a jurisdiction where he was given full discretion by a White House largely ignorant on the issue.

A few days after I arrived in Los Angeles to help Bob Troutman prepare for the opening of the Democratic National Convention in July, I was summoned to JFK's home on Cape Cod to help him respond to a surprise attack. Former President Truman, still a popular national party figure, had unexpectedly denounced him on national television, declaring that Kennedy (because of his youth) "was not ready" and that the country was not ready for him. Truman's opposition stemmed from his dislike of candidate JFK's religion, money, and father.

It seemed a harsh blow, but it provided a great opening, requiring the television network to grant him equal time to address the question of his age, an opportunity immediately before the convention to talk about his experience and his accomplishments in Congress and to cite—from my file—the names of famed historical leaders who had accomplished wonders by the time they were his age, such as Thomas Jefferson, Christopher Columbus, and Alexander the Great (JFK wisely struck Jesus from my list). When I arrived at the Kennedy home in Cape Cod, JFK's guests were Bill Battle, a friend from PT days (and future governor of Virginia), and Bill's wife. In the absence of any campaign staffers, who were all either in Washington or in Los Angeles, Mrs. Battle was recruited to help. Sitting on the porch, she took JFK's and my barely legible handwritten notes and typed up the remarks he would deliver on national television.

During the telecast, as I was standing only yards from where JFK was delivering his televised rebuttal to Truman, a young TV staffer rushed up with the news from the wire services that Jackie was pregnant. When Kennedy finished his remarks and walked backstage, I was there to greet him. "Congratulations," I said, referring to his wife's pregnancy. "I couldn't have done it without you, Ted," he replied, thinking I was referring to his television performance. We both laughed when I explained the misunderstanding. After the speech, I flew back to California. Imagine—when my grandparents got off the boat from Denmark, it took them months to get halfway across the country to Nebraska; and in 1960 I crossed the country three times in five days.

During a reception for Kennedy volunteers at our Los Angeles convention headquarters, I was asked by an eager if uninformed newcomer when I had joined the 1960 campaign. "1953," I replied. But in general my memories of the convention are filled not with receptions, but with work.

Aside from my responsibility for drafting the acceptance speech, my prime responsibility at the convention was keeping in touch with Puerto Rico, whose senior statesman, Luis Muñoz Marin, we wanted to campaign for JFK in New York City in the fall. On the recommendation of two "establishment" pro-Johnson Democrats, Abe Fortas and Paul Porter, who provided legal services to the commonwealth, Marin led a delegation supporting LBJ, the more establishment Democratic candidate, whom they had predicted would be the nominee. But JFK and I had formed an alliance years earlier at the grassroots level with the populist Jose Benitez, who chaired the "state" Democratic committee of Puerto Rico. Each rival delegation fought for formal approval from the Credentials Committee, which Kennedy-pledged delegates controlled. I mediated a solution in which all members of both delegations were each given a seat on the floor and one-half vote committed to Kennedy. An excellent compromise.

In 1960 the bargaining and maneuvering continued until the last vote was cast. As it turned out, we almost needed Puerto Rico. The roll call was alphabetical. Wyoming was the last state called, and gave Kennedy the necessary majority on the first ballot. The previous day, when two-time Democratic presidential nominee Adlai Stevenson discovered to his dismay that he had no delegates, not even from Illinois, willing to place his name in nomination, he remarked to an aide, who later reported the story to me: "What will I tell Eleanor?" It was America's last closely contested convention, at a time when presidential primaries were too few to bind a majority in advance. Today, primaries and caucuses in every state are unbossed democracy in action but, sadly, they have taken much of the fun and excitement out of conventions. Nor am I certain that the modern primary system has always resulted in the selection of the best nominee. In 1960 the "bosses" helped choose the nominee, and they chose well.

. . .

In 1983, at the age of fifty-five, I entered and completed the New York City Marathon, a 26.2-mile course through all five boroughs of the city, requiring nearly four hours of running. It was the single event in my life most comparable to a presidential election campaign: no breaks, no shortcuts, no rest, just keep putting one foot in front of the other. You know that the finish line is set, and you are spurred on both by cheers from the crowd and the knowledge that you can rest (for a month) when it's over. Truly, a presidential campaign is a marathon, twenty-four hours a day, seven days a week, month after month after month, year after year.

At the end of long days, the weary candidate and other staff members went to bed. But I went to work on the speeches for the next day and the next week, usually joined by Goodwin, summoning one or two secretaries from their rooms in the middle of the night to take dictation. Sleep deprivation was constant. Occasionally I managed to find during the day an empty motorcade car in which I could curl up in the backseat while the speeches were being delivered. One morning I was so groggy I packed and sent off to the campaign plane all my clothes, and had to call frantically for a bellman to retrieve my bag from the truck. On another, my suitcase had already been picked up for early loading on the campaign plane, when I found myself facing a strategy meeting without a necktie. JFK's friend and personal aide Dave Powers loaned me one from the senator's large traveling collection, assuring me that the senator never wore it. When I walked into the meeting thirty minutes later, his first words were:. "Is that my tie you're wearing?"

The whole experience was unlike any physical ordeal I had ever faced. The exhilaration did not always offset the exhaustion. Too many all-nighters working, too many overnight flights, and too many early morning meetings meant too little time for relaxed conversation and easy camaraderie. One critic commented, after the campaign was over, that I was "too intent on marshalling arguments and figures, and not ready enough to relax with the local leaders in the nearest bar." Fair enough.

The years between 1956 and 1961 were not easy on my family life, friendships, or health. When I was working in Washington, I made it a rule to get home each night in time to tuck my three sons into bed, crawl in with them, and tell them a story, making it up as I went along, like those I had told campers when I was a teenager in Nebraska. Often I fell asleep before they did, sometimes in the middle of a story, unconsciously repeating myself until they shook me awake. I tried to reserve weekends for time with the boys—backyard softball, occasional camping trips, Washington Senators or Washington Redskins games. Time for social life was limited, but Camilla and I dropped in on neighborhood parties whenever we could.

Much has been made in recent years of "the fog of war," the inevitable disorganization, confusion, and miscommunications in battle. The same can be said of a presidential campaign. I vividly remember one example. When my father died in late 1959, I flew home for the funeral, only to have a grieving family session interrupted by an angry telephone call from a national committeeman upset that I was not in Washington to answer his questions on campaign resource allocation in his state. When I quietly explained the circumstances, he abruptly hung up, but sent flowers the next day.

Fortunately, during the postconvention campaign, we did not make Nixon's mistake of vowing to speak in every state; and we enjoyed the thought at the campaign's end that he was tied down and freezing in Alaska while we were focusing on the big closely contested states. Even so, those months were grueling. In the only weekend interlude during that period, I was given a motel room in Cape Cod near Hyannis Port so that I could sleep all day, only to be summoned to JFK's home to be briefed, lectured, and hectored by the senator's father and Democratic lawyer Clark Clifford. Neither of them had been out on the campaign trail with us, or knew one-tenth of what the candidate knew about the electorate. As I sat there, struggling to stay awake, listening to the advice and the clichés, I made a silent vow that, if I were ever in a similar senior sidelines position, I would not attempt to provide advice to those on the front line who knew more about the campaign than I. I have tried—not always successfully—to keep that vow.

As hard as it is on the speechwriter and staff, a presidential campaign is even tougher on the candidate. It is impossible for him to remember the names of all the people whose hands he shakes, to remember the time of day, the day of the week, and the town in which he is speaking; to remember his own previously stated positions on issues, much less those of his opponents. But if he sounds temporarily inconsistent, the press calls it a weakness; if he is ambiguous, his opponent calls him a coward. Through it all, he must appear sincere and self-assured, smile through the rain and pain, protect his hand from being crushed and his suit from being torn, freeze in an open car, perspire in a stuffy banquet hall, smile at those who curse him, listen patiently to those who repeatedly advise the obvious, and repeat his own positions until he tires of his own words, restrain his natural candor, be cautious about his humor, and exude enthusiasm about the ordeal he is enduring and every person he meets. All day, the press is outside his door and window, the rooms are full of sweat and smoke, his hand is bruised, scratched, full of calluses—in JFK's case, one callus burst with blood. Everyone you meet wants something from you, your time, your endorsement, your support for some local project or measure; and then you move on to three more stops in three more states before you fall into bed. It is an exercise best suited to fanatics, egomaniacs, and superbly fit athletes.

In the postconvention campaign, JFK always stayed on message, easy because the message was essentially the same in every speech: "I'm not satisfied—We can do better." That basic message was applied to virtually any issue. Those would-be historians who have mistakenly written that Kennedy's campaign outflanked Nixon on the right ignore the fact that JFK was running on a liberal Democratic platform to raise the minimum wage, strengthen Social Security, expand housing for the poor, raise teachers' salaries, establish Medicare, increase federal aid to education, and subsidize mass transportation in large cities—all of which the Republicans opposed. Kennedy wasn't running to Nixon's right; he was simply applying his general theme—"We can do better"—to every issue, and that included the cold war competition, the overriding issue facing the country that had motivated his presidential campaign.

Kennedy believed that every voter was first and foremost an American, moved by appeals to service and the national interest, not appeals to religious prejudice, material selfishness, or regional parochialism. At JFK's instruction, his speeches after the convention all had an elevated tone, as did our campaign theme itself, "A Time for Greatness," an amendment of my earlier suggestion, "A Call to Greatness," which was coined in a meeting with Steve Smith and Mike Feldman. Throughout the campaign, we tested new ideas—Peace Corps volunteers to bring help and hope to economically underdeveloped countries; an Alliance for Progress to build strong and free economic and political institutions in Latin America; a new agency for arms control and disarmament; increased use of American food surpluses as a tool for peace and economic development around the world; a greater effort to help the poorest nations of the world, all of this in the name of strengthening the free world's defense against the spread of Communism. These were not empty promises. Within a year of his inauguration, Kennedy had established the Peace Corps and the Food for Peace program by executive order, and had promulgated legislation for a new Agency for International Development, the Alliance for Progress program, and a new Arms Control and Disarmament Administration inside the State Department.

Backing up Kennedy's gloomy warnings about the prospects for peace and security were a series of international public opinion polls conducted by the United States Information Agency, and published in the *New York Times*, showing American prestige around the world steadily declining during the Eisenhower years. Some suspected leaks by my brother Tom, a USIA employee; but his supervisor had prudently sent him on a distant foreign tour for the duration of the campaign. Others argued that Kennedy was disregarding the secrecy classifications of these documents by giving them to the *New York Times*. In truth, Senator Kennedy had no idea how these documents were reaching the *Times*. I did. The chairman of the Senate Foreign Relations Committee, William Fulbright, to whom the polls were provided by USIA, was giving them to Mike Feldman, who was under no obligation to keep them secret, and passed them along to the *Times*.

Also contributing to JFK's warnings on the prospects for peace were high-level federally appointed commissions—including the 1957 Gaither Commission and the 1958 Rockefeller Commission—that had all concluded, more by analyzing Soviet intentions than actual capacity, that the Soviet Union had or would soon have a dangerous lead over the United States in intercontinental nuclear missiles. This was termed "the missile gap" by columnist Joe Alsop and others. It fit perfectly into JFK's basic theme, and he cited it as the most alarming example of the generally lagging American performance on which his campaign was based. Like Senators Stuart Symington and Lyndon Johnson, he made much of this issue throughout 1960, as did a number of other commentators and congressional studies. Contrary to those who claim that JFK cynically exploited an issue that he knew had no basis in fact, neither of us had any knowledge or reason to believe that the missile gap described by those expert commissions would later prove to be incorrect.

In August 1960, three months before the election, the United States launched a successful reconnaissance satellite, which showed that in fact the Soviets had not produced, much less deployed, as many missiles as those commissions had estimated. Unfortunately, at the time that President Eisenhower provided a national security briefing to Kennedy, then the Democratic nominee, the results of that satellite mission were not yet available, and Eisenhower had no hard evidence to verify his insistence to JFK that there was no such gap. Ike was reportedly furious that Kennedy continued to raise this issue during the fall campaign—though many issues, particularly the stagnant economy, were more important than the missile gap in the election's outcome.

Once Kennedy was in office, new spy satellite photos revealed that the actual Soviet missile arsenal was substantially smaller than these earlier reports had projected, and that any missile gap was in America's favor. Kennedy felt that this had to be disclosed, and chose a low-key speech by the deputy defense secretary as the best way to do that. But he never felt that his overall campaign message—"We can do better"—had been invalid or unjustified.

For the nation's first televised presidential debate in history, JFK—recognizing its potential impact—prepared thoroughly. Sitting with Mike Feldman and me that morning on the roof of his Chicago hotel, he listened closely to every possible issue and question we could raise, based on Mike's comprehensive card file setting forth the position of both candidates and both parties on each one. He responded quickly to those on which he was certain of the facts, and asked for more information on others. There was no rehearsal, no debate coach, no strategy discussions on being aggressive or warm.

Finally he took a break for a nap after lunch. As the hour of his scheduled arrival at the television station neared, I was asked to wake the senator. Quietly entering his bedroom, I found him neither anxious nor discouraged, but sound asleep, covered by cards he had studied before dozing off. After washing up and dressing, he drove us to the studio himself, shaking off bromidic advice on "TV presence" from his television advisor. An estimated seventy million people, reportedly the largest campaign audience in American history up to that time, watched the face-off in that first debate on September 26. Afterward, as we walked off the Chicago television soundstage, he spotted a pay phone on the wall. A millionaire who rarely carried cash, he asked me for some coins, and dialed his father. "Dad, what did you think?" were his first words. A long period of listening ensued, while I stepped a few feet away. "Thanks, Dad, I've got to go to Ohio," he concluded, and hung up the phone. "I still don't know how I did," he said, turning to me. "If just now I had slipped and fallen flat on the floor, my dad would have said: 'The way you picked yourself up was terrific!'"

But Kennedy had not fallen on his face. All the experts had predicted that Vice President Nixon, the experienced, high-level politician who had debated Khrushchev in Moscow in 1959, would overwhelm the young senator from Massachusetts. Kennedy looked calmer, cooler, more confident, more rested, more at ease. Nixon, trying to be statesmanlike, kept agreeing with Kennedy's points. It did not sound statesmanlike; it sounded weak. Kennedy was better prepared than Nixon, more comfortable on television, and more assertive during the debate, persistently linking our social and economic failures at home to our weakness in the cold war competition with the Soviets. I disagree with those Nixon supporters who said their man won that first debate on radio, where the competing visual images could not affect the outcome. (In my own view, if JFK had looked like Nixon, the result of the debate and the election would have been the same.) "Kennedy clobbered him," was the verdict of the Chicago cabdriver who took me back to my hotel.

Claiming that in the first debate, the camera had switched to Kennedy when Nixon was speaking more frequently than it had to Nixon when Kennedy was speaking, the Nixon team demanded a new rule for subsequent debates. Each candidate (they insisted) should have equal time on camera. During the second and third debates, a Nixon aide made the mistake of further insisting on more close-ups of Nixon, which required, according to the rule they had proposed, more close-ups of Kennedy. What a great deal!

Kennedy articulated the issues both more clearly and more confidently. The debate did not switch a lot of Republican voters to Kennedy. But, by firming up the (majority) Democratic vote, and demonstrating to the country that the young senator had the talent and experience necessary to go toe-to-toe with Nixon (and therefore Khrushchev), that first debate made a difference. It was only then that all wings of his party rallied behind him, confirmed the next morning in Ohio, when previously dissenting Democrats joined our motorcade, and his crowds were bigger and more boisterous than ever— including jumpers, mostly young women who leaped from the ground to cheer him as his motorcade passed.

I had little regard for the political tactics and policy positions of Richard Nixon; but I did not hate him. On the contrary, I had enjoyed a friendly exchange with him at a Kennedy cocktail party during Kennedy's first year in the Senate when Nixon was the new vice president. He often would step across the hall from his office to poke his head into room 362 just to say hello.

Having always regarded Richard Nixon as humorless, I nevertheless gave him credit for one joke he did not tell, and will give him here credit for one he did tell.

He was the speaker at an annual Jaycees' banquet in California in 1961 honoring the winners of their "Ten Outstanding Young Men" award. Talking with some of us outside the banquet hall, when an old, gnarled waiter carrying a heavy tray of dishes hobbled up and greeted him personally, Nixon exchanged familiarities with the old man, who limped away. As we stared, Nixon turned to us and said with a deadpan expression: "That was one of last year's Ten Outstanding Young Men!"

It was such a good joke that I gave him credit for another one he had not told, by telling an off-the-record press luncheon in Washington the following week that the former vice president had spoken with me at the California banquet, saying: "Ted, there is one thing JFK said at his inauguration that I wish I had said." To which I had replied, "You mean that part about 'Ask not what your country can do for you'?" "No," he said. "I mean that part about 'I hereby solemnly swear to uphold . . .'" Even though the luncheon was off-the-record, my wholly invented joke appeared as a true story in *Time* magazine the following week. It has since appeared many times, always attributed to Nixon as illustrating his good sense of humor, appearing most recently in a collection of presidential humor by former presidential candidate Bob Dole, a funny man in his own right.

In 1972, when his bungling team was charged with wiretapping Democratic headquarters at Watergate, Nixon proclaimed loudly that everyone did it, including Kennedy in 1960. As a result, I was asked to submit an affidavit in August 1973 to the Senate Select Committee on Improper Presidential Campaign Activities. I testified that I had never heard in 1960 of any wiretapping or electronic surveillance of any Republican or Nixon office or individual, nor had I read or received any confidential information that could have been obtained only through such surveillance, nor did I see any such information in preparation for the televised debates. Decades later, I was told by Henry Kissinger, former Nixon secretary of state and confidant—and briefly a Kennedy national security consultant—that Nixon's plan to bug Democratic headquarters at the Watergate may have stemmed from Nixon's unwarranted suspicion that the Kennedys had somehow bugged his 1960 campaign plane and headquarters.

Was there a continuing Kennedy team effort, especially in the 1960 campaign, to downplay—critics would say "conspiracy to conceal"—the true state of JFK's health? To some extent, yes, and I was part of it. I've often used this analogy: If a man wooing a woman, or vice versa—as JFK was wooing the country in his presidential campaign—had a choice of disclosing that he was "on steroids for Addison's disease" or, equally truthfully, that he had "a mild adrenal insufficiency," a term used by Dr. Travell and JFK's endocrinologist, Dr. Eugene J. Cohen, which of those descriptions would any rational person choose? We chose the latter, and felt no additional disclosure on that subject was necessary.

True, the variety of statements issued by his doctors, his press office, his brother, and me may have obscured the stark truth. Shortly before the 1960 Democratic National Convention, a journalist asked me about reports that JFK was using cortisone or other medications. I replied: "I don't know that he is on anything any more than you and I are on." I may not have literally known what he was taking that year, but perhaps I should have given a more complete answer about what had been prescribed in the past.

At a convention press conference, two of LBJ's top aides questioned Kennedy's life expectancy based on their assertion that he had Addison's disease. In response, the Kennedy for President press office issued a statement from RFK that the candidate "does not now nor has he ever had an ailment described classically as Addison's Disease, which is a tuberculous destruction of the adrenal gland. . . ." Once again, this carefully worded statement was literally true but generally mis-leading.

Several years after leaving the White House, I learned from an Eisenhower political advisor of that much older president's candid reply to the close circle urging him to disregard his heart attack and run for reelection in 1956: "Okay, I'll do it," Ike said. "But, I warn you, one of these days, out on the hustings, I'll be climbing the steps to the airplane, and you and all the press will see me suddenly stop and sit down on those steps—and there goes your damn campaign." Neither Eisenhower's campaign in 1956 (when he was sixty-six) nor Kennedy's campaign in 1960 (when he was forty-three) was interrupted. In my view, each would still have won his campaign even if more medical information had been disclosed.

Political campaign contributions—some ill-motivated—have long played too pervasive a role in American politics, in some states more than others; and it would be foolish for me to claim that they played no role in the Kennedy presidential campaign of 1960. In the primaries, I heard rumors about money demands from West Virginians, and once received a letter from a newspaper executive in that state expressing a hope that Ambassador Kennedy's connections with the banking industry could help him obtain a mortgage. I forwarded the request to the Kennedy office in New York, but have no idea whether it was ever acted upon. From time to time, I also heard reports of improper activities in other campaigns. Two weeks before the 1960 convention, I sent RFK a political intelligence memorandum, noting a call from a friendly Arizona mayor who reported that his delegation's vice chairman "had been called by Johnson people promising anything he wanted, including Convention expenses, in return for his half vote." We did not match that promise.

During those early years following the 1956 convention, journalists and columnists, including Mrs. Roosevelt, began to circulate reports that JFK's father was financing a huge, well-oiled campaign machine to buy the presidency for his son. Mrs. R stated that the Kennedy campaign was being financed by his father spending "oodles of money" on his enormous organization. I can understand her misimpression. JFK seemed to be everywhere: articles by or about him in all the magazines, speaking appearances in every region, a best-selling book; all this had the appearance of a huge, well-oiled political campaign.

In fact, the precampaign was inexpensive—no staff other than me, no advance men, no headquarters, and no paid commercials or consultants. We used all the free television and radio coverage he could get. The senator's father helped; but, even after the convention, Kennedy's campaign expenditures never came close to the huge sums of money that have been spent in virtually every presidential election since. None of this mattered to his opponents, of course, who zeroed in, for different reasons, on the issue of Kennedy's wealth.

One day in his Senate office, poking fun at the image of a vaunted Kennedy machine, JFK kidded Mike Feldman, an attorney and former Philadelphian, who had handmade a chart on the decline of milk prices for use in an amateurish Wisconsin primary television commercial: "Nixon has the resources of the entire Agriculture Department and the Federal Government preparing his material, and all we have is one Philadelphia farmer."

The nastiest, most persistent post-election allegations about JFK's 1960 spending came from Republicans, who alleged Democratic voter fraud in Chicago and Cook County, Illinois. Vice President Nixon did not demand a recount, much less a grand jury investigation, once it became clear to him that (1) Republican fraud in downstate Illinois was at least as large-scale or worse than that alleged about Chicago, (2) a reversal of the vote in Illinois would still leave Kennedy the victor in the electoral college, and (3) a majority in the popular vote did not favor Nixon (depending on how one counted the decision of segregationist "independent electors" in a few Southern states to cast their ballots for Virginia Senator Harry Byrd). The Republican attorney general, William Rogers, was Nixon's best friend in the Eisenhower administration, and his Justice Department said it found no evidence of violation by the Kennedy campaign of federal election laws; no charges were filed. Nixon patriotically (or piously) stated that his decision not to challenge the outcome "recognized a need for national unity and stability"—although he later said that he had looked into the legal aspects of the situation and found no basis on which he could attain a timely victory. Some Republicans also claimed irregularities in Texas, but Kennedy's margin there was too large to reverse, even had a recount been available.

No, JFK did not buy the election by either raising or spending more money than Nixon—nor did he steal the election with voter fraud. He won it, by outworking, outorganizing, outdebating, and outthinking his Republican opponent.

The campaign was a turning point for me, as well as for the country, deepening my professional relationship and friendship with JFK. I am not now so modest that

I have not remembered with great pride some of JFK's generous expressions of confidence in me in those years. He referred to me variously as indispensable, extremely bright, his intellectual blood bank, one of his very key men, who got the work done. He insisted he wanted to keep me with him wherever he went in the campaign, saying you need somebody whom you can trust implicitly. He noted that as his own responsibilities grew, so did mine.

In his 1962 book, *Six Crises*, Nixon reported that he and Kennedy had compared notes after the election on how difficult it was on the campaign trail to use the flood of ideas, research, and speeches that came from scholars and Washington staffs who were not attuned to the day-to-day challenges on the firing line. He quoted Kennedy as saying "in the end, I found myself relying more and more on Sorensen who . . . could react to . . . up to the minute tactical shifts in our basic strategy." Nixon also told an interviewer that JFK had told him that for the last weeks of his campaign, he depended almost solely on Sorensen. No wonder the margin was so close!

Election night was long and tense at the Kennedy compound in Hyannis Port. JFK and RFK were connected by telephone to a makeshift headquarters in the nearby

Hyannis armory, and to key supporters in pivotal states. An accidental message of congratulations from President Eisenhower produced confusion and amusement, but we knew it was too early. A premature, almost defeatist statement by Nixon produced more scorn than satisfaction. Our loss of Ohio, where JFK had repeatedly drawn big audiences, was a painful blow. California, Nixon's home state on the West Coast, was late in reporting and the result was uncertain. As the night wore on, Johnson's state of Texas joined Missouri, Minnesota, California, and Illinois on the uncertain list. Finally, when it was apparent that the conclusion would not be known for many hours, JFK went over to his own house to sleep. Soon I was alone by the television in the big family house.

According to Arthur Schlesinger's theory of "cycles of American history," 1960 should have been the year when the children of the Franklin D. Roosevelt era enabled progressivism to prevail once again. But, I wondered, as I sat alone in the dark that night, with no clear victory for Kennedy in sight, where was Arthur's theoretical cycle when we really needed it? If victory was inevitable, why were we required to work so hard for so long to win a popular vote margin smaller than one-half of one percent?

My wait was rewarded when early in the morning it appeared that the uncertain states were all breaking our way, including California. I walked over to the senator's house, which I noted was now surrounded for the first time by Secret Service agents. A good sign. A member of his household staff reported hearing him arise, and suggested I go upstairs. He was still in bed, but awake. I congratulated him as our next president. He asked about California. I told him the morning news had put California in his column—mistakenly, it later turned out, after the absentee ballots were counted. Just then, his bedside phone rang. It was his mother-in-law congratulating him. My own overwhelming sense of triumph and happiness was mixed with relief. After all those years on the road, it was over. In another sense, it had just begun.

Chapter 16

The 1960–1961 Presidential Transition

Confidently anticipating victory in November, Kennedy asked two very different experts and White House alumni to prepare for him separate memoranda on what had to be done during the transition period between Election Day and his January inauguration: Clark Clifford, the prominent Washington lawyer, and Richard Neustadt, the Columbia University political scientist. Each was asked not to consult with the other or with the Kennedy staff and not to deliver his work before the election. Presidential transitions are now governed by statute, financed from a special federal fund, and subject to rules and expectations informally enforced by political observers, precedent, and the press. None of that was true during the Eisenhower-Kennedy transition, and we relied heavily on our two expert transition reports. The rest, we improvised.

Both Clifford and Neustadt submitted wise and invaluable recommendations, and the president-elect asked me to review both before he convened a meeting of his top staff a day or two after his election. In slightly different versions, both had recommended that one key post which needed to be filled promptly, in addition to that of press secretary, was that of the president's principal advisor on domestic policy and programs—his source of ideas, his draftsman of speeches and messages, the formulator of presidential legislative and administrative programs turning campaign promises into feasible action. The occupant might well be a lawyer, said Clifford.

I had never lobbied for any particular position, always assuming that JFK, if elected, would want to keep me close after eight years—although, at the time, I told my sister there were no guarantees. In one casual lunch conversation with Mike Feldman in early autumn, I speculated whether I might find a fit in the National Aeronautics and Space Administration, using my ability to translate scientific and technological terms into layman's language. Thankfully, neither I nor anyone else ever acted on that foolish notion.

But, upon reading the Clifford and Neustadt reports, I fervently hoped that I would be named to the policy-program position; and was overjoyed when the president-elect, in Hyannis Port after the election, began his first staff meeting by saying he wanted me for that post. He announced it that afternoon to the assembled press corps, saying of me: "He will begin work immediately to assist me in preparing for a new administration, having worked with me on policy matters during the past eight years." With that brief introduction, I became—with the exception of his running mate, the vice president—virtually the first member of the Kennedy administration. Now I am almost the last.

The title "special counsel to the president" had a brief but honorable history. It began, I was told by Sam Rosenman, the first to hold that title, when he served as "counsel to the governor" during FDR's years as governor of New York. When FDR became president, Rosenman became a judge. But when FDR later found that the burdens of both domestic and wartime leadership required more help, he telephoned Rosenman, asking him to leave the bench and join him in Washington. Rosenman insisted on a title like his old one, reflecting his profession. FDR agreed, but called back a week later to say that Attorney General Biddle had protested, insisting that he was "counsel to the president." Rosenman held firm; and Roosevelt called back another week later to say: "It's all settled, in a two-part compromise. You will be Special Counsel to the President and I will announce it next week when Biddle is in Mexico City at an inter-American law conference."

After Roosevelt's death, Clark Clifford became special counsel to President Truman, and he recommended that Kennedy retain that historical title, knowing that I was the lawyer likely to be given that post and that my role in the White House, as in the Senate, would include the duties that he and Rosenman had performed.

One student of the presidential staffing process remarked: "There's no question that Ted has the broadest job of them all. That's the way it's been since 1953, and that's the way it will be through 1968." The Associated Press added: "Sorensen will probably be one of the youngest men ever to hold a governmental position of such responsibility. . . ." I said jokingly of my title to Mike Feldman, who unlike me had actually been a private lawyer: "Well, I decided it was time I got back to practicing law." The choice of title was wholly Clifford's, not mine. As a "clerk" on the Senate payroll, I cared about my relations with JFK, not my title. As with Rosenman and Clifford, the title "special counsel" was adopted more to fit my profession than to describe my functions.

In December I had my first one-on-one meeting of any length with JFK since his nomination the previous July. When I mentioned the speaking invitations I was receiving, he advised me to decline them all. "Keep your head down," he instructed me. "Everyone who's held a job like yours—Sherman Adams, Harry Hopkins, Colonel House, all the rest—ended up in the shithouse. Congress was down on them or the President was hurt by them or somebody was mad at them," he added. "The best way for you to stay out of trouble is to stay out of sight." Good advice, which I faithfully followed, except on those rare occasions when he directed otherwise.

At the same meeting, I reviewed with him my choices for my deputies and assistants. Feldman, White, and Goodwin topped my list of fourteen possible names. I also reviewed with him the transition task forces that I would, on his behalf, be launching, and the names of the experts I was recommending to serve on those task forces, many of whom would later join the administration.

During those weeks between his election and inauguration, I spent most of my time not on his inaugural address, but on the transition and these policy matters. I sent a letter to each cabinet nominee—extremely presumptuous, I now realize, for a much younger man whom most of them had never met—setting forth the president-elect's requests for studies, decisions, or early actions. I conveyed twenty-one such requests to Secretary of State–designate Dean Rusk; eight, with some of them broken down into multiple sub-requests, to Secretary of Defense–designate Robert McNamara; eight to Secretary of Agriculture–designate Orville Freeman; seven to Secretary of the Interior–designate Stuart Udall; nine to Secretary of Health, Education, and Welfare–designate Abe Ribicoff (whom I later heard was offended at being so instructed by me instead of the president-elect); and twelve, including sub-requests, to Secretary of Labor–designate Arthur Goldberg. I did not send such a letter to Attorney General–designate Robert Kennedy, who had his own channel of communications with JFK, or to Secretary of Treasury–designate Douglas Dillon, with whom I was already meeting regularly on the budget. In some cases, I followed up my letters with one-on-one private meetings.

After the election, I noticed a change in my own status—my phone calls were promptly returned; my lunches were no longer confined to the Senate Office Building basement cafeteria but included invitations from the French ambassador, who informed me that France was America's oldest and most important ally, and from James "Scotty" Reston, the distinguished *New York Times* correspondent and Washington bureau chief, who informed me that governments around the world relied on the *Times* to convey accurately the administration's thinking on all issues, and therefore I should keep him informed on all our positions and plans, whether or not confidential.

Accompanied by Mike Feldman, I made my first visit to the White House to meet with The (note the capital) Assistant to the President, Eisenhower's chief of staff General Wilton Persons, who had succeeded Sherman Adams. The General informed us that no piece of paper or person (with the exception of the secretary of state and the press secretary) went into President Eisenhower's office unless he—like his predecessor—had first cleared that entry, and that other White House staff and cabinet members kept him informed on why they needed to see the president. For me, that confirmed JFK's wisdom in not granting me or anyone on his staff that kind of authority.

I also received a call from Eisenhower's outgoing Budget Bureau director, Maurice Stans, who told me that he had asked Clark Clifford to identify who on the Kennedy team should review with him Eisenhower's final budget message before it was sent to Congress; Clifford had identified me. Meeting with Stans that morning, I discovered the extent to which the federal budget involves, directly or indirectly, almost every issue in the country, ranging from tax policy to education spending to new weapons systems. As I solemnly sat and listened to Mr. Stans—trying to remind myself that this was serious business, the nation's business—I could not suppress a growing feeling that this was fun!

Chapter 17

Special Counsel to the President

Both the president and I quickly adjusted to the changes in our respective roles, the greater responsibility, the need to worry less about the next day's headlines and more about the next generation's future, the realization that the necessary response to each growing national problem was no longer merely a speech by a mere senator or candidate—sounding the alarm, raising the right questions, or criticizing our opponents' answers—but instead a solution that produced results. (Nor, I confess, was it difficult to adjust to the new salary of $21,000, roughly $5,000 more than my salary in my last year as a Senate staffer.)

The publishers of the new Congressional Directory

listed my name first under that of the president on their White House page. But contrary to the title given to me by *Time* magazine's Hugh Sidey upon my White House departure in early 1964, I was not the "Deputy President." Kennedy had no deputy president and no chief of staff. He saw no need for staff meetings, preferring the directness and increased confidentiality of one-on-one sessions, including meeting directly with my deputies, and expecting us to coordinate among ourselves. Nevertheless, years later, recognizing some similarities between my role and that of other presidents' chiefs of staff, I was invited by the University of California at San Diego to participate in a panel of—and on—White House chiefs of staff. Before it began, moderator John Chancellor gathered all the panelists backstage—including Donald Rumsfeld and Dick Cheney—and said, looking at LBJ's top aide Harry McPherson and me: "If either of you says you weren't Chief of Staff, I'll kick you off the stage."

When the Kennedy team moved into the White House, my assigned office was initially on the second floor of the West Wing with Larry O'Brien and his congressional liaison team. I raised no objection. But the president wanted me closer to the Oval Office, where he and I would have easier access to each other; and to my surprise, I was immediately moved to the large first-floor office previously used by General Persons, and later by vice presidents Mondale and Gore. The office was high-ceilinged, multiwindowed, spacious, and quiet, with a huge desk, conference table, sofa, television and—unlike any other office in the building except for the Oval Office—its own restroom. I had three secretaries in my outer office, a sharp contrast with my tiny cubicle back in room 362 in the Old Senate Office Building, where my phone was always ringing. One reporter described my White House office as "typical of the man—clean, uncluttered, businesslike, unassuming, simple, bare of obvious prestige symbols like extra-thick carpets and wood paneling."

I felt a thrill—indeed, a chill—each morning upon entering those hallowed halls in the West Wing and viewing the American flag over the front door. I never got over that combined sense of pride, awe, and overwhelming responsibility. But my clearest memory was that of exhaustion. I was too busy ever to smell the flowers in the White House Rose Garden.

Normally, my White House days began at 8 A.M., even earlier when breakfasts in the residence were scheduled, either to meet with legislative leaders or to prepare for a press conference later in the day. Sometimes I arrived still earlier for a prework tennis match with Mike Feldman on the White House court. I lunched most days in the White House mess, and often had dinner meetings there or in my office, seldom leaving earlier than 7:30 P.M. Occasionally the president would return to the Oval Office after his dinner, sometimes as late as 10:30 P.M. If I was still at my desk, I would join him for a long night of work. Even in those fourteen-hour days, there was never enough time to do all that had to be done, much less to reflect on all that needed to be considered, to read all the information pouring in, and to return all the day's phone calls.

One of the advantages and disadvantages of the White House is the iron fence that surrounds it, with guards at the gates, keeping out not only security threats but also tourists and politicians who might otherwise drop by for time-consuming chats. Without leaving the White House, I could get a meal, a haircut, and medical care. But that fence also prevents those working in the White House, who are too busy to lead a normal life, from fully understanding the concerns and complaints of ordinary people.

For me, unrelated outside activities were all too rare. I increasingly lost contact with friends from earlier stages in my life, even as I felt guilty about it. Sooner or later, under a barrage of political or press criticism, almost every White House team tends to hunker down in a bunker mentality. The Kennedy White House had a taste of that, after its 1962 crackdown on Big Steel; but it was of short duration.

"Those were the days," Robert Kennedy ruefully remarked after we stumbled in April 1961 at the Bay of Pigs, "when we thought we were succeeding because of all the stories on how hard everybody was working." The American presidency requires on the president's team the young in heart and health, if not necessarily in years, because of all the midnight meetings, the early morning briefings, the Saturday sessions, and the constant crises. There is an inevitable ebb and flow of personnel at the White House. Some burn out, drop out, or opt out for less demanding schedules or for higher pay or prestige. Happily, in the Kennedy White House, no one burned out. The youngest man ever elected president of the United States had succeeded the oldest (until then). Youthful energy and idealism were in the saddle in Washington. The test was each appointee's judgment, not the length of his years or service. Prudent performance under pressure is key to success and survival in the White House, more important than likability or even compatibility with the president.

Was the job stressful? Of course. I responded well to pressure; it spurred me to give my best, even to flourish, though it came with a cost. When unrelenting stress led to stomach ulcers, the president arranged for my temporary hospitalization at Bethesda Naval Hospital, and laughed at the humor column item citing my indisposition, which added: "Thus far the President has no ulcers—that shows who does the worrying at the White House." When White House social secretary Letitia Baldrige chided me for working day and night, I told her she did not understand; there was nothing else I would rather be doing.

Practical jokes were one way to relieve the constant pressure. One early White House day, not realizing that his fireplace in the Oval Office was a fake, JFK created enough smoke in the West Wing to cause me to rush in imitating Dolley Madison, offering to save George Washington's portrait.

When Council of Economic Advisors chairman Walter Heller gave me an obviously flawed policy recommendation on the telephone, then hours later realized his mistake and called me back with a correction, he was horrified when I told him that it was too late because I'd passed his message along to the president. Walter wanted to come over to the White House immediately to make his apologies to the president personally. He was more relieved than amused when I confessed that I had not really given his earlier message to JFK.

One morning I encountered the inimitable humorist Art Buchwald in the Washington airport, and together we concocted a scheme to rattle our mutual friend, Ben Bradlee of the *Washington Post* and *Newsweek*. Buchwald related to me that, on the previous day, lunching at a Washington restaurant, he and Bradlee had disagreed over whether Bradlee's references to Internal Revenue commissioner Mortimer Caplin in a telegram were humorous to a public that did not even know Caplin's name. They had then proceeded from table to table, questioning whether diners knew the name of the Commissioner of Internal Revenue.

As agreed with Buchwald, I telephoned Bradlee later that day to tell him that I had just stepped out of a tax legislation meeting with Commissioner Caplin, who had taken me aside to ask why Ben Bradlee would be angry at him, having heard that Bradlee was stirring up trouble in a Washington restaurant. "Oh my God," said Bradlee, immediately fearful that his tax returns would be audited: "This is all Buchwald's fault." Ben then wrote the most humble, apologetic, self-abasing letter imaginable to Commissioner Caplin, with copies to me and an increasingly gleeful Buchwald, who then called me suggesting a follow-up. But before we could implement it, we both received a note from Bradlee: "Commissioner Caplin and I are onto your game, and are cooking up our own plan for revenge . . ."

. . .

According to one associate's statement in the press: "Ted relaxes in ways most of us would never think of—he creates new approaches to old problems." That's nice, but not the whole story. Frequent visits to or from my sons always helped to relieve the stress. Weekends accompanying the president to Hyannis Port, where my boys and I were housed at Otis Air Force Base, were almost always a combination of work with him at his home and play with my sons at the base, which had a swimming pool and ball field.

But even a pleasant Saturday softball game was subject to unpleasant intrusion from the real world. One Washington weekend in May 1962, looking for a ball field on which we could play, I brought the boys down to the Federal Mall behind the White House. Before our game got under way, we saw the president's helicopter land long before schedule on the White House back lawn. Sensing that some emergency might require my presence, I brought the boys and our softball gear back to my office, where I learned that the president had been trying to reach me to discuss a bombing the previous night in Birmingham.

. . .

During my three years in the White House, my duties varied widely. A late 1963 post-assassination briefing memo by Mac Bundy to new President Johnson described my role as encompassing "all legislative programs (as distinct from legislative relations), all major speeches and messages, many of the problems of political planning, [and] at the center of foreign crises too." A fair overview, although it omitted the dozens of nonroutine matters that often took me to President Kennedy's office for the day's summary chats we had almost every evening.

During the first few months of the Kennedy administration, I undertook the formulation of presidential messages to Congress reflecting my earlier discussions with the president on the transition lists outlining the administration's pledges, goals, and programs on everything from housing to education. President Kennedy sent 277 separate new requests to Congress during his first one hundred days in office, a period in which I also had to worry about his State of the Union address, and making his new budget consistent with his proposals.

After that January State of the Union message came twenty-four "Special Messages to Congress" over the next five months, many only days apart. They spanned the breadth of the new president's agenda—from the Peace Corps and Alliance for Progress, to conflicts of interest and ethics in government, to new government reorganization plans. In May he gave what was, in effect, a second State of the Union address, called a message on "Urgent National Needs."

During those early months, I sometimes worked two or three consecutive days and nights with no sleep. In the course of one all-night session working on a draft message with Mike Feldman—on housing, as I recall—I fell asleep at my desk. Mike finished the draft while I slept. When the final copy went to the Congress and appeared in print, I read it, and commented to him that the closing portion was the best part of the entire message. He was pleased; but in truth, I had not realized it was his work.

The following year, those separate legislative messages continued, but were fewer, with topics ranging from urban affairs to the United Nations, from a federal pay raise to health, conservation, and consumer rights. In 1963, the final year of his presidency, we added "Special Messages" on civil rights, mental health, youth, and senior citizens—all growing priorities for Kennedy and the American people. Those three years of "Special Messages," compared to most of the televised presidential speeches that received far more attention, were far more important in setting the long-term course of the country and the Democratic Party.

When the president told me at the start that my duties included questions on taxes and expenditures, he might have been surprised to discover that I was as fiscally conservative as he and his father. I confess that I "rounded down" the estimated budget costs of some of the programs proposed to me by department heads, bypassing those under one-half billion dollars as of little substantial consequence to the budget. But I became increasingly skeptical of those proposals that, according to their respective cabinet sponsors, would pay for themselves. Only proposals for increasing manpower in the Internal Revenue Service, in my view, truly met that test; and the Congress consistently resisted that. I was tempted to put together an entire sample or mock budget consisting solely of proposals that would theoretically pay for themselves, so that I could tell the president—and he could tell the Congress—that his full legislative program was cost-free.

My responsibilities in the White House were much less political than my duties in the campaign. I no longer had special concerns for larger states, Democratic leaders, or voting blocs. We had no "permanent campaign" in the Kennedy White House; and until 1963 formulated no plans or strategy for reelection in 1964.

JFK's chief criterion on any question was the national interest, not his partisan advantage. When Walter Heller told me that his team of economic advisors' recommendation on a particular issue had been altered downward to take political considerations into account, I scolded him, telling him that the president and I could make the political calculations, and wanted from him and his colleagues their best and most objective substantive recommendations.

Yet, in the larger sense of the term "politics," all of us on the president's staff knew that we were in part the president's political advisors and that the White House is inherently a political institution. That is why I have not joined those, in subsequent years, who lamented that any particular president was playing politics with foreign policy or some other issue. Of course he is playing politics—the president in a democracy is required to play politics with every issue, if this country is to be governed with the consent of the governed.

In all my work, I relied on my two principal deputies, Mike Feldman and Lee White, Goodwin having transferred out of my office toward the end of our first year in the White House. Feldman and White were invaluable to me and the president. From the Senate days on, they remained my close friends, for whom I had the greatest affection and admiration. Both were brilliant lawyers. I should have asked for more deputies. In the Roosevelt administration, Special Counsel Rosenman's legal staff was said to be never larger than ten. In the Truman White House, Clifford's was never larger than eight. Mine was never larger than three. As a result, we were stretched too thin and handled too much, taking a perverse pride in keeping our staff lean, effective, and trouble-free. The work done by the three of us would later be done by seven lawyers under Johnson, and fifty or more under his successors.

Even though I was not an economist, and certainly not an expert on either fiscal or monetary policy, the periodic recommendations of what we called the "Troika" (Douglas Dillon, David Bell, and Walter Heller) were relayed to me.

In our first week in the White House, National Security Advisor McGeorge Bundy, Budget Director David Bell, and I agreed that we would meet at least weekly to keep one another informed on our respective activities and to coordinate our policy positions. Bundy, my counterpart on foreign policy, with an NSC professional staff of no more than a dozen (since then several dozen), coordinated and oversaw for the president the activities of the State Department, Defense Department, Central

Intelligence Agency, and other national security–related activities.

I collaborated with congressional liaison Larry O'Brien on the president's legislative program, helping to design it, while Larry and his team helped secure its enactment. Similarly, I worked with Walter Heller and his Council of Economic Advisors on economic questions, and with Jerome Wiesner and his Science and Technology Committee on questions relating to space, weaponry, and health. I doubt that either of those panels had more influence in any other administration. I worked with press secretary Pierre Salinger on press releases and media appearances, and with Kenny O'Donnell on politics and the president's speaking and traveling schedule. O'Donnell, as the president's appointments secretary, controlled the president's calendar, coordinated White House logistics, and served as the point of contact with Democratic Party machinery. All of us performed our respective roles together like a world-class orchestra.

I also solicited speechwriting assistance from Arthur Schlesinger, the president's resident historian. Although he was not primarily a policy advisor, the charge that this prizewinning author's role on the White House staff was nothing more than intellectual window dressing could only have been made by someone who did not understand either the extent to which JFK emphasized history and took counsel from it, or the extent to which Arthur had a keen political mind, which he had applied well before 1960 in the two presidential campaigns of Adlai Stevenson and in his brilliant books on presidencies from Andrew Jackson's to Franklin Roosevelt's. Schlesinger's subsequent volumes on both John and Robert Kennedy confirmed the wisdom of this selection.

My job also included participation in and preparation for all the president's formal meetings, including periodic meetings with the cabinet, with House and Senate Democratic leaders, and with other administration officials. Some problems faced by department and agency heads that they felt could not otherwise be settled, without taking the matter to the president, were often brought to me. I served as an honest broker, determining which decisions could be made by me and which could be made only by the president. I usually made my recommendations to the president orally, with notice to the relevant department heads. In meetings where the president was not present, I often did not distinguish between my views and his. "It's hard to figure," one cabinet member told the press, "when Ted is expressing something he really feels himself or something the President feels—maybe the answer is that there's no difference."

At the president's request, cabinet members and prospective appointees were sometimes asked to talk to me first about their confirmation or policy problems. At first, some resented this practice. When Secretary of Commerce Luther Hodges wanted to add to a cabinet agenda "the problem of Cabinet members gaining direct access to the President," I assumed that he was referring to me. I offered to leave the room, but the president deemed the question absurd and ignored my suggestion.

Among the visitors whom he sent to my office were a potential new nominee to the Federal Reserve Board; several railroad and labor executives on strike issues; the nation's top civil rights leaders; Franklin D. Roosevelt Jr. to prepare for his Senate confirmation hearing for undersecretary of commerce; Ambassador George Kennan, who was moved by congressional criticism to submit his resignation as ambassador to Yugoslavia in 1963; and Ways and Means Committee chairman Wilbur Mills to seal a compromise on legislation. JFK occasionally dispatched me to Capitol Hill visits with such Senate heavyweights as Public Works Committee chairman Bob Kerr and Republican minority leader Everett Dirksen, seeking their support on controversial legislation.

Occasionally I was asked to resolve policy or political disputes within the administration. A brief temperamental flare-up between Undersecretary of State George Ball and Secretary of Treasury Douglas Dillon gave the president some concern. "We haven't had anything like that," he said to me, and asked me—totally inexpert on international monetary policy and therefore totally impartial—to broker a peace between them. Dillon sent his deputy Robert Roosa to a meeting with Ball in my office, and we easily facilitated a meeting of the minds on what the president's policy should be.

International economic policy also led me to meet in August 1962 with a wide range of White House, State Department, Defense Department, Budget Bureau, and other officials looking for answers to the nation's chronic balance of payments deficit and gold outflow. When several diverse points of view were strongly argued, the president asked me to draft a summary memorandum combining them, and then to accompany him to a meeting with Federal Reserve Board chairman William Martin to discuss possible changes in international monetary policy. Martin was interested, but unconvinced that his fellow central bankers would approve it. Decades later, at an academic conference on this issue, a member of the Reagan Council of Economic Advisors asked me from the audience: "How could the President be sent alone into a meeting with the Fed Chairman?" "President

Kennedy was a quick learner," I replied, "and he was not alone—I was not a potted plant."

I was also drawn into a squabble between Interior Secretary Udall and Federal Power Commission chairman Swidler, who was blocking an Interior Department dam project. I telephoned Swidler and told him that time constraints had made it impossible for the pile of budget requests awaiting approval on my desk, including his, to get my attention until other troubling matters were out of the way, including his dispute with Interior. The dispute ended with that call.

I was frequently embarrassed, even before we had settled into the White House, by press overstatements about my role. In one of the first national profiles ever published about my work, Al Otten, Washington correspondent for the *Wall Street Journal*, called me "Kennedy's intellectual alter ego" an exaggeration that stuck. During my first year in the White House, even Theodore White, noted for his careful understatement, in his groundbreaking *Making of the President 1960*, gave me credit for "many of Kennedy's finest thoughts and expressions," adding that I had "become almost a lobe of Kennedy's mind." Another very silly exaggeration.

When President Kennedy, in a television interview, heard a broad description of National Security Advisor Bundy's authority and importance, he dryly commented,

"Oh, I will continue to have some residual functions," a response he would no doubt have given to the press exaggerations of my role as well. To keep me humble, my sister reported to me on the unidentified Washington dinner partner who, having asked where she was from, replied: "You are the only person I have heard of in this town who is from Nebraska, except for that jerk in the White House."

What publicity giveth, publicity taketh away. Former governor Milward Simpson of Wyoming, campaigning for a U.S. Senate seat in 1962, said I was a "Fabian Socialist." Conservative columnist Henry J. Taylor also charged that Kennedy was being led into socialism by me and other "professors-turned-politicians . . . advocates and propagandists for socialism in the United States." Having never at that time been either a professor or a candidate, I was surprised that he included me. But I was certain that I had the president's confidence, and that made all the difference.

Throughout our years together, I saw Kennedy's role and horizons expand. At each step, he wanted two things from me in addition to speech drafts and all my other tasks: First, he wanted me to brief him on all the facts, all his options, and all the pros and cons of all the options, and second, he wanted me to raise all the hard questions. Recognizing from history the danger of his becoming isolated in the Oval Office if surrounded by a bubble of yes-men, President Kennedy made certain that his staff as well as his cabinet was composed of strong-minded individuals unafraid to speak truth to power, men of different philosophies, ideologies, and backgrounds. Whenever he asked, "What do you think, Ted?" I remained candid and direct; this president did not want sycophants. Both my legal training and my Unitarian upbringing had made me a natural doubter and dissenter. During the long presidential campaign, political correspondent Stewart Alsop said I was a "no-man." The journalist Hugh Sidey called me Kennedy's "resident skeptic." It was my job to say: "Wait, why, what will the consequences be?" I was willing to challenge the rigid ideologues, either left or right, who offered easy answers and absolutes.

During Robert Kennedy's oral history for the John F. Kennedy Presidential Library, his interviewer said, "You were uniquely in a position to say No." Bobby responded, "Yeah. But there were others, I mean, Ted Sorensen did . . ." "That is the role Ted played?" the interviewer asked. "Yes," replied Bobby, "and he played it well. . . ." I was deeply touched—and, frankly, surprised, in view of the unevenness of our relationship in the early years—to discover that, when asked to whom the president turned for advice, Bobby, my friend and onetime competitor for the president's ear, answered: "Ted Sorensen was a very important figure . . . Whenever it became a difficult matter, whether it was domestic or . . . foreign policy, if it was difficult, Ted Sorensen was brought in."

Chapter 18

The President's Speeches

John F. Kennedy's speeches stood out because they revived idealism, eloquence, and progressivism, after a decade of Eisenhower's bland, dry approach and Joe McCarthy's evil tirades. JFK spoke to the country's nobler instincts, inspiring visions of a less divided nation and world. In my view, his three most important speeches, in terms of concrete impact and consequences, were his national address on the Cuban missile crisis in October 1962, his 1963 televised civil rights address, and his 1960 campaign presentation on the religious issue to the Protestant Ministers of Houston. His three most eloquent speeches were his 1963 American University commencement address, his inaugural, and his Berlin City Hall speech, in that order. Among his lesser known, but no less powerful and thoughtful speeches, were those he delivered at the University of Washington in 1961, to the Irish Parliament in 1963 (quoted by Ireland's prime minister in his own historic 2007 speech at Westminster to the British Parliament), to a national television audience on the Nuclear Test Ban Treaty in 1963, and his "Farewell to Massachusetts" only weeks before his inauguration.

His worst speech was a televised speech on the economy in the summer of 1962. After deciding not to urge a tax cut that summer, he had no specific objective. Announcing what will not be is not exciting, and economic speeches as a general rule are not exciting. Another mediocre speech was his address to the American Newspaper Publishers Association in April 1961, urging more journalistic self-censorship regarding national security issues—a mistake that he later regretted. Also unfortunate was his 1961 speech on Berlin calling for more civil defense shelters, precipitating more panic, confusion, doubt, and unfriendly sentiments than meaningful protection against nuclear fallout.

It is noteworthy that those three worst speeches all came within the first eighteen months of his presidency, and that four of his best speeches were delivered in the summer of 1963, after he and I had collaborated on speeches for nearly ten years. In part, this reflects the fact that great events can evoke great speeches, and the summer of 1963 was filled with great events. But this timing also may reflect that, in our respective roles, we had both learned as we worked together, and improved our collaborative style. That summer of 1963 was our "hot streak."

Despite being a Unitarian from Nebraska, who never knew anyone who observed St. Patrick's Day, the first full-length speech I had helped write for JFK years earlier—other than those conveying the New England Economic Program—was the speech he gave on March 17, 1954, to the Friendly Sons of St. Patrick in New York. It began with an old Irish saying about St. Patrick's Day, followed by an ancient Irish legend, and a reference to St. Patrick's dying request to an angel of the Lord. Then followed a reminder of the hundreds of millions in Communist-dominated areas who did not enjoy the liberty that had traditionally been so important to the Irish, a tribute to those leaders of the church who had suffered and struggled in resisting Communist tyranny, and a recitation of those heroes of Irish independence who in their own way had combated British tyranny. Just in case more was needed, the speech included references to the names or stories of one Irish hero after another—William Orr, Peter Finerty, Edward Fitzgerald, Oliver Bond, and others. I quoted from a bold letter by one of these heroes to the British authorities, terming it a letter "which should be reread in the cellars of East Berlin," and an equally stirring statement to a jury from still another Irish freedom fighter. At the conclusion of that quotation, the senator closed his speech with the words: "There is our message, Mr. Chairman; there is our faith and our task. Let us not fail its fulfillment." The paragraphs were longer than would later be our standard, but it was fun and a fine start for our speechwriting collaboration.

One of the most confused scenes from which any Kennedy speech ever emerged was the 1956 Democratic National Convention in Chicago where, at the last minute, JFK was asked by Adlai Stevenson to formally place Adlai's name in nomination for president. After Kennedy had left for the convention floor, Adlai's writers brought me a draft that I thought was second-rate. I had difficulty getting to the convention hall to review it with JFK, difficulty finding him on the floor, difficulty getting him off the floor, finally finding a vacant room to discuss it with him only hours before it became the convention's first order of business the next morning. He agreed that it needed to be rewritten. "I suppose I've got to do it," I said. He replied, typically, "That's right. Have it in my room by eight in the morning." I arranged for a driver and secretary to stay the night, awakened them at 6:30 A.M., had my draft typed, and took a new copy over to the senator. He quickly scanned my draft, rewrote portions, cut out portions, and added a few paragraphs. Then it needed to be retyped. When I sent one copy to the teleprompter, I found a page was missing. I mobilized an assortment of typists, including a reporter friend, Tom Winship of the *Boston Globe*, and finally got the new clean copy to JFK. The speech was a success—particularly one line: "Our candidates will be up against two of the most skilled campaigners in history—one who takes the high road and one who takes the low." Apparently a similar phrase was used in the 1948 presidential race; but after Kennedy's 1956 address, "the low road" became part of the political lexicon.

Perhaps the most consequential short speech JFK ever gave as a senator was his brief, gracious statement of concession to Kefauver in the vice presidential race at that Chicago National Convention, which helped make him almost overnight a national figure with a reputation as a decent politician. I did not contribute one word to that spontaneous statement.

Four years later, his speech accepting the Democratic nomination for president at the July 1960 Democratic National Convention in Los Angeles had three goals: reuniting the Democratic Party after a hotly contested race for the nomination, reassuring suspicious Protestant voters that his religion was not a handicap, and wooing independents and Republicans who did not know him well and mistrusted both his inexperience and his religion. Roughly two weeks before the convention, I sent the following letter to some of our more creative friends in the ranks of liberal Democrats:

> *Senator Kennedy's nomination now appears sufficiently likely that work should be undertaken now on his acceptance speech. . . . I wonder if you would be willing to try your hand at this? . . . If you do not feel you have time for a full draft of 10 double-spaced pages, would you be willing to try . . . one or more paragraphs which contain specific themes or striking phrases. . . .*

As I recall, that letter elicited more suggestions than we could use; but they helped. The inaugural address was the only other JFK speech for which distinguished outsiders were invited to submit suggestions.

The senator wanted that acceptance address to include a vivid phrase that would reflect his emphasis on the tasks and challenges confronting the American people, combining the need to change with the country's unfinished agenda, while invoking the courage and achievements of the past. Ultimately we found the phrase "the New Frontier" best fit that combination of themes. To the best of my recollection, neither the senator nor I had read or heard the phrase elsewhere, nor had we received it from any of those from whom we had solicited ideas. The relevant symbolism of the old frontier was noted, I believe, in material I received from Professor Alan Nevins, but its relationship to the Kennedy program was not developed in the Nevins materials or elsewhere. A *New York Herald-Tribune* article asserted that the phrase originated with Max Freedman and Walt Rostow, both of whom had received my letter of solicitation, but had not sent any material that was used. Bill Safire later told me that previous national candidates Alf Landon and Henry Wallace had used a similar phrase years earlier. When he asked me about it many years later, I told him that to the best of my recollection, the phrase had first appeared in one of my drafts. The fact that my grandparents were pioneers on the Nebraska frontier was not a coincidence.

The historical precedent for President-elect Kennedy's "Farewell to Massachusetts," delivered on January 9, eleven days before the inaugural, was President-elect Abraham Lincoln's "Farewell to Springfield [Illinois]." One problem facing us that probably did not face Lincoln was the obvious hypocrisy of voicing sentimental praise to a legislature—the logical site for the Kennedy speech—best known in those days for pork barrel politics and sporadic corruption. The solution was to couch the noble ideals that we wanted to cite in question form, recognizing that some of those listening in the hall might be squirming because their own records and characters did not quite match that ideal. By applying the question to himself as well as other public servants, JFK made it a declaration of the high standards to which he would hold himself. Quoting John Winthrop's statement that his community would be watched by all, as a "city upon a hill," the speech became known in some circles as the "City on a Hill" speech. Since 1961, the phrase has frequently been attributed not to Winthrop but to JFK—though many now remember its use by President Ronald Reagan as well.

Because the speech had been scheduled, conceived, and drafted at the height of presidential transition activity, in the midst of task force arrangements, budget planning, and inaugural drafting, I hope I can be forgiven for having borrowed not only the "City on a Hill" metaphor from Winthrop but also the device of stating standards in the form of questions from Franklin D. Roosevelt, who had—in the midst of his 1932 presidential campaign—paid tribute in that form to none other than Nebraska's independent Republican senator, George W. Norris, as cited in *Profiles in Courage*: "History asks, 'did the man have integrity? Did the man have unselfishness? Did the man have courage? Did the man have consistency?'" Evoking FDR nearly thirty years later, JFK said:

> When . . . the high court of history sits in judgment on each one of us—recording whether . . . we fulfilled our responsibilities to the state . . . by the answers to four questions: first, were we truly men of courage . . . truly men of judgment . . . truly men of integrity . . . truly men of dedication.

JFK's parents, according to a letter I received from his mother's secretary, were so impressed by the speech "that they wondered if he should not have kept it for the Inauguration." JFK conveyed the same concern to me. Although I adapted the Massachusetts farewell closing for the inaugural's closing with only slight changes, I assured him that we still had enough material for a good inaugural address.

JFK knew that an inaugural address stamps a brand on a new president that can last for years, both nationally and globally, as either a warrior or a peacemaker, a bore or a source of inspiration, as first-rate or mediocre. Jefferson's first inaugural, delivered after a bitterly contested election, sought to heal partisan divisions. FDR's first inaugural sought to reassure the country that it could survive the Depression. JFK's inaugural helped to change America. It was time, JFK declared, for a new generation to cope with the new problems and new responsibilities that were emerging. The speech launched an era of idealism in America. Through his speeches as well as his actions, Kennedy set an example for the world—that one person could make a difference, and that no one should accept an unacceptable status quo.

The inaugural fulfilled Kennedy's purpose and hopes, transforming the perception of him from a young president elected by the narrowest possible margin to a confident leader hailed by world statesmen and by the elders of his own party. He had approached it with confidence, though reportedly telling his wife that it was not as good as Jefferson's first inaugural. It certainly was not as good as Lincoln's second or FDR's first. But, while my opinion on this subject cannot be objective, that address surely ranks among the best of all inaugural addresses in the twentieth century. The *London Times* commentator who saw a resemblance to the cadences of Lincoln was right. Lincoln's Gettysburg Address and second inaugural had both been models for JFK and me. Carl Sandburg said that, with the possible exception of FDR's first inaugural, this was the best since Lincoln. Max Ascoli, editor of the liberal *Reporter Magazine*, said that he was neither "impressed nor stirred" by the speech. His comment both impressed and stirred the president, who in typical JFK fashion invited Ascoli to his office.

It was the fourth shortest inaugural address in history, and the shortest in the twentieth century except for FDR's fourth, which had been abbreviated under the prevailing wartime conditions. As in most Kennedy speeches, the phrases and clauses were short, as were the words. He strictly limited the use of the first-person pronoun. The speech drew extensively on his own experience and that of his generation, "tempered by war" (with which I had no firsthand experience), and was informed by his global travels. It also reflected his finely honed sense of American history, far more developed than mine.

He wanted the speech to focus on foreign policy, in part because domestic policy was more partisan and divisive, and too complex for a speech he wanted to keep short. Nor did he want it to sound like a stale recital of the Democratic platform. The speech's only domestic reference, added on the final day, after being suggested to me by our chief civil rights campaign advisors, Harris Wofford and Louis Martin, was an expansion of our reference to "those human rights to which this nation has been committed, and to which we are committed today," by adding the words "at home and around the world."

I suggested, if he wanted more, a possible question to the audience at this point: "Are you willing to demonstrate in your own life—in your attitude toward those of other races and those from other shores—that you hold these truths to be self-evident?" That line did not make the final cut.

Kennedy knew that his narrow popular vote victory, and the narrow margin of his party's control of Congress, required a speech that was not ideological. Some commentators thought the speech was a harsh cold war call to arms, with its promise to "pay any price, bear any burden." They should have read the whole speech. It called for more U.S.-Soviet cooperation, including cooperation in the struggle against war and tyranny:

> Let us never fear to negotiate. Let both sides explore what problems unite us instead of belaboring those problems which divide us. Let both sides, for the first time, formulate serious and precise proposals for the inspection and control of arms, and bring the absolute power to destroy other nations under the absolute control of all nations. . . . Let both sides join in creating . . . a new world of law . . .[waging] a struggle against the common enemies of man: tyranny . . . and war itself.

His was the last presidential inaugural to include a direct reference to the United Nations. He also issued a grim warning about the stakes in the global cold war. "Man holds in his mortal hands the power to abolish . . . all forms of human life," he said. Questioned on this afterward, my researcher assured me that it was literally true, that one thermonuclear bomb contained more destructive power than all that had been released from all weapons fired in all wars in history. In short, the speech reflected not only Kennedy's views, but our shared opposition to war.

The power of his delivery and words was enhanced by the setting, the dazzling combination of bright sunshine and deep snow, which had fallen throughout the previous day. Troops were mobilized to remove it. When the telephone rang in the office of the overworked Council of Economic Advisors, James Tobin told his comembers, "Don't pick it up. It's probably Sorensen asking us to shovel snow."

But enough volunteers and District of Columbia personnel had shoveled snow to enable all of us to get to the Capitol steps. I sat high above the back of the podium with my sister, tense, thrilled, excited but anxious as his words initially met with silence from the crowd assembled below. Was it to be a flop after all? Not until one-third or more of the speech had been delivered did the first round of applause begin. Then came more, then more; and I relaxed. For three and a half years and more, JFK and I had traversed the fifty states in anticipation of this moment. Some dignitaries later complained that they had been given obscure seats from which they could only see JFK's back while he spoke. I was accustomed to watching him from behind, as I would continue to do in the next thousand days.

The speech had undergone considerable revision. In an earlier draft, the "torch" that was passed was "the torch of liberty," but the word "liberty" was removed, then it was restored when to "assure the survival and success of freedom" was changed to "assure the survival and success of liberty." "A host of joint ventures," which Ken Galbraith rightly noted sounded like a mining company, was changed to "a host of cooperative ventures." "We shall join to *prevent* aggression . . . in the Americas" was modified to the more realistic "join . . . to *oppose* aggression . . . in the Americas." Regarding the United Nations, my draft pledge "to make it more than a forum for invective" was improved to state more positively a pledge "to prevent it from becoming merely a forum for invective." No nation or leader was referred to as an enemy. "Those nations who make themselves our enemy" had been changed a few days earlier, at columnist

Walter Lippmann's suggestion, to "those nations who would make themselves our adversary."

Traces of some themes in the inaugural can be found in themes evoked by my father many years earlier, which I may well have heard from him more than once. In 1934 my father deplored the "poverty, misery and disease facing large masses of people" around the world. In 1961 JFK deplored "the common enemies of man: tyranny, poverty, disease and war itself." C. A. Sorensen had said that "The years have taught me patience. I no longer complain if things go slowly. God did not make a tree in a day; it took Him millions of years. . . . So what if it does take a century to accomplish a reform. If we are on the right road, it matters not that the road is long. . . ." Those words, written by C.A. the year before I was born, foreshadowed JFK: "all this will not be finished in the first 100 days . . . nor even perhaps in our lifetime on this planet—but let us begin."

Not all the inaugural lines soared. "If a beachhead of cooperation may push back the jungle of suspicion . . ." is a metaphorical stretch. "That uncertain balance of terror that stays the hand of mankind's final war" sounds more profound when spoken than when read. Conversely, one line, which received comparatively little attention, was a more important statement of his administration's intent than all those that received more publicity and acclaim. That line was: "Only when our arms are sufficient beyond doubt can we be certain beyond doubt that they will never be employed." That was the Kennedy approach to war and peace. If we were sufficiently well armed, we need not attack others and they were unlikely to attack us.

The most famous line in John F. Kennedy's inaugural address was: "Ask not what your country can do for you; ask what you can do for your country." It reflected his long belief in public service, his mother's teaching that every citizen should give something back, and his campaign theme that an American citizen's obligation in a time of national trial was to assist and serve his fellow citizens. It resonated with liberals who shared Kennedy's belief in public service, and with conservatives who were weary of government handouts.

Many researchers alleged that this line was drawn from Oliver Wendell Holmes or Warren G. Harding. Others have attributed similar phrases to King George VI in his broadcast to British troops on the invasion of Europe in World War II; to Calvin Coolidge's autobiography; to a freshman fraternity pledge at the University of Texas in the 1950s; to a line in a Robert Browning poem; to a Harvard student essay in the early twentieth century; and to a Pasadena Junior High School graduation speech in 1951. The most improbable question came from followers of the Lebanese philosopher and poet Khalil Gibran. They insisted that he had used a similar phrase in a 1925 article, coincidentally entitled "The New Frontier." The Khalil Gibran Society telephoned and wrote me asking whether either Kennedy or I had read the piece, even though it had not been translated into English by January 20, 1961. Did either of us read Arabic or any of the Middle Eastern languages in which it had appeared? I was asked. No, we did not.

The most credible theory stated that Kennedy, having attended high school at Choate Academy, class of 1935, may have heard Headmaster George St. John remind his students at chapel that what mattered most was selfless service, "not what Choate can do for you but what you can do for Choate." Unfortunately, even the Choate archivist has no evidence that Mr. St. John ever said those words, and Mr. St. John's son Seymour has said that, although his father "did use the thought many a time, I do not recall any occasion on which he used the precise words; and none of the alumni can come up with a time and place when he did."

I do not doubt that all those cited said or wrote something similar, if not identical, to Kennedy's line, but I have no reason to believe that either Kennedy or I had read any of those possible predecessors before the line was inserted into one of the early drafts of his inaugural. The truth is that I simply don't remember where the line came from. Inasmuch as I tend to remember best that which I discuss most frequently, my inability to recall that line's provenance may be due to the fact that I have kept my silence all these years on that subject. As one former congressman wrote me, "sometimes mystery makes for better history than clarity." Having no satisfactory answer, I long ago started answering the oft-repeated question as to its authorship with the smiling retort: "Ask not." Certainly the line reflected JFK's lifelong philosophy, calling for sacrifice and dedication for the good of the country, emphasized by his own life of service—that makes it his line.

The president enjoyed the responses to the speech that poured in from schoolchildren, a sampling of which he read. More than one asked him what they could do for the country. A White House assistant replied to one eleven-year-old: "Study hard and obey all the rules, both at home and in school." The most touching to me among the many reports of the Kennedy line's adaptation over the years was that of the eight-year-old son of friends whose class was asked decades after the speech to define "friendship." He answered: "You should not ask what your friend can do for you, you should ask what you can do for your friend." JFK would have been proud.

The president was even willing to poke fun at his own speech. RFK cautioned against it, saying the inaugural had achieved a "sacrosanct" status in American culture; but JFK and I enjoyed the following parody for a Democratic National Committee fund-raising dinner, exactly one year after the inaugural:

We observe tonight not a celebration of freedom but a victory of party . . . For we are sworn to pay off the same party debt our forebears ran up nearly a year and three months ago. But let every Republican know, whether he wishes us well or ill, that we shall pay any price, bear any burden, meet any hardship, support any friend, oppose any foe to assure the survival and success of our party . . . Our deficit will not be paid off in the next 100 days. Nor will it be paid off in the first 1000 days, nor in the life of this Administration, nor even perhaps in our lifetime on this planet. But let us begin—remembering that generosity is not a sign of weakness and that ambassadors are always subject to Senate confirmation. For if the Democratic Party cannot be helped by the many who are poor, it cannot be saved by the few who are rich. In your hands, my fellow Democrats, more than mine, will rest the final success or failure of our course. Since this party was founded, each generation of Democrats has been summoned to give money to its national treasury. Now the Chairman summons us again. Not as a call to cast votes, though votes we need—not as a call to man the polls, though polls we are taking—but a call to bear the financial burden of a long political struggle, year in and year out, a struggle against the common enemies of all Democrats—Miller, Goldwater, Rockefeller and Nixon himself. Can we forge against these enemies a united and prosperous party, north and south, east and west? Will you join in that pecuniary effort? . . . The checks, the cash, the notes which we bring to this endeavor will light our party and all who serve it—and the smoke from that fire can truly smother the Republicans.

And so, my fellow Democrats: ask not what your party can give to you—ask what you can give to your party. Let us never contribute to our own decline; but let us never decline a contribution.

To those few of us who know the Kennedy inaugural by heart, that's funny.

Two excellent books in 2005, Thurston Clarke's *Ask Not* and Dick Tofel's *Sounding the Trumpet*, were devoted largely to the question of who had written the speech and where particular words and phrases came from. The authors of both books did exhaustive research, finding facts and files of which I was previously unaware or had long forgotten, and interviewing me at length. It was a special speech, I told them, which both JFK and I approached with painstaking care; but the process of composition and collaboration was not strikingly different from that which we had employed during the previous seven or more years and continued to employ during the three years that followed.

Clarke and Tofel concluded, from their separate research, that the speech was a collaboration between Kennedy and me, drawing upon suggestions solicited and offered from Adlai Stevenson, Ken Galbraith, and others, and upon themes and lines repeatedly used during the long presidential campaign, as well as the "Farewell to Massachusetts." They differed slightly in awarding "principal" credit, Clarke emphasizing JFK's role, and Tofel emphasizing mine. The question of the proportion of our respective contributions is confused by the fact that much of JFK's first dictation was based upon my early draft, and that portions of my early drafts were based upon his earlier campaign speeches, which were themselves most often works of collaboration between us, some of which drew from ideas and phrases from a variety of historical statesmen and writers.

The question of ultimate credit is thus obscure, as it

should be. I do know that no handwritten original will ever be found. After discussing with Jackie the conflict between JFK's rightful place in history as the true author of that speech and history's demand for every document, including those that can be misunderstood or distorted, I destroyed my handwritten first draft upon completing my book *Kennedy.* How closely did my destroyed draft resemble the final product that he revised many times? If I checked that question then, I do not remember now. One of the 2005 books, *Ask Not*, concludes, after an extensive search: "The original of the Sorensen Draft has apparently been lost." So be it. It is far less important who wrote those words than that those principles live on.

Chapter 19

President Kennedy's Ministry of Talent

Shortly after the inauguration, I attended a group swearing-in ceremony for presidential advisors and appointees throughout the administration. As I looked around, I was amazed to see in one room so many scholars, civic leaders, former government officials, and leading intellectual activists with whom I had so often been in touch over the previous four years. Truly, as JFK had pledged during the campaign, his was a "ministry of talent."

I had no formal role in their selection or recruitment, that task having been entrusted to a panel led by Sargent Shriver and Larry O'Brien. I sent two memos to Larry: one consisting largely of my own lists of suggested names, the other a list of criteria and "problems to look out for: conflicts of interest, compatibility with JFK program . . . problems of Senate confirmation or party factionalism, geographic balance and a variety of clearances." I also reminded him "not to overlook able men already in government service . . . and the use of patronage as a tool for obtaining passage of the President's program during the first year." I'm sure Larry was well aware of all those points without my reminders.

In selecting his team, Kennedy held no political grudges. Among his competitors for the Democratic presidential nomination, he brought in Lyndon Johnson initially, then Adlai Stevenson (and such Stevenson supporters as Dean Rusk), Stuart Symington's son, and some of Hubert Humphrey's principal aides and supporters. One historian badly missed the mark when he described the team as "a league of factions." Those originally committed to Johnson, Humphrey, or Stevenson all demonstrated allegiance primarily to JFK; they all took instructions from him and his top advisors; and I know of no effort by any of them to change the Kennedy team's policies.

Further proof of the quality of JFK's selections may be found in the roles they pursued after they left public service. While space does not permit a fuller encomium, many extraordinary men with whom I served in the Kennedy administration went on to further national esteem: Mac Bundy became president of the Ford Foundation; his deputy at NSC, Carl Kaysen, became director of the Institute for Advanced Study; Dave Bell became head of Harvard's School of Public Health, Jerome Wiesner became president of MIT; Freeman, Dillon, and Udall led private organizations; Arthur Schlesinger, both prior to and following his public service, was America's foremost historian; Pierre Salinger had a long career in television and the news media; and the vice president's top assistant, Bill Moyers, remains today America's most thoughtful commentator on public affairs.

Not one of his top appointees, except of course his brother, came from his own past in Boston, Harvard, the Navy, or his father's business associates. When bitter partisan acrimony followed the election via the Supreme Court of George W. Bush in 2000, one of Richard Nixon's top aides, Herb Klein, asked me to refresh his memory on how Kennedy had reached out to Republicans to unify the country after his extremely narrow win in 1960. I reminded him that Kennedy had gone to see Nixon to bury any ill feelings, and that Kennedy had appointed many prominent Republicans to top posts, including Douglas Dillon as secretary of the treasury, Robert McNamara as secretary of defense, and McGeorge Bundy as national security advisor.

For director of the United States Information Agency, he selected the country's most outstanding, if controversial, broadcaster, Edward R. Murrow of CBS. For his deputy director for policy and plans, Murrow selected my brother Tom. Tom was not yet thirty-six; and he expressed concern to Murrow that critics both inside and outside the agency might charge nepotism, saying that he had been jumped over those with more seniority because of his relationship with the president's special counsel. "I'll just tell them," Murrow replied, "I want Tom Sorensen for his qualities and his experience in his years with this agency—I would have appointed him to this job even if he were my own brother." JFK was happy with Murrow's choice. He had first met Tom in the mid-fifties, when as senator he asked my brother for a briefing on the politics of the Middle East. After the meeting, Tom said to me: "Looks like you've got a future president on your hands." Neither he nor JFK ever forgot that brief meeting. When I was in the White House, it was wonderful to have Tom nearby, providing ideas and advice for some speeches, including JFK's memorable address at the University of Washington, where he observed, as no other president ever has, the limits of American power in a world we did not, could not, and should not control.

My sister Ruth also contributed from time to time. Convinced that *Time* magazine had treated him more harshly in his first year in the White House than it had his predecessor, JFK asked me to undertake a comparative content analysis. I delegated this assignment to Ruth, who was living in Washington at the time. She found that indeed there were more negative stories on JFK's first year than Ike's. The president used her report in an Oval Office meeting with the magazine's publisher Henry Luce, an old Kennedy family friend. When I invited Ruth to join me at a White House reception for the Supreme Court months later, I introduced her to the president in the receiving line and he immediately replied with his typical charm: "Ruth, of course. What a great piece of work you did for me on that blasted magazine." And she immediately fell in love with him all over again.

The Sorensen siblings were not the only Nebraskans helping the administration. There was my deputy and former law school classmate Lee White; Evelyn Lincoln, Kennedy's longtime personal secretary, was the daughter of John Norton, a progressive Democratic Nebraska congressman who had been associated with my father.

In the East Wing, Jackie's superb social secretary, Tish Baldrige, was another Nebraskan. One evening in 1961, running late for a dinner with the Nebraska Chamber of Commerce, I asked the president's permission to be excused from a meeting. "Go ahead," he said, "we can't do any worse there anyway." He often teased me about my Nebraska roots, chiding me once during the 1960 campaign for coming not from a big urban state that could bring in more electoral votes but from a small agricultural state when I knew nothing about agriculture.

The small Kennedy staff was exceptional, as were his cabinet and sub-cabinet choices, who encountered little opposition to their confirmation in the Senate. At Labor Secretary Arthur Goldberg's brunch for the entire cabinet on the Sunday before the inauguration, I saluted them with the kind of doggerel to which my family is accustomed:

> All hail the men of new frontiers—
>   The hardy Kennedy pioneers.
>   The Georgia cracker known as Rusk.
>   The courtly Hodges, never brusque.
>   Orville Freeman, farmers' friend.
>   To Stuart Udall, a sleeping bag lend.
>   Send racy books to Edward Day.

Send lazy crooks to Bobby K.
Take health needs to Abe Ribicoff.
Blame Dillon if your checkbook's off.
McNamara's Ford is in his past.
Art Goldberg, not least, though mentioned last.

It was an administration uniformly characterized by high ideals, dedication, and integrity, an era of altruistic governance that now appears to be gone forever. Not every decision the team made was brilliant; not every action was universally admired. But no high-level Kennedy appointee was indicted for flouting the law, accepting a bribe, or lying to Congress or a grand jury; none was eased out for legal reasons or scandals. Why was the Kennedy team different? Because the president was different—because his standards were different.

A president's team reflects his character. Kennedy was honest—and he insisted that all members of his team be honest as well. When he discovered that three able and respected appointees were federal income tax evaders, he evidenced no self-righteous anger, and made no public show at their expense. He simply took quiet action to prevent one from attaining the high White House post he had been promised, and accepted quiet letters of resignation on "personal grounds" from the other two.

Of these, the saddest case was ironically one of the

most gifted and honorable men in the administration, James M. Landis, a former dean of Harvard Law School, who had been a top FDR appointee and was a close friend and business associate of President Kennedy's father. Appointed to oversee the reorganization of the powerful independent regulatory agencies, Landis had long encountered a number of problems related in part to age and alcohol. He had agreed to take his post as "Dean of the Regulators" on a six-month basis only; but JFK declined to accept his resignation letter when it arrived in July 1961. The following month, when Landis became involved in his secretary's divorce as a result of some flirtatious poems he had written her, Kennedy accepted the earlier letter of resignation. Two years later, Landis pleaded guilty to tax evasion, having simply failed to file any returns between 1956 and 1960. The Kennedys had earlier received some indication of this, and successfully urged him to pay substantial back taxes, but the IRS then calculated that amount to be insufficient. Neither the president nor the attorney general tried to protect him from indictment or his sentence of thirty days in prison, followed by a one-year probation. Nine months later, he was suspended from the practice of law, and shortly thereafter died in his swimming pool. The authorities termed it an accident, with signs of a heart attack while swimming. But when we learned that his body reportedly had a high blood-alcohol content, RFK and I wondered whether that finding was accurate. Either way, it was a tragic story of a brilliant man.

JFK regarded Defense Secretary Robert McNamara as the star of his team, calling upon him for advice on a wide range of issues beyond national security, including business and economic matters. He liked McNamara and his crisp, authoritative, no-nonsense style. Kennedy and I both observed this when during the 1961 Berlin crisis, the president convened a smaller private meeting to hear the pros and cons of declaring a national emergency. Walter Heller, Douglas Dillon, and I attended, along with the secretaries of state and defense and the national security advisor. After hearing warnings about the harsh signal his decision would send to both anxious allies and the Soviets, and the implications of emergency powers in a free market, JFK called upon McNamara, who extemporaneously presented a brilliant, logical, clear-cut argument in favor of an emergency declaration, speaking in well-structured paragraphs supported by facts. After the president decided against the declaration, we all filed into the Cabinet Room for the formal meeting of the NSC, and the president called upon the secretary of defense to open the discussion. McNamara then proceeded to deliver, again without notes, a brilliant, logical, clear-cut argument *against* the issuance of an emergency order. I was impressed.

President Kennedy was less satisfied with his secretary of state, Dean Rusk. The courtly Georgian, who stuck to his stiff, formal manner even when dealing with a young president who was anything but formal, at one time expressed pride in the fact that he was the only cabinet member whom the president did not address by his first name (not an honor, in my opinion). Always loyal and thoughtful, Rusk served Kennedy faithfully, but was not in fact the number one foreign policy maker. John F. Kennedy, more than any president since FDR, was his own secretary of state, having traveled extensively abroad in his youth, served in the South Pacific during World War II and as a member of the Senate Foreign Relations Committee, and studied and written about diplomatic history and foreign affairs. Kennedy was more prepared to lead in foreign policy and national security matters than most of his successors, possibly excepting the first President Bush.

Rusk not unhappily left the reins of foreign policy decision-making in the president's hands, but was sometimes uncomfortable with the number of White House staff participating in some advisory sessions. According to one legendary report, Secretary Rusk, in one such session, looking around the table at Bundy,

Carl Kaysen (Bundy's deputy), and me, told the president in response to a sensitive question, "There are too many people in the room for me to answer." Kennedy excused Kaysen and me and repeated his question—Rusk repeated his answer. Kennedy asked Bundy to leave and again repeated the question, inasmuch as he and Rusk were then alone. According to the apocryphal report, Rusk gave the same answer.

Although the Kennedy administration was largely an exception to the general rule of mutual distrust between the Department of State and the National Security Council staff, Rusk defended himself from criticism that he mistakenly believed was leaked by the Bundy team. The State Department was inherently more cautious than any president would like, Rusk observed, because the department was obligated to take into account the views of dozens of foreign governments as well as international law, international organizations, and American congressional and public opinion. He knew that the resultant bland product did not satisfy the White House. Not liking the message, Rusk said, they shoot the messenger.

But it was not the White House staff that said the State Department was "like a bowl of jelly," or that it "never comes up with any new ideas." Those were John F. Kennedy's words. Today, after reading Schlesinger's books, RFK's oral history transcript, and material more recently drawn from the Oval Office tape recording system transcripts, I am not as certain as I was at the time of my earlier book, *Kennedy*, that JFK would have kept Rusk as secretary of state in a second term. More than one White House tape revealed the president's impatience with Rusk, even when praising other State Department officials. Nor did JFK or RFK believe that Rusk himself was as thoroughly prepared for emergency meetings and crises as he should have been. JFK felt that, unlike the work of his National Security Council, too much of the State Department's output was unimaginative, unwieldy, imprecise, and not the kind of innovative, sharp, concrete proposals and conclusions that he wanted. In the second term, he might well have placed George Ball or McGeorge Bundy in Rusk's position.

The president's dismay with Rusk's department became clear in the summer of our first year in the White House, when the department spent what seemed like endless weeks preparing a reply to a crucial Soviet aide-mémoire on Berlin, and produced a draft consisting of nothing but decade-old clichés for which it still had not obtained clearance from either the French or the Germans. JFK decided to make a start, early in 1961, by removing Undersecretary of State Chester Bowles.

But when Chet was about to be moved out, he leaked it to the press to generate opposition, and the president suspended the move. The next time Chet's ouster was anticipated, JFK informed only Rusk, RFK, and me. After Secretary Rusk delivered the president's decision, he reported to the president that Bowles was threatening to resign in protest. I had just accompanied the president to Hyannis Port for Thanksgiving, but he sent me back to Washington on Air Force One, which was returning Khrushchev's son-in-law, Aleksei Adzhubei, to his plane. My assignment was to persuade Chet not to cause a storm. En route I kidded Aleksei, noting that he was now in the hands of the U.S. Air Force. "I know they will not deliberately crash the plane with Kennedy's assistant aboard," he replied.

Chet and I, liberal ideological soul mates, talked for hours in his office about his complaints, the new role we were creating for him, and its perquisites. The clincher came when I answered affirmatively to his last plaintive request: "Will I have a White House car? You're dead in this town if you show up in a taxi." When I reported to JFK on the success of the meeting, he replied: "Ted, that's your best work since the Michigan delegation!"—an inside joke that he would repeat whenever I did something well.

The Bowles move, however, did not solve the problem at the State Department. A number of personnel changes were still being discussed in the following two years—the possibility of shifting State Department sub-cabinet officials to new positions, sending someone from the White House to shake up the bureaucracy, or some-one from RFK's Justice Department, or even Bobby himself on a temporary basis—though RFK did not want to sink into that swamp, leaving behind his crucial duties as attorney general.

My participation in the Cuban missile crisis—at the president's direct invitation—led him to ask me, for the first time, for advice on his State Department personnel concerns. I titled my memo, dated February 12, 1963, "Overnight Observations," indicating that he had asked for my thoughts on the previous day, but also noting that I was no expert on the department's problems. I wrote that the department needed in a new chief three qualities: "solid judgment attuned to your own, imaginative ideas and initiative . . . and a tough, efficient capacity for administration and organization," adding a warning that it would be a great mistake "to make a change which increased the proportion of any one of these factors while decreasing the other two." (On re-reading this warning, I cannot remember whether it was inserted as a possible defense of Rusk.)

My memo offered possible names for addition to the

department, assuming he was talking about the number two spot—an indication that he had asked for my thoughts on the possibility of keeping Rusk but inserting new blood at a high level. I presented the advantages and disadvantages of filling the post with RFK, Bundy, or Dave Bell, who had only recently been moved from the Bureau of the Budget to head the Agency for International Development. My fourth recommendation was Clark Clifford (whom LBJ would later make secretary of defense); and behind him I listed Averell Harriman, who had already been slotted for advancement to the number three spot in the department. I also advised the president that, unless the right person was available to assure "certain improvement, it would be better to keep the present leadership team . . . and [start] to lay the groundwork for a wholesale change in January 1965."

Although I had no hint of it at the time, I learned only a few years ago that, shortly before my February memorandum, my own name was mentioned as part of these discussions. In 2001 a presidential historian brought me the transcript of an Oval Office conversation on November 5, 1962, soon after the Cuban missile crisis, in which the president contemplated moving National Security Advisor Bundy to the State Department, and making me national security advisor. "Number one," said JFK, "put Sorensen in Bundy's place; put Feldman in Sorensen's place as Counsel . . . Sorensen and Bundy are equally good." Even in the historian's presence, nearly four decades after that colloquy occurred, I was moved almost to tears by that vote of confidence from the grave.

In the course of writing this book, more facts about my possible move to the NSC became clear. In a 1970 interview with author Ralph Martin, Kenny O'Donnell explained what happened:

He [JFK] wanted Sorensen to take over Bundy's job. . . . And so he called me in one day, ruminating, more than anything else, and said, "What do you think about Bundy? Bobby thinks it might be a good idea for Bundy to go over and be Under-Secretary of State. He's a good administrator, knows how to handle it; and then Rusk can do the things he does very well—and we'd move Sorensen over to take Bundy's job." I said, "Mr. President, I'll give you two reasons why I think this is a disaster: No. 1, he's not qualified; No. 2, Sorensen is a conscientious objector. If I'm against you, I call him a draft-dodger; if I'm for you, I call him a conscientious objector. But if I'm Barry Goldwater and one kid gets killed, we might have to invade Cuba tomorrow morning. We might have a war in Berlin, or might have to go into Vietnam. And if I were your enemy, I'd say the fellow who gave you the advice, refused to go himself." . . . I said, "Politically, this is the most disastrous thing in the world. I would resent it myself: that the guy who said 'Invade Cuba' is a guy who himself would not invade Cuba . . . I know Barry Goldwater . . . he'd just tear your guts out with it . . ." [Kennedy] said, "I never thought of that. You're absolutely right," and that was the end of the move.

Had I been present, I might have protested that I had already displayed some foreign policy judgment in advising the president on Berlin, Vietnam, and especially the Cuban missile crisis; and that there might have been advantages, during those tense cold war years, to have a national security advisor who had displayed a strong moral compass almost sixteen years earlier. Even though I was disappointed to read Kenny's comments, I knew he had a point.

It was not until I read similar comments by Kenny when I researched this book, and reviewed them with my old friend and deputy Mike Feldman, that I realized the extent of Kenny's hostility toward me. Mike said Kenny's ill-will toward me was well-known in the Kennedy White House—well-known to everyone but me. "In the White House," said Ralph Dungan, my deputy for a few years in JFK's Senate office, "O'Donnell, in a political situation, would have the power to just cut [Sorensen] right out, and did . . ." I doubt that.

Recently, I learned that it was Kenny who brought to President Kennedy's attention in late 1961 the fact that Dick Goodwin was discontented working for me. Once the president became aware of this, Dick met with him and told him, as the president informed me afterward, that he could not "work well" with me and preferred to work directly for JFK, and later for the State Department and Peace Corps (the creation of which, ironically, Kenny had fiercely opposed as a "kooky, liberal idea . . ." that made him sick). In Dick's view, Kenny raised Dick's discomfort with JFK to do me some "minor damage." All this causes me to wonder whether domestic politics was the only reason Kenny advised the president not to appoint me national security advisor.

Kenny's hostility hurts and even surprises me, particularly in view of the wonderful comments about me I discovered at the same time in the taped recollections of Robert F. Kennedy, O'Donnell's hero. I had always considered Kenny a friend. Even now, I do not know what I did to offend him. Was it my reticent reserve or inability to schmooze? Was it because I was an outsider among the Irish-Catholic politicians from Massachusetts who thought they had a proprietary stake in Kennedy's candidacy and presidency? Was it because Kenny, having served in our armed forces, strongly disapproved of my registration for noncombat service? Was it because, as Dick Goodwin wrote, Kenny regarded me as a "less stalwart loyalist" than himself? I'll never know. Back in the Senate days, JFK taught me that the best way to stop a supposed friend from privately badmouthing you is to "let him know you know." Now it's too late.

The White House, by its very nature, invites factions and dissension. Those located in the East Wing envy those in the West Wing adjoining the president's office; and those located across the street in the Executive Office Building envy those in the West Wing, just as those in the basement envy those on the main floor. Some have perks that others do not—White House mess privileges; the use of White House cars with military drivers; seats on Air Force One when the president travels; attendance at meetings of the cabinet, National Security Council, and other formal bodies; a place on the distribution list of the CIA morning briefing paper; assistants and deputies of their own; an assigned stenographer or secretary; and a large office. Fortunate enough to have been granted all those perks, I had no reason to complain. I never did, but neither did I hear of complaints from others, especially about me.

My relations with my White House colleagues always seemed friendly and harmonious. It was not a White House wholly free from professional jealousy, personal differences, and occasional competition for either turf or the president's ear. Not everybody on the White House staff liked, much less socialized with, everybody else. But I can honestly say that, at the time, I knew of no personal feuds within the Kennedy White House; the fact that JFK made no mention to me of any feuds or resentments except Dick's leads me to believe that he also knew of none.

During my White House years, the only division I could have cited was the press-created division between the Professors (Heller, Wiesner, Bundy, Schlesinger, and me) and the Politicians (O'Donnell, O'Brien, Salinger, and Dungan). Social and recreational activities after hours—of which there were few—were likely to be confined to one group or the other. On the day of the inauguration, *Time* magazine reported: "A current Washington parlor game is guessing about when the close-knit Kennedy team will split in a struggle for influence between Top Aide Ted Sorensen's idea men and Patronage Adviser Kenny O'Donnell's professional politicians." Back then, I thought this division was insignificant. I was wrong. It turns out that my old friend Ralph Dungan also had resentments, dating back to the days when we worked together in the Senate, which he detailed in his 1964 oral history for the Kennedy Archives:

> Not a very pleasant working experience for the second guy . . . a great difficulty of having any kind of a direct relationship with John Kennedy . . . Ted's oppressive personality became more pronounced as time went on . . . his sharpness of manner, his brusqueness, impolite, not the warmest human being . . . If anything impaired his relationship with the principal, Sorensen would pitch anybody over. . . . Sorensen's great mistake as a human being is that he pitched over everything [for] John Kennedy . . . He screwed up his own personal life. . . . The lubricants of the Senate are these fuzzy talk-talk relationships . . . and Sorensen had a very low tolerance for that kind of palaver; the Senator did too.

I have since read enough about my "arrogant abruptness" in those days to know that the charge must have some truth to it. I am not totally astonished to learn about other complaints. Both in the Senate and later, some of my subordinates felt—as Dick Goodwin did—that I did not share with them either my access to JFK or the more important assignments that he gave me, or that I did not use their proposals and speech drafts often enough. No doubt, had I done so, that would have improved team morale and harmony. But these were basically JFK's decisions; he wanted me to perform the tasks he gave me.

Hopefully, I've learned my lesson. I schmooze more now with friends, and I like it. I regret that I did not discover it in my youth, when my abruptness appeared antisocial, offending some and unnecessarily earning enemies.

Chapter 20

My Relations with Vice President Lyndon Johnson

In the Senate, Kennedy had a realistic view of LBJ, sizing him up as a man of enormous ambition, vanity, and appetites, but also Washington political skills— skills that JFK knew he could not match. He also felt in 1960 that Johnson possessed qualities—including a mental toughness—that the White House required and others lacked, even telling Newton Minow, a confidant and later appointee, that of all his competitors for the nomination, Johnson would make the best president: "He's a son of a bitch, but he's got talent."

Back when JFK was first elected to the Senate in November 1952, he had received a congratulatory message from LBJ, who noted that the Senate Democratic leader (Ernest McFarland of Arizona) was losing that same night, that he (LBJ) had an opportunity to be the new party leader in the Senate, and that he wanted JFK's pledge of support. JFK, after his long and intensive election campaign, had other priorities—getting some rest, thanking his team, preparing his program, and selecting his staff. Nearly four years later, having forgotten about the message, JFK was privately amused when—as he and I rode on LBJ's Senate reelection campaign plane in Texas in the autumn of 1956—Johnson scolded Kennedy for not having answered his message. JFK thought that incident was particularly revealing of LBJ's priorities and personality (I didn't think at the time that it was all that meaningful).

JFK and I shared a somewhat sardonic view of the majority leader, as reflected in my letter to JFK of September 12, 1955: "Lyndon Johnson has finally come through, making up for his failure to appoint you to the Foreign Relations and Finance Committees. He has recommended that you be appointed to the Boston National Historic Sites Commission!" Our doubts were reciprocated. We heard that LBJ regarded JFK as a young whippersnapper who had not been a star member of the Senate insiders club, but had instead built his status merely on his books and many articles.

By the time LBJ neared a declaration of his presidential candidacy, JFK and I had toured fifty states between 1956 and 1959. We laughed at LBJ's repeated announcements that his presidential campaign was gaining strength through the endorsements he obtained from various Democratic senators, whom we knew did not control their respective states' national convention delegations. Later, we were given reasons to distrust him. Not only was LBJ, through his staff, the first to make mean-spirited charges at the 1960 convention about JFK's health, but we also heard, during the post-convention campaign—when he was supposedly JFK's loyal running mate—that LBJ had continued to talk privately about Kennedy's Addison's disease rumors. Could that have been true?

JFK's selection of LBJ as his running mate was not wholly surprising to me. Johnson had the precise biography that a young, relatively inexperienced Northeastern Catholic liberal needed to balance the Democratic ticket. Kennedy, somewhat left of center, regarded LBJ as somewhat right of center on many issues and a bridge to the Democratic Southerners, conservatives, and moderates whose support he knew he would ultimately need in the election and might otherwise have difficulty obtaining.

In June 1960, a few weeks before the convention, I reported that Johnson's closest associate, Bobby Baker, had taken me aside after a dinner at Joe Alsop's to confide, undoubtedly on instructions from LBJ, that the latter was now coming around to the idea that he would accept nomination for second place if he did not win first place. Years later, LBJ told RFK and me, at our 1968 reconciliation meeting in the White House, that he had been reluctant to be vice president and would rather have remained majority leader, "the best job I ever had," but that Sam Rayburn and Phil Graham had persuaded him to accept the nomination, knowing that otherwise JFK could not carry the South and Nixon would win.

In a confidential memorandum to JFK and RFK one week before the 1960 convention, I put Johnson at the top of my list of possible contenders for the vice presidential slot, noting that he "helps with the farmers, Southerners and Texas; easier to work with in this position than as Majority Leader"—where JFK said Johnson "would be just impossible . . . Lyndon would screw me all the time." Others on my list were Adlai Stevenson, "on the basis that as Vice President he would be a sort of First Secretary"; Hubert Humphrey, on the basis that he "helps with the Negroes and farmers"; Ralph Yarborough, LBJ's liberal seatmate from Texas, who I noted was "a Southerner liked by the liberals—

good civil rights and agriculture record, would help carry Texas"; Senator Claire Engle of California, on the grounds that he "would help carry California"; and Missouri senator Stuart Symington (who, like Johnson, Stevenson, and Humphrey, had initially contested for the nomination, if not vigorously), on the grounds that he "is a national figure, and would help with farmers."

I then added men who "should be considered, but [are] handicapped by being young . . . like JFK (we don't want the ticket referred to as the Whiz Kids, etc.)," including Orville Freeman, governor of Minnesota, who was "good on agriculture and civil rights"; and "Scoop" Jackson, my onetime prospective employer, who, my memo said, "has acquired stature through his inquiry on national security." Governors Docking of Kansas and Loveless of Iowa also made my list. Both had received from our camp hints of being considered in order to woo their delegations. But I identified them as "conservative, inarticulate, and reportedly sometimes ill-tempered." Neither was a serious possibility. Clearly Johnson made the most sense on that list.

Some historians have speculated that JFK's offer of second place on his ticket to LBJ was insincere, arguing that JFK knew Johnson would prefer to remain majority leader in the Senate and therefore would decline. I disagree. In my view, JFK's decision to offer the vice presidential nomination to Johnson was genuine, based on his judgment that Johnson would do the most for the ticket (for all the reasons I had enumerated in my memo), especially in the South. Much has been written about RFK's subsequent visit to LBJ, in which RFK attempted to rescind JFK's offer. Being wholly preoccupied at the time with my other convention duties, I had no role in this episode. I have always assumed that RFK was not instructed by JFK to rescind the offer. It seems more likely to me that, when RFK informed his brother that there was opposition to the choice of LBJ from labor, liberals, and others, JFK may have said something like, "Well, go see Lyndon. Nothing's official yet. Maybe he'll change his mind." It would have been typical of JFK to give that sort of casual, noncommittal assignment. Whether RFK went beyond his brother's intentions, I cannot know—though I would not be surprised to learn that he did so to advance what he believed were JFK's best interests.

In any event, Johnson's selection was consequential. JFK would not have carried Texas or any other Southern state without LBJ on the ticket, and thus would not have been elected president. More important perhaps is the fact that Johnson, whatever his limitations, succeeded Kennedy in the presidency and proved to be a strong president in securing the passage and implementation of Kennedy's pending legislative program, especially civil rights.

Neither in campaigning nor in governing did JFK and LBJ make many joint appearances. When they did, they were an odd couple—the slender, boyish Bostonian in the tailored suit, and the rangy, oversized Texan in his cowboy boots; the reserved, dignified, and scholarly Kennedy, and the rough-hewn and ebullient Johnson.

JFK knew that the vice presidency in the 1960s could be a frustrating, virtually powerless job at best—which is why he had preferred to seek the presidency in 1960 at a time when the vice presidential nomination could easily have been his without a struggle. As vice president, LBJ did not have the power of a Dick Cheney, or even the influence and access of a Walter Mondale or Al Gore. A month after JFK's death, Johnson, then the new president, told me one evening, "Your man treated me well—better than I would have treated him if our positions were reversed." He would prove this later by the way he treated his vice president, Hubert Humphrey. Yet in supporting Hubert for the Democratic nomination to succeed him in 1968, Johnson remarked to his cabinet that "Hubert has been a triple A Vice President, while I had been only about B+." JFK would have thought there was a little grade inflation in that comment.

Kennedy made a point of inviting his vice president to

all the formal meetings he periodically held—including meetings of the cabinet and National Security Council, the weekly breakfast with legislative leaders, and the breakfast preceding each biweekly presidential press conference, although formal meetings were often less important in the Kennedy White House than small informal sessions, where LBJ was not often present. The president also took the vice president with him to major Democratic Party events in Washington and elsewhere, consistently referring to the work of the Kennedy-Johnson administration. But, in general, Lyndon rarely offered advice and was not frequently consulted by the president before major decisions were made.

How far JFK went to keep the vice president fully informed, I do not know. I believe that National Security Advisor Bundy took pains to brief him regularly; I did rarely. JFK was frustrated and irritated by his inability to induce Johnson to make a recommendation or even a comment on issues that arose at policy meetings. "What do you think, Mr. Vice President?" he would ask. "Well, I don't know enough about that to express an opinion," LBJ would invariably reply. We knew he wasn't being modest; LBJ was not a modest man. That was his way of registering an unsubtle complaint that he was not being kept sufficiently informed, even on legislative matters; and JFK resented it. Kennedy had hoped that Johnson, as vice president, would employ his greater mastery of the legislative process to secure the enactment of Kennedy's creative range of domestic proposals, as largely did occur after Kennedy's death. Since I was responsible for the preparation and transmission of Kennedy's legislative messages and other policy proposals, I was as frustrated as JFK by congressional defeats and delays. As LBJ told us when RFK and I visited him in 1968, "JFK was a little irritated with me sometimes and showed it; but no one else knew." Only after Johnson became president did his performance confirm the mettle and strength that JFK had seen in selecting him as his running mate and in regarding him as the best of the other candidates for president in 1960.

The formulation of Kennedy's civil rights bill in 1963 put my relationship with LBJ to its severest test. Knowing that he had opposed President Truman's Fair Employment Practices Committee (FEPC) legislation at the very time that I was working as a young student to obtain passage of FEPC by the Nebraska legislature, but also knowing that we needed his support to win Southern votes in the Congress, I welcomed his suggestions on making the bill more acceptable, even as I quietly questioned his motives. When he supported a controversial provision, was he hoping to overload the bill with provisions that would ensure its defeat, or ensure more opposition to the president whom he hoped to succeed? (LBJ's later leadership on civil rights and his acceptance of JFK's program, as a president from the South, whatever the political cost to him and his party, was without question outstanding in U.S. history and particularly for a Southerner.)

On June 3, 1963, one week and two days before President Kennedy's landmark address to the nation on civil rights, LBJ engaged me in a long telephone conversation on the issue. I could not help but speculate later whether many of the liberal statements he was making on the issue were intended more for his tape recorder than for my work on the bill. The conversation went on for what seemed like hours, with my occasionally injecting a brief "I agree . . . I think that's very sound . . . I think that's a good idea . . . That's a good point . . . I follow you . . . That's a good suggestion." Much of what he was saying to me was advice on strategy, tactics, amendments to the draft bill, arguments that he thought the president should invoke, and individual legislators whom he thought should be appeased.

Among the tactics he recommended were the following:

I'd let a Mexican Congressman—introduce him [JFK] with that white suit on . . . put [an opponent] in the position almost where he's a bigot to be against the President . . . The President has to go in there without fussing at anybody . . . We run the risk of touching off a three- or four-month debate that will kill his program and inflame the country . . . Some specific proposals have to be weighed a lot more carefully . . . It might cost us the South, but those sorts of states may be lost anyway . . . But if he goes down there and looks them in the eye and states the moral issue and the Christian issue, and he does it face-to-face, these Southerners at least will respect his courage . . . I don't think the Negro's goals are going to be achieved through legislation . . . We get civil war going in the South, they move Kennedy in and they cut off the South from him and blow up the bridge. That's what they want to do . . . I told the Attorney General . . . I'm making it abundantly clear I'm on the team, and you'll never hear a word out of me . . . Now, I want to make it clear I'm as strong for this program as you are, my friend. I don't want to debate these things around fifteen men, and then have them all go out and talk about the Vice-President. I haven't sat in on any of the conferences they've had up there with the Senators. I think it would have been good if I had. I don't care. But if, at the last minute, I'm supposed to give my judgment, I'm going to do it honestly as long as I'm around here, and I'm going to do it loyally . . . I think that he [JFK] will be cut to pieces with this, and I think he'll be a sacrificial lamb. His program will be hurt, if not killed . . . I don't think the bill's been thought through . . . I said some of these things from nearly every train stop in the South. I looked them right in the eye and said them . . . and they respected us. They knocked Lady Bird's hat off in Dallas, but by God, they voted for us! If I can do it—they call it corn pone and all that kind of stuff—the President can sure do it . . . I don't think you'll ever pass [the bill] as it is . . . You haven't done your homework on public sentiment . . . I don't know who drafted it; I've never seen it. Hell, if the Vice-President doesn't know what's in it, how do you expect the others to know what's in it? . . . I'll tell you, when he sends this message, they're going to come running up there, and they're going to sit quietly in these appropriation committees, and they're going to cut his "outfit" off and put it in their pocket and never mention civil rights. So I'd move my children on through the line and get them down in the storm cellar and get it locked and key, and then I'd make my attack . . . Maybe I'm wrong, but you asked for it . . . This crowd, they're experts at fighting this thing, and we're not prepared for them. We got a little pop-gun, and I want to pull out the cannon. The President is the cannon. Let him be on all the TV networks, just speaking from his conscience . . . They'll say Lyndon Johnson, the traitor, and what all they've done . . . I don't agree with you it's been done . . .

It wasn't short. But it was colorful—and typical LBJ.

One afternoon in the White House, I was briefing the president on a separate issue while he dressed and his longtime black valet, George Thomas, helped him pack for a campaign trip to Ohio. The president, unhappy that he had to make this political trip, was also gloomy about reports of stormy flying weather, and said to me, as George shut his suitcase: "If this plane goes down, old 'Lyin' Down'"—as he often jokingly referred to his vice president—"will have this place cleared out from stem to stern in 24 hours—and you and George will be the first to go!"

But Johnson and I had treated each other amicably and respectfully, if warily, during the Kennedy presidency. I think the fact that I was not an Ivy League graduate strengthened his sense of trust. He told one journalist, somewhat cautiously, that I was "certainly talented. I would not hesitate to trust any political or intellectual operation to him"—very generous, inasmuch as I probably would not have said the same about him.

During JFK's years in the Oval Office, Jackie had strong opinions about LBJ, whom she sometimes referred to as "Colonel Corn Pone." Her opinions almost surely reflected her husband's. Following JFK's death, when the publishers of *Profiles in Courage* decided to bring out a memorial edition, she sent word that she did not want LBJ to do the foreword. Her feelings, as well as her sense of her husband's true feelings, became crystal-clear to me when she agreed to read the manuscript for my book *Kennedy*. She wanted me to delete or at least modify virtually every favorable reference I had made to Johnson, and scribbled the following comments on the manuscript:

This is the first of several glowing references to LBJ, which I know do not reflect President Kennedy's thinking; he thought perhaps more highly of him while in the Senate and at the convention than he ever did afterwards. You must know—as well or better than I—his steadily diminishing opinion of him then. As his term progressed, he grew more and more concerned about what would happen if LBJ ever became president. He was truly frightened at the prospect.

Where my manuscript said JFK "learned from Lyndon Johnson," she said emphatically, "I don't think he learned anything about campaigning from Lyndon Johnson—because Lyndon's style always embarrassed him, especially when he sent him around the world as Vice-President." Where my draft mentioned "a deep mutual respect" between JFK and LBJ, she commented, "I think you overstate this a bit—from JFK's side. But it doesn't matter." Then she crossed out that last sentence. It mattered to her.

Chapter 21

My Relations with President Kennedy's Family

Like me, John Kennedy grew up in a large and loving family that taught, inspired, and helped him along the way. I did not know Joe Kennedy Jr., who was killed in World War II, nor his sisters Kathleen and Rosemary. I admired Jack's sisters Eunice, Pat, and Jean—all strong women, politically savvy and seasoned campaigners for their brothers. I knew well Jack's brothers Bobby and Ted. Though the three Kennedy brothers I knew were very different, each had the same innate capacity for continuing intellectual growth. Unlike most politicians in Washington, who think they know it all once they have reached the nation's capital, all three Kennedy brothers kept learning, growing, expanding their horizons, broadening their agenda.

Jack and Bobby were very different. Bobby was more volatile and intense. He particularly admired physical courage, whereas JFK particularly admired moral and intellectual courage. Bobby was less likely to keep his emotions concealed than Jack. Jack was more likely to accept people as they were, while RFK was more likely to love a person or hate him. Both were quick to grasp a problem, although RFK was more prone to make snap judgments, a trait he later outgrew. Both cited the axiom, "Forgive, but never forget," but the angrier RFK was less likely to forgive, and the gentler JFK was more likely to forget. The difference could be seen on television, where Jack was cool, and Bobby often red-hot.

Bobby and I were not close friends, but our relationship evolved over three stages. The range and change of my opinions about RFK are best reflected in the following response I gave to an ABC News interviewer in 1967, as a possible RFK race for the presidency loomed:

When I first met him, in 1953, the year I went to work for his brother Jack, I would not have voted for Bob Kennedy for anything. He was militant, aggressive, intolerant, opinionated, somewhat shallow in his convictions, and I suppose some people would say more like his father than his brother. But he has changed over the years. When he became a candidate in his own right [for the Senate] in 1964, he became a man appealing for people's votes, their hearts, and that brought out a new Bob Kennedy. Then, for the first time, he had asked for their help, and he found that he could do it. He was shy, just as Jack was very shy; he had a reserve about him, which is still sometimes difficult for him to break out of. I've been with him many times since he entered the United States Senate, and I still find him growing and changing.

Shortly thereafter, I received the following handwritten note from RFK on United States Senate stationery:

> *Teddy, old pal—Perhaps you could keep down the number of adjectives and adverbs describing me in 1955 and use a few more in 1967. OK? Bob.*

We first met when I was a new assistant in JFK's Senate office and he was on the staff of Senator Joseph R. McCarthy's subcommittee, working on investigations into government operations instead of anti-Communist witch hunts. In those days, he was a conservative, very close to his father in both ideas and manners, sharing his father's dislike of liberals. No doubt he viewed me with as much suspicion, if not disdain, as I viewed anyone working for McCarthy. When members of my family in the early 1950s expressed reservations to me about RFK's relationship with McCarthy, I simply replied that it was a subject I did not wish to discuss.

Our friendship was not enhanced on the occasion when—in a photo opportunity for a magazine article—JFK, RFK, and I went across the street to the Capitol lawn to simulate a touch football game in which JFK threw me a pass with RFK defending. As I reached up for the ball, I felt a powerful and unsportsmanlike shove and went down onto the muddy grass in my one good "Senate suit." I took that as an indication of how he felt about me. The feeling was mutual.

We saw relatively little of each other until the 1956 Democratic convention. By the time JFK ran for reelection to the Senate in 1958, RFK knew me well enough to borrow my only overcoat as the Boston autumn turned colder. By the time he returned it weeks later on Election Day, I had had more than one frozen thought about the Kennedy family's sense of entitlement. As his work on the Senate Labor Rackets Committee investigation ended and he became more involved with the JFK presidential campaign after the Palm Beach summit meeting in April 1959, we saw more of each other.

Even then, he seemed somewhat suspicious, maybe even jealous, of my role and relationship with his brother. Once he embarrassed me by asking that I leave the room so that he and JFK could have a confidential talk about the primary in Wisconsin, where I had spent months making contacts, lining up delegates, and building support. Momentarily flushing with resentment, I understood, and immediately went back to my office.

I was initially disappointed when my job became more narrowly confined to speechwriting after Bobby joined us and took over many of my earlier campaign responsibilities. But I bowed to the inevitable, recognizing that it was what JFK wanted and was in the best interests of the campaign. During the 1960 convention and postconvention campaign, we continued to collaborate without becoming personally close. He did not interfere with my writing, I did not challenge his role as campaign manager, though I heard reports that he was angry whenever campaign staffers still came to me for advice or instructions.

The atmosphere improved during my days in the White House—the second stage in our relationship. We learned to appreciate and respect each other more in our separate roles, though I was not among those invited to weekends at Camp David or to the well-publicized parties and seminars that he and his wife, Ethel, hosted at Hickory Hill. I did not expect to be included and was too busy to feel excluded.

Bobby and I may have occasionally competed for the president's ear on policy matters, but rarely if ever on legal questions. He and I were in touch regularly, but neither of us gave or took directions from the other. We did not find it necessary to arrange a formal treaty, such as existed in other administrations between the White House counsel's and attorney general's offices. Nor did my office subject the Department of Justice to any of the reviews that we required of other departments before they sent their legislative proposals to Congress.

As RFK began to realize that more coordination between our two offices could help the president's objective of putting forward a coherent legislative package, and as more experience and the passage of time improved relations between us personally, he began to request my office's review and input on some Justice Department matters, including the juvenile delinquency program that would later be expanded into the War on Poverty. On civil rights, we worked closely together and had no differences of opinion. I accompanied him on a trip to Prince Edward County, Virginia, which was defying a court order for racial desegregation. We also collabo-

416 · TED SORENSEN

rated in the efforts he led to roll back the inflationary steel price increase in 1962, and on the Justice Department's position before the U.S. Supreme Court regarding congressional reapportionment standards.

In retrospect, it may have been an error for President Kennedy to name his brother attorney general, although he was a remarkable one. Constitutionally, a principal role of that position is to hold the president legally accountable. Had such a question ever arisen, that would have been a difficult role for RFK to play, although he was far less servile to the president than some of the attorneys general who have served since. Journalistic exaggerations of his White House policy role and influence on JFK ignore the vast areas of government policy and presidential decision making in which he was not involved, and—in view of his heavy responsibilities at Justice—could not have been, although he certainly played an important role in the Cuban missile crisis.

The third phase of our relationship followed his brother's assassination. In the weeks after November 22, Bobby and I, each realizing the depth of that event's impact on the other, became closer than we had ever been. As Mac Bundy wrote about me immediately after the assassination, in a memo for LBJ, summarizing the role of each member of the White House staff: "He was

so close to JFK that his sorrow is that of a brother."
On the Saturday afternoon following that terrible Friday, Bobby walked into my West Wing office, his puffy, reddened eyes hidden behind dark sunglasses. It was a brief meeting. Neither of us said much; neither of us had to—it was a grieving session.

Our personal closeness deepened when I moved to Hyannis Port to write my book *Kennedy*, and I saw a great deal of him. Jack's death changed Bobby. It humbled him, softened him. He became a gentler, warmer person, a change also occasioned by his own growing responsibilities in public life. While he started out more like his father than JFK, he ended up far more liberal than both his father and JFK. When, in the mid-1960s, a newspaper reported that I was more temperate on some issues than he, RFK, amused, wrote Jackie: "Can you imagine what you-know-who would say if he heard me described as more liberal than Ted Sorensen!"

In 1964, I agreed to his request that I go to New York and campaign for him in his race for the United States Senate. Thereafter I saw him frequently in his years as a senator. He would call me in from time to time, asking my advice on questions ranging from what to say about Vietnam to whether he should run for president.

As a senator and member of the United States Supreme Court bar, RFK kindly agreed to make the formal motion for my admission to practice before the United States Supreme Court. As *Time* magazine reported, "Senator Robert Kennedy, who certainly knew what he was talking about, pronounced the introduction: 'I am satisfied that he possesses the qualifications.' U.S. Chief Justice Earl Warren smiled down from the bench . . ." On a photograph taken of us on the Supreme Court steps that snowy day in January 1966, RFK inscribed: "Two future Justices of the Supreme Court discuss legal decisions and strategy after winning their first case. Ted—with appreciation for many things."

The acrimonious, adversarial relationship between Bobby and Lyndon Johnson has been exhaustively covered in many books and articles; but I had a ringside seat to this battle on one occasion. In the late 1960s, it appeared that President Johnson and FBI director J. Edgar Hoover were conspiring to smear their two most respected detractors, RFK and Dr. Martin Luther King Jr., by leaking to the press—through Drew Pearson and others—the claim that RFK as attorney general had greatly expanded the use of FBI wiretapping, specifically including the tapping or "bugging" through hidden microphones of Dr. King's alleged conversations with Communist advisors. The apparent Johnson-Hoover instrument was Edward Long of Missouri, a

Democratic senator with close ties to Hoffa's Teamsters. Johnson remained piously above it all, repeatedly stating that he had stopped all wiretapping when he became president.

One day in December 1966, RFK asked me to take a look at the entire file and determine what could be done to stop this series of insidious attacks. After reviewing the situation, I recommended that he fight fire with fire. I prepared for his signature a letter to Senator Long urging that his subcommittee hold a "comprehensive" hearing on the subject, with which RFK would fully cooperate. To be both comprehensive and balanced, the hearing, I suggested, would need to call and cross-examine under oath as witnesses not only RFK, but also J. Edgar Hoover and LBJ's closest aides. Any such hearing that complied with all of our conditions would have been explosive for both Johnson and Hoover. I cleared the text with RFK, and, on my next trip to Washington handed the proposed draft to President Johnson's informal advisor, Clark Clifford, telling him that things were getting out of hand and that RFK would have no option but to send this letter if the nasty leaks and one-sided statements continued. The leaks stopped and the letter was never sent.

My last service to Robert Kennedy was to serve as

legal counsel for his posthumously published memoir on the Cuban missile crisis, *Thirteen Days.* It was not the only Kennedy family memoir on which I advised. When the family matriarch, Rose, decided to write her autobiography, I agreed to serve as her lawyer and book agent, as I had on another RFK book, *To Seek a Newer World.* I smiled when Rose called me in my office upon receiving news of the author's advance of $1.5 million I had obtained from her publisher: "Ted," she said, in her strong Boston accent, "thanks a million—and a haaf."

I first met JFK's brother Edward, then a Harvard student, in the fall of 1953, when we visited the Kennedy family home in Hyannis Port on the same weekend. We didn't see each other much in the next few years. But I got to know him better when he played a key role in the 1960 presidential campaign, particularly in the Western states, and still better when he sought the Democratic nomination in Massachusetts for JFK's vacated Senate seat in 1962.

Ted's chief competitor for the Democratic nomination was Edward McCormack, the favorite nephew of House Democratic speaker John McCormack, a powerful and influential longtime legislator who had better ties with many House members than did JFK as president. Ambassador Kennedy very much wanted Ted to seek the nomination and become senator, and JFK had had enough disagreements with his father over policy issues not to add one more. In addition, the president had already come under fire for nepotism when he appointed his brother Bob attorney general, particularly from the *New York Times*. The White House, JFK insisted both publicly and privately, would remain neutral in the Senate Democratic primary in Massachusetts. Secretly he sent RFK and me to the Cape to coach Ted on his campaign in general, and on his upcoming televised debate with Eddie McCormack in particular.

As RFK and I sat with him in the family dining room, I employed the same format that I used in the president's pre–press conference breakfasts, going through a long list of possible questions and issues, making certain that he was comfortable with the facts and adequately prepared on his positions. That evening I sat in the back of the hall in which the debate was conducted, watching McCormack flabbergast Ted with the charge: "If his name were Edward Moore . . . his candidacy would be a joke."

Jack's death, followed by Bobby's death less than five years later, deeply changed Ted. He matured rapidly.

He knew he bore responsibility for the family name, assumed the mantle of family leadership from his brothers, and took on the job of nurturing and guiding their children, comforting their widows, and supporting their causes.

In 1968 he ruled out a run for president in RFK's place, disappointing those of us who were prepared to rally the convention around him. In 1969, his tragic automobile accident on Chappaquiddick Island—which has been too overwritten and overanalyzed in the past to deserve further comments here—ended his presidential prospects, apparently for all time. During the week of anguished discussions that followed, his brother-in-law Steve Smith asked me to join other advisors at the family home on the Cape. I decided that, as a friend as well as a lawyer, I could do no less, even though I was not surprised later when that participation was used against me in my own brief political career. In long emotional sessions, as Teddy recovered from his own trauma and injuries, he related the facts to me; and, together with his longtime speechwriter, the talented Milton Gwirtzman, and others, I had a hand in the preparation of his televised statement of apology and despair. My own subsequent television interview, in which I struggled for answers, convinced me to say nothing more on that subject. It was not the high point of either my career or his.

I continue to see Senator Ted occasionally, just as I have occasionally accepted assignments from him. One such assignment came in the 1970s when he was a senior member of the Senate Judiciary Committee, and wanted me to interview a leading candidate to serve as counsel for the committee. My schedule was so busy that I asked that young lawyer-professor to meet me at LaGuardia Airport so we could have our conversation during a taxi ride to Manhattan. I was impressed with the candidate, and endorsed him to Ted, who wisely hired this future Supreme Court justice, Stephen Breyer.

For one man to have survived so many tragic and traumatic blows—the assassinations of the two brothers he loved, the airplane accident that almost killed him in 1964 (after which I visited him in the hospital, finding him amazingly brave, determined, and cheery), and the fatal automobile accident in which he was involved, as well as the final frustration of his presidential ambitions—and still be able to lead, laugh, and offer hope to others, is testimony to Ted's amazing resilience and capacity for survival.

More respected and effective today than some presidents have been, Ted long ago came to terms with the fact that he need not be president to fulfill his portion of the Kennedy legacy. Today he enjoys his service to the nation too much to contemplate the less tiring and less controversial life of retirement; I think he will ultimately die in the Senate. More active and at home in that august body than either of his brothers, Ted was—and still is— the most relaxed campaigner of the three, with an easier style on the public platform, the best politician, better able to work with other senators in both parties to make the most of the often cumbersome legislative process. Always the liberal lion, he has proven to be a courageous battler on the cutting edge of issues both domestic and foreign, maintaining the liberal tradition of his brothers even when others in the Democratic Party showed less courage. Conservative columnist William Safire has called Ted the "scourge of conservative judges and free-market medicine . . . trying to keep the liberal flame burning under the rich and powerful." Jack and Bobby would have been proud.

Both his national role and its limits were made finally clear when he concluded his race against incumbent President Jimmy Carter for the 1980 Democratic Party nomination by his eloquently moving concession speech at the convention: "The dream shall never die." I wrote to him that his campaign had been a "great personal victory . . . which overcame the doubters and naysayers who underestimated your ability to defy your detractors, adhere to your principles, and to accept defeat with grace instead of bitterness. . . . You emerged a winner . . . the conscience of this party, the hope of this nation . . ." Nearly thirty years later, he still is.

The father of these increasingly liberal sons was Joseph P. Kennedy, former ambassador to Great Britain, a major factor in the president's life—providing money, encouragement, occasional contacts, practical guidance, and always interesting, often entertaining conversation. When I first met the Ambassador on Cape Cod shortly after I started working for JFK in 1953, he said, "You couldn't write speeches for me. You're too much of a liberal. But writing for Jack is different." I agreed with every word.

Of his numerous colorful expressions, the one I most liked and adopted for my own use was his way of emphasizing rejection: "Not for chalk, money, or marbles!" In the Senate campaign of 1952—I was told years later by the campaign's ad agency representative—JPK Sr. sat reading one evening in a corner of the living room while JFK, his mother, and sisters giggled about stories they would recount on an upcoming family campaign film, including a story of young Jack, on a family blueberry-picking expedition, falling into the thorny bushes and coming out with both pains and stains—a silly episode, but one they all thought would amuse Massachusetts voters watching the show. JPK Sr. said nothing. But the next morning, exiting the house as the young advertising executive was walking in, he did not even pause to utter three words that said it all: "Blueberries are out."

Although he would occasionally call the Senate office with a suggestion, asking the staffer on the other end to "see what Ted thinks," my interactions with the Ambassador were limited in those early years, but grew as I worked on *Profiles in Courage* in 1954–1955, a period during which we corresponded occasionally. In late summer 1955 I received a letter from him criticizing an obscure paragraph, and asking that it be made clearer:

> [These passages can be] stated much more simply and forcibly . . . I think Harper's should have an excellent editorial writer go over the whole book, particularly these two chapters, with the idea of punctuation and simplifying the structure. It's a fine job as it is, but I remember when Lindbergh spoke to me about the real success of his book, he said he almost did not recognize it after the editorial writer at Scribner's had finished working on it—he brought so much more clarity and punch to it . . . Harper's . . . should have a man of top caliber to do this same job. If he is very good, I am

sure you will have a worthwhile and profitable piece of literature, and worthwhile financially if properly exploited.

Following all the furor over the authorship of *Profiles in Courage*, I had been exceedingly careful never to claim authorship and always to minimize my role. I was therefore stunned years later to learn that, when talking with John Siegenthaler, who had assisted RFK with his first book, *The Enemy Within*, Joseph P. Kennedy had given John a "lecture on not taking credit for his son's book, [and] had conveyed a little hostility toward Sorensen . . . [who] takes credit all the time for writing *Profiles in Courage*." If there was a little hostility, I doubt it lasted long, and I never sensed it.

In 1958 the Republican candidate opposing JFK's reelection to the Senate was so unknown, at a time when JFK had become a national hero and presidential prospect, that the slogan agreed upon for the Kennedy campaign, already reproduced on hundreds of posters, yard signs, pamphlets, and buttons, was the appeal: "Be Proud of Your Vote!" The Republican candidate, Vincente Celeste, looked certain to be buried in an avalanche of Kennedy votes. But Joseph P. put his foot down, wisely observing that the slogan might well be interpreted as an ethnic slur, offending Italian-

Americans throughout the state, possibly even throughout the country. The posters, yard signs, pamphlets,
and buttons were all discarded.

During that same campaign, Ambassador Kennedy
called me with his suggestions for a proposed speech on
inflation by Senator Kennedy. He concluded his advice
by noting, "At least that's what I would like to hear."
Delicately, I responded to the millionaire ambassador,
"But Mr. Kennedy, maybe you don't reflect what the
typical voter would like to hear." "Hell," he replied.
"I'm the only typical one around here."

He and I also had occasional contact during the 1960
campaign. On New Year's Eve 1959/1960, he called me
at home to give me a message he wanted delivered to
the president of the United Steelworkers Union. Later,
in February, I received the following letter: "Dear Ted:
I continually hear about Nixon's experience . . . for the
most part that is a term used to describe a lifetime of
mistakes."

Ambassador Kennedy probably wearied of reading
constant reports about how much of JFK's success was
owed to my help on speeches and campaigning. Both
JFK and I smiled at constant reports about the Ambassador's influence in Democratic Party circles, how he
was the one pulling the strings in the campaign, making the decisions and obtaining most of the endorse-

ments, reports that we both knew were not true and very likely came from the old man himself. In truth, Ambassador Kennedy did not have much power and influence in the national Democratic Party in 1960; and JFK and I had to work hard, winning over local voters and leaders, before his father could press his case with those few leaders whom he did know. Rumors that old Joe obtained the backing of mob figures in Chicago for his son were particularly unfounded and irksome. The senator and I had worked hard for years to win support from many Democratic members of Congress and local leaders in Chicago and Cook County. They could deliver thousands of votes; the mob could not.

JFK's own remarks about his father were always couched in affection, gratitude, and admiration, but he made it clear to me on more than one occasion that his father's friends were not necessarily those whom he would have chosen and that he had a different philosophical approach. As an occasional guest at the family dinner table in Hyannis Port, I observed that Joseph P., an imperious man, was sometimes a domineering conversationalist, but the senator did not argue, preferring often to remain silent. As JFK reflected, upon hearing that Martin Luther King Jr.'s father had initially planned to vote against him on religious grounds: "Well, we all have our fathers." Ultimately, whatever names might have been hurled at him by his critics—bigot, right-winger, isolationist, ruthless capitalist—the fact remains that Joseph P. Kennedy fathered the most idealistic, open-minded internationalist president since World War II, and he deserves much credit for his family's many other remarkable accomplishments. So also does Rose Kennedy, an enduring source of affection, strength, praise, and uncanny political advice, as well as sharp reminders of standards of proper English and personal appearance.

I can think of no other family in the history of twentieth-century America—or, with the exception of the Adams family, in the entire history of America—where a father could be so proud of three sons in high federal office at the same time. It was a wonderful moment. I could tell how much the three brothers enjoyed it simply by looking at them. Yet, as I reflect now on that period when all three shone in Washington, I realize how tragically brief it was. Less than one year into his son's presidency, Joseph P. suffered a debilitating stroke. Shortly afterward the president flew to Palm Beach on Air Force One to visit his father, asking me to make the trip with him in order to work on the plane on the 1962 legislative planning we had just begun. After that, I saw the Ambassador only once, when, in the midst of RFK's 1968 campaign, I stopped with Bobby in Hyannis Port for lunch. It was a sad sight.

. . .

If Ambassador Kennedy was the powerful patriarch of the family, Jacqueline Bouvier Kennedy was, in some ways, its most powerful woman. Strong-willed but never arrogant, gentle but never weak, Jackie was unlike any other powerful women I have met. I saw her rarely in the early years—only on those occasions when she would come to the Senate office, or I would visit the senator at home. Her pregnancy kept her largely uninvolved in the 1960 campaign, except for her concerns about JFK's poor diet on the trail and his lack of a warm coat in cold climates. My relationship with her in the White House was friendly but distant, our encounters warm but rare. Her priorities as first lady were to assure the privacy, safety, and education of her children and a happy, affectionate home for her husband. With a few notable exceptions, she did not participate in policy decisions. When construction of Egypt's Aswan Dam threatened to flood thousands of historic sites and artifacts on the banks of the Nile, including the ancient Temple of Ramses at Abu Simbel, Jackie persuaded her husband to ask Congress for money to support a UNESCO rescue effort. In addition, while JFK shared with his wife a desire to elevate the quality and importance of American cultural life, his establishment of an

Advisory Council on the Arts, the first formal government body "to which the artist and the art institutions
can present their views and bring their problems," was
in large part due to her inspiration. The National Foundation on the Arts and Humanities soon followed. The
number of symphony orchestras, opera companies, and
dance companies in the country multiplied, and the ar-
chitecture of Pennsylvania Avenue became inviting as
well as dignified. All thanks to Jackie.

In all her roles—senator's fiancée, wife, first lady, arts
advocate, grieving widow, attentive mother, cherished
friend—she was a special person whom I uniformly
regarded with awe, admiration, and affection, for more
than forty years, until she died in 1994, still vibrant and
beautiful. The extraordinary outpouring of grief at her
death, redoubled by the tragic death of John Jr. a few
years later, was an indication of the continuing attraction that this remarkable family still had on the hearts of
Americans and others around the globe.

We became good friends when I lived for more than
a year on Cape Cod, writing my book *Kennedy*, visiting her often, sometimes discussing the book. During
the second of those two summers, she asked me as a
neighbor and friend to be her only guest at an otherwise lonely birthday dinner. I could think of no available present of possible interest to her, other than sheets

of yellow paper from my files containing JFK's doodles during the Cuban missile crisis. She loved it. The
following Christmas, she returned the doodles to me,
beautifully framed, with her own special inscription:
"For Ted—who saved them then; and gave them to me
in Hyannis Port on my birthday last year. I want you to
have them now, with my love always, for all you were
to him." On those visits in Cape Cod, we would discuss whatever she wanted to tell me of her life, laughing
over the foibles of the world and Washington as they
went on without us. Over the years that followed, she
had occasion to write me some wonderful letters in her
inimitable style, which I cherish, such as this one, dated
November 8, 1977:

Dear Ted:

*It must get to be a bit boring having people tell
you how brilliant you are. But you are and you must
suffer people telling you so—I am filled with wonder
and a reverence like one is meant to feel when one
sees the Grand Canyon, whenever I see that mind
behind your calm face hone in to the vital nerve. I
think people should stand back and revere that. I
feel privileged to have seen it with you so often with
Jack, all that you made possible. In addition . . . you
have such a great, deep heart. All the things that you*

*have done for various members of the family, heroic
things and sweet things . . . and now the patience
and the insight that you give to me . . . I think that
life is so fast-paced, everyone is trying to create
their new life out of their old anguish, and it goes so
fast, sometimes people don't take the time to tell the
people they love and use how much they are moved,
how much they are beholden. I just don't want to
be hit by a taxi before I tell you all that. I can't ever
help you the way you will always help me, but you
are Androcles and I am the lion; and you never
know when you will want that lion to pop up. The
lion is always there unasked, but I pray that one day
you will—not ask, because you are too proud—but
indicate—that would be kind—because you would
correct an imbalance.*

All that in a letter asking me to "rattle the sabres"
to a mutual friend, her lawyer, to take action against
the latest media attempt to portray her life in a way she
regarded as "unspeakable."

Another touching letter was in response to a letter
I sent her at a time when many former JFK associates
were expressing outrage that she had married Aristotle
Onassis, not that it was in any way their business. I

understood her need to find security and privacy for herself and her children away from the turmoil and danger of American public life.

Dearest Ted,

Thank you for your letter. It makes me cry. You said something that was in my most secret heart— that I didn't think anyone but me would realize— that [the remarriage] is what Jack might have wished for me—could he see and know all that has happened to us all since he died. Thank you for your great heart and understanding. In the end, there is only the alliance of the heart, but I don't think there are many people like you who see it so.

Please know that all the things you said to me, I say to you. I will be your friend forever, dearest Ted. I always would have anyway, but you touched me so much in saying that you will be my friend in my new life and will do anything for me. I hope you will come and see us when we come home.

With much love, Jackie

I did not see her during her time with Onassis, and never asked her about it. Her longtime companion thereafter was one of my closest friends and clients, the wise, warm, and supportive Maurice Tempelsman; and their mutually caring relationship gave me many more opportunities to see Jackie socially. My law firm represented her on more than one occasion—she adored our senior partner, Judge Simon H. Rifkind—but I was not directly involved in those representations.

Jackie Kennedy's greatest accomplishment in life was not the beautification of the White House or Pennsylvania Avenue, or the publishing and civic chores she took on during her years in New York City, but her children—two healthy, intelligent young people whom she raised by herself during the turbulent sixties and seventies when so many teenagers strayed into drugs, alcohol, or delinquency, while hers were model students who became model citizens.

JFK had dearly loved his two little children. They were so small when he was president, so delightful in the White House that he permitted them to wander into his office at any time. He arranged for Eisenhower's putting green on the lawn behind the White House to be converted into a children's playground for the little White House school, all to help create a normal environment for Caroline and John; occasionally he would step out of his office to watch the children play.

John Jr., in the years before his tragic early death,

was already a young man with a bright political future, blessed with the good looks, charm, intelligence, and drive that his father had enjoyed. That future was not to be, when his small plane went down in fog en route from New York to Cape Cod. Just as his father had been the subject of so many speculative articles about why he was seeking the presidency, so was young John, both before and after his death, the subject of equally unfounded and wildly inaccurate stories about his career choices.

Caroline is the keeper of the family flame, an eloquent spokesperson for all her father represented. One day in 1974 I received a telephone request from Jackie that Caroline, then a young teenager, be permitted to visit me in my law office to hear me expound at length on what her father had stood for, accomplished, and meant to the world, and why he was such a special leader at a time when she was too young to know and understand it all. The reason for Caroline's interest was a paper she was undertaking for her social studies class. When it was completed, boldly entitled "The Foreign Policy of President John F. Kennedy," the paper ran twenty-five pages. Her social studies teacher praised it, calling it "a thoughtful and sensitive testimony to your father, his aspirations, his beliefs and his ability to influence the thinking of others (like yourself—I would not minimize the importance of this for you personally)." Caroline's accompanying note when she had submitted the paper had acknowledged that she could not be "objective" on that topic. To this her teacher replied: "You have [well] documented your evaluation of Kennedy's beliefs and actions. You've approached your work as a student of U.S. history. There is rarely a vagueness or inaccuracy in your paper. I hope you'll let your family read it—they will be proud and pleased."

Reading that student paper decades later, I was not surprised that it showed a remarkably mature understanding of the role of the presidency in American foreign policy during the cold war, and accurately reflected her father's views: "Restraint is essential, and because we are strong, we can afford not to use our strength." Clearly her father's daughter, though the paper always referred to him as "Kennedy" or "President Kennedy," and was objective enough to include a criticism from British Prime Minister Harold Macmillan, who had stated that JFK was best on specific issues but "lost" on broader principles (the opposite of Macmillan, I would have told her).

Around the same time, I received another moving letter from Caroline's mother, en route to Europe on the Onassis plane.

*You were so incredibly kind to give all the time
you gave at a moment's notice in your busy life
to Caroline. She has a wonderful history teacher
who cares about JFK and who cares about her, and
he steered her into doing her term paper on him,
because he thought it would help her. At first she
was happy, but it really became traumatic for her.
The more she read, the more it made her miss her
father. She read every book, but yours meant the
most to her, and then it was you who spent the most
time with her. Others just weren't as welcoming as
you were. You told her things she could never have
found in books. Her professor, who is stern, told me
that her paper was so deep and so moving. It doesn't
matter that it is an A-paper—it just matters that she
found her father through doing it.*

*Dear Ted, all our lives have gone into different
orbits—that is sad, but it is survival. I pray we will
see each other more; but if this plane doesn't make it
to the other side of the Atlantic, someone will rescue
the mailbag, and tell you that I will never forget the
past nor the present, all you were to Jack, to me, now
to tiny Caroline.*

Rereading that letter from the Onassis plane—"for
the time you gave to Caroline—long, long precious $$$

Judge Rifkind time—for a little girl's term paper"—
thirty years later moves me. But I am equally moved
by the more recent request from Caroline that I perform the same service for her children, who never had
a chance to know their grandfather.

I ultimately found that the writer of such moving,
sensitive, and beautiful letters could also be volatile on
rare occasions, turning those eloquent words and powerful feelings against even close friends if they seemed
to err. I had heard of Jackie's explosive fury when she
thought Bill Manchester was commercializing the subject of her husband's death by selling his book *Death of
a President* for serialization in *Look* magazine. Later,
angered that the Kennedy Institute of Politics at Harvard appeared to be in danger of being swallowed up
in conventional academia, she wrote—but apparently
did not send—an explosive letter to its blameless new
director, beloved by us all, saying:

> *We are at cross-purposes . . . Our objectives are
> completely different . . . If the Institute continues
> as it is, it will become a monument to everything
> that President Kennedy was not . . . We must not
> let happen to Robert Kennedy's memorial what
> happened to President Kennedy's once we let it
> become part of an institution. . . . I do not think*

that the family should raise any more money for a
memorial which is so little in keeping with the spirit
of President Kennedy. . . . I do not think he would
ever have been permitted to be its director, because
he was not "safe" enough.

Believing sincerely that the Institute of Politics has to the contrary become a wholly appropriate reflection of JFK's spirit and interests, I can only assume that the fires raging in that letter were ultimately banked. But I can also imagine the crushing effect that letter would surely have had on its intended recipient, if he had ever received it. I know I was crushed upon receiving an even angrier letter from Jackie in 1987. It was written when she initially misunderstood both the purpose and the nature of a book I was planning to compile and edit, only with her consent, bringing together JFK's most notable speeches, statements, and writings under the title *"Let the Word Go Forth."* Somehow she mistakenly thought that this volume would represent an effort by me to claim authorship of all its contents, despite the care I had taken for more than thirty years not only to avoid any such claim, but to attest to the opposite. She thought that I was exploiting JFK's name for my own financial gain, as well as confusing the question of authorship. Never before had I been the object of her wrath, and a rebuke from my own mother could not have hurt more. When I tried to call her or find others to intercede, she was uninterested in my protests that she had been misinformed or was misunderstanding the entire project.

I tried to explain—through Senator Ted Kennedy, Maurice Tempelsman, and Steve Smith—that all of JFK's speeches and statements in the book were in the public domain, not subject to copyright; that the only copyright was in my introductions to the book and each chapter, in which I again made clear that the author was JFK; that half the proceeds from the book were being donated by me to the John F. Kennedy Presidential Library, with the other half going to my three sons, who, I noted in an abject letter of apology to her, "did pay a price for my years of commitment to Jack"; that assembling his most important speeches was not some form of glorification for me but a recognition that his legacy deserved to be compiled and organized in one volume available to readers and researchers everywhere, much like the works of Churchill and Lincoln. In my letter, I assured her:

> [I] would not under any circumstances undertake this project if it has only your grudging consent. I treasure our relationship too much to risk your ever

doubting my motives and loyalty . . . I'll gladly call it off . . . But harder to bear than I can ever express to you is the knowledge that you, for whom I have such deep respect and affection, could believe, after all these years, that I would consider a step that would advance my interests at Jack's expense. You must believe me, Jackie, when I assure you that nothing was further from my mind . . . I pray that we can put this behind us and continue our friendship.

Fortunately, with a helpful explanation from Steve, she in time understood the project better; but I have never forgotten the impact of that one brief but ferocious rebuke.

Chapter 22

Kennedy's Civil Rights Initiative

In the late 1950s and early 1960s, most white South-erners—even progressives and moderates—were fearful that the Southern way of life, in which blacks were segregated, exploited, and consistently mistreated, would be changed by Northern forces inciting violence and trouble. For nearly a century, every man in high office in the Deep South supported racial segregation. Not all were as racist and demagogic as others, but most felt that segregation was so widely accepted throughout the South that it must be morally right. It was not. The dramatic change, in effect a moral revolution, was not initiated by John F. Kennedy or his brother Robert. On the contrary, both were slow to recognize the moral imperative underlying the need for change.

The civil rights issue was not a high priority for JFK in the Senate years, and so it was not an issue on which I frequently worked, despite my long-standing commitment to the cause. In 1957, after being advised by Harvard legal scholars that amending the pending Voting Rights Bill to provide for jury trials in contempt of court cases would not seriously weaken the legislation, Kennedy voted for the amendment to assure passage of the bill. An imperfect bill was better than no bill at all, he replied to his critics, and I agreed. But in casting his "aye" vote, Kennedy antagonized many of his pro–civil rights supporters in Massachusetts and elsewhere. Some of my liberal friends, disappointed by Kennedy's politics of pragmatism, also criticized me for viewing the Senate civil rights debate strictly from a tactical angle.

My involvement on civil rights during the 1960 campaign was also minimal—in part, I'm not proud to say, because the issue was not central to the campaign. Both Kennedy and I believed it was morally as well as politically permissible to compromise on tactical moves to preserve a long-term strategic goal of overriding importance—in this case, defeating Nixon and changing U.S. policy at home and abroad.

In December 1959, when Robert F. Kennedy was about to join the campaign in a major role, and was preparing to make an exploratory visit on behalf of the campaign to several Southern states, I sent him a memorandum entitled "Southern States and Civil Rights." My memorandum argued, in essence, that the case for the South supporting Kennedy at the convention did not rest on his being against civil rights, citing the two roll call votes on the Civil Rights Bill of 1957 in which Johnson and Kennedy had voted together and Symington and Humphrey had voted the other way. Johnson, my memo noted, was obviously the choice of the Southern states; but, if he decided not to run or did not make it to the convention, the other possible choices for Southerners were either Symington, who, I noted, had voted with other Northerners "of anti-Southern prejudice," or Stevenson, who, I noted, had "never taken any position on these specific legislative proposals, although his views in general would appear to be like Kennedy's." The memo continued:

> In the last few years, Kennedy has visited every southern state, several of them more than once. He has always been willing to listen to southern needs and problems . . . Stevenson has made no such trips

and does not have this same background . . . The South needs a winner. A Democratic President—to help southern agriculture, small businessmen [and] industrial expansion . . . Senator Kennedy has won five elections beginning in 1946 . . . He could be that Democratic president—but Stevenson, the two-time loser for the Presidency who lost several Southern states, could not.

Late in the campaign, a Georgia judge sentenced Dr. Martin Luther King Jr. to four months in prison and hard labor for a traffic technicality, reflecting the ugly face of racial prejudice in a gross miscarriage of justice. After an intensive hotel room debate among his advisors, Kennedy called Dr. King's pregnant wife, Coretta, to offer his consolation and concern. I acknowledge with shame and regret that I was among those arguing against a call, cautioning prudence and delay. I thought it was a symbolic act that would lose JFK more votes among white Southerners than it would win him among blacks. I reasoned that black voters already opposed Nixon, and would oppose Republicans even more as their economic plight worsened under the Eisenhower administration, and Nixon continued to make clear that his campaign's "Southern strategy" was focusing on Southern whites. I was wrong, both morally and politically. The Kennedy call was a bold and important stroke that sent a message of hope to blacks all across America. News of the call, when it reached black churches around the country, helped swell the tide of black voter support in the key states that produced JFK's election.

In the early White House days, civil rights was not among the legislative messages that the president asked me to draft for transmittal to Congress. There was no Kennedy administration civil rights program in 1961. Democratic legislative leaders convinced him that merely sending civil rights legislation to Congress—which, in its previous session, despite a larger proportion of liberal Democrats, had bottled up a modest civil rights bill— would produce no legislative gains on the civil rights front, but would ensure Democratic legislative losses on every other front. JFK decided to do what he could through executive orders. It was easy for his critics in the civil rights movement to say be bold, send up a bill; but there was no hope of getting a bill passed. Kennedy knew that his legislative program—particularly its provisions to increase the minimum wage, provide aid to economically distressed communities, and build more public housing—would materially help blacks, and that the empty gesture of sending up civil rights bills to certain defeat on Capitol Hill would accomplish nothing except the defeat of his other legislation and increased frustration among those who were being denied their rights.

Given my own background and convictions, I was frustrated by his caution in moving the full powers of his presidency behind the civil rights movement, but I was also sufficiently pragmatic to understand the importance to blacks of both his legislative program and his future reelection; and I did not want to see either jeopardized by a premature purely symbolic move. Moreover, I had confidence that he would ultimately do the right thing.

One week after he issued his executive order establishing the Peace Corps, early in his first year, he issued Executive Order 10925 establishing the Committee on Equal Employment Opportunity "to promote and ensure equal opportunity for all qualified persons regardless of race seeking employment with the federal government or on government contracts." The order declared it to be the obligation of all government contractors to "take affirmative action to ensure that applicants are employed, treated, recruited and upgraded without discrimination." This may have been the first official use of the term "affirmative action" in the drive to assure equal opportunity and employment around the country. There was no reference to quotas or equal results—the emphasis was on equal opportunity.

Black civil rights leaders, including my old friend from Omaha, Urban League president Whitney Young, recognizing that the president hoped to use executive orders instead of legislation, urged him to consider "one monumental Executive Order to cover everything, a second Emancipation Proclamation, including education, housing, travel, public accommodations and employment, regardless of whether presidential power could actually, constitutionally override the Congress and the states in these areas." "Why don't you call Ted Sorensen?" JFK told them. "Write him a memo. We'll see what comes of it." They did prepare a long memo, and came to meet with me in the White House in February, after first meeting with the president. According to NAACP president Roy Wilkins's later recollection, I accepted the memo "and promised to consider it," but worried that, in the absence of pressure from the public, moving ahead too rapidly on housing might jeopardize the nomination of Robert Weaver, a prominent black, as administrator of the Housing and Home Finance Agency.

Under mounting pressure from civil rights leaders,

JFK expressed regret that he had mistakenly given the impression during the 1960 campaign that civil rights in housing could be advanced merely with "one stroke of the pen." "Did you write that phrase?" he asked me one day. When I replied that I had not, he said, "Oh, well I guess no one wrote that."

Executive action also included executing and implementing the laws of the land. The president was obligated under the Constitution to ensure the enforcement of court orders, including those requiring the admission of qualified black applicants to the all-white state universities in the South, inevitably pitting the federal government's chief executive against some Southern governors. When Governor Ross Barnett of Mississippi defied such a federal court order regarding the application of James Meredith to the University of Mississippi, Attorney General Robert Kennedy encouraged the president to be firm.

I was confined to Bethesda Naval Hospital with ulcers, trying to keep up with the situation by reading newspapers. My daily pocket calendar for that month says simply "HOSPITAL" for the days of Friday, September 21, through Sunday, September 30, and my hospital checkout was originally scheduled for Monday, October 1. I had, in fact, temporarily checked out for

one night on the town when I attended the premiere
of Irving Berlin's *Mr. President* on September 25. The
real Mr. President called me in Bethesda on Saturday,
September 29, and asked me to put my thoughts on
paper, because a television speech on the crisis appeared likely. Late Saturday night, I called my longtime secretary Gloria Sitrin, and asked her to come to
the hospital so that I could dictate my thoughts. Gloria
discussed with her husband whether it would be a
violation of Jewish New Year restrictions to do so. They
agreed, she later said, "that the nation came first." I
dictated and dispatched the following memo to the
president:

> My greatest regret is that I am immobilized at a
> time of domestic crisis. You and the Attorney Gen-
> eral have been handling the whole Mississippi affair
> excellently, however, so I doubt that my presence
> would have made any difference. While the fol-
> lowing thoughts may be of little value because of
> my removal from the scene, they are offered in sup-
> port of what I judge to be your present course:
>
> Stay out of it personally for the time being. The
> defiance should be against the majesty of the United
> States, not John F. Kennedy.

Soren Pedersen and Mette Sorensdatter Pedersen, Ted's great-grandparents.

Chaikin family, 1896. *Left to right*: Phineas, Morris, Annis (Ted's mother, age eight), Dora, and Stella.

Annis Chaikin
Sorensen, Ted's
mother.

Christian Abraham Sorensen,
Ted's father.

Sorensen siblings reading *Life* magazine. *Left to right*: Ted, Ruth, Robert *(center)*, Phil, and Tom.

Sorensen siblings celebrating their mother's eightieth birthday. *Front, left to right*: Robert, Annis Chaikin Sorensen, Ruth Sorensen Singer. *Back row:* Tom, Ted, and Phil.

Senator John F. Kennedy with Lucy Torres administering oath to Ted (1952).

Senator Kennedy and Ted at work in Senate office (late 1950s).

Senator John F. Kennedy, Jacqueline Kennedy, and Ted being greeted in 1958 by José Benitez upon their arrival in San Juan, Puerto Rico.

Ted reviewing a sample ballot for a May 1960 primary election.

President Kennedy and Ted in Oval Office (1961).

JFK's 1960 general election campaign. Ted standing between fellow
speechwriters Dick Goodwin *(left)* and Mike Feldman *(right)*.

Tom Sorensen and Ted in Ted's White House office.

Poet Carl Sandburg, Secretary of the Interior Stewart Udall, and Ted at Interior Reception (October 12, 1961).

Saturday softball game with sons (August 1962). *Left to right*: Steve, Ted, Phil, Eric.

Visit to the Open Air Museum in Copenhagen, Denmark, with sons (summer 1967). *Left to right*: Steve, Ted, Eric, Phil.

Pre-presidential campaign announcement session (March 1968) in dining room of Hickory Hill, home of Ethel and Robert Kennedy. *Left to right*: Steve Smith *(seated)*, RFK, Senator Ted Kennedy, Ted, and William vanden Heuvel.

Ted speaking at an RFK-for-President campaign rally (spring 1968).

Gillian Martin and Ted greeting Arthur Schlesinger at their engagement party (spring 1969).

Ted in his law office (winter 1969).

Ted campaigning during the 1970 New York State primary campaign for U.S. Senate.

Charles Evers, Mayor of Fayette, Mississippi, endorsing Ted's candidacy.

Ted and Gillian at campaign appearance.

Costa Rican President and Mrs. Oscar Arias greeting Ted on his 1987 visit to San Jose with New York City Mayor Ed Koch.

Arthur Ashe and Ted after a pro-celebrity fund-raising tennis match in Westchester.

Ted and Cuban President Fidel Castro.

Ted and Arthur Schlesinger in front of a Soviet missile at the Havana, Cuba, military museum (October 2002).

President of South Africa Nelson Mandela at the United Nations with Ted and Gillian Sorensen.

Sorensen family at the wedding of Juliet and Ben Jones. *Left to right*:
Ted, Steve, the bride and groom, Eric, Phil, and Gillian (2000).

Gillian and Ted in Pound Ridge.

Ted at New York City residence.

Senator Barack Obama and Ted at DePaul University, Chicago
(October 2, 2007).

Similarly, no press conference when all this is over. There are too many questions you should neither evade nor answer directly.

Keep moving, but move slowly. There can be some action every day, preferably in court—without sending troops until all litigation is at dead end. You are demonstrating how many graduated steps there are between inaction and troops.

Mobilize other means of changing the climate . . . the citizenry of Mississippi may be more receptive if a few voices of moderation, including Baptist and other Protestant clergy, could be heard. The businessmen backing the Governor may be more nervous if big federal contracts in that state were held up for fear that violence may interfere with their being carried out . . . The students may be less enthusiastic if Ole Miss lost her accreditation, some of her football opponents for this fall, or her eligibility for post-season bowl games.

Finally, if it comes to the point of troops, I suggest you consider taking 15 to 30 minutes of nationwide TV time for an address to the citizens of Mississippi.

All this may not be worth much . . . but I am available by phone and hope to be back Monday.

On Sunday the president called again: "You might as well come back now." I did. It turned into a long night of work. If Saturday, October 27, 1962, in the midst of the Cuban missile crisis, was my most intense afternoon in the White House, Sunday, September 30, 1962, only a few weeks earlier, was my most intense night.

At 10 P.M. that night, JFK delivered to the nation a speech, which I had prepared, based partly on the notes I had dictated to Gloria the night before. It had two themes:

(1) The rule of law. "Even among law-abiding men, few laws are universally loved, but they are uniformly respected and not resisted. Americans are free to disagree with the law, but not to disobey it. In a government of laws and not of men, no man, however prominent or powerful and no mob . . . is entitled to defy a court of law."

(2) The honor of Mississippi. "Thanks . . . to those Southerners who have contributed to the progress of our democratic development in the entrance of students regardless of race to [other] state-supported universities of [the South] . . . Mississippi and her university are noted for their courage, their contribution of talent and thought to the affairs of

this nation . . . The most effective means of upholding the law is not the police . . . It is you . . . your courage to accept those laws with which you disagree . . . The eyes of the nation and of all the world are upon you . . . and the honor of your university and state are in the balance."

My draft speech stated lofty principles, but it accomplished nothing. Even as the president spoke, the mob scene at Ole Miss was worsening.

During that long night, Attorney General Robert Kennedy tried to make certain that enough tear gas was on its way to arm and protect the federal marshals on the campus. While waiting, the president and I talked about a number of other things. The transcript of that chat included my one-sentence comment on the Mississippi rioting: "Sad day in our country."

Present around the table that night in the Cabinet Room, in addition to the president, attorney general, and me, were, as I recall, Kenny O'Donnell, Larry O'Brien, and Burke Marshall, Assistant Attorney General in charge of civil rights. Our principal political liaison with the South, Vice President Johnson, was not present. It was a disorganized discussion, with constant phone calls informing us of new developments. Cynical humor still prevailed. "I haven't had such an interesting time since the Bay of Pigs," said JFK sourly. Picking up on the comparison, I suggested the attorney general might want to provide air cover for his marshals.

All this time, James Meredith was being guarded by federal marshals in a building on campus. Near the end of the night, there were fears that some student rioters would discover his presence and storm the building, raising concern in O'Donnell's mind that there could be a lynching. Before the night was over, two people were dead as a result of rioting on the campus. To stabilize an otherwise lawless scene, the president dispatched twenty-three thousand federal troops to Mississippi. After a long night, they arrived by morning, and a long battle and a constitutional crisis subsided. Although the arrival of troops seemed agonizingly slow at the time, I could not help but think of these events forty-three years later, when the devastation of New Orleans by Hurricane Katrina produced another lawless scene of looting and shooting, and the federal government's response was subject to disastrous delays.

Racial tensions continued to rise throughout the nation, with marches, protests, and demonstrations across the South, while Southern police, using tear gas, fire hoses, dogs, and beatings, intensified their repressive tactics. Early in May 1963 I sent the president a memorandum entitled "The Range of Alternatives in Birmingham," a site of increasing unrest. I recommended five possible steps:

Private presidential telephone calls to the involved parties, including the local newspaper publisher;

A public presidential statement to a business organization by telephone loudspeaker, and a statement to both sides urging them to sit down with Burke Marshall and Secretary of Commerce Hodges [a North Carolinian];

A meeting in the White House of Negro and business leaders from Birmingham and its new Mayor;

A special board of fact-finders and mediators appointed by the President;

Legal actions: a Department of Justice criminal action under the old [1957] Civil Rights Act. For Alabama generally, Justice Department actions against the state police and a suit on voting rights, federalization of the Alabama National Guard before the Governor could mobilize it, and an appeal to major Birmingham employers to improve their hiring practices, including U.S. government agencies in the city.

Nationally, I suggested that the President call a conference of business, labor, and Negro leaders on the subject of "equal public accommodations as well as new legislation."

On June 11, 1963, eight and a half months after the Mississippi confrontation, we faced a similar situation at the University of Alabama. The leading segregationist politician in the South, Alabama Governor George C. Wallace, had gained notoriety and local popularity by vowing to stand in the "schoolhouse door" of any institution that a Negro student, armed with a court order, tried to enter.

During one of our crucial strategy sessions, RFK arranged for filmmaker Robert Drew and his crew to be present in the Oval Office, recording the events for history. Entering the room, I stopped short when I saw the lights and camera. "It's OK, it's been arranged," RFK said. Upon watching the footage many years later, I was embarrassed to see myself yawn during that historic discussion. I had not slept much that week.

We were better prepared for the Alabama crisis than we had been for the crisis in Mississippi. This time, the president and attorney general were ready well in advance with a plan of action, an armed force sufficient to keep order on campus, and an advance agreement with the governor that he would have his few minutes in the doorway, in the limelight and on national television before stepping aside when informed by Deputy Attorney General Nicholas Katzenbach that the Alabama National Guard had been federalized by presidential order and that two qualified Negro students were entering to register by court order. Although we were uncertain whether Wallace would in fact step aside as agreed, that little dance was peacefully performed as choreographed, while the president and I watched on his Oval Office television set.

As Wallace left the doorway, the president turned around and said to me, "I think we'd better give that speech tonight." What speech? For weeks, as our civil rights strategy and legislation were being formulated, there had been much talk about whether and when the president should address the nation on the topic. But no decision had been made, and no draft had been prepared. O'Donnell and O'Brien were both opposed to JFK making a speech because of its effects on his political future and legislative program. I had my own reservations for the same reasons, despite my long hope that he could exert leadership on the issue.

Those reservations had increased during the months between the Mississippi and Alabama campus confrontations, as violence in the streets of the South and demands for action across the nation grew rapidly. We had been preparing comprehensive civil rights legislation, but it had not yet been completed, as both objections and suggestions for change continued to come in from a variety of sources inside and outside the executive branch. I felt that a major speech on civil rights should await the completion of the legislation and cover its contents. Moreover, the situation at the University of Alabama was not a constitutional crisis, was not directly related to the most controversial parts of the legislation, and seemed an unlikely basis for a major presidential speech.

Nonetheless, JFK decided that 8 P.M. was best for televising this major presidential speech, and Press Secretary Salinger requested that time on all TV and radio networks. It was then after 4:30 P.M. I made some noises about limited time. RFK, who had arrived with Burke Marshall, said, "Don't worry, we have a lot of good material over at the Justice Department that we can send to you." I worried anyway.

In Washington, few thought there would be a speech. When McGeorge Bundy sat down to dinner at Joe Alsop's that evening and everybody said, "Let's tune in the president's speech," Bundy replied, "There isn't going to be a speech. I just left the White House 30 minutes ago and Sorensen didn't have a draft yet." That was true. I didn't. I could not draw upon a previous Kennedy civil rights speech file, because there was no such file. But I had a memory full of JFK's remarks during the campaign, plus issues and proposals we hoped to cover in the legislation, and a personal background of involvement in an issue about which I had long cared deeply, beginning with my high school oration at Nebraska Wesleyan University roughly twenty years earlier. Unfortunately, I had no copy or even memory of that speech, which read, in part:

> We have said the Negro could study and pray, but not in our schools and not in our churches. We have said he could work, but not through our unions. We have said he could vote, but warn him away from the polls. We have said he could live but not on our level, and we have said he could be free, and then subjected him to discrimination and poverty. . . . [And when] an American soldier on the German Front . . . wounded and decorated, returned home . . . he did not find his American liberties . . . Why? Because his skin was not white.

Those sentiments must have surfaced from deep within my mind when I drafted remarks for the president on that evening of June 11:

Are we to say . . . that this is a land of the free except for the Negroes; that we have no second-class citizens except Negroes; that we have no class or caste system, no ghettos, no master race, except with respect to Negroes? . . . when Americans are sent to Vietnam or West Berlin we do not ask for whites only.

It was the only time in my three years in the White House that JFK came to my office to ask about a speech. "Don't worry," I replied. "It's in the typewriter now." My secretary was typing up my handwritten draft. "Oh," he joked, "I thought I was going to have to go off the cuff on national television."

RFK later recalled that, when he returned to the White House around 7 P.M., my first draft was unsatisfactory. In a Cabinet Room markup session with RFK and Burke Marshall, JFK made the following edits, mostly changes in tone: "The cesspools of segregation and discrimination exist in every state" was changed to "difficulties over segregation and discrimination exist in every city . . ." "The Negro cannot enjoy the free and full life that makes life in America worth living and worth dying for" was changed to "He cannot enjoy the full and free life which all of us want." The sentence "A social revolution is at hand, and our task is to make that revolution peaceful and constructive for all" became in the final version "A great change is at hand, and our task . . . is to make that revolution, that change, peaceful and constructive for all." The phrase "But the pace is still shamefully slow" became "But the pace is very slow." "The orderly implementation of the Supreme Court's decision on education cannot be left to haphazard cases brought by individuals willing to brave possible reprisal" was changed to "cannot be left to those who may not have the economic resources to carry the legal action or may be subject to harassment." In short, my speech was toned down, but its substance remained.

Both JFK and I wanted a speech that would pay tribute to the conduct of those students of the University of Alabama "who met their responsibilities in a constructive way," implicitly contrasting them with the rioting students at the University of Mississippi eight months earlier. We emphasized that the National Guardsmen on the campus were from Alabama, that the judge who ordered the admission of these two students sat in Alabama, and that the two students themselves were "clearly qualified young Alabama residents who happened to have been born Negro."

It was the centennial year of Lincoln's Emancipation Proclamation of 1863—that had to be noted. Public resentment, not confined to the South, against civil rights demonstrations had to be taken into account by references to legislation that would settle these disputes "in the courts instead of the streets." We cited broader national interests to provide "liberty for all Americans and their posterity—not merely for reasons of economic efficiency, world diplomacy, and domestic tranquility but, above all, because it is right." As LBJ had urged, Kennedy declared civil rights to be a moral issue, "as old as the Scriptures and as clear as the American Constitution." Taylor Branch, Martin Luther King's biographer, said that the speech evoked King's own style by placing one foot in the language of patriotism and one foot in the Scriptures. In fact, several weeks later, JFK would admire the eloquence of King's "I Have a Dream" speech at the August 1963 civil rights march on Washington; and J. Edgar Hoover's allegations that a Communist Party functionary was influencing Dr. King did not alter JFK's admiration of King in the slightest.

My draft closing for that June 11 speech—declaring that we must all "live up to the cause of liberty for all . . . in our public action and private lives, in our every word and deed . . . in all the years to come. With God's help, that cause will succeed"—was deleted to make room for the last several paragraphs that JFK had been scribbling while waiting for me, fearing I might produce nothing and he would have no text at all. I was still working on my draft at four minutes to 8 P.M., leaving the president only a few minutes to look it over. If one studies the final text with care, there is a discernible point where the rhythm and style change slightly. But those closing passages, emanating from his scribbled notes, were eloquent and powerful. By oversight, they repeated some of the same statistical contrasts that had appeared earlier in the speech, and included a statement I might not have used: "We have a right to expect that the Negro community will be responsible and will uphold the law."

Despite the rushed rewriting and additions, it turned out fine. Decades later, Reverend Walter Fauntroy, one of Dr. King's closest associates, told me that he and Dr. King sat together watching the speech on television. At its conclusion, Dr. King leaped to his feet and said: "Walter, can you believe that white man not only stepped up to the plate, he hit it over the fence!"

The basic principles of equality voiced in that speech ultimately helped black, Hispanic, female, Jewish, gay, and all Americans historically subject over the years to exclusion and discrimination.

A few days later, the president began the most intensive use of the educational powers of the presidency that I have ever seen. Week after week, he convened White

House meetings with the leaders of American society—business executives, union leaders, clergymen, lawyers, educators, and others—meetings in which, accompanied by the attorney general and vice president, he exhorted those attending to help in this effort, to do their part in their respective segments of society.

Following the speech, JFK made unprecedented civil rights legislation his top priority. According to RFK, LBJ was opposed to sending the legislation up shortly after the speech, believing that we should first do more work in Congress, a wise suggestion. The president also took time to canvass all the key congressmen and senators, delaying the submission of the legislation by another week. On June 19, he sent to the Congress the most comprehensive civil rights bill in history, accompanied by a message "making clear to all that race has no place in American life or law." Propelled by LBJ, that bill became the Civil Rights Act of 1964. It was followed by the Voting Rights Act of 1965, which authorized the Department of Justice to speed educational desegregation, outlawed discrimination in federally funded projects and contracts, and extended the life of the Civil Rights Commission.

Like the aristocratic Founding Fathers who sowed the seeds of their own group's fall from power by broadening democracy, Kennedy and Johnson paved the way for a string of national Democratic Party defeats by promulgating civil rights legislation that has alienated Southern and border state voters for fifty years. Ever since the Democratic Party of their era conscientiously split North and South over the single greatest issue ever to confront our country—the status of our black citizens—the Republicans have won seven out of the last ten presidential elections; and no Northern Democratic presidential nominee has won since Kennedy in 1960. Nevertheless, I believe deeply that it was the right thing to do—and I am certain JFK felt the same way.

Kennedy understood the political risks of supporting civil rights. Both he and LBJ were warned that Southern politicians, including Democrats, would not accept provisions for increased voting rights or facilitating admission to public schools; that laborers North and South would object to working side by side with blacks on assembly lines or construction projects; that both men and women, North and South, would object to blacks entering such intimate places of public accommodation as lunch counters, swimming pools, and boardinghouses. Some polls showed that even white liberals were privately opposed to integration in their own neighborhoods and schools. Other polls showed that Southerners who had supported JFK for president in 1960 would not vote for him again. Many Southern moderates told Kennedy that segregation and prejudice could not be legislated out of existence, that he had to wait for a change in public sentiment at the local as well as national level, that attempting to force such a change would be neither feasible nor peaceable.

RFK would later say that the president "felt that maybe that [June 11] speech was going to be his political 'swan song,'" and "discussed whether that was the right thing to do," joking that RFK had "gotten him into so much difficulty." Privately, the president confided to one black leader that "this issue could cost me the election, but we're not turning back." In August–September 1963, the American people were asked in a Gallup Poll whether the Kennedy administration was "pushing racial integration too fast or not fast enough?" Fifty percent said "too fast." Asked about this poll at a news conference, JFK replied, "great historic events cannot be judged by taking the national temperature every few weeks . . . I think we will stand after a period of time has gone by." He still stands.

Chapter 23

The Cuban Missile Crisis

Following months of rumors about possible new Soviet military activities in Cuba, the president called me into the Oval Office on the morning of Tuesday, October 16, 1962, with urgent news. He had just been informed that pictures taken the previous weekend by a U-2 spy plane over Cuba had shown what photographic intelligence interpreters had concluded were the beginnings of installations for Soviet intermediate range missiles, capable of carrying nuclear payloads to the United States and most other parts of the Western Hemisphere.

At the first meeting of his advisors that same morning, we were advised that the missiles themselves were not yet in place and no threat had yet been uttered by

Khrushchev. Nonetheless, the sudden secret initiation of those missile sites represented a dire warning, a warning that Kennedy immediately decided to take seriously and formulate a counterplan. In the years since, I have compared the position of the United States, upon learning that the Soviets had secretly rushed nuclear missiles into Cuba, to the position of two American shrimp fishermen in a small boat in the Florida Straits, a few months after the Cuban missile crisis, when Cuban MIGs buzzed them. When asked at his press conference whether he thought the planes "attacked" or merely "harassed" the boat, the president replied: "if you are on the boat, that is regarded as an attack." In October 1962, we were in that boat, and had every reason to believe that the United States was the target of those missiles.

Clearly, the president told me, the assurances that he had received from Khrushchev in their back-channel correspondence, and the assurances that I had received from Soviet ambassador Anatoly Dobrynin in an earlier confidential conversation—assurances that the Soviet government had done nothing "new or extraordinary in Cuba"—were false. Kennedy felt strongly that the United States had to respond quickly. He was, he told me, convening a meeting of his top advisors at 11:45 A.M. that same morning. He wanted me to attend, and asked me to bring copies of the two warning statements about

Soviet offensive weapons in Cuba that he had made at news conferences during the preceding months.

For this meeting, the president did not summon the National Security Council, where attendance was determined largely by statute, and was often too large to keep a secret and efficiently reach a decision; the only people he wanted in that room were those in whose judgment John F. Kennedy had confidence. Serving on the ExComm, as it came to be known, was for me a unique and bonding experience shared with a select few. No postcrisis controversies soured these friendships. My enhanced relations with McNamara and Bundy in particular, and my admiration for Ambassador Llewellyn (Tommy) Thompson, a former ambassador to Russia, remained strong for decades. In general, each participant both publicly and privately praised the others, including those on the other side of the hawk/dove divide. (Although I use those terms here to simplify, we did not use them in the ExComm. Those terms were coined after the crisis was over. The dedicated officials sitting around the cabinet table during those thirteen memorable days could not so easily be reduced to one-dimensional labels.)

There were two exceptions to the mutual admiration of those who served on the ExComm. Robert Kennedy later expressed privately his surprise and disappoint-

ment that Dean Rusk did not feel he should chair meetings and didn't seem to have an agenda. He also said
that he was "shocked" that Soviet expert Chip Bohlen,
after the first day or two, "ran out on us" when he decided to sail to Europe (instead of flying later) to begin
his duties in Paris as the new American ambassador. In
hindsight, that may have been for the best, inasmuch
as Bohlen's only memorable contribution to the group's
discussions was to quote Lenin, "Probe with the bayo-
net. If you meet steel, stop. If you meet mush, push."
Nor, unsurprisingly, was RFK impressed by LBJ's
contributions to our meetings.

This crisis was a threat to global survival, but I did
not take time during those days to ask myself why it
was happening. Contrary to speculation that Khrushchev had gambled with Soviet missiles because he had
judged Kennedy at their 1961 Vienna summit meeting
to be weak, Khrushchev's son later recalled that his father returned from Vienna "with a very high opinion
of Kennedy as a worthy partner and strong statesman,
a sensible politician." My own view is that Khrushchev,
who was determined to see his country regarded as a
superpower equal to the United States, deemed Soviet
missiles in Cuba the equivalent of NATO missiles in
Turkey. Once the weapons were there, Khrushchev
did not want to back down and thereby look soft to

his Chinese and domestic critics. Similarly, JFK knew that Western allies' confidence in the United States depended on his not backing down and looking soft in the face of this threat. He acknowledged in our ExComm discussion that our allies already thought we were obsessed with Cuba, and would think us crazy if we invaded. Were both men now thinking the unthinkable and gambling on world survival largely for reasons of appearances? If so, that is indefensible in hindsight.

To prevent press and Soviet speculation that crisis meetings were being conducted at the White House, the president urged us in that first meeting to avoid large numbers of official limousines parked behind the White House, and to adhere—as he would—to our respective routine schedules, including even campaign speeches and social commitments. My pocket calendar for those thirteen days shows nearly every planned activity crossed out, including "Bermuda," the only boondoggle opportunity afforded me during my years in the White House, an invitation to address a meeting there of the International Junior Chamber of Commerce. Also crossed out for October 27 was a reference to "the boys"; I could not see my sons for their usual Saturday visit on that penultimate day of the crisis.

As the days wore on, I found my time almost wholly consumed by the crisis, and asked Mike Feldman to take over all my chores on domestic policy, giving him several grim assignments: Find out all you can about the bomb shelter under the White House and how to access it; obtain copies of previous U.S. declarations of war; determine who would be in charge of the government if the president, vice president, and senior cabinet members were all killed in an attack; and what plans, if any, exist for the evacuation of Washington (in the event of an attack, I was to stay in the White House with the president, although the president, always able to laugh at adversity, joked to me: "You know there's not enough room in that basement bomb shelter for all of us!"). By then, one week into the thirteen-day period, both emotions and fatigue were affecting our ExComm discussions, as many ExComm members, including even RFK and McNamara, shifted their positions between passive and aggressive responses from time to time. After a meeting toward the end of the crisis, the president shared with me his concern that Dean Rusk had overworked himself to the point of mental and physical exhaustion. If the crisis had lasted thirty-one days instead of thirteen, who knows what would have happened?

In one sense, the urgent pace of those thirteen days helped us all to cope emotionally with the crisis. We were simply too busy to be scared. But I still remember the night when the enormity of the crisis sank in. Looking up at the stars, and remembering the planetarium sky show I had seen years earlier, I thought about those planets or stars that, at some unknown time in ages past, had been extinguished, blinked out, self-destructed. Were we about to join them?

From the beginning, the president made certain that all his options were reviewed, including the option of doing nothing at all. Virtually everyone's initial choice, at that first October 16 meeting, was a surgical air strike against the nuclear missile sites before they could become operational. U.S. bombers could swoop in, eliminate the sites, and fly away, leaving the problem swiftly, magically ended. But further questions—JFK always had further questions—proved that solution illusory. First, no cruise missiles or smart bombs existed in those days to assure the precision and success of the strike. The Air Force acknowledged that it could only be certain of eliminating 60 percent of the missiles, leaving the others free to fire and destroy us.

Second, the Air Force was unwilling to send its planes and pilots over Cuba unless they had previously bombed all Soviet surface-to-air missile sites, then all Cuban antiaircraft sites, and then all Soviet and Cuban airfields, incapacitating enemy fighter planes and preventing enemy bombers from darting to Florida while our Air Force was otherwise engaged. Then, once most of Cuba had been bombed, said our military, we would need to restore order and assure U.S. control by following up the strike with a U.S. invasion. So much for the surgical strike. I vividly recall one hawk saying: "Mr. President, this is your chance, your excuse, to go in there and take Cuba away from Castro." I later learned that the Joint Chiefs were discussing an airdrop by the 82nd Airborne, which would "mop up Cuba in 72 hours with a loss of only 10,000 Americans more or less." The same source told me he used his lunch hour that day to purchase "knapsacks and provisions" for his family's evacuation.

During one ExComm meeting, Treasury Secretary Douglas Dillon, who favored the air strike plan, passed me a note across the table:

Ted—Have you considered the very real possibility that if we allow Cuba to complete installation and operational readiness of missile bases, the next House of Representatives is likely to have a Republican majority? That would completely paralyze our ability to react sensibly and coherently to further Soviet advances.

It took Dillon, a stalwart Republican who had served in the Eisenhower administration and contributed generously to Nixon in 1960, to point out the political implications of the president's decision.

By midweek, another option gaining strength in our meetings was a blockade to keep out shipments of more Soviet weapons and nuclear equipment, possibly including the nuclear warheads, which we could not locate with aerial photography. Those favoring a military solution argued that the air strike would remove the missiles quickly, which the blockade would not, and that the air strike was the kind of strong response that the Soviet threat and deception justified, while the blockade was not. The blockade option was gradually reshaped—to permit food, medicine, gasoline, and the necessities of life; to prohibit the sinking of ships stopped for inspection; and to avoid language inviting a reciprocal blockade of West Berlin. Instead of "blockade," a bellicose label, we would call it "a quarantine against additional offensive weapons in Cuba."

When JFK returned Wednesday evening, October 17, from a brief campaign trip to Connecticut, RFK and I met him at the airport. His first question, upon entering the limousine, was "Any leaks yet?" I replied: "Only your talk with Joe Alsop." He reacted so instantly, I thought at first that perhaps my intended joke was not a fiction—then he realized it was a jest, relaxed, and laughed. We then told him that we had noted that day more candor on the part of those ExComm participants from middle-level positions, worrying less about disagreeing with their superiors when the president was not in the room. He understood, and thereafter absented himself that first week from many of our meetings; and I summarized the discussions for him at the end of the day.

Earlier on Wednesday, former secretary of state Dean Acheson had been brought in as an outside consultant. Asked for his recommendation, Acheson replied that, based on his intimate knowledge of Soviet motives and conduct, he thought the United States should bomb Soviet missile sites in Cuba. Asked how the Soviets would react, he predicted they would then bomb NATO missile sites in Turkey. Asked how we would react to that, he said the United States under its NATO commitments would be obligated to bomb Soviet missile sites inside Russia. Asked how they would react to that, he paused and replied: "by then, we hope cooler heads will prevail." It was distinctly cool in that room. Long after it all ended, Acheson told an *Esquire* magazine interviewer that the Kennedys showed no great talent in handling the Cuban missile crisis—just "luck." Asked by the press for a comment, I replied: "we were lucky—lucky we did not take Mr. Acheson's advice."

Acheson did, however, perform ably on the morning of October 22 as JFK's emissary to brief the usually obstinate President de Gaulle on the missiles and our intended response. After his initial presentation, when Acheson told the French president that an Air Force colonel sitting outside was prepared to review the CIA aerial photography with him, de Gaulle brushed the offer aside: "No, the word of the President of the United States is good enough for me."

In our Thursday, October 18 deliberations, after RFK advised the ExComm that a surprise bombing strike on island military installations—killing innocent civilians—would be compared to the Japanese bombing of Pearl Harbor in 1941, thereby tarnishing America's place in history, we debated whether some form of notice should be given. The military was uncomfortable with the idea of warning the targets of an air strike, fearful the missiles would be moved under cover or camouflage. Finally, I was asked to draft a warning note from President Kennedy to Khrushchev. Practically everyone at the table had a condition to impose on my draft. It must withstand the scrutiny of the American people, foreign diplomats, and posterity. It could not read like an ultimatum, because a superpower would not yield to an ultimatum. It should not be complicated, because Khrushchev would tie us up in negotiations for weeks while the missile sites were completed. It should not be so soft that he would think he could get away with it, or so hard that the world would blame us for a nuclear holocaust. It must not provoke Khrushchev into notifying his forces that the missiles had been discovered and should be immediately fired, thereby launching World War III.

I tried my hand at a draft of that Kennedy-Khrushchev note that Thursday:

I am entrusting [this note] to a courier who has my complete confidence . . . [This] note is to inform you that, shortly after the close of your conference with my emissary, I have no choice but to initiate appropriate military action against the island of Cuba. Should you . . . be able to give to my emissary your unequivocal assurance that this work [assembling the missiles] will halt . . . and all . . . offensive weapons removed, United States military action can be withheld while continued surveillance makes certain that this is done. In this event, I would be glad to meet with you . . . I have instructed my emissary to explain this position in detail, to inform me promptly in order that military action . . . may be started if no satisfactory response is forthcoming . . . Any other response . . . cannot deter this nation. . . . I am serving similar notice upon Premier Castro.

Our intention is not war with the Soviet Union but to remove this threat to peace . . . The United States possesses both the will and the weapons to take whatever action is needed . . . [Do] not underestimate either our determination . . . or our desire for peaceful relations . . . I shall await the report of my emissary . . .

Fortunately, that draft letter—which did not meet all the ExComm's conditions or mine—was never completed or accepted by the president, nor delivered to Mr. Khrushchev, who I believe would have reacted violently. When I reported to the ExComm that no draft could meet all its contradictory conditions, that diminished the number of supporters for the "air strike plus invasion" option. In long continuous debates, turning points are difficult to recognize at the time they occur. But my failure to produce an acceptable notice may have been a turning point toward building a consensus behind the blockade option, which RFK and I were already supporting. That evening, after the ExComm met in George Ball's conference room, one floor below the State Department dining room where Soviet foreign minister Andrei Gromyko was the honored guest, we traveled back to the White House to share our conclusions and recommendations with the president, only to discover in the midst of our presentation that Mac Bundy (possibly at the president's urging) was insisting that the "sit-tight and do nothing" option be discussed again. In support of that position, perhaps quoting the president, Bundy pointed out that our European allies had learned to live in the Soviet nuclear bull's-eye and maybe we could do so as well.

Friday morning the president met privately with the Joint Chiefs at their request. General Curtis LeMay bitterly criticized the blockade approach as "almost as bad as the appeasement at Munich," insisting on "direct military intervention, right now." Marine Corps commandant David Shoup agreed: "You'll have to invade . . . we must go in with plenty of insurance . . . and as quick as possible." The president coolly held them off. After this tense meeting, encountering me in the hall outside his office as he was about to leave on another scheduled campaign trip, he was still seething. "You and Bobby have to pull this thing together. It's falling apart," he said, knowing, I believe, that I would work for the blockade option, not the air strike. Certainly, from our work together on Berlin and other foreign policy crises, he knew that I preferred any possible diplomatic resolution to military confrontation.

That afternoon, RFK convened the ExComm, which promptly reopened discussions on an air strike. I sourly but vigorously protested that the rediscussion of an option rejected the night before was doing "neither our national security nor my [previous month's] ulcer" any good. But in the president's absence, no firm course was set. We remained divided.

Finally, the blockade/quarantine group, recognizing that whichever path the president ultimately selected would require a televised address to the American people, asked me to formulate a draft speech as a means of articulating, for the consideration of the group and the president, all the components of the course we were recommending. When I reflected on that task in my office, I found too many unanswered questions, and returned to the meeting with those questions, asking the quarantine backers why that plan was best, how it would get the missiles out, how it could prevent them from being finished and fired, and how could we avoid the blockade's indefinite extension. The answers helped clarify their thinking and mine, and enabled me to spend that night drafting in my office. I was in the midst of writing when I remembered that I had a long-standing invitation to dinner that night at the home of Washington matron Florence Mahoney. I called her to explain that I had to work late. She asked why; I could not say. A short time later, her housekeeper arrived with a full dinner in a covered dish, a huge help. By 3 A.M. Saturday morning, I had produced a draft speech, which the ExComm and the president reviewed the next day. Although that first draft ultimately went through more changes in the following forty-eight hours than any speech I wrote in my life, it provided a framework of basic policy around which an ExComm consensus could be formed and a presidential decision made.

Decades later, when Bob McNamara and I were invited to a Moscow screening of the film *Thirteen Days*, he told the attending press and the movie's producer that the film contained one fundamental error: "It was not Kenny O'Donnell who pulled us all together—it was Ted Sorensen." That was an overly generous description, but I do believe that draft speech helped pull together all the components of the plan later adopted, integrating in one document the various military, diplomatic, multilateral, and other strategies under discussion.

There is still a minor mystery as to who, if anyone,

was asked to draft an alternative speech announcing and justifying an air strike on the missiles. There was, I discovered only recently, such a draft with a chilling start: "I have ordered—and the United States Air Force has now carried out—military operations with conventional weapons to remove a major nuclear weapons build-up from the soil of Cuba."

A copy of this "second speech" was among the documents circulated at the November 2002 reunion in Havana of Cuban missile crisis participants. I asked the conference organizers where it came from, and was told: "We thought you wrote it." But I am certain I did not. I could not have articulated a policy I so strongly opposed, nor forgotten such a wrenching experience if I had been required to do so. The draft did not appear to have been typed on my White House secretary's typewriter; it bore classification stamps, which I never put on my speech drafts. It also included a statement of America's intention to use nuclear weapons if necessary—a statement I would never have written, knowing JFK never would approve it. I do not believe that second speech draft was ever presented to JFK.

The confusion may have stemmed from that earlier effort to write the high-level emissary warning note that never went forward. It is that draft note, I believe, that formed the basis for the speculation that I had been asked to write a second speech as an alternative to the quarantine speech. But it is also possible that someone in the air strike group, probably Mac Bundy, knowing their group would need a draft to present to JFK as an alternative to mine, prepared that second speech version, taking some language from both my earlier draft warning note and from my draft blockade speech (some passages in the attack speech are identical to passages in my blockade speech). Bundy would say later that the air strike camp was at a disadvantage because, unlike the blockade camp, it had no one who could put its case in words they knew the president would speak.

When the president returned to the White House from Chicago on Saturday morning, October 20, I gave him, in addition to my draft blockade speech, a one-page memorandum outlining, from my perspective, the divisions in the ExComm and the choice he faced.

There are two fundamental objections to air strike which have never been answered:

1. Inasmuch as no one has been able to devise a satisfactory message to Khrushchev . . . an air strike means a U.S.-initiated "Pearl Harbor" on a small nation which history could neither understand nor forget.

2. Inasmuch as a clean, swift strike has been abandoned as militarily impractical, . . . the more widespread air attack will inevitably lead to an invasion.

There are two fundamental advantages to a blockade . . . :

1. It is a more prudent and flexible step, which enables us to move to an air strike . . . at any time it proves necessary . . .

2. It is the step least likely to precipitate general war while still causing the Soviets . . . to back down. . . .

To me, that said it all. The president then summoned the ExComm for the critical meeting at the residence in which he effectively selected the blockade option (he did not give final approval until the following morning). From our first meeting on Tuesday morning, October 16, to the president's return from Chicago on Saturday morning, October 20, it had taken us only four days to formulate a unified response on how to get the Soviet missiles out of Cuba.

The president chose the blockade option because he felt it was more likely to lead to a peaceful outcome. He knew that the approach had risks. He knew that it could drag on without resulting in the withdrawal of the missiles. He knew that he was inviting a wave of domestic political criticism and possibly the defeat of his party in the congressional elections the next month. He knew that a more aggressive course of action, like an air strike or invasion, would be more popular, whether it succeeded or failed.

It is not difficult to amass public support for a belligerent policy against a national adversary. In 1962 the easy, popular target would have been Cuba. It could have been invaded and liberated from both Castro and Communism to the delight of the American electorate, possibly even without triggering a Soviet military response, provided Soviet troops and missiles were left alone. But that course of action would not have guaranteed elimination of all the Soviet missiles, much less prevented their being fired at the United States. JFK knew that the Soviet Union, not Cuba, posed the real threat to the security of American and Western freedom. He rejected that easy choice of a strike at Cuba, and pursued the more difficult and possibly more dangerous confrontation with our real major adversary in the longer struggle that had no victory in sight—a choice that required diplomacy and risked the charge that he was appeasing Castro and afraid of war. Remembering today JFK's leadership during that crisis, I believe that a president who refrains from going to war may actually be showing more courage than one who follows the more politically popular course and launches military combat.

Had the president in October 1962 opted for the air strike/invasion option, we now know that it would have produced a nuclear war. Such an air strike and invasion, we have learned, would have brought in response an immediate nuclear assault upon our forces by Soviet troops in Cuba, equipped with tactical nuclear weapons and authorized to use them on their own initiative, thereby precipitating the world's first nuclear exchange, initially limited perhaps to the tactical weapons level, but inevitably and rapidly escalating to an all-out strategic exchange, very possibly lasting until little remained in either country other than radioactive ash. A "nuclear winter," I was later told by scientists, might have made this planet uninhabitable for thousands of years before another, perhaps more rational, species emerged. I shudder to think what would have happened had the angry, neurotic Richard Nixon been president during those crucial thirteen days.

JFK's choice of the blockade option was challenged when he met with congressional leaders only hours before his Monday night, October 22, national television address. In that meeting, Senate Armed Services Committee chairman Richard Russell called for an invasion: "You should assemble as speedily as possible an adequate force and clean out that situation!" Also favoring an invasion, "and an all-out one, as quickly as possible," was the usually dovish chairman of the Senate Foreign Relations Committee, William Fulbright. Again the president stood firm. "It would be foolish," he said, "to expect that the Russians would not regard [an invasion] as far more direct and more offensive than a blockade . . . Invasions are tough, hazardous . . . Thousands of Americans get killed . . . very, very difficult and very bloody."

A few hours earlier, not yet having had an opportunity to confide to my two deputies, Mike Feldman and Lee White, all that was happening, I asked them to come into my office and handed them each a copy of the president's speech. Each read it in silence, until the irrepressible White said: "What a shame—they just finished sanding that building across the street." One of my secretaries was kept completely out of the loop throughout the crisis because her roommate worked for conservative Republican senator Kenneth Keating.

That day, too busy for interruptions, I accepted only three phone calls from politicians. One was from Wilbur

Mills, the powerful chairman of the House Ways and Means Committee, asking if the situation was severe. Another was from Birch Bayh, who was running for the Senate that year. The last was from Ted Kennedy, asking, "Can I continue giving my standard speech on Cuba?" "No," I answered. "Wait for the president's speech tonight."

Before settling down the previous Friday night to draft the speech, I had quickly reviewed Franklin Roosevelt's 1941 speech on Pearl Harbor and Woodrow Wilson's 1917 speech declaring war on Germany. My final line, "Our goal is not the victory of might, but the vindication of right," came from Wilson's speech. But the Kennedy 1962 speech was not a declaration of war. Nor was it undertaken without congressional participation, the leaders of both parties in both Houses having been consulted before the speech; and a wide-open congressional resolution, authorizing any form of executive action against Cuba, having been enacted the previous summer, as noted in the speech. Nor was the U.S. response open-ended; it had one limited objective: the dismantlement and withdrawal of the Soviet nuclear missiles in Cuba.

That televised address to the nation on the night of October 22, 1962, was not the best speech of JFK's presidency, but it surely was his most important. It fully informed the American people and the world of what appeared to be the greatest danger to our country in history, without creating national panic, despair, or a cry for either surrender or war. It was used as a state document for presentation of the American case to the heads of every government around the globe at a moment when maximum support from other governments and world opinion was essential. It was also handed to the Soviet ambassador to Washington by our secretary of state as official notification of the U.S. course—a notification that told the Soviets their missiles were no longer secret.

The speech, delivered at 7 P.M. on October 22, 1962, was addressed to many different audiences:

First, to potential critics in Congress, the press, and the public, lest they accuse the administration of napping in the face of an unprecedented threat, reassuring them that, "as promised, the closest surveillance" had been maintained, and that the administration felt "obliged" to report this new crisis "in full detail."

Second, to the United Nations, lest its members deem the U.S. blockade an unauthorized act of war, reminding them that Soviet actions represented a "flagrant and deliberate defiance" of the 1947 Rio Pact and the UN Charter, justifying a regional defense authorized by the charter.

Third, to reassure the world that "we have no desire to dominate or conquer any other nation or impose our system upon its people," and that the United States instead sought "to join in an historic effort to end the perilous arms race and to transform the history of man." This proved critical: When the small countries of Guinea and Senegal denied landing and refueling rights to Soviet cargo planes bound for Cuba, that helped convince Khrushchev that his gamble had failed.

Fourth, to warn members of the Organization of American States (OAS) that Soviet missiles posed a threat not only to U.S. cities, but to "Mexico City, or any other city in . . . Central America or in the Caribbean area." The speech referenced the Western Hemisphere eighteen times in twenty-nine paragraphs, calling for an emergency meeting of the OAS Organ of Consultation.

Fifth, to American hawks, lest they fear that a quarantine was too passive by leaving the missiles in place, reassuring them that "these actions may only be the beginning . . . Should these . . . preparations continue . . . further action will be justified." Several days later, when Khrushchev appeared not to be taking the blockade seriously, State Department spokesman Lincoln White, when asked at a press briefing whether there was any improvement in the situation, called attention to the line that any attack on the United States would "require" a "full retaliatory response," the most ominous line in the whole speech. The president, furious, called up Lincoln White personally to reprimand him sharply. When later we learned that Khrushchev had pulled out the missiles in part because he became concerned that the crisis was getting out of control, the president ruefully remarked to me: "Maybe that White statement helped." But I don't think he ever thanked poor Lincoln.

Sixth, to the Cuban people, lest they feel targeted by the United States, hailing their "aspirations for liberty and justice for all," but warning them that "your leaders are no longer Cuban leaders inspired by Cuban ideals. They are puppets and agents of an international conspiracy . . ." Those paragraphs were drafted and translated with the help of our Hispanic Assistant Secretary of State, Arturo Morales Carrion, and broadcast across Cuba through a hookup on U.S. radio stations, arranged by FCC Chairman Newton Minow.

Seventh, yet most important, to Soviet Chairman Khrushchev, lest he believe America would yield to his threats or at most seek a summit meeting, warning him that, while we seek to avoid the risk of nuclear war, "neither will we shrink from that risk at any time it must be faced."

And, finally, to reassure our European allies that America was acting with "patience and restraint, as befits a peaceful . . . nation, which leads a worldwide alliance . . . This nation is opposed to war." In a nod to our commitments in Berlin, the president further informed our European allies that the Soviet missiles signified a "deliberately provocative and unjustified change in the status quo which cannot be accepted . . . if our courage and our commitments are ever to be trusted again by either friend or foe."

Historian Michael Beschloss has called President Kennedy's speech of October 22 "probably the most alarming ever delivered by an American president." I regret that judgment. That was neither JFK's intention nor mine. In fact, JFK decided not to show pictures on television of the kinds of missiles we knew were being built, not even pictures of the rudimentary sites, because he thought that might contribute to a panicked public reaction. Rather than incite fear, we wanted to reassure Americans and the world that the president knew what was happening, that the missiles would not be permitted to stay, and that a prudent, limited response had been formulated and was ready to be implemented.

Ambassador Adlai Stevenson's performance in the United Nations Security Council on Tuesday afternoon,

October 23, in which he stood up to Soviet Ambassador Valerian Zorin, greatly impressed the president, who had been annoyed by Adlai's earlier ambivalent advice: on the one hand, "if they won't remove the missiles . . .we will have to do it ourselves" . . . but on the other hand, "you should have made it clear that the existence of nuclear missile bases anywhere is negotiable before we start anything."

On Friday night, October 26, we received a long letter that appeared to be the work of Chairman Khrushchev himself, reflecting in part his wish for agreement on at least somewhat reciprocal terms. But we received the next morning a second letter distinctly cooler in tone, more likely the handiwork of the Politburo. During the ExComm meeting Saturday afternoon, I joined RFK and Ambassador Thompson in urging the president to respond to the positive elements buried in the Friday evening letter and delay for twenty-four to forty-eight hours a response to the second letter's insistence on a Turkish missile deal, arguing that there was always a chance that he'd accept our position, and "meanwhile we won't have broken up NATO over something that never would have come to NATO." JFK was concerned about the risks of ignoring Khrushchev's second letter. It was not so unreasonable, he felt, and should be answered to avoid giving Khrushchev an excuse or provocation to attack us.

Increasing the pressure and anxiety as I worked on the afternoon of October 27 on the president's reply, was the fact that that Saturday was already a dark, worrisome day for several reasons. A Soviet surface-to-air missile had shot down one of our high-flying U-2 reconnaissance planes over Cuba. (Its pilot, Major Rudolf Anderson, would be the sole fatality of the crisis.) Our lower-level surveillance flights over the island had also been fired upon, this time by Cubans. In view of the indispensability of continued U.S. reconnaissance, the Joint Chiefs forcefully reminded the president of Ex-Comm's informal understanding that the United States would retaliate promptly against any Soviet surface-to-air missile (SAM) downing a U-2. The president replied by saying, in effect: "Let's wait and see how this exchange of letters plays out." He also ordered cancellation of the next day's highly provocative, low-level surveillance flights.

As if all these pressures were not enough, a fatigued and anguished ExComm also learned, during those same tense hours, that an Alaska-based American U-2 pilot, on an air sampling mission to ascertain whether, and how extensively, the Soviets might then be testing nuclear weapons (as we were), had accidentally entered Soviet airspace over the Chukotski Peninsula, causing the Soviets to scramble their fighter jets on the not unreasonable assumption that World War III had begun. Ruefully shaking his head, JFK said, "There's always one son-of-a-bitch who doesn't get the message."

Years later, we learned that, around the same time we were drafting our letter to Khrushchev, Cuba's Fidel Castro was sending his own message to Khrushchev through the Soviet ambassador to Havana. Predicting that the Americans were about to invade in the next seventy-two hours, Castro urged the Soviet leader to use that "moment to eliminate this danger to global Communism forever. . . . However harsh and terrible the solution would be, there is no other." It appears that this letter so alarmed Khrushchev that it became another factor in his decision to pull back. At the 2002 "reunion" of crisis participants in Havana, I used a luncheon toast to Castro both to thank him for helping to alarm Khrushchev and to chide him for urging our elimination; he replied that his request was limited to the start of an American invasion.

After RFK and I drafted the reply to Khrushchev and once our draft letter had been cleared with President Kennedy, with the full ExComm, and with UN Ambassador Adlai Stevenson, the ExComm dispersed, and the president convened a smaller meeting in the Oval Office with RFK, McNamara, Rusk, Bundy, Ambassador Thompson, myself, and possibly others. His decision to limit attendance implied to those of us present that it was a move about which the other members of ExComm did not need to know. The purpose of the session was to instruct RFK on his upcoming meeting with Soviet Ambassador Anatoly Dobrynin, at which he was to deliver JFK's letter. We discussed at length Khrushchev's proposal that we give up NATO missiles in Turkey for his withdrawal of Soviet missiles in Cuba, the quid-pro-quo our letter had essentially ignored. Rusk devised a wise response: While no formal deal was possible, why not indicate that the president was determined to remove the Turkish missiles and would do so once the crisis was resolved? President Kennedy agreed. The outmoded, unreliable Jupiter missiles, which had been foisted on the Turks by the Eisenhower administration, were set to be removed in any case as nuclear-armed Polaris submarines under the Mediterranean became the regional deterrent; and no loss of American life or security would result from conveying to Khrushchev private information that could help him save face.

The letter was simultaneously dispatched both to our embassy in Moscow for delivery to the Soviet chairman, and to RFK for delivery to Ambassador Dobrynin during their meeting at the Justice Department that evening. As instructed in our Oval Office huddle, RFK forcefully urged the ambassador to secure Khrushchev's acceptance of our proposed terms, warning that hawks on the ExComm were rising and threatening to launch an air strike and invasion within a matter of days. The Soviets should understand, RFK said, that if they did not remove their nuclear missile bases, we would remove them; and that this was "not an ultimatum, just a statement of fact." He called for a Khrushchev commitment to withdraw the missiles the next day: "Otherwise, there will be drastic consequences." (Despite that warning, and despite the growing pressure on the president, I did not believe that JFK would start bombing—nor do I now.)

RFK—probably acting on his own—varied slightly the language in our letter, I learned later, by conditioning the U.S. non-invasion pledge on Castro's halting subversion in other Central and Latin American countries, and by limiting the pledge to not permitting an invasion "from American soil." He also assured the ambassador that, if it was any comfort to Mr. Khrushchev, our removal of the NATO missiles in Turkey would be accomplished in a matter of months, provided the Soviets did not make any public claim that this was part of the bargain and the result of their pressure—in which case, the attorney general said, the understanding would be off and the NATO missiles would remain. Many years later, we learned that RFK's second oral message—about our ultimately removing the missiles in Turkey—reached Khrushchev only after the Soviet chairman had decided to end the confrontation on the basis of our letter (as translated and delivered by our embassy in Moscow). No U.S. or NATO offer about the missiles was ever formally received and accepted. Thus there was no deal.

Nonetheless, concerned that our actions would be interpreted as cutting a deal with the Soviets, we decided to keep this part of the discussion secret, lest our allies or domestic hawks charge that we had sacrificed Western security for American safety, or that Kennedy had backed down from a Soviet threat. In deleting RFK's reference to these events in his posthumous memoir of the crisis, *Thirteen Days*, I explained, in a confidential letter to Senator Edward Kennedy, that the omission of certain unspecified understandings would result in one paragraph that "may not be regarded as precisely accurate by the Russians and by a few Americans in the know—I doubt that anyone will contradict it publicly, but they might sometime . . ."

Instead, the Turkish missile understanding was first made public ten years later, in a *Time* magazine article cosigned by the surviving participants of that small Oval Office meeting; John and Robert Kennedy were dead, and those of us who knew about it felt the disclosure would do no harm to national security.

Later that grim Saturday night, October 27, 1962, the full ExComm reconvened without the president for an after-dinner meeting in the Cabinet Room. The discussion became heated, as the hawks loudly insisted that they had been proven right, that the blockade had not succeeded in inducing Khrushchev to pull back. Suddenly Vice President Johnson, who had largely remained silent in our discussions since the beginning, spoke up: "All I know is that when you were walking along a Texas road and a rattlesnake rose up ready to strike, there was only one thing to do—take a long stick and knock its head off." His uncomfortably clear meaning was chilling.

Meanwhile, I was preparing to fly the next morning to Boston to brief senatorial candidate Ted Kennedy before his televised *Meet the Press* appearance, at JFK's request. The president felt that, whatever the outcome of our letter, any comment made by his brother on national television would be regarded around the world as the views of the president. Before departing, I left word with the president on how to reach me should he need to, and I added advice on three pending ExComm questions he might need to decide in my absence:

(i) No need to intercept the Soviet ship headed for the quarantine barrier; "We can afford to avoid an incident which might unnecessarily lead to escalation . . . **(ii)** With respect to communications with Khrushchev . . . indicate that both his . . . offers are negotiable, but only after work on the missiles ceases . . . **(iii)** I assume no extreme military action will be ordered over the weekend . . . We may be underrating the role of the blockade and its effect on the Soviets . . .

When I fell asleep that Saturday night, the crisis was still unresolved. If Khrushchev did not pull back, I feared, the pressure inside ExComm to use military force would continue to grow. It had been the bleakest day of the crisis—a day when the two inconsistent Khrushchev letters made it look as though a negotiated conclusion was impossible, and the firing on our high-flying reconnaissance plane and low-flying surveillance plane made it look as though a shooting war was inevitable.

It was not until decades later, at one of our missile crisis reunions, that I learned just how close we had come to war that day. Unbeknownst to us at the time, a Soviet submarine accompanying the Russian tanker that was approaching the quarantine zone was equipped with a nuclear-tipped torpedo. When an American destroyer's sonar detected the submarine, it began dropping grenade-sized depth charges to signal the submarine to surface and identify itself, making the submarine crew feel "like we were sitting in an empty barrel, while somebody constantly beat it with a stick."

The Soviet submarine's commanding officer had discretionary authority to fire its nuclear torpedo if attacked, and his shaken and frightened crew pleaded with him to fire it. He did not do so, because he was unable to communicate with Moscow to receive authorization. That careful Soviet bureaucrat, anonymous to history, may have prevented nuclear war and possibly global destruction.

I could hardly believe my ears when I heard the good news on my bedside radio upon waking the next morning. Whatever the relative importance and impact of each of the medicines—the letter, Bobby's oral warning, his oral assurances—in our package to Khrushchev, the package had worked. A carefully balanced combination of deterrence and diplomacy, communications and negotiations, backed by an overwhelming U.S. naval superiority in the Caribbean and overall nuclear superiority worldwide, had succeeded. Khrushchev was backing down. I immediately called Mac Bundy. "It's true," he said. Khrushchev was withdrawing the missiles. "Our 10:00 A.M. ExComm meeting in the Cabinet Room has been postponed to 11:30 so the President and Jackie can go to church; and he advises everyone else to do the same."

When John F. Kennedy entered the Cabinet Room later that morning, all members of the ExComm stood and applauded. He urged us all to remain cautious, not to gloat, and to recognize the statesmanship of Chairman Khrushchev. He issued a public statement congratulating Khrushchev on "an important contribution to peace," adding that he regarded the two letters they had exchanged "as firm undertakings on the part of both our governments . . ." He then directed work on arrangements for inspecting and certifying the full missile withdrawal. Just as he had after the Bay of Pigs, he also directed that a postcrisis review be undertaken to examine where we had miscalculated and what we had done right.

In the weeks to come, he would sweat out the long-delayed removal of Soviet bombers from Cuba; express concern about the visiting German leader who, unaware of Kennedy's negotiations with Khrushchev, had stated to the president that his success proved that the Soviets would always back down when the United States threatened or deployed superior force; and listen with amazement to Soviet emissary Mikoyan's explanation for the crisis that Khrushchev's fear of a U.S. invasion of Cuba had been triggered by campaign speeches containing that vow made by, of all people, Richard Nixon in his race for governor of California. It showed an extraordinary misunderstanding of the American political system, the president told me; "but then," he added, "we don't understand theirs too well, either."

In my lifetime, there have been three occasions when credible intelligence gathering indicated potential threats to the American homeland—first, radio interceptions in the months preceding the Japanese attack on Pearl Harbor in 1941; second, in the photos of Soviet missiles in Cuba in 1962; and third, intelligence reports in the months leading up to the terrorist attacks of 9/11. Each involved different facts and circumstances. Only in 1962 did our government and military readiness thwart the attack.

After the crisis ended, I made my first national TV appearance on *Meet the Press*—largely because the president had confidence that I was able to say without error or sounding defensive what it was necessary to say about the crisis—and no more. When the show ended, as the microphones were removed and the lights dimmed, a telephone rang in the studio. The show's host and his assistants looked bewildered, not realizing there was a telephone in the room. It was handed to me, and I immediately recognized the familiar voice on the other end: "They didn't lay a glove on you," said JFK.

Some weeks later, USIA director Edward R. Murrow invited my brother Tom and me to a dinner at his home. By prearrangement with Tom, I had Mike Feldman telephone me during the evening. Within earshot of the others, I pretended he was giving me an urgent message, and said into the phone, "Tell them I'll be right down." I swung around and informed the others present that new missiles had been sighted in Cuba, and an emergency meeting of ExComm had been convened. Murrow, having been unable to attend an earlier session to which he had been invited, began preparations to attend, and voiced deep concerns about the implications. When Tom and I immediately told him I was just kidding—it was a practical joke—he was not amused by our hoax.

In subsequent weeks and months, articles appeared everywhere about the White House's handling of the crisis, including one highly publicized *Saturday Evening Post* article. According to more than one historian, the president asked the authors of that article, Stewart

Alsop and Charles Bartlett, to delete most mentions of my name and role on the grounds that hard-line conservatives might protest the involvement of a onetime conscientious objector in a military crisis. Upon inquiring with Charlie, I learned that this request was not made by the president but by his military attaché, who in fact had no role in the ExComm and no influence on—or authority to speak for—the president.

Some months after the crisis ended, addressing a religious audience, I was asked an impassioned question: "By what moral right did the President of the United States threaten to incinerate the world because of Soviet missiles in Cuba?" I replied that it was a legitimate question, a question that the president had asked himself, and that it illustrated the insanity in which the world had enveloped itself, but that the principle of reciprocal deterrence—the doctrine of mutually assured destruction, mad as it was—had prevented war. It had worked on this occasion, I added, because we had a president who did everything possible to avoid war. In short, threatening war, as immoral as that normally is, was in this unique instance an appropriate means of preventing war. As proud as I am of my role in the Cuban missile crisis, I am still not wholly comfortable with that answer. All public servants face a series of difficult moral dilemmas that cannot always be resolved.

A distinguished British visitor to my White House office in 1963 called Kennedy's peaceful resolution of the Cuban missile crisis "not only a great turning point in history, but the start of a golden age." He seemed prophetic. Less than eight months later, President Kennedy reflected on those October dangers in his commencement address on peace at American University: "We are both caught up in a vicious and dangerous cycle in which suspicion on one side breeds suspicion on the other, and new weapons beget counterweapons . . . Nuclear powers must avoid those confrontations which bring an adversary a choice of either a humiliating retreat or a nuclear war . . . [in which] all we have built . . . would be destroyed in the first 24 hours."

The missile crisis, and the American University speech, led to the first arms control step in the nuclear age, the Limited Nuclear Test Ban Treaty, signed in Moscow in the late summer of 1963. The crisis also led to the U.S.-Soviet "hotline." Clearly, both countries had needed a better, faster way to communicate. Decades later, Soviet ambassador Dobrynin told one of our reunions his method of reporting to Moscow during the crisis: A Western Union boy on a bicycle picked up his coded telegram, and biked it back to Western Union, which transmitted it. "I hoped," said Dobrynin, "that he did not have a girlfriend in our neighborhood."

By then, the world had stepped back from the precipice, as an ironic result of its most dangerous crisis. But was this the only way to achieve that result? Surely JFK's incurrence of domestic political wrath from hardline super-patriots (by doing nothing) would have been by comparison a minor and transitory risk, although their takeover of the U.S. government would have made world war even more likely.

In the forty-year cold war contest for the leadership of the world, the United States peacefully prevailed for the same reason we prevailed in October 1962—because we acted with vigilance, patience, and restraint. In the eyes of history, our greatest presidents have proved their qualities of greatness when confronted by great challenges—war, depression, and moral issues from slavery to civil rights. The discovery that the Soviet Union had secretly rushed nuclear missiles into Cuba tested JFK's wisdom, courage, and leadership as no president since Lincoln and FDR had been tested. No other test so starkly put at stake, depending on the president's choices, the survival of our country. It was for that moment that he had been elected; and it was for that moment that he will most be remembered.

Chapter 24

President Kennedy's Foreign Policy

In retrospect, the Cuban missile crisis required the application of every element of Kennedy's foreign policy. It would be simplistic to summarize that policy as merely antiwar, although that cannot be minimized, no matter how often we cloaked it in his spontaneous rhetoric on competing with, and standing up to, the Soviets during the cold war. It would be more accurate to say he was pro-peace, promoting peace in conflict areas around the globe, preventing them from spinning out of control. The American University commencement address may have been my draft, but it was JFK's policy. He summed it up best in his November 16, 1961, remarks at the University of Washington in Seattle:

We must face the fact that the United States is neither omnipotent nor omniscient—that we are only 6% of the world's population . . . that there cannot be an American solution to every world problem. . . . In short, we are neither "warmongers" nor "appeasers," neither "hard" nor "soft." We are Americans, determined to defend the frontiers of freedom, by an honorable peace, if peace is possible, but by arms if arms are used against us.

It is no doubt tempting for any commander in chief to use America's overwhelmingly superior military might. President Kennedy was urged to send troops into East Germany at the time of the Berlin crisis, but he did not. He was urged to send troops to tear down the Berlin Wall, but he did not. He was urged to send combat troop divisions to the Congo, and to Vietnam; but he did not. Kennedy would have had the support of the American people had he undertaken any of these actions, but he did not. Most importantly, he was urged to bomb Soviet nuclear missile sites in Cuba and use an invasion to take Cuba away from Castro, but he did not. The destroyers that formed the quarantine barricade in the Cuban missile crisis, the tanks that tested the Autobahn access to West Berlin after the Berlin

Wall was built, and the troops readied for deployment to Laos never fired a shot; but they helped advance our security and foreign policy objectives. It is easy to start wars, or become involved in the wars of others. But he never did.

Instead he sent Peace Corps volunteers to perform educational, medical, engineering, and other tasks in the poorer countries of the world. He launched the world's first government agency dedicated solely to the study of disarmament programs, making possible a cadre of professionals in this extremely complicated field. He sent diplomats armed with the unprecedented proposals generated by his new Arms Control and Disarmament Agency to international conferences. He sent American food and agricultural surpluses to hungry peoples as part of his expanded Food for Peace Program. He sent a higher proportion of America's gross national product to undeveloped countries in need of economic and humanitarian aid than any subsequent president. He urged on his fellow citizens vigilance, service, and sacrifice in the long cold war; but he never asked them to kill anyone. Abroad, his speeches sent clear signals that America wanted peace and international understanding. At home, he encouraged peace advocates. When representatives of the American Friends Service Committee, an early source of my pacifist leanings, called upon him at the White House, expressing opposition to larger military budgets, and concluded with an apology for taking up his time, he replied: "No, no, keep the pressure on. You know the other side of this argument is pressuring me constantly. That's how our system works—systole and diastole."

Kennedy resisted calls by pundits for a Grand Design in foreign policy, and yet there it was. Prudent and pragmatic, it did not satisfy those looking for some sweeping, simple ideological answer, but it worked. His mixture of realism and idealism, prudence and innovation, made Kennedy difficult to define on an ideological spectrum, but those are the facts.

I entered the White House with no foreign policy experience, expertise, or responsibility. But I soon learned that foreign policy, domestic policy, budgetary policy, congressional relations, and the president's own political fortunes all intersect and overlap. In foreign policy, much more than in domestic policy—where congressional legislation and appropriations are the key—*a president's words are policy*; and I had a responsibility to help shape those words and thus help shape that policy. Occasionally he would ask me to look at international issues, ranging from U.S. bases in Portugal's African colonies to international gold and wheat sales.

Department and agency heads asked me to reflect their views to the president on issues within their respective jurisdictions, domestic or foreign, which I did.

It also became my responsibility to help him shape the new agency and program for foreign economic development assistance. I reviewed with program veterans, outside experts, and the president himself the following questions, as set forth in a memorandum I sent the president in March 1961:

- As to its name, we faced a choice between the Agency for International Development (AID) or the "Growth Administration For Freedom" (GAFF). That was easy.
- Should the new Administrator report to the Secretary of State or directly to the President, and should he have the rank of an under secretary or report to the Under Secretary for Economic Affairs?
- Should military assistance be part of one Presidential message and agency (along with economic assistance), or kept separate, or reduced to help finance economic development?
- In view of the consistent Congressional practice of cutting foreign aid requests, should we ask for more than we need and expect?

These were just a few of my questions, most of which have never been answered.

Early in his presidency, several days in advance of his initial conference in Paris with President de Gaulle, the president sent me on my first trip abroad, to ascertain from French foreign policy intellectuals the dimensions of de Gaulle's views and French opinion at that time, to prepare me for the drafting of JFK's Paris speech. When I came to report to him in the French government guest house, he immediately put his finger to his lips when I started to talk, asking: "or don't you think our oldest and closest ally would be capable of bugging my bedroom?"

In his typically casual way of assigning odd topics to various aides, JFK also asked me to keep an eye on U.S. relations with Iran, and its shah, Mohammad Reza Shah Pahlavi, who was reportedly jealous of Kennedy's charisma, intellect, world standing, and domestic popularity. The shah, I was told by a State Department contact, thought Kennedy's inaugural words "Those who make peaceful revolution impossible make violent revolution inevitable" were aimed at him personally. He may have been right.

Like many other North Americans on both sides of the border, Kennedy did not have cordial relations with

Prime Minister John Diefenbaker of Canada, whom JFK, on a state visit to Ottawa, hoped to enlist in the Organization of American States (OAS). Upon departing, Kennedy accidentally left behind a memo pad on which he had, in his illegible hand, scribbled some reminder on this subject. Diefenbaker, who appropriated the pad, thought it referred to him as an SOB, and later threatened to "expose" JFK's vulgar diplomatic breach if Kennedy did not concede in a U.S.-Canadian dispute on North American air defense installations. When I reported this to the president, he told me: "I couldn't have written that he was an SOB, because I didn't know he was one at that time."

In 1962 JFK planned an internationally televised two-man debate or discussion with Khrushchev, permitting the Soviet leader to address the American people while the American president addressed the Russian people. This Khrushchev-Kennedy television exchange had been carefully negotiated. We had solicited ideas from U.S. ambassadors Thompson in Moscow, Kennan in Belgrade, and Gavin in Paris, all of whom suggested that the president emphasize his commitment to peace and disarmament, avoid cold war issues like Berlin, make no statements humiliating Khrushchev in front of his countrymen, and keep in mind that the average Soviet citizen—who would be our principal target audience—had been filled with a lifetime of propaganda about the evils of U.S. capitalism and racial discrimination.

JFK planned to say a few words in Russian, to invoke the name of FDR, and to ask the Soviets to reverse the course that Stalin had begun. The purpose was not to score more debating points but to convey goodwill. My brother Tom, who, with White House press secretary Pierre Salinger, had negotiated the arrangements with Khrushchev personally, said in a memorandum to me that "the President will have the same advantages in his TV appearance with Khrushchev that he had in the Nixon debates—obvious sincerity, obvious ability, obvious youth and vigor." When Tom and Pierre visited Russia to negotiate with Khrushchev, they complained, on a private phone call to a colleague in the United States, that the only thing missing from their government dacha was alcohol. Upon returning to the dacha after a day of meetings, they found the refrigerator filled with beer.

At the last minute, when Khrushchev and his colleagues decided that Kennedy's speech announcing the resumption of nuclear testing was "atomic blackmail" and too aggressive, they canceled the debate, which had never been officially announced. It was a missed opportunity. After the president's death, I proposed to

LBJ that he seek a similar joint TV appeal for peace on a global hookup of networks, reopening the negotiations that Pierre and Tom had launched with Khrushchev on behalf of JFK years earlier. Again, nothing came of it.

The Bay of Pigs

Much as West Berlin was regarded as a splinter in the heart by Soviet Chairman Khrushchev, Cuba was all that and more to John F. Kennedy, pitting the charismatic young president against the fiery young revolutionary Fidel Castro. Like West Berlin, Cuba was a symbolic reminder of unfinished business, its continued existence under Communist control a taunt to be exploited by critics at home and abroad. In the three short years of his presidency, that small island would prove to be the scene of John F. Kennedy's greatest failure— at the Bay of Pigs—as well as his greatest success—his peaceful resolution of the Cuban missile crisis.

As originally hatched under the Eisenhower administration, the CIA invasion plan, ultimately located at Cuba's Bay of Pigs, called for a brigade of twelve hundred Cuban exiles, organized, armed, and trained by a team from the CIA, to sweep into Cuba in April 1961, initiating, it was assumed by its authors, a chain of events that would lead to the overthrow of Fidel Castro. The plan was at first accepted by Kennedy, partly because of his unwillingness to be labeled "soft," and partly because he was unable to devise any politically acceptable means of dismantling and dispersing the brigade assembled by the CIA. He received a series of assurances from its principal salesmen, CIA director Allen Dulles, deputy director for plans Richard M. Bissell Jr., and others; assurances that the invasion would succeed with the help of a concurrent uprising by the Cuban people; that American involvement would be invisible to the rest of the world; and that any failure at the beachhead could be followed by brigade members taking refuge in the same mountain range into which Castro had led his own rebel forces years earlier.

It all sounded easy, almost too easy to be true; and it was. None of these assurances was valid. Exiled Cuban politicians, Kennedy later discovered, could not be relied upon to reflect public opinion in their former homeland, or to keep operational plans confidential, or to inspire or lead effective military action. They distrusted one another and they distrusted their American sponsors, who, in turn, distrusted them. Exiled leaders predicted that the invading forces would be welcomed as liberators and have an easy military victory, despite the warnings of appalled U.S. allies. I now wonder how the CIA intelligence officers could have been so deluded. How could they think it would be easy to overthrow Castro when he still enjoyed widespread popular support, and most of the Cuban leaders opposed to him were either in jail or in Miami?

Long after the operation's failure, secret minutes emerged of a November 15, 1960, CIA meeting—prior to briefing the new president-elect—in which the CIA's own reviewers concluded that the invasion was "unachievable . . . There will not be the internal unrest earlier believed possible . . . nor will [Castro's] defense permit the type [of] strike planned," they said. Not a single one of these concerns was communicated to Kennedy during his CIA transition briefing in Palm Beach three days later, the skeptics being unwilling to challenge their superiors in front of the new president-elect. To me, that fiasco earned for the CIA the motto frequently ascribed to it: "Often wrong, but never in doubt."

At the time, I was wholly preoccupied with the president's domestic agenda. Had I been in the mix, I like to think I might have appealed to Kennedy's other side, the skeptical, cautious, prudent leader who had seen enough of war. I recognize that, even had I been a part of those secret planning discussions, I too might have accepted the assurances of the expert planners. But, then again, I might have questioned the experts, as I often did in other areas, raised doubts, and challenged their evidence. I might even have asked about the invasion's impact on the moral authority of the United States, on America's reputation, and on world opinion, as I would during the Cuban missile crisis.

As it happened, my only conversation with JFK about the operation, before its execution, came in early April, when Mac Bundy and Dave Bell, in one of our weekly policy coordination meetings, confided in me—almost accidentally—the existence and imminence of the plan, but did not feel free to inform me fully. I went promptly into the Oval Office and asked the president. He grimaced in a way that indicated he did not really want to discuss the subject with me, so I did not press him—I wish I had. All he said, in his occasionally earthy way, was that all those knowledgeable on the subject were trying primarily to protect themselves: "I know, everyone's grabbing their nuts on this one."

We had no real conversation on the matter until after it failed. Then we walked the White House driveway behind the West Wing. Anguished and fatigued, he was in the most emotional, self-critical state I had ever seen him. He cursed not his fate or advisors but himself. "How could I have been so far off base? All my life I have known better than to depend on the experts. How could I have been so stupid, to let them go ahead?" he said, reciting the wholly invalid assurances on which he had relied. It was the worst week of his public life. Fortunately he had had the courage to recognize, albeit belatedly, that the plan had been misconceived, and he halted it, wisely and courageously rejecting the CIA's request that he send in more U.S. airpower that would almost surely have antagonized the world and possibly incited a Soviet military response. But courage is not enough for a leader who is neither infallible nor omniscient; he also needs luck.

After it was over, I held a background session for the press in which I tried to put the debacle in context, indicating that although Kennedy had fired the weapon, it had been built and loaded by his predecessor. Kennedy publicly rejected my efforts. "I am the responsible officer of the government, and that is quite obvious," he announced on April 21. Later that week, in an address before the American Newspaper Publishers' Association, he cited a quotation recommended to me by Edward R. Murrow: "An error doesn't become a mistake until you refuse to correct it." Determined to correct his errors, Kennedy ordered a complete postmortem, pressing the investigators to be objective and comprehensive, letting the chips fall where they may. CIA inspector general Lyman Kirkpatrick, in his own report that summer, blamed the plan's collapse on "institutional arrogance, ignorance, and incompetence." That sums it up pretty well.

I admired Bundy's courage, integrity, and perspicacity in preparing for the president, at his request, a memorandum on what went wrong at the Bay of Pigs that did not omit the president's own failings. I only wish that in later years Mac had written LBJ a similar memo on Vietnam.

Kennedy was particularly scornful of those advisors who had not opposed the Bay of Pigs operation, but then changed their stories after the operation's failure, and told the press or even the president: "I told you so, I knew it, I predicted it." That posture was one of the factors that led the president to shift Chester Bowles from the State Department to a special roving ambassador position, later appointing him ambassador to India. It was also a factor, I believe, when he asked the Secret Service a year later to install a special taping system on his telephone and in the Cabinet Room and Oval Office, following the precedent set by Eisenhower, and possibly earlier presidents. JFK wanted to record everyone's position at the time it was stated—at least for the history of his administration that he intended to write. Fate did not permit him to do so. But that oral record proved to be a boon for the works of historians and other writers, including (in this book) me. None of his advisors, with the possible exception of his brother Robert, was aware that much of our advice to the president was being recorded on the secret taping system. I was neither annoyed nor astonished to learn about it many years later. Nor do I believe I would have changed any of my advice had I known it was being taped.

In general, my involvement in U.S. policy toward Cuba was limited. I heard scattered references to "Operation Mongoose," a CIA plan to sabotage and weaken the Cuban economy, presumably undermining the popularity of the Communist Party on the island and its leader. My only contribution was a memorandum, listing nonviolent ways to end Communist control of Cuba, including (1) broadcasting to Cuba's citizens the Castro regime's betrayal of its revolution by subjecting itself to foreign control by Moscow, and (2) increasing the number of Voice of America Spanish broadcasts into the country.

Later, I participated in the "Standing Group"—a successor to the ExComm, established by RFK and Bundy after the missile crisis. The Standing Group devoted one meeting in the spring of 1963 to considering the widest possible range of alternatives in Cuba. The assassination of Castro was not on that list; and I am confident that JFK would never have been involved in any plot to kill Castro—confident because the possibility of a president's complicity in assassination comes down in large measure to his character, and I knew JFK's character as well as anyone. I was with him in 1961 when he first received word that General Trujillo of the Dominican Republic had been assassinated; he was surprised and unprepared. I was with him again when he first heard of the violent death of South Vietnam's Premier Diem in 1963: Though he surely had to have known that his government had given the South Vietnamese army a green light for the overthrow, he was visibly saddened that Diem was killed. Years later, one CIA operative testified that he had interpreted a casual presidential remark, expressing Kennedy's hope that Castro would one day be "deposed," as proof of JFK's "indirect" acknowledgment and approval of an assassination plan. That is absurd. In 1956 JFK wanted "Onions" Burke deposed as chairman of the Massachusetts State Democratic Committee. That did not mean he wanted him murdered. He did not always act to protect or prop up despotic foreign leaders in jeopardy; but he did not support their assassination.

There are a number of paradoxes in the story of the Bay of Pigs: The largest covert operation in CIA history was too large to remain covert and too small to be successful, with too few men on the ground, too few pilots in the air, too few ships in the water, and too little ammunition in reserve. From conception, it was a doomed project—doomed if JFK placed too few restraints on the operation, and doomed if he placed too many. It was planned in too much secrecy to permit the necessary vetting and the inclusion in that process of outside skeptics. The Cuban exile community in Miami, which had the largest stake in the operation's secrecy, surprise, and thus success, proved to be the chief source of advance leaks to the news media, even exaggerating the size of the exile force, which stimulated Castro to increase his defenses.

Interestingly, the same CIA official who was partly responsible for the Bay of Pigs disaster in 1961 also deserves some of the credit for preventing a third world war in the Cuban missile crisis of 1962. Richard Bissell developed the aerial photography capacity of the U–2 aircraft that enabled the United States to detect the Soviet missile buildup in time to formulate a prudent response, paving the way to the peaceful resolution of that crisis.

Some good came out of the Bay of Pigs. Kennedy learned that taking full responsibility, instead of blaming others, actually improved his standing in the polls, although he flashed a rueful smile in telling me that it would not last unless he stumbled into several more disasters. He also became a better leader, making important changes:

- He changed his attitude, no longer assuming that he had a golden touch that never failed. Shortly after the Bay of Pigs, he asked each of the military chiefs to prepare recommendations on what course the United States should follow in Indochina, realizing when he reviewed the mishmash of answers that they were no more expert on that part of the world than they had been on Cuba. "Thank God the Bay of Pigs happened when it did," he said to me later. "Otherwise we'd be in Laos by now and that would be a hundred times worse."

- He changed his policies—emphasizing economic, administrative, and political reform in Latin America to isolate Castro and reduce his influence, instead of listening to any more military remedies. The ineffective CIA effort to topple Castro through a campaign of sabotage and subversion showed Kennedy the futility of that effort.

- He changed his advisors, easing out the intelligence and Pentagon experts who had given him the invalid assurances, and asking RFK and me to participate in subsequent National Security Council sessions.

Perhaps he believed the Bay of Pigs scenario might have unfolded differently had we been involved. He trusted RFK and me to give him the sort of candid, critical assessment he did not feel he had received on the planning of that inherently flawed operation.

✦ He changed his decision-making process—fortunately in time for the next Cuban crisis, the missile crisis of 1962. He no longer accepted one recommended option without examining all others.

✦ He did not, in the second Cuban crisis, unlike the first, exclude allies and international organizations from his planning.

✦ He no longer felt the demands of secrecy made it impossible for him to be open with the American press, public, and Congress.

Conversely, in the first crisis the president had sought to reassure some officials of their standing by their inclusion; in the second, he consulted only those advisors in whom he had confidence, and did not rely solely, if at all, on the advice of his generals.

The Bay of Pigs operation was an immediate failure for the United States, for JFK, for the CIA, for the brigade itself, and for Cuban-Americans generally. But

I cannot help but wonder, more than forty-six years later, whether that was true in the long run. Perhaps JFK's short-term failure was in one sense part of a long-term success—the global success of the United States and West emerging successfully from the cold war, keeping the peace by practicing vigilance, patience, and restraint. If that analysis is correct, the lessons President Kennedy learned at the Bay of Pigs, and applied the following year during the Cuban missile crisis, helped save the world.

Berlin

Khrushchev had been threatening to take over West Berlin since 1958; but, in the summer of 1961, war over Berlin actually seemed likely. Soviet citizens' anxiety about the possibility of war—as well as their sense of humor—were conveyed to me by a Russian joke I heard from Khrushchev's son-in-law, Aleksei Adzhubei:

Q: What do we do if the bomb drops?
A: Cover yourself with a sheet and crawl slowly to the nearest cemetery.
Q: Why slowly?
A: To avoid panic.

By July 1961 the president had solicited recommendations from all relevant advisors on how he should respond to a Soviet aide-mémoire declaring that a normalization of relations treaty with East Germany, extinguishing West Berlin's special status, would soon be signed; and what, if anything, he should say to the American people. The president asked me to analyze the resulting amassed advice, to give him my own conclusions, and, at the same time, to start work on a speech.

On July 17 I sent him a detailed four-and-a-half-page memorandum entitled "The Decision on Berlin." In that memo, I criticized the more militant options then being offered, which included a presidential declaration of a national emergency and a call-up of army reserves and National Guard. That course of action, I wrote, might engage Khrushchev's prestige to a point where he could not back down from a showdown, and arouse both domestic and foreign critics who were fearful of trigger-happy actions by the new, inexperienced Kennedy administration, thereby creating domestic and Western divisiveness that could encourage Khrushchev. After proposing a televised presidential address on the subject, I switched into my customary questioning mode, adding, "Is a wholly negative diplomatic posture necessary now?" proposing that the State Department explore the possible use of the UN or World Court on this issue. I doubt any other president would have taken those proposals seriously; but JFK discussed them with me at length.

On October 6, 1961, the president asked me to prepare an outline of points to make in his upcoming discussions on Berlin with Soviet foreign minister Gromyko. I proposed that both sides "strive for agreement, after a 'cooling-off-period' in which we can both consult with our respective allies and Congresses"; and undertake "no more unilateral acts or threats that make a negotiating climate impossible."

Later, in March 1962, when the State Department drafted a modus vivendi proposal for the president to offer to the Soviets, he again asked my views. I advised him that the package might be immediately rejected by Moscow. If we truly wanted to reach agreement, I wrote, "Would it [not] be desirable . . . to make the package more appealing bait. . . ."

Throughout the Berlin crisis, Kennedy took steps to keep America's possible use of nuclear weapons credible to both the Soviet Union and the West Germans; but he made no specific decision ever to use those weapons. Contingency plans existed; memos were sent; meetings were held; options were listed; the president listened, asked questions, expressed doubts; and calculations were made. Some historians have concluded, from all this, that Kennedy seriously contemplated the use of nuclear weapons. It would have been irresponsible for him never to have considered their use, in view of the tinderbox in which we lived at the time, the importance of West Berlin to the global cause of freedom, and the Soviets' enormous advantage in conventional forces in any armed conflict over West Berlin. But none of those historians ever pointed to a specific decision or commitment by JFK to use nuclear weapons under any circumstances—because no such decision or commitment was ever made.

Surprisingly, two of Bundy's more peace-minded National Security Council staff members concocted a scheme under which the United States would lob nuclear missiles onto the Soviet nuclear testing site in the hope of disrupting Soviet tests in a way that enabled the U.S. to deny responsibility. They brought this scheme to me, and received a brief response: "You guys are crazy—get out of my office." I have no doubt that the president would have responded similarly.

Kennedy's strategy on Berlin required a strong Western alliance. But there were strains in that alliance. General de Gaulle feared a U.S.-led NATO might succeed without him. German Chancellor Konrad Adenauer feared that Kennedy might agree with Moscow on concluding the cold war without him. Kennedy, hoping to appeal over the heads of these two obstinate elders to their younger constituents, flew to Europe in 1963 to strengthen the alliance with a message of hope, hope not only for a positive, united Western alliance, but also for a reunited Europe, East and West, in a future post–cold war era of prosperity and democracy. He also used that trip to curb Europe's chronic postwar anti-Americanism.

I still remember West German Minister of Economic Affairs Ludwig Ehrhardt, then new at his job, joining JFK's motorcade. Noting the president's success with his distinctive American-style wave to the crowds lining the route, Ehrhardt decided to try it—first only with his hand; then with half his arm, and finally with a big sweep of his fully extended arm. It still didn't look Kennedyesque.

JFK's short speech in front of the West Berlin City Hall (the Schöneberg Rathaus) was one of his best, and most remembered—a speech designed to salute the citizens of West Berlin for their courage and patience in peacefully maintaining an island of freedom amid a sea of Communist military and political power. The speech was a hopeful prophecy for the future, looking to the day when "all who stood for freedom would be able to look back with pride and satisfaction, when that day finally comes, as it will." His speech contrasted West Berlin with the sterile economy and politics on the other side of the wall, calling it the best proof that Communism represented neither the wave of the future nor a path to progress for newly developing nations. If there are those who disagree, he said, "let them come to Berlin."

It was a beautiful day and the largest, most enthusiastic crowd I had ever seen. As I stood behind JFK on the city hall steps on June 26, 1963, I looked out on a vast area totally carpeted with people in every direction, filling every window of every building on the square, not far from that offense against humanity known as the Berlin Wall—a wall, erected nearly two years earlier, that represented not the triumph claimed by its builders but a fundamental failure in the Communist system, a failure to build a society sufficiently attractive to keep its most talented people at home.

The last line of the city hall speech, in which the American president identified himself with the citizens of Berlin, was its most famous and beloved. It set off a fifteen-minute ovation, despite the fact that it contained—I have been repeatedly told—an unintentionally humorous grammatical error, for which I take responsibility. "*Ich bin Berliner*" means "I am a Berliner." Inserting the word "*ein*" before Berliner (I presumably thought it was necessary to include the article "a") means, in common German parlance, "I am a jelly doughnut."

The distinguished West German statesman Willy Brandt subsequently wrote in his memoirs that I had rehearsed the line with him at dinner in Bonn the previous evening. I do not believe he would invent such a discussion; but neither do I believe that he would have permitted such an error. It was not long before mail began to pour into my office pointing out my mistake, and it has not entirely stopped. One commentator speculated that the applause that greeted that line was wild at least in part because people thought Kennedy was deliberately making a humorous play on words in a foreign language. I don't think so. Another speculated that I had knowingly and deliberately left the error in his text in the belief that it would humanize Kennedy to his audience. Untrue. I believe that everyone in that vast audience knew precisely what Kennedy meant by that phrase.

Three years later, when a USIA book tour of Germany took me to the University of Hamburg, I jokingly explained to the students in my audience why President Kennedy had not been able to visit their city, and say *"Ich bin ein Hamburger!"* Before I even uttered that closing word, the savvy bilingual audience cut me off with laughter.

During the luncheon inside city hall after the president's speech, Mac Bundy talked to me about the need to correct the tenor of the speech, particularly its reference to the West's inability to work with the Communists, weeks before negotiations were to begin in Moscow on a nuclear test ban treaty. We inserted new material into his afternoon speech to students at the Free University of Berlin, talking about the winds of change blowing over the Iron Curtain and the rest of the world, and a prediction that the "power of historical evolution would be felt in Eastern Europe too . . ."

Closing his brief luncheon remarks, after the cheers had died down and the crowd outside had left, JFK proposed a toast "to the people of Berlin on both sides of the wall, to the German people on both sides of the wall, and to the cause of freedom on both sides of the wall." At day's end, when a weary JFK cheerily climbed into Air Force One, he sank into a chair opposite me and said: "We will never have another day like this one." Sadly, that was true. But the day, the speech, and its inspiring (though erroneous) last line are still remembered.

Thirty-one years later, I delivered a speech in a reunited Berlin, in a reunited Germany, in a reunited Europe, recalling my earlier visit with JFK and his efforts to sustain the hope and pride of the one million or more Berliners gathered in front of him that day. Were he still alive in 1994, he would not have claimed all the credit for the peaceful survival of Berlin and its freedom, I said. He would have shared that credit with many, East and West. But I could not help but think what a sense of satisfaction he would have experienced to see the wall come down without a single American shot being fired.

In the year prior to that speech in Berlin, after staring at each other down a nuclear gun barrel over missiles in Cuba, both Kennedy and Khrushchev had come to the realization that there had to be better ways of resolving the conflicts and disagreements between East and West. Kennedy's commencement address at American University in Washington, D.C., on June 10, 1963—a speech combining eloquence, high principles, effective proposals, and idealism—had been planned for some time in the hope that it might break the deadlock in negotiations with the Soviet Union on a treaty to halt nuclear testing.

The president and I had each been advised in separate conversations with Norman Cousins, the innovative *Saturday Review* editor and peace activist, that the Soviet leadership was ready for a breakthrough if Kennedy could make the first move. Cousins believed that Khrushchev faced a critical choice at the next Soviet Central Committee meeting later in June. Under pressure from the Chinese because of his withdrawal of missiles from Cuba the previous year, he had either to denounce the United States as an imperialist warmonger who had failed to respond to his policy of peaceful coexistence, or show some concrete change in response to his statesmanship. The United States, argued Cousins, should therefore speak first, demonstrating our peaceful intentions. Mac Bundy agreed with this notion, and asked some of his aides to send their best thoughts for such a peace speech to me, and to keep the plan confidential.

Kennedy was committed to spending the days preceding the American University commencement on a Western speaking tour, ending in Hawaii with the U.S. Conference of Mayors. I had hoped to go to Hawaii with him for personal reasons, but he asked me to stay in Washington to work on the speech, then fly to Hawaii and work with him on it on the long return trip. As I left for Hawaii, I sent a copy of the completed draft to Bundy, who convened a small group—his two deputies, in addition to my brother Tom and Arthur Schlesinger—to review it.

The president, after reviewing the speech with me

en route back to Washington, discussed it with Bundy by telephone, urging him to show it to the secretary of state and the secretary of defense, but not to circulate any copies within their respective departments. The president knew that the unprecedented message of the speech would set off alarm bells in more bellicose quarters in Washington, possibly producing leaks and political attacks in advance of his talk.

He spoke to the U.S. Mayors Conference on Sunday, June 9, and we started back that same evening, arriving Monday morning at Andrews Air Force Base outside Washington. I went directly to the American University campus. The president stopped at the White House to change his clothes. The commencement ceremony was held on the university athletic field. I sat in the back of the platform, again thrilled by the president of the United States stating principles so fully consistent with my own, touching briefly on civil rights in the United States but primarily on peace—"not a Pax Americana enforced on the world by American weapons of war," but a peace that was beneficial for all mankind. "For," said John F. Kennedy that fine June day, "in the final analysis, our most basic common link is that we all inhabit this small planet; we all breathe the same air; we all cherish our children's future; and we are all mortal." In that unprecedented speech, JFK called for a reexamination of the cold war, a reexamination of our relations with the Soviet Union, and a reexamination of what kind of peace we truly wanted.

In that speech, Kennedy became the first American president to demonstrate not only appreciation of Russia as a great power—a recognition that Khrushchev dearly wanted—but also empathy for Russia's enormous toll of human casualties in World War II, which the Russians felt had been largely unrecognized in the West.

JFK and I had agreed that Woodrow Wilson's call "to make the world safe for democracy"—which sounded like imposing our system on mankind, exactly what he did not want the Communists to do with their system—should be changed to "making the world safe for diversity," thereby envisioning the day when each country, including those within the Communist orbit, would be free to choose its own system.

Kennedy's unilateral initiation of a moratorium on nuclear testing in the atmosphere (which he added to the draft on our return trip from Hawaii as a concrete demonstration of the speech's noble principles) was approved that morning by the chairman of the Joint Chiefs and the chairman of the Atomic Energy Commission. It led promptly to negotiations in Moscow on a nuclear test ban treaty, negotiations that JFK personally monitored closely from Washington. During those negotiations in Moscow, Soviet chairman Khrushchev told our delegation leader, Averell Harriman, that more than anything else, Kennedy's speech—which the chairman allowed to be rebroadcast throughout Russia on Western radio and to be published in full in the Moscow press—had paved the way for the treaty.

On July 26, 1963, six weeks after the American University speech, the president delivered a televised address to the nation hailing the initialing in Moscow of the Limited Nuclear Test Ban Treaty. For that speech, I made certain that suggestions were solicited and received from sources throughout the government, to support our argument that the treaty's curb on nuclear weapons development would enhance the security of the United States, and that the risks of Soviet violation or repudiation were minimal. Fortunately, the president's early 1962 speech justifying our country's resumption of nuclear testing had been worded with sufficient care to prevent its being cited against him in that 1963 test ban effort. Kennedy sent the treaty to the Senate, with a request for ratification in a comprehensive message answering all possible objections from the hawks in that body. He succeeded, and I was proud when the president sent to me one of the pens he used to sign the treaty after its ratification.

That spring and summer formed a remarkably intensive but productive period in Kennedy's curtailed presidency. On the day before the American University speech, June 9, he spoke to the nation's mayors in Honolulu, calling for their help on the civil rights crisis. On June 10, the same day that he spoke at American University, he also signed the Equal Pay Act prohibiting wage discrimination against women. The next day, June 11, he directed from the Oval Office the admission of the University of Alabama's first two black students, despite Governor George C. Wallace's theatrically staged stand in the doorway, and went on nationwide television to give the strongest presidential declaration since Abraham Lincoln that race discrimination in this country was to end permanently. The next day, June 12, he established the first National Advisory Council on the Arts. One week later, he sent Congress the most comprehensive civil rights legislation of all time, and announced the joint U.S.-Soviet establishment of a direct communications link between our respective capitals, the so-called hotline. By June 23 he was in Germany on his trip to solidify the Western alliance. To paraphrase Wordsworth: Bliss was it in that dawn to be alive, but to be young, and in the service of that president, was very heaven!

In 2003, forty years after the president's death, when

America's reputation abroad was in tatters, I was in Rome for a speaking engagement, and invited by a local foreign policy group to give an address. "On what subject?" I asked the chairman. "Tell us about the good America, when Kennedy was president," he said. I did. I talked about an America admired for its values, respected for its principles, not feared for its might or resented for its success; an America that led by listening, worked with the rest of the world, and respected international law; an America that stood for peace, not one that started wars. That was America when Kennedy was president.

The Peace Corps

The Peace Corps was one of John F. Kennedy's proudest achievements, the epitome of his call for service and sacrifice, and an important new instrument to communicate to other countries the best of American values. Given his penchant for invoking the old saying that success has a hundred fathers and failure is an orphan, he would have been the first to acknowledge that the Peace Corp really did have a hundred fathers: a bill by Senator Hubert Humphrey, a speech by James Gavin, another by Fritz Hollings, an article by Milton Shapp (later governor of Pennsylvania), a bill by Congressman Henry Reuss, a campaign strategy memorandum from the brilliant Fred Dutton prompted by Senator William Fulbright, the example of the Mormons and other religious organizations.

Many of those paternity claims stretch back years before the 1960 campaign. But this baby took its first breath late in the night of October 14, when neither our campaign headquarters nor I had completed our initial formulations of the Peace Corps idea. I do not believe candidate Kennedy even had a speech text in hand when we arrived at the University of Michigan campus hours late, after one of the Nixon TV debates, and found a huge crowd of students still waiting outside the student union. He mounted its front steps, and spontaneously launched into a heartfelt description of what would ultimately become the Peace Corps:

> I think we can make the difference. . . . How many of you who are going to be doctors are willing to spend your days in Ghana? Technicians or engineers, how many of you are willing to . . . spend your lives traveling around the world? . . . not merely to serve one year or two . . . but to contribute part of your life to this country. On your answer depends the answer to the question whether a free society can compete with totalitarians. I think it can, and I think Americans are willing to contribute, but the

efforts must be far greater than we have ever made in the past. . . . Unless you comprehend the nature of what is being asked of you, this country can't possibly move through the next 10 years in relative strength. So I come here tonight . . . to go to bed! But I also ask you to join in the effort . . .

As he spoke, hatless and coatless in the autumn chill, I stood at the bottom of the steps, listening, admiring, and instantly recognizing that a full-scale speech on this subject would soon be necessary. The students responded with cheers and applause that night, and with intensely organized efforts in the following weeks, signing a petition to Kennedy asking for a government-sponsored endeavor they could join, and asking the Kennedy campaign's chief Michigan coordinator to arrange with me a plan to present that petition to JFK the next time his plane landed within driving distance of their campus.

The final full-scale speech on which I worked, drawing on all the sources noted above, was delivered a few weeks later. It was JFK's signal speech on world peace in San Francisco on the night of November 2, 1960. He called for "A peace corps of talented men and women willing and able to serve their country" as teachers, engineers, doctors, or nurses in developing nations around the globe.

Between his election and inauguration, he appointed a transition task force to develop and refine the proposal. The Peace Corps proposal first entered the official national agenda in his State of the Union address on January 30, 1961.

Forty days after he moved into the Oval Office, the Peace Corps became a reality through an executive order and the dispatch to Congress of a message and proposed bill to establish a permanent independent agency. The executive order enabled the president to organize—under his energetic brother-in-law Sargent Shriver—and to staff fully an operation that was in place by the time the bill passed six months later. Shriver was the perfect choice to run the new program—idealistic, tireless, and deeply committed to public service, as he demonstrated in a variety of official positions both before and after JFK's death. Shriver, too, was dedicated to helping the least fortunate among us, both at home and around the world.

Kennedy issued his executive order on March 1 without waiting for Congress because he knew there would be debate and delay. Many Republicans opposed it. Many liberal Democrats initially demeaned it. Many conservatives initially dismissed it. Many Communist governments denounced it. Well-intentioned academics wanted to study it. His State Department and Agency for International Development both wanted to control it. The CIA wanted to use it. Some leaders in neutral nations, even those most in need of help, heaped ridicule upon it.

Ultimately, both liberals and conservatives embraced the idea, showing the American spirit of generosity through face-to-face contacts and practical assistance, building goodwill not through a bureaucracy, propaganda, wealthy tourists, or American businessmen, but through friendly, courteous, helpful Americans from all walks of life interacting daily with ordinary locals. The whole program helped make young Americans feel reconnected to the national interest.

The Peace Corps not only embodied my own youthful ideals, but was central to JFK's presidency. In time, that proud effort, together with JFK's civil rights program and antiwar decisions, combined to overshadow in my thinking any few brief disappointments or disagreements I might have had on other fronts. In government, to decide is to risk. Even the Peace Corps, that noblest and most widely supported of JFK's innovations, could have resulted in an expensive failure, resented by beneficiary governments, a source of complaints from overworked or endangered young volunteers and their parents, or a constant source of medical, security, and other problems for young Americans far from home. But little or none of that happened, thanks to able administration by Shriver and his team.

In August 1961 President Kennedy spoke to the first group of volunteers about to leave for Ghana and Tanzania. The fifty-one volunteers who landed in Accra, Ghana's capital, made an immediate impression on their hosts by forming a chorus on the airport tarmac, in front of the Ghanaian minister of education and other officials, to sing the Ghanaian national anthem in Twi, the local language.

The corps began that year, 1961, with five hundred volunteers, and rose to nine hundred by 1963, and twelve thousand by 1965. Twenty-three other countries developed their own Peace Corps initiatives, imitating ours. In dozens of countries, U.S. Peace Corps volunteers worked in education, agriculture, health care, and community development. As the number of volunteers serving and the number of countries served increased, the president's pride in his creation, in these ambassadors of American idealism, increased as well. He took every opportunity to meet on the lawn behind the White House with new groups of volunteers about to go overseas and often with those who had just returned; and he took every opportunity to sing their praises.

Over the years, Peace Corps volunteers and their skills have been welcomed in countries from Afghani-

stan to Sri Lanka, from Iran to Venezuela. It is still helping people help themselves—and helping America win
new friends—all over the world. I have frequently met
former Peace Corps volunteers around this country,
serving in high business, political, diplomatic, medical, educational, and nonprofit executive positions.
All tell me the Peace Corps "did more for me than I
did for it."

By the time I addressed the thirty-fifth anniversary
dinner of the National Peace Corps Association in 1996,
some 144,000 volunteers had shown America's best face
to the world's most needy people. In my speech, I compared the words of my "favorite President" with the
words of my "favorite Peace Corps volunteer," comparing the president's original hopes with the actual
experiences almost thirty-five years later of one young
volunteer living out that dream:

> "I am convinced," said John Kennedy in San Fran-
> cisco, "that . . . men and women in this country . . .
> anxious to respond to the public service, dedicated
> to freedom, are able . . . to join in a worldwide
> struggle against poverty and ignorance."
>
> My favorite volunteer wrote: "Life here . . . is
> hard by American standards—there is no electric-

ity or running water, the health center . . . is insufficiently supplied . . . and large numbers of women give birth at home, without ever receiving prenatal care."

"The life will not be easy," said my favorite President on March 1, 1961, but "it will be rich and satisfying. For every . . . American who participates in the Peace Corps . . . will know that he or she is sharing in the great common task of bringing to man that decent way of life which is the foundation and a condition of peace."

True to his prediction, my favorite volunteer wrote: "I now feel what . . . months ago seemed nearly impossible: that this is my home . . . its inhabitants are generous and friendly. I arrived not knowing a soul but left feeling as if I had many new friends."

After his death, Peace Corps volunteers in many countries were called "Kennedy's children." One of them, I'm proud to say, was also one of mine—my daughter, Juliet, my favorite volunteer, whose letters home from a village at the edge of the Sahara Desert in Morocco proved that all those years later, JFK's legacy was still alive.

Outer Space

At the height of the cold war in the middle and late 1950s, the race between the two superpowers to demonstrate superior achievements in science and technology turned increasingly into a competition for superiority in the exploration of outer space. It was a difficult competition for the United States; our competitor could advance in secret, largely uninhibited by press criticism, public opinion, legislative priorities, or constitutional and budget limitations. Increasingly, Russian space launches contrasted sharply with highly publicized American failures, as one rocket after another fizzled and failed on the launching pad during the Eisenhower years. The possibility of the Soviet Union's military occupation of space was a nightmare to the West. In the 1960 campaign, space became a leading example of candidate Kennedy's insistence that new leadership was needed to "get this country moving again."

During the 1960 transition, I met with Jerome Wiesner and many of his scientific colleagues, questioning whether the enormous amounts of money being poured into U.S. space exploration programs were worthwhile. I was deeply impressed by his recounting the scientific by-products that could come from that exploration, not only advances in communication, health, information, astronomy, and meteorology, but possibly the unlocking of mankind's oldest mysteries: the origins of the universe, of the planet Earth, and of life itself.

When, on Wednesday, April 12, 1961, Soviet cosmonaut Yuri Gagarin became the first human to be launched into orbit, Kennedy recognized that feat as an important cold war gain for the Soviets and graciously sent sincere congratulations to Chairman Khrushchev. On the following day, mindful that he had an upcoming interview on America's space posture (with Hugh Sidey of *Time* magazine), he asked me to gather a group whose expertise might be helpful in determining how the United States could best respond. Although I had no real aptitude for science and astronomy, I benefited from the extensive efforts of my colleagues to instruct me. Space, like so many other issues, was one that I learned on the job.

It was a subject that the president also learned on the job. When NASA administrator James Webb brought into the Oval Office a desk model of a future U.S. space capsule, Kennedy, who had no real grasp of the enormous technology involved, and remained skeptical about the cost and importance of space missions, quipped to me, "I think he stopped in a toy store on his way to town."

That Friday, April 14, I gathered in my office administration officials both expert and responsible in this area—budget director David Bell and his key assistants, White House science advisor Jerome Wiesner and his space experts, and deputy space administrator Hugh Dryden. Their consensus view was that the Soviet Union had been required to develop larger rocket thrust for their strategic arsenal years earlier when the United States had already developed lighter thermonuclear weapons, which did not need excessively powerful rocket launchers. Consequently, the Soviets had a sizable advantage in the space race and would continue to score firsts for some time. I asked what would come next, after Gagarin's orbit. My group reviewed a number of likely future launch products—a capsule with two men in space, a space platform or laboratory, an unmanned vehicle to the far reaches of space, taking pictures and mineral and air samples. Regarding each ascending rung on that ladder, I asked what were the prospects of the United States impressing the world by doing it first. Each time, the answer was the same—the Soviet lead in rocket thrust would continue to beat us to every milestone, even to putting an unmanned vehicle on the moon.

"What about a manned vehicle?" I asked. That project, they agreed, was so large, so complex and so far off, requiring so many new scientific and engineering developments, components, and studies, that the United States might have time to overcome its rocket engine lag, undertake those new developments, components, and studies, and thus possibly have as much chance as the Russians had to be the first to achieve this goal. That ray of hope, after all the previous pessimistic answers, caught my immediate attention. I asked more questions. Although the several meetings that would ultimately be held that day merge in my memory, I believe it was at this meeting that we first discussed the possibility of sending a man to the moon.

The very notion of a manned flight to the moon, as impossible as that seemed, was one that I knew would engage President Kennedy's keen interest. It embodied everything he had said for a year and longer about striving to get this country moving again, about joining the Russians in peaceful space exploration, about crossing "new frontiers."

That evening, Hugh Sidey joined President Kennedy, me, and several other advisors for a meeting in the Cabinet Room, where we discussed the range of options confronting the president. As the meeting concluded and the president got up to leave, Hugh asked about going to the moon. "Wait here," the president said to him, summoning me into the Oval Office.

Our meeting was brief, and I do not recall precisely

what was said. The president was incredulous about sending a manned vehicle to the moon, but excited. He immediately sensed that the possibility of putting a man on the moon could galvanize public support for the exploration of space as one of the great human adventures of the twentieth century. "Get it staffed out," he said. "Go find out what McNamara's department thinks."

As I left, I approached Hugh, waiting outside the Oval Office. In my excitement, I prematurely told him that I thought the U.S. answer to the Gagarin flight would be strong and dramatic. "We're going to the moon," I exultantly confided, adding that much still needed to be reviewed and confirmed before the president could make his decision public.

Six weeks later, JFK would deliver to Congress what was, in effect, a second State of the Union, a message on "Urgent National Needs." During those forty-two intervening days, intensive study on a possible lunar landing had been undertaken by Vice President Johnson as chairman of the Space Council, by McNamara, and by Webb. The president fired off a constant stream of written questions to them on costs, risks, manpower, alternatives, and administrative responsibility. He heard from hundreds of individuals in the process of making his decision—scientists, engineers, experts of all kinds—and became convinced that the United States must not remain second in this race. A tentative premise grew into a firm conclusion only after it had been carefully studied, the estimated costs calculated, the risks weighed, and the responsibilities allocated.

Along with requests for new funds and authority to confront the nation's escalating domestic and international crises, his "Urgent National Needs" speech made public his decision to "go to the moon before this decade is out," and sought congressional funding and approval. The president initially sensed—as a good speaker can—that his audience was skeptical, if not hostile, and that his request was being received with stunned doubt and disbelief by the members of Congress, both Democratic and Republican, in joint session that morning. He then deviated from his prepared text—the only time I can recall his doing so in a formal address—to add a personal note of urgency on the importance and difficulty of this commitment and the need for support from all.

His self-imposed deadline, "this decade," was chosen and inserted by JFK himself to exert pressure on NASA. The phrase deliberately left some flexibility—it could mean within the decade of the sixties, or within the next ten years. The moon landing actually took place on July 20, 1969, little more than eight years later. Kennedy, in setting that deadline, surely expected to be alive at the end of the decade, and was prepared to be either chastened or triumphant.

One night that summer of 1961, I sat on my front steps, gazing at the moon, wondering whether it was really possible, or was it all crazy? I partly agree with those who said these enormous financial resources—tens of billions of dollars in 1960s currency before it was over— may have been better devoted to combating our own planet's ills and helping our own country's poor. But I do not believe for a moment that those billions would have been approved by Congress for those compassionate purposes, nor do I believe that Congress would have voted for the many less dramatic science programs proposed as alternatives by many scientists. The "moon shot" was the making of America's superiority in space, and all the scientific, diplomatic, and national security benefits that followed.

The president's Science and Technology Advisory Council under Jerry Wiesner recognized the historic importance of manned space flight, comparing it to the Wright Brothers' first flight and Lindbergh's flight across the Atlantic, but also warned of possible health dangers. They worried about NASA's inability to simulate in the laboratory not only weightlessness but also human exposure to such extraordinary speed, heat, and atmospheric pressure. One of Wiesner's top advisors said to me: "If doubts arise, substitute an animal for a man." The decision was not mine to make. Some months later NASA actually used a chimpanzee on one flight, enabling the president, in his biweekly news conference, to announce that the chimpanzee "took off at 10:08 this morning . . . He reports that everything is perfect and working well."

On May 5, 1961, America's first attempt to send a man, Alan Shepard, into space, at least into sub-orbital flight, occurred in full view, while gloating Russians, undecided Third World neutrals, and concerned allies awaited the outcome. Untold numbers of the American press insisted for weeks that all their reporters must receive passes to be present; that their editorial writers and columnists must be free to deplore the media circus atmosphere resulting from so many reporters being present; and that such a big buildup would worsen our national humiliation if the flight were a failure. When Shepard's mission was successful, JFK, his wife, LBJ, several other aides, and I, watching on a little television set in Evelyn Lincoln's office, heaved a collective sigh of relief, and cheered.

The flight of Alan Shepard, and John Glenn's subsequent encirclement of the globe, however limited in scope, were hailed by the president as a triumph for America and the free world, and deepened the patriotic pride of most Americans, increasing both their morale and their support of the president. He was lucky again, said the politicians. It was not luck. JFK had inherited a disorganized and ridiculed space exploration effort, and boldly transformed it into a successful program.

But the most important test of President Kennedy's global greatness was not whether he could get a man to the moon and back but whether he could achieve peace on planet Earth. The lunar landing program, by accelerating and organizing our effort to avert the Soviet militarization of space, and by increasing the possibility of international scientific cooperation, including work with the Soviet Union, helped his efforts for peace. Part of the motivation for JFK's decision in April 1961 had been a Soviet refusal to join with us in a cooperative international space effort, as he had requested in his inaugural, to assure the world that neither superpower would dominate this new ocean through hostile, military means.

After JFK's death, LBJ and I agreed the program should continue. As he said at a press conference:

President Kennedy asked me, [during the 1960 transition] at Palm Beach, to assume responsibility for the space program and try to give it some leadership and direction . . . The President talked to me a number of times about the desirability of setting a goal to go to the moon in this decade, and the dangers of it and the wisdom of it. He asked for my recommendation, which we made in writing. I recommended this goal for this decade. Mr. Sorensen and I discussed the goal at length in view of the fact that our beloved President had set that goal. Naturally we have religiously adhered to it. [Okay, so he exaggerated a little.]

One manned flight during the Johnson presidency ended in tragedy with the 1967 death of Virgil "Gus" Grissom, one of the original astronauts and one of the best, whom I knew personally. We had both been named among 1961's Ten Outstanding Young Men. I continued to support the manned space exploration program, knowing that it inevitably involved some risk, as most important scientific advances and explorations do, and as Grissom himself knew. But we also knew that man was still the most delicately tuned machine— his powers of observation, detection, and deduction could tell us things in space that computers and cameras could not.

In 2001, when I was invited to speak at Chicago's Adler Planetarium on the fortieth anniversary of American space flight, I noted first that I was an unlikely choice for that assignment, not knowing the difference between a black hole, a brown dwarf, and a red shift. Long before I went to Washington, I had visited that very planetarium and watched its spectacular show on the grandeur of our universe, which had caused me as a very young man to think about the measurement and meaning of time and distance, the insignificance of the life of one person, or one nation, or one planet in the vast cosmos—a humbling perspective.

Science historian Lawrence Suid has said that hundreds of years from now, assuming we do not destroy ourselves in the meantime, the fact of man's leaving his planet for the first time in 1969 would rank as the most significant event of history, "the culmination of technology, dreams and science." I hope so, provided the U.S. preserves space for peaceful uses and the benefit of all mankind.

Those modern writers who say that opposition to JFK's peaceful and prudent foreign policy was strong among hard-line cold warriors in the military and intelligence agencies are correct. But top civilian officials in the Defense Department, McNamara and Roswell Gilpatric, chief of staff Maxwell Taylor and CIA director John McCone, were sincere admirers of and loyal to the president, and too firmly in control of their own departments to permit any serious revolt, however much some of them may have grumbled in the privacy of their fellow-hawk discussions or later in their memoirs.

Chapter 25

My Role in Press Relations

One veteran journalist told me recently that Kennedy's presidential press conferences, with all their frank and funny answers, seem as distant now as candlelit dining rooms and clipper ships. JFK did not approach these conferences with the dread that other presidents have acknowledged. On the contrary, he regarded them as an opportunity not only to inform and persuade the country and Congress of his positions and proposals, but also—we discovered in the first year—an opportunity to inform and instruct the members of his own administration, particularly those in the middle and lower ranks of the departments and agencies who rarely had direct communication with the president, but could learn from his news conferences the direction of his thinking.

President Kennedy prepared for those news conferences like a student preparing for a final exam. On the prior evening, each department and agency head in the government was required to submit a report on any important developments, problems, or proposals, good news and bad, after being warned that the president would not take kindly to being surprised on television at his news conference by a question about some problem in that department's work on which he had received no information. JFK, a speed reader, pored over these departmental reports.

On the morning before an afternoon press conference, the president, accompanied by the vice president and secretary of state, conducted an intense 8 A.M. breakfast review, usually lasting until 10 A.M., for which Feldman and I prepared a list of all possible questions, as had press secretary Pierre Salinger and others. In a process reminiscent of his preparation in September 1960 for the first televised debate with Nixon, I would list topics, often in the form of a question. He would respond with a nod if he knew the answer, or with a request for more information or an alternative reply. Sometimes he would add questions not on either my list or Pierre's. Often, at the end of the session, Walter Heller would give the president a one-page update on the national economy, should that question arise. The president would assign

Feldman and others the task of developing over the next few hours any additional information he needed on any topic. If he wanted to open the conference with a statement, I was usually responsible for providing the first draft.

His press conferences were customarily held at 4 P.M. He wanted the requested material by 2 P.M., and held a follow-up meeting with a few of us at 3 P.M., when Bundy, Salinger, and I—and/or our deputies—would bring him updated questions and information to review in his bedroom before he left for the State Department auditorium where the news conferences were generally held. The president would often be eating lunch or resting, having just finished a bath. Sometimes he would be sitting up in bed, sometimes shaving. These bedroom sessions were informal, and often very amusing.

It was in one of these final preparation sessions in June 1962 that I asked for his response to the Mexican ambassador to the OAS who had criticized his policies and, in effect, urged him to cancel his forthcoming trip to Mexico City. JFK tried out on us a stiff, elaborate, verbose, evasive nonanswer, talking loftily of our national interests and comity in international relations. When I imprudently asked exactly what that meant, he replied with a smile: "It means that no little SOB in the Mexican government is going to stop my trip!" When asked that very question an hour or so later in his press conference, JFK's actual answer was a gracious "This is really a matter between the representative and his government rather than between this government and the representative."

JFK's spontaneous humor at presidential press conferences sometimes had to be restrained. I could see in his eyes and smile an internal struggle to resist a tempting quip that could get him in trouble. Usually he contented himself with a gentle response to a pointed question. Asked for a comment on Senator Margaret Chase Smith's "proposal that a watchdog committee be created," he simply replied: "To watch Congressmen and Senators? Well, that would be fine if they feel they should be watched." He was later privately amused when his reference to Senator Smith as a "great lady" was incorrectly printed in the official government transcript without the letter "d"; the mistake was quickly corrected.

One afternoon, when Bundy, Salinger, and I were briefing the president in his bedroom on last-minute developments that might be raised in that afternoon's news conference, the subject under discussion was the French government's decision to embargo American poultry exports on the dubious grounds that the U.S. practice of injecting hormones into hens to give them larger, meatier breasts affected the libido of French consumers. When one participant in our group sardonically asked whether France's aging president, General Charles de Gaulle, had any personal concern about the issue, I interjected the line: "And he dances divinely, too."

The president, laughing, asked, "Do you know that joke?" When I replied that it had circulated among my brothers and me for years, he noted that he had heard it, but only within his circle for many years. The others present insisted on hearing the story, and the president insisted that I tell it, the punch line being the one I had just uttered. The joke, not to be repeated here, is about a specialty poultry worker identified to an inquiring female as a "pheasant plucker." When I finished telling the story, JFK laughed harder than the rest, acknowledging that for years he had told and retold that story, mistakenly using the phrase "chicken plucker" and not getting many laughs. It was one of the few occasions I knew more about something than he.

His remarkable self-restraint enabled him to avoid even partial sentences that could be distorted out of context or deemed offensive to some—a skill he demonstrated on the presidential campaign in Anchorage, Alaska. I had briefed him en route that the new state was sharply divided over the location of its new state capital, and that any indication of a preference on his part for

one of them, Anchorage, Fairbanks, Juneau, or Nome—
would guarantee him a negative vote in all the others.
When asked upon arrival where we thought the state
capital should be located, Kennedy replied: "Let me
say that I don't know enough about that to comment on
it—or at least I know too much to comment on it . . ."

The president did not object to hostile questions at
his news conferences, occasionally answering them with
quips, and never berating the questioner. However,
nettled that one questioner had irresponsibly identified
by name alleged security risks in the State Department,
whom the president was certain were being unjustly
accused, he did chastise the questioner for her lack of
consideration. He liked an older woman reporter from
Maine, Ms. May Craig, and knew that she took pride in
asking complicated questions that often seemed off the
wall to others; for that very reason, he called upon her
whenever he could to add some flavor to the event.

Helping him prepare for those news conferences was
not my only role in matters relating to the press. Although I had no formal responsibility for media relations, I constantly fielded telephone and other inquiries
from journalists, and made it a rule to try to return each
day every call I possibly could before I left the White
House in the evening. JFK almost never asked me to
call a journalist to complain about a story, unlike LBJ

who did it constantly during the few months I served him in the White House.

From my earliest days in the Kennedy Senate office throughout my stay in the White House, my relations with the press were generally friendly and frank. Both JFK and I liked journalists, finding much in common with them. JFK liked individual journalists more than he trusted them as a group, although he usually spoke so honestly and openly to them that they believed he trusted them. Echoing a warning I once received from JFK, I reminded one of my best friends in the press, Al Otten of the *Wall Street Journal*, that he and I should "never forget that, even as good friends as we are, our objectives are different."

In mid-September 1961, shortly after Congress adjourned its first session during the Kennedy presidency, Larry O'Brien and I made an off-the-record presentation in a private home to a group of some thirty reporters representing most of the major media markets in the country. I handed out copies of a three-page memorandum headed "for your information in writing your stories . . . not to be attributed to the White House," detailing the administration's legislative accomplishments that year, which (unsurprisingly) my memorandum said were "substantial," considering the majorities enjoyed in both houses of Congress by the Republican-Southern

"Dixiecrat" coalition. The copy that I found in my Kennedy Library files had been correctly labeled by its first recipient in a red pen scrawl as "Propaganda."

An uninvited correspondent from the conservative *Chicago Tribune*, who obtained a copy of the memo, as well as an oral report on the session from skeptical journalists who were present, reported that someone shouted out during my presentation: "Do you expect us to swallow this bunk?" The *Tribune* story asserted that representatives of more conservative newspapers were not invited, and that many of the journalists present related reactions "ranging from irritation to disgust at what they labeled a brainwashing." The writer justifiably felt that I had gone too far, expecting them to write the material as their own. I was not only new in those days, I was naive.

Recognizing the press as a powerful influence on public policy, I have never agreed with those who worry about antagonisms between press and government. I have as a private lawyer traveled and worked in too many countries where press and government, instead of holding each other in check, are in bed together. I like the press's role in America as watchdog, but I recall the old saying that the watchdog never barks when a family member passes by. I want the watchdog to keep on barking.

Chapter 26

Planning for JFK's Reelection and Second Term

During the autumn of 1963, the president and I began for the first time to think seriously about his presidential reelection campaign in 1964 and his second term, looking ahead to his agenda for reconciliation abroad (the Senate ratified the Nuclear Test Ban Treaty on October 7) and at home (the House Judiciary Committee approved his bipartisan civil rights bill on October 29).

On November 12, the president convened his first campaign strategy meeting for 1964. Attending with the president and me were the attorney general; Kennedy brother-in-law Steve Smith; the Democratic National Committee chairman, John Bailey; White House aides Kenny O'Donnell and Larry O'Brien; an O'Donnell liaison with the national committee, Richard Maguire; and Richard Scammon, who, in addition to being director of the Census Bureau, was a skilled political scientist with an impressive command of voting statistics. Vice President Johnson was not present, although I believe JFK had every intention of keeping the ticket the same for the 1964 race, particularly in view of his increased need to firm up Southern support; Johnson was not part of the inner circle and did not have the warmest relations with—or full confidence of—everyone in that room. Today I am the sole survivor of that group.

It was decided that each of those present would have essentially the same job he had in the 1960 postconvention campaign—with Steve Smith coordinating fundraising and spending, Kenny O'Donnell scheduling and logistics, Larry O'Brien organization at the grassroots level, and John Bailey organization at the political chieftains level. I would continue to be responsible for issues, policies, the platform, debates, and speeches. Robert F. Kennedy, staying on as attorney general, would direct the entire effort behind the scenes but would not have the title of campaign manager. That would have fooled no one; and to make the attorney general campaign manager was probably a worse idea than making RFK attorney general.

Having prepared, well in advance of the 1960 convention, an analysis of the number and allocation of delegates at that convention, and the significance of those numbers for JFK and his more liberal and Southern opponents, I prepared a similar memorandum for that November 1963 meeting. I also noted "the unique opportunity offered the Democrats in 1964 to amend their Party structure at a time when no presidential nomination contest would be affected, altering the distribution of voting power in the Democratic National Convention to adhere as closely as possible to the concept of political equality, one person, one vote, no preferred class of voters." My memo continued:

the present system is substantively illogical, harmful, and unfair, if not unconstitutional. It not only inflates excessively the power of the smaller states in general but also treats unfairly those states which have larger numbers of Democrats and larger voter turnouts . . . Both law and equity call for an abolition of the present system and its replacement by one based on the fundamental principle of "one

man-one vote" . . . It would over the years improve
the quality and prospects of Democratic [presiden-
tial] nominees by selecting those whose strength
in the convention reflected true strength in the
country. . . .

That grand if unrealistic suggestion received no attention.

At the meeting, the president was in a confident
mood, proud of his accomplishments, satisfied that
by then he knew how to manage the bureaucracy and
get along with his global allies. Our meeting discussed
the challenge he faced to win votes in the following
November (1964), particularly in the South and suburbs,
and whether to establish an "independent citizens" organization alongside the Democratic National Committee. Later that month the president was to fly to Florida
and Texas to help unite the warring factions of the party
in both states, and to lay the groundwork for their 1964
campaign. The president totally dismissed rumors that
LBJ or some other Southerner might attempt to mount a
contest within the Democratic Party over the civil rights
issue. We speculated on whether the Republicans would
nominate Barry Goldwater to appeal to the South and
far right or Nelson Rockefeller to draw votes from inde-

pendents in the center. JFK disagreed on almost every issue with Goldwater, but liked him personally and felt that Goldwater was at least intellectually honest in expressing his extremely conservative views.

Moreover, the combined approval of the president's Nuclear Test Ban Treaty and the prospects of a Goldwater nomination by the Republicans gave JFK an increasing sense that world peace would be a principal theme of his 1964 campaign. Earlier that fall, after the Limited Nuclear Test Ban Treaty was initialed, JFK had set out on a tour of Western states, intending to talk primarily about his new proposals for conservation and the environment, but increasingly shifted his emphasis to peace as he encountered a favorable response to that issue.

In Great Falls, Montana, he had extemporaneously strayed from the text of a prepared speech on the administration's nine-point program on resource development to say the following:

> . . . this generation of Americans has to make up its mind for our security and for our peace, because what happens in Europe or Latin America or Africa or Asia directly affects the security of the people who live in this city.

In Hanford, Washington, in a speech devoted to energy issues, including nuclear power, he extemporaneously inserted the following:

It may well be that man recognizes now that war is so destructive, so annihilating, so incendiary, that it may be possible, out of that awful fact . . . [to] develop a rule of reason and a rule of law . . . it may be possible for us to find a more peaceful world.

In Las Vegas, Nevada:

Behind this shield, behind this increased strength . . . behind those evidences of our desire to be strong in a free world, we have also attempted to work for peace, and we see nothing inconsistent with being strong and trying to live in peace.

I was back in the White House, marveling at the change in subject matter, and not the least bit disappointed that I had devoted so much time preparing draft speeches on conservation that were in large part unused. After he returned and we discussed the trip, it became clear to us both that presenting the American voters with a clearer choice on the overriding issue of peace would be good for both the campaign and the country.

Around the same time, as I contemplated the strategy for reelection, I jotted down the following confidential notes on the political impact of the national economy:

In the crudest political terms, we should hope that full employment would peak in the summer and fall of 1964, and that a recession between the fall of '63 and the fall of '64, if inevitable some time, would be better sooner than later, and that the [optimum] timing of Congressional action on our tax and economic program should be evaluated accordingly, also that a tax cut would not mean much to an unemployed man with no taxable income; that, even if unemployment did not substantially lessen and remained at roughly 5%, as [seems] likely, there would be no identifiable Kennedy recession or Kennedy stock market boom.

Shortly after our early November planning and strategy session, I returned to Nebraska to deliver the keynote address at the Annual State Democratic Dinner in Omaha. I made clear the president's intention to run for reelection in 1964. My speech was subject to no instructions or clearance, but reflected our earlier White

House discussion. Testing another possible theme for the 1964 campaign, I described JFK as "a president who cares about America." I noted that there were three "overriding qualities needed in a president—a creative mind, a compassionate heart, and a courageous spirit."

Reelection planning had advanced to the point where we were already discussing the details of the 1964 Democratic convention. A few days after our strategy session, on November 19, I wrote to movie producer and Democratic Party fund-raiser Arthur Krim to thank him for the hospitality that he and his wife, Mathilde, had provided to me on a brief holiday in New York City the previous weekend. I concluded: "I will be sending some materials on convention movies to you, Arthur, as soon as I get the President off to Texas on Thursday . . . I hope we can all be together again soon."

Goldwater would later comment that he would have had "a chance. The tide was turning against Kennedy. . . . [He] certainly couldn't have carried the South. The business fraternity was against him. I felt that I had a fair to middling chance of defeating him. I wouldn't have bet a lot of money on it. . . . Kennedy would not have been afraid to debate, as Johnson was." Goldwater even had a notion of the two candidates' scheduling a series of debates "in town after town on the . . . issues," and thought Kennedy would agree to that. It is true that Kennedy enjoyed debating, but I'm not certain he would have agreed to build Goldwater's audiences for him.

When Goldwater said he had a chance, he had a point. Kennedy's support in the polls was already slipping in late 1963. While a Gallup Poll in September had shown him with a 53 percent to 40 percent lead over Goldwater, an October Harris Poll showed the opposite result, with Goldwater coming out ahead, 54 percent to 38 percent. Civil rights was heating up. We tried to downplay the issue politically, and were gratified by such newspaper headlines as "Sorensen: Civil Rights Not '64 Campaign Issue"; and an article quoting me: "I am sure the Republican party, which is the party of Lincoln, will not want to become the party of white supremacy."

Still, I believe that John Kennedy would have won a second term in 1964. His steadily increasing hold on the respect and affection of the American people, the increasing domestic recognition of his victories for peace in the Berlin and Cuban missile crises, and the economic impact of his tax cut and legislative programs, would all have enabled him to repeat the kind of campaign mastery he had demonstrated in 1960 when he had won an even more difficult presidential election campaign against a tougher opponent than Goldwater, and against an incumbent administration. The 1960 charges of youthful inexperience, and the religious issue, would have disappeared in 1964. Election Day defections in the South over civil rights would, I believed, be more than offset by gains in the rest of the country.

I also have no doubt that his second term would have been a triumph. He would have brought a more heavily Democratic Congress in with him, laying the foundation for strong legislative accomplishments. His experience as a leader, working the levers of government, would have made his second term even more innovative and effective than his first. The Medicare program he had favored as far back as 1960 would have been enacted in 1965, as would his tax reduction and civil rights legislation. Antipoverty legislation would have been pushed through.

All of us in the White House, in a second term, would have been able, I believe, to perform our jobs better, working just as hard, perhaps with more coordination and harmony. Before the end of a second term, I would have been in my forties, old enough, as JFK and I once discussed—in very general terms—to serve in a cabinet post or, like Harry Hopkins, as a kind of special emissary abroad, although I am not certain he would have been willing to part with my immediate proximity in the White House.

. . .

We would have celebrated his fiftieth birthday on May 29, 1967, and it would have been a moment of great laughter and affection. Had he lived (and won a second term), he would have served in the White House five more years, still pressing us in one meeting after another, still grinning impishly at press conferences on a regular basis, still talking intimately with visiting heads of state, chatting happily with his growing son and daughter, speaking solemnly on television to the American people, and moving gracefully through the golden years of his life and leadership. Unlike Eisenhower, he would not have suffered the loss of his top advisor in a corruption scandal. Unlike Nixon, he would not have been forced to resign over "high crimes and misdemeanors." At the end of two full terms, he would have been full of hope, energy, and confidence, leaving the presidency to begin his next challenge, perhaps as president of a great university, editor of a major newspaper, or secretary of state in his brother Bobby's administration.

The only controversial foreign policy issue that he deliberately, explicitly postponed to his second term—when he would have larger popular and congressional majorities—was U.S. relations with China, a power whose Communist takeover and involvement in the Korean War had made it an almost untouchable topic in American politics, but a topic that Kennedy knew had to be faced. He had already expressed sympathetic interest in helping China at a time of famine, but was unable to break through Chinese resistance to serious Western contacts at that time. For Kennedy to build relations with China might also have required a new secretary of state, given Rusk's resolute resistance to change—but that change in personnel might have been forthcoming anyway.

Castro's Cuba, the site of Kennedy's greatest blunder and greatest triumph, was another nettle that he was willing to grasp as he thought about the long term. Kennedy opposed Communism in the Western Hemisphere, but he was not obsessed with hatred for Castro personally. Gradually, he acquired a grudging respect for Castro, in whom he discerned remarkable qualities of leadership. He and Castro, despite the ideological gulf between them, would no doubt someday have enjoyed a personal dialogue, in which private mutual admiration might well have played a part.

Through his former campaign staffer and Stevenson UN aide, William Attwood, and other indirect channels, JFK carefully explored the possibility of a rapprochement with Castro, even the possibility of the latter banishing Soviet forces from Cuba and providing a commitment to end Cuban subversion in the Western Hemisphere. Kennedy would not have insisted on Castro's leaving the Third World nonaligned movement, which had several leaders friendly with Kennedy. A neutral Cuba was exactly what Kennedy wanted. While he continued to deplore its politics and repression, JFK hoped that he might someday be able to turn Castro into another Marshal Tito, the Yugoslav Communist leader who broke with the Soviet system and Moscow without adopting anti-Communist policies. There is evidence that both Kennedy and Castro were considering more contacts, possibly along these lines, at the time of Kennedy's death. In a second term, in which he would never again need to worry about facing Cuban-American voters, many changes might have been possible.

Vietnam was the most difficult foreign policy conundrum JFK faced as he looked ahead in November 1963. The Communist Vietcong insurrection against the government of South Vietnam was gaining strength. Knowing that the survival of a free West Berlin was much more important to the maintenance of world peace and Western democracy, he shrewdly avoided letting Vietnam seem more important in the eyes of the American press and public, or even in his own state and defense departments, than he knew it really was. But perhaps in retrospect it was a mistake to give the issue too little attention.

The best speech he ever made on Vietnam was made not in the White House but in the Senate in 1954, after a congressional visit to Vietnam in 1951. As a new senator, he warned President Eisenhower and the American people that America could not replace French colonialism in Vietnam, that the conflict there was nationalistic war, and that the Vietnamese were sick of foreign troops on their soil. No Western power, he added, neither the United States nor the French, was going to win such a battle. Young Senator Kennedy said it would be futile for the United States to send combat troop divisions there, and President Kennedy never did.

Although some historians note that the U.S. commitment to an independent South Vietnam began under Truman, Eisenhower recommitted the deployment of U.S. military advisors and instructors to Premier

Ngo Dinh Diem. Diem was viewed by the U.S. government, the Catholic Church, and, until his corrupt family moved in and took charge, American liberals like Mike Mansfield and Justice William Douglas, as a patriotic nationalist who represented the best hope of saving an independent South Vietnam from both Communist rule and French colonialism. But Kennedy as president came to feel strongly that Diem's struggle for anti-Communist control of an independent South Vietnam was unwinnable unless Diem and his family undertook the reforms—land, tax, and political reforms—that Kennedy and his team urged. He also knew that the Diem family, as long as it was confident that the United States would never abandon Vietnam to the Communists, had no intention of agreeing to those reforms.

In that context, the division within the Kennedy administration over whether to defend Diem against his own army, or to permit a coup to install a new leader, became the deepest division over any issue during Kennedy's years in the White House. Kennedy did not think Vietnam's prospects for survival would be improved by the United States objecting to or blocking a Vietnam army coup removing Diem from office. Perhaps he should have guessed that, in that part of the world, the overthrow of Diem by the South Vietnamese army could well lead to Diem's death. But I could see from the look of shock and dismay on JFK's face when he heard the news of Diem's assassination that he had had no indication or even hint that anything more than Diem's exile was contemplated.

Nor could the president's main foreign policy advisors reach a consensus on other aspects of Vietnam policy. During one National Security Council meeting, I listened silently as two members (one military, one civilian) reported on their recent mission to Vietnam. Their findings on the struggle's progress and prospects were so contradictory, one optimistic, the other pessimistic, that the president intervened: "Are you sure you two fellows went to the same place?"

On those occasions when the president asked for my views on the issue, I expressed doubts about a military solution, preferring instead a search for a peaceful settlement. I believed then and now that my hopes reflected his. In a memorandum to the president on April 28, 1961, I expressed skepticism of the latest U.S. plan: "The outcome is highly doubtful" to the extent it depends on unlikely Communist reactions; to the extent that it depends on wider popular support among the Vietnamese and on reforms by Diem, "the outcome is speculative at best." The plan, I wrote, had no timetable, no clear division of authority, no realistic estimate of long-run costs and effect, and too many miscellaneous ideas vaguely thrown in without any serious consideration (including a UN appeal and a five-year economic plan). I summed up: "There is no clearer example of a country that cannot be saved unless it saves itself."

In a subsequent memorandum, on November 24, 1961, I proposed, as I had during the Berlin crisis, a televised presidential address on our policy in Vietnam and Laos, arguing that, in such an address, the president could dispel the

> wildly inaccurate speculation and debate . . . on what we are going to do in SE Asia . . . In general, such speeches have proven useful this year as a means of explaining policies more precisely than a news conference permits . . . Only the Vietnamese can defeat the Viet Cong, we cannot do it for them. Troops of a different country, color and culture are not . . . effective in combating civil disorders, guerrilla actions and most local wars. . . .

Reminding him of his words a few weeks earlier to the University of Washington—"We are not omnipotent or omniscient" and there "cannot be an American solution to every world problem"—I added, "Our role as the chief defender of all the free world requires that our strength not be drained or diverted away from the main lines of defense by action against guerillas and satellites."

In still another November 1961 memorandum, I cautioned against significant military escalation by listing other unanswered questions—whether American troops will be welcomed or resented once they arrive; whether Khrushchev will regard such a move as "more stupid than bold," and "feel we are sufficiently weakened and diverted to permit him further moves"; whether American troops can actually accomplish much more than Vietnamese troops "that already outnumber Communists 10–1"; and whether "all other courses have been explored or exhausted." I was not in the loop on Vietnam, but I sensed those memos met with his approval.

Kennedy, with his narrow popular and congressional majorities, facing accusations from the far right that he was soft on defending freedom against Communism, did not feel that he was in any position to abandon Eisenhower's commitment, and ultimately increased the number of U.S. military advisors in South Vietnam to more than sixteen thousand in 1963. But, recognizing that the struggle between Diem's religious and capitalist backers and Ho Chi Minh's Communists involved nationalists on both sides, Kennedy did not want to insert the United States in the middle of a civil war in a country whose history and culture were little known to American decision makers. He was constantly asking one advisor or outside expert after another: How can we ever get out? On more than one occasion, he asked whether Vietnam was the right place for the United States to fight and take a stand.

Feeling that his careful management of the problem was handicapped by unfavorable press coverage, he made the mistake of urging the *New York Times* to replace David Halberstam as its correspondent in that country. I know of no other instance when he made such a request of any newspaper. Halberstam and other correspondents covering the country were right. The president was not getting an accurate assessment of what was going on in Vietnam at that time, either on the battlefield or in the political arena, where the Diem family was increasingly isolated from its own people, a serious drawback in a guerrilla war.

When his 1952 Republican senate opponent, former UN ambassador Henry Cabot Lodge, expressed interest in an international appointment, Kennedy, as part of a bipartisan solution, sent him to Vietnam, hoping his political and diplomatic skills and intelligence could help solve that confused situation. When I was told that Lodge was being appointed to Vietnam, I replied, deadpan, "You mean, North Vietnam?" As it turned out, Lodge was not as effective as everyone had hoped—like most American politicians, he talked too much to the press, did not do his homework, did not trust the CIA, and antagonized both the military and civilians in the Defense Department.

Kennedy tried to find or open a back channel to the North Vietnamese through his confidant, friend, and ambassador to India, Ken Galbraith, who was close to Indian foreign secretary Desai. In the late spring of 2005 Galbraith confirmed in an interview with the *Boston Globe* that he had discussed the matter with President Kennedy in the spring of 1962, that he had expected JFK to "pursue the Indian channel," to advise the North that if it stopped its guerilla action in the South, we would, in the words of JFK's assistant secretary of state Averell Harriman, "withdraw to a normal basis." Was an informal mutual nonescalation understanding possible? Relying on Harriman archive documents newly uncovered by Gareth Porter, the *Globe*'s Bryan Bender reported that Harriman had been instructed by the president to direct Galbraith to proceed, but that "Harriman [later] met with Kennedy and apparently persuaded him to delay . . . and the overture was never revived." In that same 2005 interview, Galbraith confirmed that while he expected to pursue the matter with his Indian friends, he never received official direction to do so. This is another indication of Kennedy's hopes for a resolution of the conflict in Vietnam, and his willingness to communicate and negotiate with his adversary.

Just before he was killed, the president's focus had been on his announced intention to reduce the U.S. presence; but I do not know whether the McNamara plan to withdraw one thousand Americans by the end of 1963 was intended primarily to put pressure on the South Vietnamese. JFK recognized the desirability of withdrawal, but also the fact that it would not be easily achieved. He saw no merit in a withdrawal plan that would so antagonize the political right in this country that he would be replaced as president in 1964 by someone who would make matters worse by sending in more troops. But neither Arthur Schlesinger nor I believed the report that Kennedy privately told advisors that he would withdraw U.S. troops from Vietnam after the 1964 elections, as Kenny O'Donnell later asserted; that sounded too politically calculating for JFK.

Nevertheless, the president learned in the Laotian, Cuban, and Berlin crises that essentially political problems do not lend themselves to essentially military solutions; and I believe that he would have continued to look for a negotiated way out. At a press conference on November 14, he said "our object" was "to bring Americans home." Earlier that year, in a May 1963 press conference, he declared that if the South Vietnamese government ever suggested it, "we would have some troops on their way home the next day." In September he said of the South Vietnamese: "In the final analysis, it is their war. They are the ones who have to win it or lose it." In October he said, "It would be our hope to lessen the number of Americans" in Vietnam by the end of the year.

However, looking back, I realize he made many conflicting statements, both public and private, simultaneously commencing a withdrawal to answer his dovish critics while increasing verbal and military support to answer his hawkish critics. Complicating further any discernment of his intent was my own observation in his meetings on a declaration of emergency during the Berlin crisis. The president was capable of holding one meeting with one set of advisors when the real decision had already been made with a different group.

In truth, JFK understood and from time to time supported two clearly contradictory propositions: (1) that a takeover of free, democratic, and independent South Vietnam by the Communist North would strengthen the Soviet Union's drive for worldwide domination in the cold war; and (2) that the increasingly corrupt and unpopular government of South Vietnam could not defeat the North, fueled by nationalistic aspirations as well as Communist supplies, without the intervention of American combat troops and airpower, thereby sinking the United States into a quagmire contrary to his most basic beliefs and principles. He temporized between the two, by steadily contributing money, military advisors, and covert action, postponing the key decision to intervene militarily, which President Johnson ultimately made. Kennedy did not have a win-at-any-price philosophy, particularly when the price would be paid in the blood of young Americans.

In the end, all we can conclude with certainty is what he did not do. Despite a steady flow of recommendations from missions to Saigon headed by Vice President Johnson, chairman of the Joint Chiefs Taylor, and Deputy National Security Advisor Rostow, that he should send combat troop divisions to fight in South Vietnam and U.S. Air Force planes to bomb North Vietnam and the troop trails heading south, Kennedy never did. The Joint Chiefs recommended that the president send sixty thousand U.S. soldiers into Laos. He never did. McNamara suggested that he deploy forty thousand troops to Laos in 1962. He did not. He was determined not to precipitate a general land war in Asia. He never reversed Eisenhower's commitment, but neither did he escalate the conflict to a level anything like that reached under LBJ. By October 1963 he had left the United States neither fully in nor fully out.

Because of my own strong opposition to the subsequent escalation in Vietnam under Johnson, I would like to believe that Kennedy would have found a way to withdraw all American instructors and advisors. But even someone who knew JFK as well as I did can't be certain, because I do not believe he knew in his last weeks what he was going to do. It was the only foreign policy problem handed off by JFK to his successor in no better, and possibly worse, shape than it was when he inherited it.

Chapter 27

The Death of President Kennedy

Promptly at 10:45 A.M. on the morning of Thursday, November 21, 1963, the president walked out of the Oval Office to the helicopter that would take him to Andrews Air Force Base to board Air Force One for Texas. The weather was cool and cloudy when I ran out the back door of the White House to catch him and hand him the material on "Texas humor" that he had requested earlier that morning. I don't remember exactly what we said to each other, as we spoke for the last time under the roar of the helicopter rotors. Perhaps he thanked me for the humorous anecdotes I had collected. Perhaps I noted some emerging issue we would need to discuss when he returned. But I placed no significance on that brief talk at the time; it was just another departure. The previous day I had provided some suggestions to Jackie's assistant for her scheduled appearance before a Spanish-speaking audience in Texas.

After the president left, I met with seven or eight American Political Science Association Congressional Fellows to answer their questions and show them the Oval Office, available that day, I told them, because the president was on a trip to Texas, on a mission involving political divisions in a state where "he had many enemies." One of those in my audience remembers that I used the word "dangerous"—but I have no recollection of either saying or thinking that. That evening I had dinner at the home of columnist Joe Alsop, and then returned to the White House, where I joined Arthur Schlesinger for a screening of *From Russia with Love*, a movie I know JFK would have enjoyed.

It was the time of year when work on the legislative, State of the Union, and budget messages for the following January had to be commenced, and my hands were full. The next day, Friday, November 22, brought a routinely busy morning at the White House, even though I had expected it to be a slower day than usual, with the president and vice president in Texas, and most of the cabinet scheduled to depart for Tokyo for a joint meeting of the American and Japanese cabinets that the president had hoped would further cement relations between our two countries.

After confirming with Mac Bundy that my presence was not required, I bowed out of an afternoon session at the Pentagon to review the defense budget, and left for the Carlton Hotel, where I had a noon lunch meeting in suite 1412, with the distinguished president and editor of the *Kansas City Star*, Roy Roberts, a moderate Republican who wanted to discuss both the leadership and the program of the Kennedy administration. Roberts asked me about the rumors that JFK would drop LBJ from the ticket in 1964. I responded that the president had every intention of keeping LBJ. For some reason, Roberts's mere mention of the vice presidency reminded me that Abraham Lincoln had a vice president named Johnson. Eerily, that caused me to note the ugly statistic that had recently been published—that, beginning in 1840, every president elected in a twenty-year cycle had died in office (Harrison, Lincoln, Garfield, McKinley, Harding, FDR).

Since I was no longer expected at the Pentagon after lunch, I asked my White House driver to stop briefly at my apartment in Arlington, before I returned to work. Just after leaving my apartment, the White House dispatcher called my driver. "Do you have any passengers?" "Yes, Ted Sorensen." (He probably used my code name, which I have forgotten.) "Return immediately to the White House, and bring him to the West Basement entrance." With the president away, what could be so urgent? I rushed back, expecting some new political crisis.

Greeted by a sea of tears and ashen faces, I was told by Gloria Sitrin, my longtime secretary, that the president had been shot. She handed me the UPI ticker bearing the news. Gloria and Toi Bachelder, another secretary, suggested I go to the office of lead Secret Service agent Jerry Behn, who, they said, had an open line to Parkland Hospital in Dallas. With no pronouncement yet from any doctor, I silently clung to whatever faint hope I could summon. When I reached Jerry's office, he was on the phone with Roy Kellerman, a Secret Service agent who had been riding in the president's car. A short time later, Jerry put down the phone, and turned toward me: "He's dead."

There was no chaos, no shrieking or wailing, at least none that I remember—just disbelief and grief. I felt numb, helpless, clueless about what to do. A few times later that day, I tried to force myself to think about the future—including my future—but could not. I could think only about the horror of what had happened. I felt as if I were on automatic pilot, fulfilling a role in a sur-real drama for which there was no script and for which there had been no rehearsal.

With no other senior White House staff present, I felt some responsibility, but no idea how to fulfill it. It did not matter. Everyone in the White House that terrible afternoon looked to RFK for direction. The attorney general asked me to notify House speaker John McCormack who, upon the swearing-in of the new president, Lyndon Johnson, would become second in line for the presidency. I did so, with difficulty. I could barely get the words out, but I felt useful trying. RFK asked my opinion on whether the cabinet plane should turn around over the Pacific and I replied, of course, they should come back and be in their offices in Washington as soon as possible during this national emergency. He also mentioned that he had received a call from LBJ, who, uncertain about the precise word-ing of the oath of office, had posed the question to the attorney general. I reminded Bobby that it was in the Constitution. None of us was thinking clearly.

In the conference room across from the Oval Office then known as "the Fish Room," a television set was on, and I sat there for what seemed hours by myself, half paralyzed, unable to function, sinking deeper and deeper into myself, listening to Walter Cronkite grimly repeat the events of the day over and over again. The news kept showing clips of the president delivering a speech earlier that day at a breakfast in Texas—the same speech I had gone over with him in the Oval Office on the morning of his departure.

The previous summer, as the president boarded Air Force One in Shannon Airport to fly back to Washington after four joyous days touring Ireland, he said to the crowd, "I certainly will come back in the springtime." (Those words still have special poignancy for the Irish and for me also.) In preparation for that trip to Ireland, I had come across a ballad on the death of Owen Roe O'Neil by Thomas Davis; and, as I sat there in the Fish Room on November 22, with intermittent waves of grief washing over me, one verse kept repeating itself over and over in my mind: "We're like sheep without a shepherd when the snow shuts out the sky, how could you leave us, Owen, how could you die?"

When the day began, according to my 1963 pocket calendar, nothing was scheduled for that weekend except a dinner and movie with my Chaikin cousins. Later, I would cross out that and all other appointments for days, if not weeks, simply putting in the space for November 22 an exclamation point with a black circle around it.

Back in my office, I accepted few calls that afternoon. One was from my brother Tom, who later came by my office and insisted that I join his family and my brother Philip, who was in town on business, for dinner at Tom's home so that I would not be alone that evening. Another call requested my presence at Andrews Air Force Base where Air Force One would soon be returning. Otherwise my system virtually shut down. With others, I went out to Andrews to meet the plane bearing the president's body, and Jackie, LBJ, and various aides. In the chopper to Andrews, I sat next to George Reedy and Walter Jenkins, two top LBJ aides. "I feel sorry for your position," I said. "I'll help as best I can. But I hope you don't mind if I don't think too much of the state of Texas."

In her newspaper column, Mary McGrory described me at Andrews as "looking white-faced and stricken, unseeing and unhearing in the nightmarish light and noise." I spoke to no one, but watched silently the unloading of the casket, the descent of Jackie and LBJ and their departure in official limousines. There was nothing I could do. I was having trouble controlling my emotions. I recalled the last time I had seen JFK at Andrews; he was energetic, laughing, and planning for the future. For the first time that day, I wept. As others went to the Bethesda Naval Hospital, where the president's body was being taken, I returned to the White House.

Before leaving for Tom's house in suburban Maryland, I said good-bye to Gloria and tried to comfort her, as she let out the sobs she had been restraining all day. As we were finishing dinner at Tom's house, around 9:30 P.M., LBJ called from the vice president's office in the old Executive Office Building. Kindly, strongly, generously, he told me how sorry he was, how deeply he felt for me, how well he knew what I had been to President Kennedy for eleven years, and that he, LBJ, now needed me even more. (Many years later, Bill Moyers told me that, on the plane back from Dallas, LBJ repeated over and over that he needed to keep the Kennedy team, "especially Sorensen.") The new president asked me to come see him in his old office in the next day or two. I said, "Good-bye and thank you, Mr. President," hung up the phone, and broke down sobbing, unable to face the fact that I had just addressed that title to someone other than John F. Kennedy. Deep in my soul, I have not stopped weeping, whenever those events are recalled.

After taking a sleeping pill that night, I returned to my office at 9:30 A.M. on Saturday morning and shortly thereafter received two calls. The first was from Pierre

Salinger, asking me to see Art Buchwald and Teddy White. Not functioning too well, I forgot all about Pierre's request, until reminded later. Buchwald wanted for his column examples of John Kennedy's humor, which I gave him, though I did not think the request entirely appropriate. To Teddy, interviewing me for a future *Life* article, I said, "I don't want to see everything go down the drain because of some nut in Dallas."

The second call I received was from Bobby, inviting me to attend a Mass in the East Room of the White House. It was there that I spoke to Jackie for the first time. She came over to me and gave my arm a hard squeeze, looking me in the eye, trying to comfort me. It was a look of shared sadness. Despite the unimaginable shock and grief she had suffered from her husband's murder in her presence, she went out of her way that dreadful first week to comfort me, knowing that I was devastated as well.

Today I can still remember the Senate and presidential campaign days in some detail, but I cannot remember the details of that awful weekend. The days blur in my memory. I believe it was that same miserable Friday afternoon that RFK, his brother-in-law Sarge Shriver, and I first gathered to talk about church and funeral arrangements, as well as precedents. The final decision on all matters was left to be cleared with

Jackie when she felt ready, including whether to bury this fallen sailor in Arlington National Cemetery "so that he would belong to the nation" rather than in the family hometown of Brookline, Massachusetts. I do not recall whether at that moment I supported his burial in Brookline or Arlington, a cemetery I had never visited, but which I regarded with some dread as a funeral factory; but I do recall that an internal debate erupted over his burial place, with Kenny and Pierre attempting to persuade me to support Brookline.

Funeral planning continued Saturday afternoon, with discussion of readings, what and by whom, both at the Monday services scheduled for St. Matthew's Cathedral and at graveside. Having never attended a Catholic Mass (other than earlier that day), I felt my participation as a reader would be inappropriate. I did prepare a list of possible readings and quotations, as I would in subsequent weeks and years for memorials across the globe, including both biblical passages and excerpts from JFK's speeches. I took them to Bobby and Jackie, who was doing her best to keep the atmosphere from becoming too depressed, kidding with me about my not drinking even ceremonial wine. When she suggested a favorite JFK verse from Ecclesiastes: "a time to be born, and a time to die," I knew it was just right. She mused that Jack had once read that line to her, adding, as if he were still quoting Scripture: "and a time to fish and a time to cut bait."

At one point, Ethel called to ask whether Communion would be distributed at the funeral Mass. I expressed my concern about the difficulty of distributing Communion to more than a thousand people; but she was adamant.

Reprising my longtime ironic role of liaison with Catholic clergy, I joined Sarge on a visit that night to Washington Archbishop Patrick O'Boyle's home to meet with Boston Archbishop Richard Cushing, and Francis X. Morrissey, a Kennedy friend and Boston pol. Our White House driver got lost on the way there. At 10 P.M. Sarge got out to ask directions. When we finally arrived, I stressed to Cushing that the service should be as simple as possible, as Jackie wanted. "Yes," he said. "We'll leave him like a Jesuit." The meeting went well, there were no major disagreements, although Archbishop O'Boyle grumbled about interrupting Mass to read "political speeches."

On Sunday, the president's casket was taken from the White House to the Capitol rotunda, where he lay in state until the next day. I waited in line to pay my respects at his flag-covered bier, refusing all official suggestions that I be moved ahead of those who had been standing in line for hours. It was in that line that I learned that assassin Lee Harvey Oswald had been murdered by Jack Ruby. This makes it worse, I thought. My God, when will it all end?

Early Monday, I received a call from Bobby, expressing concern that none of the passages to be read at graveside included civil rights. I found one and sent it to him. Then I joined the procession from the White House to St. Matthew's Cathedral for the funeral Mass celebrated by Cardinal Cushing, carrying with me, at the suggestion of my secretaries, the top hat I had received as a present to wear at the inauguration. After the Mass came the graveside ceremony at Arlington, where I wept again when his body was lowered into the earth, grimly attesting that he was gone forever.

The entire week seemed unreal and unbelievable. I was constantly drawn to watch television with fascinated horror, but unable to stomach what I saw and heard. Almost instantly there were countless rumors and exaggerated reports about who did what. No one knew anything for certain—but everyone thought they did. In the end, one clear fact remained—John F. Kennedy was dead. As my late law partner Judge Simon Rifkind would say years later at a memorial service for RFK, referring to the murder of both Kennedy brothers:

"What have we done—all of us—to deserve to live in a generation in which the sheep devour their shepherds?"

"Did he suffer?" I asked a navy medical officer. No, I was told, his death had been instantaneous. That, while comforting, was not true, I later learned. According to official testimony, the president, after the first shot wounded him in the neck, continued to show weak vital signs. In those last minutes, before the next shot to his head killed him, he wore a "quizzical" expression. I knew that man too well to believe that his magnificent mind was either blank or paralyzed with fear. I believe that he was quickly asking himself many questions: Which of my enemies would do this? What will happen to the country if I am killed? Who will take care of Jackie and my children? After all that I have endured and survived in war and in office, is this how it's going to end? For almost eleven years, it had been my role to answer all his questions. Those I could not answer.

I felt helpless. Previously, I had been called in on every kind of crisis—the West Virginia primary, the Truman attack before the convention, the Houston ministers challenge, the aftermath of the Bay of Pigs, the Cuban missile crisis, the Berlin crisis. For more than a decade, it had been my job to help him. In Dallas, there was nothing I could do to help. I was not even present. During the four years before his election as president,

I had traveled with him to every state, including Texas, but never internationally. After his inauguration, I traveled with him internationally—to Europe and Central America, but never domestically. By that twist of fate, I was not with him in Texas that day.

For the next two weeks, many good friends supported me, inviting me to dinner almost every night—some of the grand dames of Washington, including Kay Graham, Florence Mahoney, Katie Loucheim (an appointee about whom JFK once said, "I wish we had a dozen Katie Loucheims to appoint") and some of my old neighbors—the Wernkes, the Yntemas, and the Schifters, as well as my brother Tom; Joe Alsop invited me more than once to lunch. Those days and weeks were a blur of pain and tears, trying to comfort people who were trying to comfort me. Throughout, a variety of White House and administration colleagues kept dropping by my office to express their own grief, anger, and suspicions, their sympathy for me, and often their loyalty to RFK.

My whole world had suddenly changed—indeed, ended. I had loved my years with Kennedy, my three years in the White House, my opportunity to help shape our country and its role in the world. For more than a decade, he had filled almost every inch of my life and thoughts, and suddenly it was all over. Suddenly, without warning, he was gone. There was still a peace to be won, new goals to be pronounced, new proposals and principles and priorities to declare, new frontiers to cross, but my leader, my guide, my chief source of inspiration and motivation was gone.

It was the most deeply traumatic experience of my life. The unreality of it, the unacceptability of it, the sudden desperation of it all, an eloquent voice suddenly stilled, a compassionate heart suddenly stopped, a brilliant brain shattered, that handsome smile gone forever. Of course I could not believe it. "They wouldn't even give him three years," I was heard to say—the country, the world, fate. My old friend and Senate office mate Ted Reardon, another longtime Kennedy aide, came to see me in my office, and virtually shouted: "I'd like to take a fucking bomb and blow the fucking state of Texas off the fucking map." I felt anger and rage, but knew they could accomplish nothing. The president's killer was soon killed. Vengeance was not JFK's style. He would not have blamed Dallas. He would have wanted me to get on with my life, my work, his legacy.

His death hit me much harder than had the death of my own father. When my beloved father died, it seemed inevitable, expected; he had been fading for so long, his suffering was over at last. JFK's death in Dallas was totally different. After nearly eleven years, we never had a chance to say good-bye or even to thank each other one last time. I never had the chance to offer one last statement of my affection and respect—it had always been unspoken—and suddenly, it was too late to tell him. We had both always been too busy and unsentimental in our daily work, subjected to daily pressures, and we always knew there would be an opportunity for those expressions some other time. I had never considered a future without him. I had always assumed I had years, if not decades, to enjoy our collaboration and friendship. I had never even asked for an autographed picture of us together. Why would I, when I saw him every day?

Intellectually, I knew that it would all end someday—nothing in life lasts forever. But I could not have imagined it would end like that. I thought it might end after he had won and served a second term, seen the fulfillment of his plans and dreams, grown old, said good-bye, and been hailed in farewell. I assumed the end might come in illness, as I think he himself long suspected, slowly, predictably, with time for smiles and laughter and hugs for his children. But not like this, so suddenly, savagely, mindlessly.

Within days of his death, I was overwhelmed with letters of sympathy from friends, associates, and strangers. Remembering JFK's 1960 campaign comment that "the nuns were all for" him, though he was "not so sure of the monsignors," I found myself particularly moved by the beautiful letters from nuns all across the country. But one of the most touching condolence letters came from my middle son Steve, not yet ten years old and then living in the Midwest:

> *Dear Daddy, Our whole family is so sorry that President Kennedy was shot. I'm told you have your same job. I am doing very good in basketball. We have one puppy here. I am bringing him up, and I am having a lot of fun. . . . Your son, Steve.*

Another moving letter came from JFK's good friend and source of ideas, the conservative syndicated columnist Joseph Alsop:

> *It is harder to know what to say to you than to almost anyone else, for no one else had quite your relationship to him. To all the others—even to Jackie and Bobby—I've written of him, and of my gratitude for what he gave our country and the world . . . in this wonderful time which will not and cannot come again. But it is useless for me to tell you . . . it is fruitless for me to say to you that he set our country and the world on a new and*

*better course and gave us that most precious of all
gifts, new hope! From the beginning of his serious
career, hour after hour, day after day, you shared
in it all. He was lucky to have you to serve and aid
him; and we are lucky, too, that you did so . . . You
strengthened his arm and extended his reach. One
thought has filled my mind in these dark days . . . I
suspect that you, too, have had the same thought . . .
Every century or so, a great country like ours, with
great burdens to bear and goals to aspire to, needs
a new moral exemplar . . . George Washington, the
first of our models . . . Lincoln attained the status
of the great American saint . . . In our century, the
two Roosevelts . . . Cynical and trivial people would
laugh if they could read this letter; for the President
cared not a pin, for the petty morality of the back-
fence gossips . . . But more than any other public
man I have ever known, he exemplified the higher
morality—the morality of courage, of generosity of
heart, of hearing without quailing or shrinking back;
taking the blame and being chary to blame others,
however blameworthy. Above all, he exemplified
the morality of practical citizenship . . . a genuine
concern for all Americans, putting the country first
and yourself second when that hard need arises.
Unless I miss my guess, he will provide our country*

with its new moral exemplar, to serve the generations
yet to come as Lincoln did and Washington before
him. . . . I think of those years now like a harvest
time—golden and bright and full of good gifts. To
you, who shared so richly and usefully in this great
adventure, I feel I ought to say "God keep you" for
you will need help. But I am not a religious man, so
I shall simply say thank you.

Affectionately, Joe.

A few weeks later, my colleague Arthur Schlesinger invited me to attend another screening in the White House theater. I gloomily replied, "Too soon." Told that the president's sister and brother-in-law would be attending, I realized that gloom was not a sufficient response. Life went on; and yet it didn't. I still had duties to fulfill; yet I didn't. What was the point? I wrote and spoke about JFK's death as little as possible, chilled by that constant question from friends and strangers: "Where were you on November 22?" Passersby whom I encountered on the street, who had the best of intentions, had a compulsion to tell me where they were when they heard the news, and to ask me where I was. They still do.

Months earlier I had accepted an invitation from the daughter of an old family friend to speak at Wellesley

College on December 13. After some delay, I finally decided to keep my commitment under the condition that my words would not go beyond the walls of the college—it was my chance to deliver a eulogy, exactly three weeks after his death. "Elders who had scoffed at his youth felt suddenly that they had been orphaned," I said. "Youth, who had been impatient with his patience, felt suddenly older and grayer." I talked about his extraordinary qualities, his accomplishments, his uniqueness, "the first president born in this century, the first of Catholic faith, the first to reach out to space, the first to bear throughout his presidency the awful and awesome obligations of the age of mutual destruction." I quoted the poet Shelley's words on the death of the youthful Keats: "'til the Future dares forget the past, his fate and fame shall be an echo and a light unto eternity." I quoted Tennyson: "And so the stately ships go on to their haven under the hill, but O for the touch of a vanished hand and the sound of a voice that is still." I took no questions and returned to the White House.

This period was all the more difficult for me because in the late summer of 1963, Camilla, my first wife, after three years of mutual separation had culminated officially in divorce, had moved back to her previous home in Wisconsin with our three sons. Their departure pained me deeply. Although Camilla generously assures me now that neither of us was to blame—that we were very young when we married in 1949, and in Washington grew in different ways at different paces and in different directions—I still feel responsible. The constant travel and heady life of a presidential campaigner and counsel had undermined our marriage. As early as 1960, when asked by a reporter how my family felt about my almost complete absence from home during the campaign, I replied: "They're used to it—it's been that way for a long time." As one writer put it, with all too much accuracy: "It's almost as if Ted says to his family: 'Look, you have my love, but this man has my life.'" During a few months late in 1963, I lost my family, my best friend, and my purpose for living.

In time, I realized that there was no reason not to continue my efforts to advance the ideals and objectives that John F. Kennedy and I had shared. Gradually, my grief turned into a determination to carry on, not to let "them" (whoever "they" were) imperil the goals, programs, and ideals for which JFK and I had been working. The poet W. H. Auden summed up my feeling perfectly in his elegy: "What he was he was; what he is slated to become depends on us . . ." I vowed then that I would do all I could to keep John F. Kennedy's legacy alive. For eleven years, it had been my full-time job to advance his interests, invoke his name, and articulate his message in the struggles for justice at home and peace around the world. For the succeeding forty-plus years, I have made it my part-time mission to do the same.

Because I prefer to recall my wonderful memories of his life, and not my terrible memories of his death, I have never visited the Dallas museum commemorating the event or viewed the Zapruder film of his murder, nor have I described in detail or full candor my feelings at that time; and I find it heart-wrenching to do so even now, so many decades later. I am not alone in feeling this way. Even Dean Rusk, who was not particularly close to President Kennedy, wrote me in 1988: "I have never tried to put into words the supreme agony of the assassination because words are simply not up to the task. This year was a twenty-five-year reminder that I have never been the same since."

I do not know whether I have ever fully recovered from John F. Kennedy's death. Time passed. Love and laughter helped. But the deep sadness of that time remained, only to be reinforced five years later by the murder of his brother Robert. Those two senseless tragedies robbed me of my future.

• • •

The impact of his death on me was insignificant compared to its impact on our country and world. In my lifetime, I have seen many traumatic events shake the American people—the Japanese bombing of Pearl Harbor in 1941, the death of Franklin Roosevelt, the assassination of Martin Luther King, the terrorist attacks on New York City and Washington in 2001. But none of these had the same impact on the American psyche and spirit as the Kennedy assassination. An era of hope and pride was suddenly transformed into an era of cynical despair and pessimism.

Many historians share my conviction that the world would have been different had Kennedy lived. The Vietnam War would not have been escalated. The cold war would not have long continued. He would have set the country and world on a course of peaceful multilateralism much as FDR did. LBJ's Great Society, civil rights and other domestic programs, largely based upon JFK's 1963 legislative initiatives, would have been enacted in time. The 1968–1970 riots in our college campuses and inner cities would not have occurred with a president still in the White House whom young and black Americans knew listened and cared. He had given so much for so many people, and still had so much more to give to the world when he was struck down by someone he had never wronged for reasons that no one knows. Truly, as JFK had, years earlier, said in a memorable press conference, "Life is unfair."

President Kennedy was not universally beloved. His death was mourned by governments of every ideological stripe and economic stage, with two notable exceptions. In the paranoid pariah state of Communist Albania, the unyielding dictator Enver Hoxha was reported to have expressed satisfaction with Kennedy's removal from the world scene. In the tragic kleptocracy of Haiti, the repressive François "Papa Doc" Duvalier declared a national carnival to celebrate.

I have neither the wish nor the power to reopen the painful debate about who killed John F. Kennedy or why, nor do I have any new knowledge on the subject. I have not paid much attention to the conspiracy theories about the assassination, in part because the subject is too painful for me to study, and in part because none of the conspiracy theorists has produced any credible evidence to prove a plot by higher-ups to hire Oswald to kill Kennedy. Nor is there any convincing evidence to confirm Oliver Stone's imaginative but grim movie *JFK*, which I finally brought myself to watch as preparation for this book, and which for an amazing number of young people represents the truth about the Kennedy assassination.

RFK was unable to quash his own suspicions that his brother's enemies were behind his death. Yet Bobby told his deputy Nick Katzenbach, who told me, that he was not interested in receiving or reading conspiracy theories.

I have personally reached the point where, incredible as all the conflicting conspiracy theories are, it is equally hard to believe that none of JFK's enemies was behind his death and his brother's less than five years later. I have no new facts to reveal and no new conclusions to add. Yet I remain torn on the question. On the one hand, what good would it do to find out now who killed John Kennedy? It would not bring him back or resurrect his policies and standards. On the other hand, many people all over the world, including me, would feel somewhat better knowing, with a certainty, even now, that John F. Kennedy was killed by ideological adversaries, and thus died a martyr for a cause, and not simply in a senseless killing at the hands of a crazed lucky sharpshooter.

I do not join in the abuse that some have heaped upon the Warren Commission, a distinguished bipartisan body of eminently fair and intelligent patriots whose approach realistically could never satisfy all the critics nor be allowed all the time that would have been necessary to make a comprehensive test of every allegation and theory then circulating. However, I no longer regard the repeated doubts about the single bullet or lone assassin theories as unreasonable, nor can I be certain that the Warren Commission report closed the books forever on the question of who killed Kennedy.

Some of the published conspiracy theories are ludicrous as well as lurid, possessing a grain of logic without a shred of proof. Most of these conspiracy theorists place Castro on the list of possible suspects. I do not. Castro was wise enough to know that Kennedy was not a threat to him, and that such a move would risk Cuba's survival. Gore Vidal, Jackie's distant if unbeloved relative, whom I met briefly during his limited period of hoping to help write for JFK, believed—or at least wrote—that organized crime was instrumental in both JFK's election and his assassination. I don't think so.

Some conspiracy theorists have undertaken serious and extensive research, trying to connect dots that no one else has connected. Others have an ideological motivation, hoping to prove that Kennedy was killed by the extreme right or extreme left. Nearly all are well-intended, attempting to solve a crime for which it is at least theoretically possible some person, organization, or government agency is yet to be held to account. But however many shots they claim to have heard, however many coincidental deaths they claim to be related, it all comes down to one death from one gun that really mattered.

I hope all the conspiracy theorists whose invitations to comment I have declined, or whose theories I have not read, or whose meetings or press conferences I have not attended, understand my inability to do so. I have endorsed none of them, preferred none of them, accepted none of them. When they scoff that I was not informed about the secret operations, findings, and conspiracies that lay behind the murder, they are right; and I doubt anyone else was informed. Many of these theorists have said they had actual documents and revealing photographs to show me, so confidential they could not be published.

While the conspiracy theorists cannot prove that any one of their targets of accusation was involved in the assassination of JFK, neither can I prove that none of them was involved. Deep in my heart, I cannot fully and permanently exonerate any of them—pro-Castro Cubans, anti-Castro Cubans, the Soviet KGB, the Mafia, the CIA and militarists, alarmed by Kennedy's soft American University speech on peace and his announced inclination to draw down American military advisors in Vietnam. All could have had motivations to get rid of JFK and the resources to cover it up. That is not enough for a court of law, but it is enough to leave an entire nation with uneasy feelings. I do agree that, had some of his detractors on the extreme right been able to peer deep into his heart, their worst fears would have been confirmed.

On November 22, 1963, the country was enjoying at least surface peace and prosperity; but deep beneath that surface, the fires of rage burned. President Kennedy was aware of the hostile climate in Texas. One right-wing leaflet distributed in Dallas blared: "John F. Kennedy—Wanted for treason." Nevertheless, with divisions in the Texas Democratic Party between the John Connally establishment wing and the Ralph Yarborough reform wing—as well as divisions between white and nonwhite—all threatening Johnson's ability to ensure that Texas would be in the Kennedy-Johnson column a year later, Johnson suggested the president's visit. It was an act of courage and determination on JFK's part to enter hostile territory. But he felt that, as president, he could not afford to shun any state or city merely because his adversaries were present. Like Colonel Davenport, in the story with which JFK closed virtually every 1960 campaign speech, on his Day of Judgment, John F. Kennedy preferred "to be found doing his duty."

Death was a subject about which he could easily talk and jest in private. As he drove me home from the Senate to Virginia one evening, too fast, he joked about which of us would be featured in the Nebraska press if we were both killed in a fatal crash. Fortunately, intervention by a D.C. police car prevented our putting that particular hypothesis to the test. When he signed his will in his Senate office, he asked me and one of his secretaries to act as witnesses, assuring us that it was "perfectly legal because there's nothing in here for either of you." When his vice president was unhappy about leading a fact-finding mission to war-torn Vietnam, the president reportedly said: "Don't worry, Lyndon, if anything happens to you, Sam Rayburn and I will give you the biggest funeral Austin, Texas, has ever seen." More seriously, he once said to me that there was no real defense against a lone, unpredictable sniper, if that madman was both determined to succeed and lucky. Exposure to sniper attack is an unavoidable part of every active president's position. Some of his decisions are bound to stir passions and controversy, his whereabouts are never difficult to ascertain, and his appearance before crowds is unavoidable.

November 22, 1963, in Dallas was the second time that a madman had attempted to kill JFK. Less than six weeks before his inauguration, the Secret Service and Palm Beach police informed him that a would-be assassin had been arrested, his car loaded with dynamite to be exploded inside the walls of the Kennedy estate. The deranged seventy-three-year-old had stopped his car on the previous Sunday a short distance from the gate, waiting to blow up the president-elect on his way to Sunday morning Mass, but had changed his mind at the last minute when JFK's wife and two little children appeared with him. The would-be assassin came so close, wrote the Secret Service chief later, "it was appalling . . . just how near we came." With the Secret Service fearful of copycats, the incident was disclosed only to JFK, who confided it to me. He seemed more bemused than frightened.

If fate somehow decreed that sooner or later some madman would succeed, better that it happened after JFK saved mankind in the Cuban missile crisis, paved the way for equal rights in this country, launched America's leadership in space, established the Peace Corps, and set a standard for leadership and eloquence that has inspired people all over the world. Better that we had his leadership—even for one brief shining moment—than not at all.

Chapter 28

President Johnson's 1963 Transition

Beginning with his call to me on the night of November 22, 1963, LBJ urged me to stay on as his assistant and advisor. He could not have been more gracious. Not known for his soft and tactful manner, particularly when he was engaged in the power of persuasion, Johnson was the picture of tact in his relations with me during the three months I remained at the White House. I knew—even though I had the same office, the same title, the same pay, and—when necessary—almost the same access to the president—my job had changed. My previous role in the White House had stemmed from my eleven-year relationship with the man who had mattered most to me, and he was gone.

The new president and I had a totally different relationship, not surprising inasmuch as Lyndon Johnson was totally different from John F. Kennedy—in philosophy, personality, style, and intellect—and the less visible differences were even greater. The powers and pressures of the presidency revealed Johnson's true nature in a way that the vice presidency could not. With all his taste for power, Johnson as president was paradoxically an insecure man with a massive ego, uncomfortable with his intellectual superiors. To me, he personified the kind of hyperbole and hypocrisy that defined the worst aspects of politics in my eyes— the side of politics that had disillusioned me when I first witnessed it during my lunch hour visits to Capitol Hill as a young Federal Security Agency employee in 1951.

Johnson suffered from what has been called the paranoia of power. I believe that those presidents who are comfortable accepting and exercising their responsibilities and leadership as part of their daily duties did not feel the need to talk about power frequently. During my brief time in the Johnson White House, I noticed that, unlike JFK and me, LBJ and his aides often talked about power. Describing the difference between the Kennedy and Johnson White Houses, Lee White, my deputy, would later note, "There was something more fun in the Kennedy White House." How true. Improving the world should be fun.

The differences were apparent even to my ten-year-old son. When Johnson learned one day in December 1963, during our Oval Office conversation, that my three sons were waiting for me in the White House mess, he immediately interrupted our meeting, saying, "Let's go join them!" We went downstairs, and sat down with my boys at their table. LBJ was not as good as JFK in small talk with small folk, and soon left to go back to his office, whereupon my son Steve, who had previously met only one president, turned to me and said: "He doesn't look like a president." I smiled.

For all these reasons, I knew that my life in the White House could not be the same. I knew that JFK would not have approved my leaving during the brutal, grim post-assassination transition, but I never expected to stay much longer. The White House staff is not part of the government bureaucracy but a personal extension of the president. Neither professional nor political staff members expect to go from one president to the next. In that context, together with other senior aides, I had promptly submitted a pro forma resignation letter to President Johnson, advising my deputies Mike and Lee to do the same, thereby enabling LBJ to feel free to bring his own people into the West Wing as quickly as he could. Johnson rejected all these offers of resignation—contrary to the advice he received from his friend John Connally and others, he would later tell me.

My letter, dated November 23, 1963, read:

Dear Mr. President:

Because I strongly believe that you should have complete freedom to select your own associates in the difficult position in which you have been placed, I hereby submit my resignation as Special Counsel to the President effective upon your acceptance at whatever subsequent date you should specify. You may be assured that my loyalty and respect for you will continue whatever action you may take on my offer of resignation.

On that Saturday evening, in Johnson's vice presidential office in the Old Executive Office Building across the street from the White House, with his aide Bill Moyers sitting in, LBJ and I talked, as he had requested during his phone call the night before. We had scheduled the meeting earlier, but I bumped into LBJ that afternoon in the West Wing basement, and he said he was running late.

Almost immediately, LBJ asked, "What would you think of the possibility that a foreign government was involved in this?" "Do you have any evidence?" I asked. He handed me a government memorandum, not identifying any specific source, saying in effect that a foreign government had hoped to assassinate President Kennedy. "Meaningless," I said. He persisted. Concerned that there was an international conspiracy, he raised the issue of his own safety and security.

I mentioned the letter of resignation I had sent him earlier that day. "I know. I got it." That was the last time he mentioned it. "I want you to draw the threads together on the domestic program," he told me. "But don't expect me to absorb things as fast as you're used to." I didn't. I handed him a list of eleven matters that required early decision or action on his part—a list based on material that I had asked my deputies Mike and Lee to pull together earlier that day. I do not recall much of that hour and a half meeting, but I was blunt and unsmiling. I was not in a good mood in general, or toward him in particular. I advised him to speak to the Congress, and cautioned him that he faced "two kinds of problems: those appointees who will not make themselves available to you, and those who will be too available."

Most of the hour and a half was devoted to his request that I stay: "I need you more than he needed you." I was reported in the press—probably accurately—to have replied: "I've given eleven years of my life to John Kennedy, and for those eleven years he was the only human being who mattered to me"—an emotional over-statement at an agonizing moment in my life. I am truly sorry that my grief-induced utterance was so inconsiderate of my family's feelings, and I hereby belatedly apologize to my three sons and their mother, Camilla. But it did convey to LBJ the depth of my pain.

Later that same tragic weekend, when he asked me to draft his first presidential address, which he planned to deliver to a joint session of Congress on Wednesday, November 27, the day before Thanksgiving, I agreed. I wanted to help commit LBJ to carrying on Kennedy's program for 1964, and Kennedy's legacy for the ages; and I wanted him to invoke those policies and words specifically, as well as the late president's name.

Alternative drafts for the address were submitted by LBJ aides Jack Valenti, Charlie Murphy and Horace Busby; and by Adlai Stevenson and Ken Galbraith, who left his draft on my desk, saying, "If I say so myself, this one's perfect so you won't have to change it." But when I finally sat down in the White House mess to work on the speech on Monday evening—after burying the president at Arlington a few hours earlier—I reviewed all these drafts, and decided to start fresh. Later that night, LBJ and I spoke by phone about the legislative agenda and its timing. Offering his thoughts on the upcoming speech, he said:

> I'd like to have a little more along the lines of "date" stuff [deadlines for action]. . . . I think if we have a given date, we're going to fall on our face. I think they'll say the Kennedy program was defeated and Johnson is repudiated . . . I think we'll just have to try to do that . . . maybe Thanksgiving . . . if you haven't quit me completely by then . . . This is a mighty hard life . . . You didn't tell me it was going to be this kind of life when you made me Vice President.

"It is a hard life," I replied. "It is going to get harder. I think you ought to think about going away for Thanksgiving." "I'm afraid to," said Johnson. "I don't have enough time to keep abreast of this, Ted. I just haven't read one third of the stuff I need to read and I read until 2:00 in the morning. . . ."

The following evening, I submitted my draft of the speech to President Johnson. He glanced at it, saying a bit insincerely that he wouldn't "change a word." Leaving his office, I went to Mac Bundy's office, where I found McNamara and Rusk. Before that gathering had adjourned, Johnson walked in with his advisors Abe

Fortas and Walter Jenkins. "We made some changes because it sounds too much like President Kennedy," I was informed. I didn't see the draft again until just prior to delivery. Tuesday afternoon, I saw Johnson in the Oval Office, Kennedy's office—that upset me all over again.

Johnson would later say that my draft was "a great tribute to a great man . . . but the Congress wanted to know how I was going to stand on these things." So he shortened my list of Kennedy's accomplishments, instead putting more emphasis on what he, LBJ, would do in the future. He understandably deleted one opening statement that I had suggested: "I who cannot fill his shoes must occupy his desk." At the time I resented the deletion, but now acknowledge that this and other changes were wise. That speech had to reassure the country and the world that the United States still had a functioning government and president, and that Kennedy's initiatives would be continued in the future, helping bring the country back to reality, awakening it from a terrible nightmare.

To have my speech draft changed by the president, even to have him incorporate material from others, was not new to me. JFK had done that more than once. But Kennedy's changes to my drafts were consistently good; these, I thought, were mostly poor. In the past,

I had always held final editing responsibility, making certain that any new material was consistent with the organization and substance of my basic full draft. This time I did not hold that final pen. So many drafts and constant rewriting resulted, I felt, in a speech that was repetitious and poorly organized.

Two days later, Johnson insisted that O'Brien, Salinger, and I accompany him in the presidential limousine to Capitol Hill for the speech to the joint session. Knowing that I had been grumbling about the changes, LBJ turned to O'Brien and Salinger: "This is a fine speech, 90 percent Sorensen, only 10 percent Johnson." "No, sir, that's not accurate," I protested, "not more than 50 percent Sorensen." "Well, anyway," said Johnson, "your 50 percent is the best." To that I replied in a more presumptuous fashion than I had ever used with JFK: "On that point, Mr. President, we agree." Everyone, including LBJ and me, laughed, and the tension was broken.

At lunch later that day, Joe Alsop complained that the Johnson speech, unlike JFK's, had a "corny" ending—a quotation from the song "America the Beautiful," meant to emphasize the concept of "brotherhood" that had meant so much to President Kennedy. I did not tell him it was my work.

Looking back, I am amazed that I was able to work at all during those first few days. Even then, I knew keeping busy would be part of my healing process, helping me manage my mental stress and depression. For nearly eleven years I had always been too busy. My salvation on November 22 and the weeks that followed was to keep being too busy. Better to be fully preoccupied than reliving that day in my mind. The only disadvantage of returning to my West Wing office to work each day was the constant reminder of my departed leader. Day after day, I did what I could to console and counsel my colleagues (and in so doing, myself), reminding them of our obligations to the nation.

In those first difficult days and weeks, I tried to keep occupied. I ate. I slept. I took no pills. But in my loneliness and grief I took one step more self-destructive than any pill could have been. In the space of a few months, having lost so much, my family, my boss, my role, feeling so alone in the world, I reached out—within a few days of the president's assassination—to Sara Elbery, a young woman I had previously dated, and asked her to come to Washington and marry me. She accepted. For both of us, it was the wrong move with the wrong person at the wrong time for the wrong reason. We were totally different—in background, in-

tellectual interests, personality, religion, and in almost
every other way. My friends and my siblings told me not
to go through with it. As the months wore on, and the
enormity of my folly became even more clear, I stub-
bornly insisted that I must be a man of my word, and
embarked seven months after the president's death on
a marriage that was doomed to be brief and painful for
both of us. Shortly before Sally's untimely death, some
years after our 1966 separation, we forgave each other
our mutual mistakes.

Jackie, knowing that my hasty marriage had become a cause of shame and regret, much later wrote
to me: "None of us should be blamed for anything we
thought or said or did during that first awful year." But
I have never forgiven myself for deciding on a second
marriage when I was in no condition to make far less
important decisions. Having grown up in a family that
frowned upon divorce, I will be embarrassed until my
dying day that I was divorced twice. My mother's view
of the subject, as well as her antipathy to commercialism, was made clear to me after that second marriage
failed, when she said: "There are two things I want to
see happen before I die: you remarry your first wife,
and your brother Robert get out of the advertising business." I didn't; he did.

The Monday after President Johnson's speech, the

Washington Post's Katharine Graham, whom I admired as I had her late husband, told LBJ in a recorded telephone conversation that she didn't think I "looked very well . . . He is very hurt." Presumably referring to an encounter on the day of the president's death—when I had unceremoniously asked her to leave a funeral planning meeting in the White House at which I did not think she belonged—she said, "I know the mood he was in and I don't forgive him for it . . . he was just unforgivable . . . We all have to just imagine how he feels . . . Instead of crying, he did this really naughty trick of being cantankerous . . . because he had that peculiar relationship with President Kennedy . . . I think he is going to come around . . . if you just give him a little love." "I've done as much as I can and have any pride and self-respect left," Johnson replied.

That same day, the president asked to meet with O'Brien, O'Donnell, and me, repeating that he and our country needed us, and that JFK would have wanted us to stay. O'Brien and O'Donnell agreed to stay at least through the transition period. When LBJ looked at me and asked if I was "with him," I replied, wanting to be both candid and cooperative, in the same noncommittal mode I had maintained from the start: "I'm still here, Mr. President."

Perhaps he sensed my ambivalence. In the ensuing

months, Johnson went out of his way to refer to me in the presence of others as "my trusted counselor." He was wooing me, in a sense, to stay on. In a speech to the National Business Council in early December, he even plugged my small book of lectures, *Decision-Making in the White House*, and introduced me to a luncheon with labor leaders by saying: "Judgment is not worth anything without information . . . Here is a man with both judgment and information."

In fact, it was becoming increasingly difficult to remain in the White House. The continuing ill-will between LBJ and RFK put the JFK holdovers on the White House staff in an impossible position. I no longer knew how open I should be about my relations with RFK. The antipathy among some White House staffers toward Johnson—almost as if he were an undeserving, unworthy usurper—combined with the emotional and political support for RFK, who was still in the cabinet, rose to the point that it threatened to divide our previously close-knit team into open factions.

On Thursday, December 5, for the first time in all my years in government, I decided to jot down some confidential notes for history, entitling them "Notes on What Happens to Government When the President Dies."

O'Brien, Dungan and Reardon and others come to my office uncertain of the future

Eisenhower and Robert Anderson [former Treasury Secretary] tell new President to take this opportunity to cut the budget

Secretary Dillon moves in absence of Heller, saying budget cut is only way of getting tax cut and claims JFK had so pledged

Secretary of Labor Wirtz stalks out of LBJ talk to Business Council, saying "I've had enough"

Freeman and Udall lobby for liberal budget

Bundy and Rusk compete as to who can (a) flatter LBJ the most, (b) take over new functions, (c) control foreign policy, on which LBJ knows nothing

The organization, if any, of decision-making is unknown and confused; Washington lawyers in and out of the White House, newsmen on the phone or at home, Texas hangers-on moving in, snap decisions made by LBJ on appealing-sounding proposals without checking

Press reaction more important than ever

First message to Congress altered, no longer a tribute to JFK

O'Brien and O'Donnell splitting re: National Committee

LBJ delivering flourishing speeches to small, informal groups and meetings of one or more, complete with Texas stories more earthy than tasteful,
and folksy or obviously trite homilies, and repeated
stories on how LBJ will really cut budget more than
JFK

I see now that memo was written in anger as well as
sorrow.

In the three months I remained in the White House
under Johnson, I had no difficulty working with him,
and did not withhold my candid views from him. On
January 27, 1964, after I advised Johnson on how to
respond to the scandal surrounding his friend Bobby
Baker, I later learned that LBJ told his confidants in the
Oval Office:

I tell you, the smartest man I've met in this White
house is Sorensen. He told me tonight he just
thought I was a big, fat, cigar-puffing, pot-bellied
numbskull [not true] by following the advice to get
out here in front of the press, that that's all they
want you to do.

After that first speech to a joint session of Congress
came an address to reassure the United Nations that the

United States would continue in Kennedy's multilateral path to peace; then a separate State of the Union message to Congress in January 1964. That State of the Union message was probably rewritten more times, by more people, than any Kennedy speech, with the exception of the October 22, 1962, speech during the Cuban missile crisis. I did not change my style in drafting speeches for Johnson, nor was I asked to do so. According to Bill Moyers, Johnson knew he did not have Kennedy's ease in conveying thoughts to big audiences through the intimacy, subtlety, and nuance of television, and believed I could help with that.

At his Texas ranch over the Christmas–New Year holidays, President Johnson and I reviewed the proposals I had compiled for inclusion in that first State of the Union. The final item on my list, which had grown out of a Kennedy-sponsored White House Conference on Narcotics in 1962, proposed not only expanded federal jurisdiction and enforcement over a growing national problem, but also new provisions for long-term treatment and rehabilitation. Johnson, weary from our late night session, suddenly erupted: "Drugs? I don't want to have anything to do with them. Just lock them up and throw away the key!" I retired for the evening, deleted the reference from the speech, but kept the provision in his legislative program. The Drug Abuse Control

Amendments of 1965 and the Addict Rehabilitation Act of 1966 were the result.

This was not the only Johnson program that originated in the Kennedy presidency. The highlights of Johnson's Great Society legislative accomplishments included a number of measures that can be traced back to Kennedy task forces, conferences, advisory councils, executive orders, even his speeches. I am happy to acknowledge that Johnson's legislative skills were required to enact Kennedy's domestic agenda in the form of concrete legislation.

Unfortunately, Johnson reversed some of Kennedy's foreign policies—halting the planned withdrawal of U.S. Army instructors and advisors from Vietnam, suspending a series of confidence-building agreements with the Soviet Union, abandoning Kennedy's plan to explore relations with China in his second term, and gradually ending Kennedy's Alliance for Progress with Latin America.

Johnson had inherited most of Kennedy's national security team, along with most of Kennedy's foreign policy problems. But he did not have the same ability and understanding to balance and evaluate those advisors in the same way. He was more skilled than Kennedy in getting House and Senate leaders to pass his legislative program, including bills on civil rights. But he did not have Kennedy's understanding of the world, including the pitfalls of Vietnam. Johnson thought all problems could be solved by making a deal with a leader. But some constituencies have no single leader, and some leaders cannot always deliver their constituencies. As Senate majority leader, Johnson knew how to use the levers of legislative power—appointments, budgets, and publicity—but presidential power is primarily moral power, the power to persuade and inspire by conveying values and ideals. Johnson never fully understood this.

Attempting to persuade Johnson to make world peace a theme of his presidency—as JFK had hoped to make it a theme of his 1964 campaign—I wrote a memorandum to the new president in January 1964, recommending a "U.S. Peace Offensive," including the distribution of food surpluses to the hungry in all nations, the transformation of the Bering Strait into a "Sea of Peace," and a demilitarized and denuclearized boundary between the United States and the Soviet Union. Regarding Vietnam, I urged him to propose publicly to Khrushchev the neutralization of both parts of Vietnam, and a cessation of all military activity by both the United States and North Vietnam in South Vietnam. My proposals fell on deaf ears. The timing of my departure was fortuitous; I could not have stayed in the administration once LBJ made his decision to send combat troops to Vietnam.

Moreover, I had no intention of staying beyond the immediate transition. Johnson had his own longtime aides, like Reedy, Moyers, Valenti, Busby, and others, who had relations with him at least similar to mine with Kennedy. It was not only appropriate for them, once he became president, to continue in that relationship in my place; it made for a better organized White House if they had the title, the office, and the role that I had previously held. I felt that LBJ was entitled to have a top aide whose allegiance was solely to him. Because mine was not, it was awkward and unfair to him for me to continue serving him.

I had also decided that I would write a book about JFK and my years with him. He had planned to write such a book with me after the presidency. Now that he was gone, I felt some obligation to write it. When Evan Thomas of Harper and Row, the same publisher and editor who had produced *Profiles in Courage*, and with whom both JFK and I had long enjoyed a good relationship, asked me to write such a book and made a generous offer, I decided it was time to leave the White House.

On January 14, approximately seven and a half weeks after the president's death (my mind having been made up weeks earlier), I walked into the Oval Office to inform the president of my decision, handing him my formal letter of resignation, effective February 29:

> Having largely completed my work for you on the 1964 legislative program and messages, and with increased confidence in both your dedication to the policies of the late President Kennedy and your election next November, I feel an obligation to devote the next several months to writing a book about the late President and my eleven years of service with him.
>
> I am deeply grateful for the many kindnesses which you and Mrs. Johnson have shown to me—especially during these difficult weeks since November 22 . . .

He immediately began to protest, saying, "You and I know that he is up there looking down on us and wants us to work together, carrying out his ideals, and he would not want you to leave here." His speech grew only more saccharine, finally reaching a point where he talked about his relations with his staff, and declared that, once I got to know him better, I would discover that he treated his staff as if they were his own children. Having observed on several occasions that LBJ could lavish praise and gifts on his staff—his personal court—one minute, and crush their dignity and self-confidence the next, I replied quietly, "Yes, I know." LBJ had kept the victorious American Davis Cup tennis team waiting in the Cabinet Room more than an hour as he tried to talk me out of leaving.

His formal reply to my letter came that same day:

Reluctantly and regretfully, I accept your resignation.

I know your decision to leave was a hard one. So was mine to let you go. For while many men may appreciate the scope of your work, only one—the President himself—can fully appreciate its impact on the Office itself.

In the past three years, I came to respect you greatly—as you served John F. Kennedy. In the past seven weeks, I came to rely on you greatly—as you worked faithfully and brilliantly to make this Government succeed. Those "great and lasting decisions in human affairs," of which you once wrote [in *Decision-Making in the White House*], will be more difficult to make without you.

But I accept your decision, appreciative of the motivations which led to it. I know that as the

Nation has been made stronger by your service, so will the memory of John F. Kennedy be made richer by your book.

When it is finished, I intend not to let you forget your promise to be available for future tasks.

On that day I became the first member of the Kennedy White House team to leave. It is amazing how a staff member, whether in the White House, a law office, or any other institution, on the eve of his departure, will suddenly become endowed, by those with whom he has worked, with qualities of wisdom and indispensability that none of them had previously attributed to him. A farewell party in my honor was held in the ornate Benjamin Franklin Room at the U.S. Department of State on February 19. The gathering was a reprise of my Washington career. The lawyer who first invited me to Washington, Stan Gewirtz, was there, as was my early boss on the joint congressional committee, Senator Paul Douglas. Some journalist friends attended, including Walter Lippmann and Kay Graham. The guests ranged from one of JFK's earliest supporters—Teno Roncalio—to LBJ's trusted lieutenants, Bill Moyers and Jack Valenti; they included all members of the cabinet, along with members of the White House staff and U.S. Supreme Court, including Chief Justice Warren, Justice William Brennan and Mrs. Brennan, and Justice Byron White. The president and Mrs. Johnson dropped by.

Justice Arthur Goldberg, who had been the senior cabinet member under Kennedy, served as master of ceremonies. The wonderful Margaret McNamara spoke a kind word of tribute on behalf of the cabinet wives. Dean Rusk said, "I've rarely seen such a gathering of what Chairman Khrushchev would undoubtedly call Washington's ruling class. It's not true that we got them all here by saying, 'You have to come—he's going to write a book.'" My deputy Mike Feldman told the gathering that I had been required to leave as a result of multiple violations of LBJ's economy edict requiring lights off late at night in the White House, the very hours when I continued to work. He also joked that the White House medical dispensary, no longer required to take care of my bad back and ulcers, would be able to cut its staff in half to save still more money in the LBJ economy drive. In the atmosphere of conviviality and generosity, forgotten by these cabinet chiefs were all the times that I had shaved their budget requests or altered their proposed inserts into the State of the Union message.

The presence of so many distinguished guests—some of whom I had helped win to the Kennedy cause years earlier, and all of whom I had worked closely with for over three years—nearly brought me to tears—which I was close to anyway most of the time in those first few months after November 22. When the festivities ended, as the marine band played "For He's a Jolly Good Fellow," an impromptu press conference took place outside. "Will you feel outside the mainstream of history now?" a reporter asked. I answered "Yes."

Columnist Bill Shannon of the *New York Post* called it "a final fond farewell to the Kennedy era." A *Washington Post* editorial, "Eminence Grise" read:

> The resignation of Theodore Sorensen as special counsel to the President ends a sadly brief but brilliant chapter in our political annals . . . In the breadth of his interests and the clipped resonance of his writing, Mr. Sorensen exemplified much that was admirable in the Kennedy era in Washington.

The *New York Times* proclaimed, "the country gained enormously from [JFK and my] relationship." *Life* magazine's Hugh Sidey's article was headlined "Departure of a 'Deputy President'" and referred to me as Kennedy's "all-purpose aide and co-author of The New Frontier . . . Most aides had specific spheres of operation; only Sorensen seemed to pop up everywhere, doing everything. . . ." Perhaps it seemed so to outsiders, but throughout our years together, JFK was receiving advice on every subject from RFK, political advice from O'Donnell and others, and substantive advice from throughout the White House and executive branch.

After I left, I continued to hear from President Johnson. On my honeymoon with Sally in June, he sent me a cable parodying the Kennedy inaugural. When I asked his advice about a television network's invitation to me to serve as an analyst during the 1964 convention at which he would be easily renominated, he replied that it was a mistake to mix the roles of participant and observer. (My guess is he was really thinking: "I don't want this SOB raining on my parade.") In a similar conversation, when I began to evaluate negatively some of his potential running mates, he offered me some wise counsel I have applied ever since: "Never piss in a well you may later be drinking from."

Occasionally I would see Johnson on friendly visits to the White House and in receiving lines during Democratic Party functions. As he bowed out of the White

House in 1968–1969, we had an exchange of friendly letters in which he generously declared:

> *You and I worked together in a time of grief and great pressure, when the stakes for the country were high. One of the reasons why we came through it reasonably well is that you and a number of other men put country first and served it, and me, as capably as you had served Jack Kennedy. I share your hope that we will see each other in the coming years . . .*

When Bobby Kennedy and I visited him in a reconciliation meeting shortly after Johnson's withdrawal from the 1968 presidential race, I still had mixed feelings. Whatever my policy differences with LBJ, and my discomfort with his style compared with JFK's, I had enormous admiration for his leadership skills; and as I left that table and said good-bye, I felt an immense sympathy, almost pity, for the man who had fought the good fight against poverty and racial injustice, who had pushed through so much important legislation for those who, in the end, had turned against him. Then I thought of the tens of thousands of young Americans he had needlessly sent into an escalating war in Vietnam, and all the innocent civilians killed by the tons of American bombs he dropped on the North Vietnamese without breaking their will to battle for independence, and all the federal health and housing programs that had been financially starved because of that war—and I could not find it in my heart to utter more than a few words of routine praise and gratitude for Lyndon B. Johnson. For all his brilliant successes, I would always revere the tragically abbreviated thousand days of John F. Kennedy's New Frontier far more than the nearly two thousand days of war and waste in Johnson's Great Society.

PART III
New York City, 1965–2007

Chapter 29

Return to Private Life
and Authorship

As I drove my convertible out the White House gate at the end of February 1964, I remembered the taxi that took me by that same gate upon my arrival in Washington on the evening of July 3, 1951. Both were trips into the unknown, but a lifetime of events had transpired in between.

The dedicated team assembled by JFK scattered after his death—some went home, some went to work for RFK, some stayed with LBJ. Through the good offices of Senator Ted and the Kennedy Library, we stayed in touch. Beginning in 1966, I had the good fortune to live in New York, where I saw McGeorge Bundy and Arthur Schlesinger on a regular basis. Mike Feldman, though he stayed on in Washington, remained a close friend.

Contacts were also kept through my rare appearances on New York's social circuit, including my attendance at Truman Capote's Black and White Ball at the Plaza Hotel in 1966 to honor *Washington Post* president Kay Graham, a party filled with familiar faces. I also kept in touch with Florence Mahoney, one of the "grand dames" of Washington, still feisty when she died at age 103, and still flaunting her sofa pillow with the inscription: "Age is just a number, and mine is unlisted."

In 1969 many of my Washington friends attended a party at the St. Regis in New York, hosted by John and Helen Martin to mark the occasion of my engagement to their daughter Gillian. I met Gillian in February 1968 at the home of Robert and Ethel Kennedy. Like me a Unitarian interested in current events and public affairs, like me descended from a moderate Republican father and activist mother from the Midwest, Gillian had worked in television in New York. In early 1968 she was the assistant producer of a charity telethon in Washington in which Ethel Kennedy was involved. At an event-related dinner at the Robert Kennedys' Hickory Hill home, I met this very bright and attractive young woman, thirteen years my junior. When I noticed that she was being subjected in the buffet line to some unwelcome attention from an inebriated football star, I invited her to sit with me on the stairs to eat dinner. Later that spring Gillian joined the RFK presidential campaign, and the rest is history. We were married in June 1969 in her home town of Grand Rapids, Michigan, the beginning of what she described, in a 2001 e-mail to our daughter, as an "unbelievably lucky . . . partnership for 32 years . . ."

It was more than luck. Initially shy and reserved, Gillian became an accomplished advocate and public speaker, throughout her career choosing positions that complemented my own interests and activities. Her work in the RFK campaign and subsequent political campaigns led to her joining New York mayor Ed Koch's cabinet in 1978 as his commissioner for the United Nations and Consular Corps, then a stint as President of the National Conference of Christians and Jews, and thereafter to sub-cabinet positions at the United Nations, working with Secretaries General Boutros Boutros Ghali and Kofi Annan. Gillian is now with the United Nations Foundation, addressing audiences across the country on the importance of the UN to the U.S.

Gillian introduced me to ballet, and I introduced her to opera, both of which were on our West Side doorstep, at Lincoln Center. The birth of our daughter, Juliet, in March 1973 significantly and delightfully changed our lives on Central Park West. We shared chores from dishwashing to diaper changing, and found great joy in raising our wonderful little girl.

In 1974 several old Kennedy hands gathered in our New York apartment to watch *The Missiles of October*, a television drama of the Cuban missile crisis. Jacqueline Kennedy Onassis, Jean and Steve Smith, Mac Bundy, Carl Kaysen (Bundy's White House deputy), Arthur Schlesinger, Don Wilson, and their wives were there. We all enjoyed laughing at the actors impersonating us. But reunions like that were all too few.

For my fiftieth birthday in 1978, Gillian gave a splendid party, inviting dozens of friends from the old days, as well as new acquaintances. Jackie sent Gillian a nostalgic note:

> *Dear Gillian—Ted's birthday was one of those watershed evenings that don't happen often in anyone's life. . .*
>
> *Treasured friends, noble figures, great moments, shared endeavors, all of what mattered most in their lives . . . all linked to Ted—all celebrating together. . .*
>
> *And the wit of friends and family—the closeness. All was the best, what you and Ted exemplify.*
>
> *I went home feeling moved and grateful and happy. I love to replay it over and over again in my mind.*
>
> *I hope that is what you have been doing too. Lucky Ted to have married you. Lucky all of us who have been in Ted's life.*

What a way to start a glorious new decade . . . all
my thanks for those precious hours I will never
forget.

These days, I continue to see my friends in the Kennedy family—though less frequently—Ted, Jean, Ethel, Eunice, and more often, Caroline.

It took time in 1964, 1965, and 1966 for me to adjust to my new life. I wrote Mike Feldman, upon his appointment as my successor as special counsel: "Don't leave that great place without consulting me. It is a shock." In Washington, as in life, when it's over, it's really over. I no longer had too many phone calls to return at the end of a day, nor were my own phone calls returned as quickly. My calendar was no longer full. Less than two weeks after my departure, my White House secretary wrote me: "So far no one has moved into your quarters. They are using the office as a spare room—meeting in it one day, staff lunchroom another."

Robert Kennedy ruefully told me on the golf course in Hyannis Port that summer that he had the same experience—adding that the FBI's J. Edgar Hoover had been pleased to tell him that he would no longer be reporting to the president through the attorney general. Others in the cabinet and Washington were simply less deferential. "Someday I'm going to write a book about that," said Bobby, singling out Robert McNamara as genuinely friendly with both him and Johnson, but mentioning others who had professed friendship when he was the president's brother, but no longer seemed interested when the president was dead.

I really did not miss the power and perks of the White House after I left—although my sister, Ruth, claims it took years before I remembered to close the door behind me when leaving a car, no longer having a White House driver to do so for me. She may be right. I did miss travel on Air Force One—when the captain wanted to take off or land, he took off and landed, no circling while waiting for a gate, no taxiing down the runway while awaiting permission to leave, no walk to the terminal to get my luggage, or squeezing into tiny seats three abreast.

My new status became particularly clear to me during my first year as a practicing lawyer in 1966 when one client's assignment required an appointment with an obscure assistant postmaster general. He kept me waiting in his outer office for at least one hour, while I could see, through his open office door, that he was not otherwise engaged. At that point in our respective careers, he had power, and I was merely another supplicant. It was a good lesson.

What I missed most were my responsibilities. At first I suffered what might be called the ex-cop syndrome.

The label comes from a Jimmy Breslin column about the retired policeman who, walking down the street, still worried about every unlatched back door and suspicious lurker. Like the retired cop, I still worried about problems of domestic and foreign policy over which I no longer had any jurisdiction.

Occasionally I heard from friends on the LBJ staff, including this Jack Valenti gem on life in Washington: "So the Washington River runs. Many times I have a nagging feeling I am riding it in a frail canoe, with rapids at every turn in the bend, and angry natives on the shore howling at me and daring me to try to reach the landing." Another letter from Jack noted that he had been with the president in Omaha, but the non-political nature of the visit made it "impossible for the President to make any overt . . . gestures to the next lieutenant governor of Nebraska [my brother Phil]. If we go back, I have been instructed to 'lay it on right' with him."

In December 1964 President Johnson conveyed feelers as to whether I would draft his January 20, 1965, inaugural address, saying that I had "promised" to do so when he agreed to my resignation. I declined, adding in my letter to Bill Moyers that "it would be a mistake for anyone so far removed from the Washington scene to attempt a draft of the Inaugural Address."

Then I relented and provided a one-page memorandum of "Thoughts on 1964 Inaugural," but I am uncertain whether LBJ and his team accepted any of my advice. It included, among other suggestions, "Rebuke those who teach hate and violence . . . the fanatics, foreign and domestic . . . the bigots, foreign and domestic . . ." Forty years later it is still timely advice.

It was just as well that I did not play a major role. I was still too shaken by the events of 1963 to participate in the nomination or inauguration of a candidate other than JFK. I did not attend the 1964 Democratic National Convention in Atlantic City, where Johnson was nominated. Instead, I was devoting all my time to writing the book that President Kennedy had intended to write with my help after his second term. "If I don't write it now," *Time* magazine quoted me, "I'm not sure I'll ever write it."

I had never written a full-length book. Two Columbia University lectures I had delivered while still in the White House had been published as a book, *Decision-Making in the White House*—for which President Kennedy had written a generous introduction (drafted perhaps by Arthur Schlesinger), stating that I had "been an astute and sensitive collaborator in the presidential enterprise . . . a participant as well as an observer, of important decisions in difficult days." But writing those two lectures was different; and I was still unfamiliar with the challenges of writing a book.

In February 1964 I gathered my thoughts and papers, and requested relevant facts and documents from former Kennedy colleagues. I started writing in June, optimistically hoping to have a completed draft by Labor Day 1964, and a finished manuscript by New Year's Day 1965. I was lucky to finish it by Labor Day 1965. The book was a good transition for me. It kept John Kennedy in my thoughts, and at the center of my work. It allowed me to feel I was still serving him, and to continue doing my part to help him be remembered as the greatest president of the twentieth century, which had been my goal for the previous decade and longer.

The book served as my emotional decompression chamber, a healthy undertaking for me at the time, a chance to write all I knew and believed about that man— a catharsis in one sense and a joy in another. It lessened the pain.

I wrote *Kennedy* much the same way I wrote his speech drafts—beginning with an outline, gathering all my relevant notes and materials, dividing them into piles that corresponded to the outline, and then composing a first draft based on the materials in each pile, editing each paragraph and page as I went along, writing the final version one chapter at a time.

Kennedy was written in solitude, with only my files, piles, and memories. As I wrote, I turned often to the transcript of the interview Carl Kaysen conducted with me for the Kennedy Library Oral History Program.

I could not draw upon a diary, because I had never kept one. Sensing an obligation to history in late 1960, I had tried to start one, but the days were too short to record faithfully and fully the reports, recommendations, statements, memoranda, and meetings that had consumed my time.

Writing a book requires uninterrupted, undistracted, unending hours of work. I immersed myself in my subject, working from the minute I awoke in the morning until I could no longer keep my eyes open at night. It dominated my life. I pulled more all-nighters writing that book than I had during all the many crises in the White House. I felt guilt when I took a break to rest. An unwritten or unfinished manuscript is always there, waiting in the next room, justifying no distraction. Exercise, sleep, companionship, sometimes even food, were slighted.

Logistically, my arrangements were far from perfect. In a cottage I had rented in Hyannis Port, I wrote, in longhand, with pen on a yellow legal pad, mailing each draft chapter to Gloria Sitrin, who had retired from her secretarial chores in the White House but still lived in the Washington area. She typed each chapter, sent it back to me for revision, and I sent the revised drafts to my editor, Evan Thomas of Harper and Row. Evan was horrified at all this reliance on the U.S. mails, and insisted that I hire a local stenographer to take dictation and make copies. He was still more horrified to learn that it was my practice to destroy my files, manuscripts, articles, memos, and old speeches once they were dictated or transcribed and the edited version had been revised—which I did to avoid both confusion and subsequent leaks about my original intent. He feared that, should the book manuscript be lost or destroyed, I would not be able to reconstruct it, having destroyed all my research material. But the manuscript survived.

My original title was *Promises to Keep: A Portrait of John F. Kennedy.* My second was *A Time to Hope.* When both of these encountered doubts, I settled on simply *Kennedy,* after I noticed on a library bookshelf that many of the world's finest biographies had been titled with only the name of their subject.

Carl Kaysen industriously served as a book advisor and fact checker, sending chapters and even passages in the initial manuscript to experts in the administration for review. I wanted to be certain both that the manuscript was accurate and that it did not compromise national security. One of the experts who reviewed the manuscript, Roswell Gilpatric, deputy secretary of defense, wrote to Carl: "Having read the foreign policy chapters of Ted's work, it is my judgment that, generally speaking, they do not present security problems and therefore I do not consider clearance procedures necessary." Ultimately, I received only one request for change in a reference to CIA programs, "not because they raised security questions, but [because they] might lift the curtain on too much covert activity of a type that may be useful in the future." I changed the text accordingly. The CIA was also concerned, I later learned, that my reference to Kennedy's belief that "the camera"—satellite and U-2 photography—was becoming our best source of intelligence—might be telling too much to our adversaries, but I was not asked to delete it.

Despite my insistence on accuracy, I confess to at least one creatively inspired account in that book. In one of my letters to Gloria, I wrote: "Secret: as a manner of getting in a tribute to JFK that would otherwise have been edited out as idolatry, I am closing the Cuban missile crisis chapter by recalling that I read to you from the *Profiles* frontispiece. You remember that, don't you?" Always loyal, she replied: "I remember very clearly your reading to me from the *Profiles* frontispiece in connection with the Cuban missile crisis!"

In addition to other administration colleagues, I wanted Bobby to review my book before it was published, primarily to make sure that I had my facts right. In a phone call, he advised me to delete the reference to my conscientious objector status after World War II, which he (rightly) considered potentially harmful to my political future, and to omit as well my private visit with Justice Douglas—an innocent visit that he thought might raise too many questions. He also recommended that I remove the names of individuals who had provided confidential advice to the president during the Cuban missile crisis, lest the press sensationalize these revelations. I agreed. But, after I hung up the phone, I realized that I had already sent to the publisher the book's introduction, which included missile crisis statements by Adlai Stevenson and Douglas Dillon.

Years before she would assume her editorial responsibilities at Doubleday, Jackie agreed to read the manuscript of *Kennedy*. She proved to be a superb editor, correcting typographical errors, challenging mistaken assumptions, defending some of her husband's personnel decisions, suggesting useful clarifications, and repeatedly setting the record straight on matters not known to me, specifically noting whom JFK privately admired and whom he did not, all in handwritten notes on several sheets of lined yellow paper. In addition to asking me to tone down my references to JFK's praise of LBJ, she made a number of other specific suggestions:

[JFK] never had brandy in his life . . .

He so admired Walter George [conservative senior Democrat from Georgia], saw him at every Senate opportunity and would always quote to me at night whatever Walter George had said to him during the day. All that he admired in senators he saw in Walter George.

If JFK ever went into a crowd, he did it because he was beginning to feel more relaxed in crowds.

I suppose your footnote 6 is necessary—so that you don't seem too biased, but as JFK's ambassadors were so extraordinary, it strikes a jarring note—and joggles your thinking as you are reading about all the good men. Why don't you put this footnote at the bottom of the page if you have to put it in. When you think of some of Eisenhower's ambassadors— Guggenheim to Portugal—[another] requested to leave because of lechery—Zellerbach—Gluck etc— Earl Smith's "past record of performance in diplomacy" was not what made him unacceptable to Switzerland—it was banking interests—but I understand that you must be critical somewhere . . .

Perhaps you have to say this—I know he was sensitive to press criticism in the beginning—but in his last 2 years in the White House—he accepted it as part of every day's agenda—[Jack] had learned how to roll with the punches and they bemused rather than upset him. He became so tolerant— like a horse you see in the field in summer—the flies have annoyed him at first—but there are long months before they will go away—so he does his work—which is eating grass—and just flicks his tail—Whenever I was upset by something in the papers—he always soothed me and told me to be more tolerant—if you want examples of this—I have many to give you. They even extended into international relations . . .

"He thought *The New York Times* the greatest newspaper in the world"—Are you sure? He had a great deal of disillusionment about them—nepotism—their columnists who never left DC—etc— just don't give them that much of a plug—perhaps "one of the greatest newspapers"—(he liked *le Monde*)—because he really had a lot of contempt for the *Times* . . .

"John-John, as his father called him." His father never called him John-John—only John. That nickname now plagues the little boy—who may be stuck with it all his life. I know your book deals with more important things—but it would be great if you could put that nickname to bed. I don't know where it started, as both of us hated nicknames—our own—Jack and Jackie we thought a most unfortunate combination—and we always called our children by their first names. I can only think it started when I was hugging John as a baby and saying nice things to him—like John, John—and some newspaper woman—it may have been dear old Laura Berquist—picked it up—John gets angry now when strangers call him John-John—because he thinks it is babyish—He has many fights in the park about it. You could help him if you said his father never called him that . . .

Not vodka and tomato juice in the afternoon . . . On vacations he had a drink before lunch—otherwise never—just one before dinner . . .

"Kennedy rarely if ever used the putting green . . . although he kept it with that in mind." It was part of the children's playground once the White House school was started—Forts were dug in the sand pit and flags and toys and digging went on all over the putting green—That amused him and he would come out to watch the school playing on it—He never cared about it—though the gardeners kept it clipped—but it was pretty pockmarked by children . . .

Caroline "firmly ordering cameramen at an air-port 'No pictures'" Please delete—not fair to her—She is such a shy tender little girl and she got that horror of the press from me—She used to put her hands over her face when she saw cameramen—then I saw I had erred in my desire for privacy for the children—so I had to teach them all over again—that cameramen were all right—a part of their father's life and they must behave in front of them in a way that would show they had the same good manners their father had. This was a hard lesson to teach them. I think Runnymede [British Memorial Ceremony for JFK] shows I did. I just object to your phrase because it makes Caroline sound too tough—and she is the most vulnerable little girl that ever existed . . .

You are wrong—he read poetry a lot—at least with me . . .

Couldn't you make it clearer that he quoted his father saying S.O.Bs just about the steel industry? Later on you say that is what he meant—and I know he did, but I had to refer back to this page to check the statement—which less interested persons will not do. That quote caused him so much unnecessary hatred—Just really make clear the context in which he said it the first time . . .

I was fascinated by what Jackie chose to correct.

Later, the author William Manchester incorrectly claimed that the Kennedys had pressured me with demands for changes, perhaps reflecting his own unfortunate experience with Robert and Jacqueline Kennedy. In fact, I welcomed most of their suggestions in the interests of accuracy. No other member of the family saw the final manuscript, much less attempted to censor it. Still, at the time I wrote the book, I thought I might soon return to government, and felt it prudent to limit my criticisms of LBJ, the Democratic Party, and the Kennedy family to avoid burning any bridges.

The book was finally published on October 4, 1965, nineteen months after I drove out of those White House gates for the last time as a presidential aide. I refused all suggestions that the publication date be delayed until the November 22 anniversary. Reviews varied. One said I was "likely to gain the reputation as Kennedy's Boswell." Some wrote: "meticulously accurate . . . historians will use it indefinitely as a basic source . . . the intimacy, throughout, is immensely impressive . . . more revealing than if President Kennedy had written it himself." Others complained that it was "agonizingly analytical" and "expensive—$10.00, but excellent." Some critics thought it was unseemly for me to write so soon after the president's death and to report confidential advice and conversations. Other reviewers said the book was not objective, detached, or nonpartisan. One even said it was "almost unadulterated hero worship." I had said that already—in the book's prologue: "This book, let it be clear at the outset, praises John F. Kennedy and what he has done, not merely out of loyalty and affection, but out of deep pride and conviction."

Through its many editions, *Kennedy* sold well. *Look* magazine, in publicizing its serialization, called it "the most important publishing event of 1965." That would have made my father proud. Two days before my ninth birthday, he had sent me a penny postcard from Washington: "Dear Ted, I am sorry I will not be home on your birthday. Some day you may write a book that people all over the world will read."

Mine was not the only book on JFK being written at that time by a former staffer. Pierre Salinger wrote his own book, as did presidential secretary Evelyn Lincoln and aides Larry O'Brien, Kenny O'Donnell, and Dave Powers. One columnist summed it up: "the major industry in New York City this summer is handling words about John F. Kennedy." When Arthur Schlesinger disclosed that he would be writing his own book, *A Thousand Days*, the media created a story. Which book would come out first, his book or mine? Even the British serialization rights of the two books were in a contest between the *London Sunday Times* (his) and the *Observer* (mine). One article measured the speed of my handwriting compared with Arthur's typewriter. At a White House farewell party for Arthur, the cake decorations depicted two cowboys racing down the path to a pot of gold-wrapped chocolate drops, with a legend "May the Better Man Win," one cowboy identified with the initials "TCS" and the other "AS Jr." A few years later, I just smiled at the response of Israeli prime minister Eshkol when I announced my intention of presenting him with an inscribed copy of my book on JFK: "Oh, yes," he exclaimed, "*A Thousand Days!*"

As our respective publishers raced to serialize in U.S. magazines—his in *Life*, mine in *Look*—and then publish our books, a minor feud was generated by the press, alleging that we had written different treatments of Kennedy appointees, such as Dean Rusk, who were still in office when our books came out. Arthur wrote me, stating his belief that I had "launched an unmistakable, if indirect, attack" on him and had tried to "dissociate" myself from any "contaminating association" with his book, both of which I quickly denied in a personal letter to him. Our friendship was temporarily strained, but it quickly recovered.

The furor over the Sorensen–Schlesinger books ultimately spilled over into the subsequent furor over Bill

Manchester's book on Kennedy's assassination, *The Death of a President*. Bill had interviewed me at length for his book, while I was writing mine on Cape Cod. I found it difficult to talk about the assassination, and from time to time broke off the interview simply to recompose my thoughts and emotional balance. When it was finally published, his book stirred enormous hostility to the point of litigation from the Kennedy family. For personal reasons, I could not bring myself to read it, and have never read it. Arthur Schlesinger's is the only book on President Kennedy that I have ever read in full.

Years after writing *Kennedy*, I was told by a professor that he required his students to choose between my book and those by Clark Clifford, Dick Neustadt, and others who had served several presidents, implying that my book might be less valuable because I served principally only one president. "Yes," I replied, remembering *Gone with the Wind* author Margaret Mitchell's expression of satisfaction that she had written only one book, "but my one President was quite a President."

Chapter 30

New Life in New York

Upon the publication of my book, I spent several months addressing dozens of educational and civic audiences, seeing most of the country from the lecture platform, after seeing it for so many years from the political platform. I spoke in England and Ireland; East St. Louis and Austin; Wichita, Ithaca, Arlington, Chicago, and on the West Coast, even taking an around-the-world trip to deliver a lecture series in New Zealand.

The title of my lecture was "The Legacy of John F. Kennedy." When told by my lecture agency that I must offer three separate titles for its client brochure, I responded that I preferred to continue talking primarily about the Kennedy legacy. "You do not need three different speeches," I was informed, "just three different titles." That was easy. Ultimately I chose to schedule my own lectures. Whenever the title was required by a host far in advance, I responded that my title would be "The Road Ahead."

I learned some valuable lessons on the lecture circuit: Student audiences are often better than adult audiences—more open minds, more penetrating questions, more enthusiasm; and foreign audiences are often more responsive and interested than American audiences. Most of the questions I received from all kinds of audiences were about the Warren Commission report and various conspiracy theories; who wrote *Profiles in Courage* and who wrote President Kennedy's inaugural address; and what was the solution in Vietnam, what would President Kennedy have done in his second term. There were occasional jarring moments—the audience member who said, "I don't care what anybody says about your book, I thought it was good"—or the number who referred to the late president as "Jack," though they did not know him—those who insisted that it was unpatriotic, if not treasonous, for me to charge the CIA or military with errors at the Bay of Pigs, but permissible to make such charges against the president.

All this traveling across America was both a book promotion effort and a minor source of income, while I was looking for and deciding what would be my next job. On a trip to California, I visited Governor Pat Brown and former RFK assistant Ed Guthman. I also met with University of California president Clark Kerr to discuss the possibility of my accepting a high position in the University of California system; but a friendly informant warned me that "the conservative bloc on the Board of Regents is not prepared to accept the kind of direction which a person of your background and instincts would give." Good advice, and I heeded it.

As I traveled, I carried in my pocket a list of job possibilities, often asking close friends like Burke Marshall, RFK's assistant attorney general, and Mike Feldman which they would recommend. That list included all kinds of possibilities—to join *Newsday* as a syndicated columnist; the *Saturday Review* as a contributing editor; Princeton's Woodrow Wilson School to conduct a weekly seminar; a variety of law firms in Boston, Washington, and New York City; a federal position (presumably part-time) as a member of the National Historical Publications Commission; a position as full-time roving lecturer under the auspices of a high-powered speakers' bureau; two university presidencies; one foundation presidency; and even elected office—shortly after I left the White House, both Nebraska's Democratic national committeeman Bernie Boyle and Democratic governor Frank Morrison encouraged me to enter the senatorial race in Nebraska against incumbent Republican senator Roman Hruska. That idea was a nonstarter.

The one job my three young sons most wanted me to get was commissioner of baseball. Most of the friends I consulted laughed at that one, asked me a few questions, and then told me whatever they thought I wanted to hear. I did not tell all those potential employers interviewing me what they wanted to hear. When the Major League Search Committee was reported in the press, on the same day that I was interviewed, to be considering General Curtis LeMay, the would-be nuclear bomber during the Cuban missile crisis, I told the members of the committee: "If what you want is a retired Air Force general, you do not want me." It turned out that what they did want was a retired air force general, a LeMay subordinate who got the job.

In truth, throughout 1964 and much of 1965, still writing and promoting my book, I remained undecided. One friend said: "It was the only time in the years I've known him that he seemed confused and indecisive." My brother Tom explained it this way: "I think Ted really only wanted one job; and I kept telling him that the job of Special Counsel to John F. Kennedy was no longer available."

By that time, at least one job possibility had faded. While I was still in the White House, my friends in the movie business, Arthur Krim and Bob Benjamin, had explored with me whether, once my book was finished, I would be willing to take over the leadership of the Motion Picture Association of America.

LBJ, when informed of that possibility, saw it as an opportunity for him to keep me close at hand for occasional speechwriting and other chores, inasmuch as the MPAA main office was less than two blocks from the White House. Deciding to help get me the job, LBJ telephoned his close friend, Edwin Weisl, as I sat across from him in the Oval Office, listening to the classic "Johnson Treatment":

> **LBJ:** "I got some bad news for you and some good news too."
>
> **Weisl:** "What's the bad news?"
>
> **LBJ:** "Well my friend Sorensen is sitting here at my desk and he's decided he's gonna write a book. And he's the most competent man we've got on the staff and he's gonna write a book about the President. But I don't see how I can get along without him. Well he's got to do it and he doesn't want too many memories around here to just live with him every hour. And he's almost as emotional as I am, as sentimental as I am. So he wants to go work for

the motion pictures producers and I told him I thought maybe I could get you to help him. And he could still work for me too."

Weisl: "I certainly will do that.

LBJ: "He's the most competent man we have, as a lawyer, as a counselor, as advisor, he's got all the contacts, and by far the most skillful writer . . . I've just never had anyone that compares with him and I just think in the campaign on the big speeches where I've just got to measure up he'd just be the best one available. And I believe you could do that job for me if you really tried at it . . ."

Weisl: "Well, what does he want . . . ?"

LBJ: "He wants to take Eric Johnson's job [as head of the MPAA]."

Weisl: "Oh . . . Has he been approached on it?"

LBJ: "No . . . You just go on and get it for him."

Weisl: "Well, I'll do my very best . . . What's the good news?"

LBJ: "The good news is that you're getting him and the bad news is I'm losing him. . . . Eddie, if I had the money I'd give this fellow 200,000 dollars a year myself. Now he's not interested in any . . .

job. Unless he can be the head of it, there'll be 20 people wanting him for anything. But I just thought we had some friends in this outfit and I didn't think they could find anybody better than one of my best men. . . . I'm gonna lose him either to this outfit or some other outfit that I control. I'm not gonna just turn him out into the pasture, let him go his own way, cause I want to use him myself."

Shortly after that conversation, Weisl informed me that the members of the MPAA Board seemed intent on offering me the position, and would be ready to proceed once my own state of mind was made known. I wrote him a long, presumptuous letter about my requirements for the job—to which I immodestly added:

> . . . the contract should provide for the contingency of my accepting from the President a Cabinet or Ambassadorial position . . . I am hopeful, in short, that this post can be developed into a more broad and positive role that makes the most of the industry's capacity for education, communication and cultural development . . . I hope we are thinking along the same wave-lengths . . .

Apparently we were not. A few months later, I was told that an MPAA contact had said "their only interest in Sorensen was because of the President's interest and . . . the President was no longer interested." The job ultimately went to Johnson's loyal aide and my friend, the multitalented Jack Valenti.

The one government job for which I was briefly considered—having been recommended to LBJ by Mac Bundy in the summer of 1965—was to replace Adlai Stevenson as ambassador to the United Nations, Adlai having died suddenly in London of a heart attack. But I could not have guessed at LBJ's tactical planning at a higher level—that he would somehow persuade my old friend Arthur Goldberg to resign from the U.S. Supreme Court to take the UN position, enabling Johnson to appoint his longtime confidant Abe Fortas to the Court. Only LBJ could have persuaded someone to resign from a lifetime position of unsurpassed honor and influence on the Supreme Court. According to rumor, he told Arthur that the UN post, where he could "solve" Vietnam, was a better path to higher office, perhaps governor of New York, and after that, who knows, perhaps the first Jewish president? Neither Johnson's capacity for persuasion nor Goldberg's ambition should be underestimated.

Eventually I decided that the profession for which I had been trained would provide the best long-term base. A dozen years earlier, when still a young assistant to Senator John F. Kennedy, I had become friendly with Arthur Goldberg, who was then a leading labor lawyer, and I asked him whether my legislative and political post would ultimately be helpful in the private practice of law, "or was I straying too far from my chosen profession?" He replied, long before I went to work in the White House, that he thought my work was excellent preparation for law in the larger sense in which it was practiced in the major law firms. Remembering that advice gave me some measure of confidence that I could dive right into the profession.

In 1965, while considering my future, I came across an April 1951 letter from the distinguished Washington lawyer Thurman Arnold to my law school dean, Fred Beutel, thanking him for his letter of recommendation but stating: "Unfortunately we do not have any openings in this office at the present time and do not contemplate expansion in the near future." I sent that letter to my new friend and Johnson advisor Abe Fortas, a longtime partner in the Arnold firm, appending a cover note: "One can never be sure how the pendulum of history will swing." Fortas immediately replied by sending the following letter to "Judge" Arnold, with his own cover note:

> You either have a cloudy crystal ball or a lack of scruple in dealing with friendly professors who refer to you their outstanding students. At the time you wrote rejecting Sorensen, there were nine lawyers in this firm . . . [Now] we have dozens—sometimes I think hundreds . . . you told Professor Beutel that we did not have any openings . . . that we do not contemplate expansion . . . what the hell were you contemplating? If you are going to carry this burden of contemplation, you must . . . be forthright and honest . . . I don't know what you can do to make amends to Ted Sorensen. I expect you will attempt to persuade him that you rejected him for his own good. But this will get you nowhere. Rejection is rejection . . . it is true that Sorensen's name is known throughout the nation, indeed . . . throughout the world. It is true that his words—even though spoken by others—have achieved immortality . . . but he has retired at an early age and is about to make a million dollars merely by writing a book. It is true that his ideals, his imagery, the nobility of his sentiments, the power of his principles, have raised

*this nation and the world to a new plateau . . . It was
palpably insincere for you in your letter to refer to
your "appreciation" of Beutel's letter. It is perfectly
obvious that you regarded his letter as such a hell of
a nuisance that you did not even consider the clear
and unmistakable merits of Ted Sorensen. When this
firm finally faces up to the fact of its insolvency, I
just want you to remember that this disaster could
have been averted, if you had merely faced the future
squarely, girded your sleeves, rolled up your loins,
and hired Sorensen.*

When my wise counselor and journalist friend Joe
Kraft opined that I should enter the legal profession, I
explained in a letter to him:

*. . . my guess [is] that 95% of all legal business
is boring—particularly in comparison with my
previous responsibilities. I do not want to knock it
too hard because I may join the [profession]. But my
hope is to find work that will interest me on its own;
and I wonder how many firms could assure me that
I would be working primarily in that five percent of
public law, administrative law, international law and
the like that to me represent a worthwhile challenge,
and not merely reorganizing corporations, drafting
wills, or fighting against progressive legislation.*

One Washington lawyer, full of kind words, advised me at length about joining his law firm with the understanding that I would be devoting substantial time to outside public interest activities and handling only those cases that were consistent with my conscience and national interest policies. He asked me not only to consider joining his firm but to return to Washington at a time when he could have a dinner at his home in my honor, "perhaps 30 or 40 of your closest friends from the Congress and downtown." Time and circumstance did not permit me to act on either offer—the job or the dinner—and I have no doubt that was in the end best for both me and my friendly recruiter, the conservative Republican lawyer, and later indicted and imprisoned Nixon White House official Chuck Colson. Again, one can never be sure how the pendulum of history will swing.

Around that same time, I also met with Judge Samuel Rosenman, a friend who had been FDR's leading speechwriter and the nation's first White House special counsel, and was by 1965 a distinguished senior partner in a prominent New York law firm that bore his name. He took me to dinner and showed me around his firm's luxurious suite of offices, in an effort to induce me to join his firm. After he told me how much money his partners made, noting especially the expensive art on their office walls, I asked him: "Are they having any fun?" He looked at me thunderstruck. "Fun?" said Judge Rosenman. "They make all this money so they can have fun on weekends and during their summer vacations." Having had the good fortune to find fun in all my roles with John Kennedy, I decided that money was not the main test for me; that I would be spending so much time in my office, whatever firm I joined, I wanted my life in the law to continue to be "fun."

But the private practice of law was not nearly as satisfying as public service had been. No legal memorandum I ever wrote gave me half the satisfaction I received from drafting Kennedy's letter to Khrushchev during the Cuban missile crisis. Even working on the Tajikistan constitution was not as satisfying as my involvement in Kennedy's 1963 civil rights message and legislation. The heady sense of pride I experienced in providing advice to Sadat, Mandela, and other heads of state paled in comparison with JFK welcoming my report on a manned lunar landing. The sense of accomplishment I felt when my client's Panama pipeline was completed was not comparable to helping to coordinate Big Steel's reversal of its inflationary price increase in 1962.

JFK chum Chuck Spaulding had recommended me to his lawyer, Jack Massengale, a Paul, Weiss partner. Coincidentally, another JFK chum, Bob Troutman, had recommended me to his fellow Georgian, a new Paul, Weiss partner, Morris Abram. After a round of interviews at Paul, Weiss, I made my decision; and on January 20, 1966, five years to the day after JFK's inaugural address, the *New York Times* reported that I was moving to New York City to join the Paul, Weiss firm.

That spirit of camaraderie and fun that characterized my years with JFK partly explained what drew me to Paul, Weiss, Rifkind, Wharton & Garrison. It was best expressed by Judge Simon H. Rifkind, the leader of the modern New York City firm, "If you are not having fun practicing law, you're not doing it right." I was fortunate in the four decades of fun that followed.

I had initially assumed that my career at the firm would be temporary, a base for interesting private and public activities until 1972 or later when I hoped and expected that Robert Kennedy would run for president, win, and bring me back to Washington. I'm lucky that I gave as much consideration to my choice of the firm as I did as to my selection in March 1966 of Marge Hornblower as my secretary. She handled all my assignments with the same immediate and expert attention that had previously been accorded me by three secretaries in the

White House. Our productive partnership at the firm was dissolved only by Marge's retirement in 2000. Our friendship remains intact; we maintain our mutual admiration and affection; we continue to collaborate; and we still seek advice and assistance from each other.

I chose Paul, Weiss because of its high intellectual quality, its reputation as a bastion of progressive politics, and its commitment to public service. "I wanted a firm that would encourage, not just permit, me to be active in public affairs," I told a *New York Times* reporter. Judge Rifkind repeatedly emphasized in his public speeches that the law was a profession, not a business, that we served clients, not customers. Unfortunately, the law today is not what it was in Judge Rifkind's day; commercialism, advertising, and more emphasis on profits than public service have become widespread; and public-minded intellectuals like Judge Rifkind and other early Paul, Weiss Partners, devoted to pro bono tasks and codes of ethics, are increasingly rare. The firm's practice was never entirely pro bono (free legal services), of course. When asked by a wealthy group of clients how they could "ever repay" him for saving their company, Judge Rifkind wryly replied: "The Phoenicians solved that problem a long time ago."

I learned only after selecting Paul, Weiss that, in order to practice law in New York State, I had to have practiced law for five or more years in another state, or, alternatively, to have taken and passed the difficult New York State bar exam. I wondered: Did my government service constitute the practice of law? In the course of discussing the matter with representatives of the New York State Bar Association, I learned that Richard Nixon's move from politics in California to a law firm in New York a few years earlier had set the precedent for former government officials being admitted to the New York State bar without taking the bar exam. Upon encountering the former vice president on Madison Avenue in 1966, I told him that I was following in his footsteps. He generously asked if I wanted to see his file, and I quickly accepted. With the help of his file for guidelines and the precedent of his admission, I was admitted to the New York State bar shortly thereafter. It was a spontaneously friendly offer to help me; but when Nixon later became president, my name appeared on his self-styled "Enemies List" (reportedly more Chuck Colson's doing than his), a recognition that rewarded me with congratulations from my law partners and an annual audit of my income taxes from the Internal Revenue Service.

Early in my first year, just back from Christmas vacation with my boys in the Virgin Islands, I assisted a Paul, Weiss client that had a subsidiary in the islands.

I traveled to St. Thomas, successfully made my pitch to my friend, the governor, and returned to New York the same day. The partner in charge reprimanded me for setting a bad example, in not even taking time for a swim. I knew then that I had chosen the right firm.

When my old friend Arthur Goldberg came to Paul, Weiss after his stint as U.S. ambassador to the United Nations, he insisted, not surprisingly, that his name be added to the firm's name. Arthur's series of prestigious positions—cabinet secretary, Supreme Court justice, UN ambassador—had modified the humble modesty that had previously characterized him as a labor lawyer. His self-importance was a subject of humor around the firm: "Question: What should we call you, Mr. Goldberg, Mr. Secretary, Mr. Justice, or Mr. Ambassador? Answer: Oh, a simple 'Your Excellency' will do." He frequently peppered his remarks with ". . . when I was on the Supreme Court."

Choosing Paul Weiss also meant choosing to work in New York. Joe Kraft had urged me to join one of the large New York law firms as a base for future public service and a variety of outside activities. Robert Kennedy thought I should practice in New York City, not Washington, so I could continue to play a role in real politics. Roswell Gilpatric, a distinguished leader of the New York bar who had been Kennedy's deputy secretary of defense, also supported the choice of New York over Washington—for the opposite reason. He thought my knowledge of Washington would be a unique asset in the New York bar. Another friend advised me not to be a lawyer in Washington: "If you are a lawyer in Washington, the burden is on you to prove that you are not engaged in lobbying or influence peddling." For my first year at least, I had the best of both worlds; I was a Washington lawyer in New York.

Though Nebraska was still my true home, I found New York City a better place to live than to visit. Earlier trips had been a constant hassle—finding transportation, accessible lodging, and inexpensive restaurants. Once I lived here long enough to familiarize myself with the city, and walked to and from my office each day, I found it was more enjoyable, interesting, and diverse than almost any city in the world. Recalling Harry Truman's quip, I soon discovered that the average New York City cocktail party guest, equipped with hindsight, is smarter than any president of the United States.

In 1966 I finally had a new home and a new job—actually, several new jobs, having concluded that several of the possibilities on my job list could be combined with the private practice of law—writing articles for *Saturday Review* as a contributing editor, offering a weekly opinion on local television, and conducting a seminar at the Woodrow Wilson School at Princeton. My course for seniors, entitled Presidential Leadership in Foreign Policy, included a weekly classroom lecture and discussion, and a public lecture at the end of the school year. (It also included, when my second year of classes ended, a touch football game with my students in which I cracked a rib; soon thereafter I retired from both touch football and Princeton.) I also maintained my advisory relationship with then-senator Robert F. Kennedy.

When I was in the White House, I had little regard for those academic, journalistic, and other critics who mistakenly thought they always knew more than the President. After leaving the White House, I became one of them. In the ensuing decades, I wrote articles, essays, and opinion pieces not only for the *Saturday Review*, but for roughly fifty different publications, ranging from the *Wall Street Journal* to the *Westchester Wag*, from the *New York Times* to the *New India Digest*, from the *Catholic Mind* to *Playboy*, from *Redbook* to Germany's *Die Welt*. I wrote about everything from the Cuban missile crisis to "Why I Love Paddle Tennis," from the role of faith to the role of humor in politics. My articles covered presidential power in the U.S. and countries on nearly every continent—from Panama to Iran to Germany and China. Lecture series formed the bases of my subsequent books—*Watchmen in the Night* on Watergate's effect on the presidency, and *A Different Kind of Presidency* with its emphasis on bipartisanship to break the political deadlock and end the recurring bitterness that characterized politics in the mid–1980s.

I also served for many years on the boards of non-profit and nongovernmental organizations whose mission or goals were similar to my own. Two of my favorites were the Twentieth Century Fund (now the Century Foundation) and the Council on Foreign Relations, to which I had the honor of successfully nominating Governor Bill Clinton of Arkansas for membership.

Frequently on the anniversary of either the Cuban missile crisis or JFK's death, I wrote or spoke about the Kennedy legacy, even producing a book on that subject, *The Kennedy Legacy*, published in 1969, that deserved much of the scorn heaped upon it by some reviewers. I also played a part in helping to establish the Kennedy School of Government and the Institute of Politics at Harvard, and the John F. Kennedy Presidential Library and Museum in East Boston—institutions that were initially intended to be combined in one location, Cambridge, until a Cambridge matron complained that the library and museum would bring thousands of tourists to town, and she could not "bear the thought of Winnebagos from Nebraska parked in Harvard Square." Nebraska!

Chapter 31

Practicing Law

Having never been engaged in the private practice of law, in 1966 I began at Paul, Weiss working in the one area I knew something about—government regulations and relations. By my second year, half my time was spent representing clients on relations with foreign governments, my interest in international matters having been enhanced by my participation in the Cuban missile crisis. Soon my practice was almost entirely international. My previous association with Kennedy helped me get appointments to see key decision makers around the world.

Often the legal issues in my assignments were only a small part of the challenge. I liked to think my trouble-shooting legal work on a global scale resembled the kind of work C. A. Sorensen did on a local scale in his early days as a young lawyer traveling around Nebraska. I found myself working on problems and projects of every variety and in countries of every type. As I flew over endless miles of jungle in Africa, it seemed to me a continent filled with infinite varieties of beauty, danger, opportunity, and peace, if man did not disturb it— just like the world itself. Like those bossy schoolboys who want to settle every schoolyard fight, I wanted to help smooth every international dispute and civil war. Of one fact I was certain—that was better done by law than by military force.

When I returned to New York from some little-known (in New York) country—like Macedonia or Fujairah—some of my colleagues would ask how deals could be made in such forbidding, far-off lands. Frequently I was warned, before landing in one place or another, that I would find it to be the most corrupt country I had ever seen, reminding me of my days on the campaign trail in 1956–1960, when JFK and I were constantly told in Kentucky, or Louisiana, or Arkansas, or Nevada, and elsewhere, "Oh, this is the most politically corrupt state you've ever seen."

During my years with Kennedy, I had learned to function on a few hours of sleep. I mistakenly thought those years of sleep deprivation were over when I began private practice. But one overnight flight often followed another. My sensitive stomach often made these long, sleepless trips even more uncomfortable. Although my Nebraska palate was accustomed to plain, bland, simple fare, I ate a variety of unidentifiable substances in Africa, China, and elsewhere, some even more unappetizing than the eyes of one crustacean I had declined to eat with JFK in Hawaii. I was offered fried ice cream in Singapore and baked porcupine in the Congo—the latter so fiery that I needed a liquid to douse the flames in my stomach, only to find that alcohol was fuel on that particular fire.

Within my narrow specialty, my practice thrived. I knew much less about other fields of law. Having been assigned to the firm's corporate department, for want of a better fit, I attended periodic departmental lunch meetings, often understanding comparatively little of the legal complexities of the work reported, wondering, in a clear case of what is known among psychologists as the "impostor syndrome," whether my ignorance would someday be exposed and lead to my ouster.

Other than those major firm clients whom I was able to assist abroad, I was cautious in accepting new matters. I once rejected a request that I intervene in Washington on behalf of a U.S. arms manufacturer, a good client of the firm, protesting that I would have neither comfort nor credibility presenting such a case. I declined to represent two convicted felons—one a politician, another a prominent New Yorker—who asked me to help them secure pardons. I declined an Israeli friend's request to represent the South African apartheid-created state of Bophuthatswana as a homeland for blacks. A liberal friend, then serving as an American public relations man for the Somoza dictatorship in Nicaragua, asked me to help secure U.S. congressional or executive branch approval for normalization of U.S.-Nicaraguan relations. I told him that I was unwilling to represent Somoza, but was willing to be retained by my friend to help his public relations firm understand what human rights failings would need to be corrected by Nicaragua before normalization was possible. He declined my offer, telling me later that a prominent Washington Democrat had taken the Somoza account.

Unfortunately, I never learned any foreign language. My fluently multilingual wife Gillian excused me by quoting Lady Churchill, who reportedly said: "My husband speaks only one language, but he speaks that one beautifully."

Because English by 1970 was increasingly becoming the basic language of international commerce, and where it was not, translators were available, my lack of foreign language skills posed few problems—except once in England, of all places. The African government with whom I was negotiating a mining contract was represented by an attractive young female solicitor in a London office. When she insisted that a clause that I wanted in the contract would merely cover an issue already covered by another clause in the draft, I replied, using an old American adage, that I believed in using, for safety's sake, "both belt and suspenders," not realizing why she blushed a deep purple, until—after the session—another British lawyer informed me that the word "suspenders" means a ladies' garter belt on that side of the Atlantic.

My most terrifying air travels included a trip with Gillian over the Andes from Argentina to Chile, when our plane encountered what the pilot later told us was a "clear air pocket," and dropped straight down a few thousand feet. The papers on my lap, like one passenger not buckled in, rose to the ceiling before falling to the floor. But I told Gillian not to bother picking up the loose pages, questioning whether that was a good use of what little time we might have left. I heard years later that that particular air route had been abandoned as too dangerous.

I felt unsafe in Angola, when the pilot of a chartered plane flying my client and me to the interior, for a meeting with rebel leader Jonas Savimbi, warned us, as we disembarked, to be back on board before dark, because both government and rebel forces sometimes shot at unidentified aircraft at night. When we returned to the relative safety of the capital, as my client and I stood outside our hotel before dawn, in preparation for a vigorous walk, we were startled when a dozing sentry dropped his automatic rifle, which clattered down the steps in our direction—fortunately without discharging.

In Ghana, my urgent need to see the minister of finance necessitated my interrupting him in a cabinet meeting in the castle, after which he introduced me and my client's local representative to a kindly, graying, grandfatherly man emerging from the meeting, who talked with me warmly. As we departed, the client's representative whispered that the late addition to our conversation was "a killer"—the president's chief of security, with a reputation for brutal enforcement of state law and order.

In Sierra Leone I took a break from negotiations, changed into swimming trunks, and walked to a beautiful beach—followed by a fully-clad and armed bodyguard.

I never carried a gun, nor felt the need for one; but they were often in evidence in other countries, both near and far. In Cuba my local host, a red-bearded professor from Columbia University, took me about in a car with what looked like, to my untrained eye, a machine gun on the backseat.

One Latin American president, wrongly accused in a *New York Times* article of receiving secret anti-Communist funds from the CIA, asked me to represent him in a lawsuit against the *Times*, noting that in his country the allegation amounted to an impeachable offense. To keep my visit with him secret, he arranged for his presidential limousine to meet my commercial flight at the bottom of the airplane ramp, whisk me away to his private home for a long talk, and return me the following day to the steps of my departing airliner, thereby altogether bypassing all customs, immigration, and other record of my ever having been in his country at that time. I did not get him a public retraction, but did obtain, for his own satisfaction, a private letter of apology.

In the newly independent, formerly Soviet Republic of Tajikistan in 1993, I was asked by the prime minister to help draft a new constitution for the country. Unfortunately, the president had a very different approach from the prime minister—so different that the latter soon became the former prime minister about the same time my proposed constitution was approved. During my first meeting with the prime minister in his office, with a civil war in progress, I heard a shot outside his window, followed by a shout—translated for me by the prime minister as "Halt!" I asked: "In this country, they shoot first and then cry 'Halt!'?" Earlier that afternoon, as my client and I were about to depart the government guest house to visit the prime minister, a black sedan roared around the corner, blocking our way. The client and I stayed in our car. Four uniformed, armed men emerged; then the president emerged, to bid us farewell—a gracious, if slightly unnerving expression of his hospitality.

Leaving Israel for Jordan, my driver from the U.S. consulate in Jerusalem parked his official car in the only shade on the Israeli side of the Allenby Bridge, to await the representative from the U.S. consulate in Amman to meet me halfway across the bridge for a "hand-over." Behind us came a voice: "Move the car please, you are in the line of fire." It was then that we spotted gunnery emplacements facing each other on either side of the bridge.

When a Venezuelan army general and I boarded his plane to fly to the interior, his mechanic informed him that all necessary engine checks had been completed and bid us a hearty farewell. "No," said the general, "you are coming with us." The surprised mechanic then said there were a few more checks he wanted to complete.

The deep impression that President Kennedy had made on other countries remained evident wherever I went around the globe. Foreign leaders all wanted to talk to me about the Kennedys. When I visited Israel with a client in 1966, former prime minister Ben-Gurion came over to my table in the hotel dining room, sat down, and proceeded to advise me on presidential campaign strategy for Robert Kennedy, which included as a first step meeting secretly with the Russians to find a solution to Vietnam.

Over the years, I also received many letters from presidents and prime ministers, expressing their admiration for John F. Kennedy. A typical example read: "I followed the career of John F. Kennedy with great interest, joy and eventually sadness. The model he set as a political leader is one I seek to follow."

Foreign leaders were not the only ones who attempted to emulate JFK. So did I. What I had learned from JFK was invaluable to me as an international lawyer—to listen and learn from leaders of other countries; to be cautious on matters of war and peace until I knew the case for each side and all the facts and alternatives; to recognize that cultural differences can lie at the heart of political, policy, even legal disagreements; to be flexible, curious, friendly with all; and to keep my hopes high but my expectations low regarding the results that can be achieved and the amount of time they will require.

While I made more trips to Africa than to any other continent, side trips on my business travels also took me and Gillian to Peru's Machu Picchu on a private railway car, stopping along the way to sample the wares of trackside vendors; I recall visiting La Paz, the world's highest capital city, and touring the ancient cities of Uzbekistan. I played tennis in Bonaire and Zaire, in Caracas and Contadora. Frequently I would doze off in an airport waiting room—all of which look alike the world over—and upon awakening be uncertain where I was. In early 1961 when I helped write the words in Kennedy's inaugural about the "peoples in the huts and villages across the globe struggling to break the bonds of mass misery," I had never seen them. Now I have, including homeless boys begging on the streets of Kinshasa, legless mine-field victims in Angola, and slum dwellers picking over the town garbage dump in the hills outside Caracas.

I have had the privilege to meet at least a hundred prime ministers, presidents, premiers, chancellors, kings, and queens on nearly every continent. One of them, the president of Bolivia, Gonzalo Sanchez de Lozada, had retained me to prepare a new charter for his party. That draft charter was termed by his opposition faction the "Statutos Sorensenos," which was not meant as a compliment. Many luminaries I met only casually—

Pierre Trudeau of Canada on a New York dance floor, François Mitterrand at the French consulate, Prince Sihanouk of Cambodia on an airplane, President Zia of Pakistan at an art museum, King Abdallah of Saudi Arabia at a formal audience in his palace.

Some of my acquaintances included the former foreign minister of a Latin American country, subsequently murdered in Washington; a Middle Eastern businessman whose mysterious disappearance I was asked to investigate; a Vietnamese refugee turned American banker; two United Nations officials from the Soviet Union, both believed to be KGB agents; a British businessman once barred from the United States on suspicion of being too close to China; an Iranian businessman-scholar and one of his thirty brothers, both of whom had to leave their fortunes, carpets, and antiques behind when they fled their country.

My status as a foreign visitor with some standing in the United States was sufficient to enable me to obtain meetings with dissidents without any fear of reprisal—Jews in the Soviet Union before glasnost, collaborators in Namibia before the end of apartheid, Tibetans in China who supported genuine autonomy, and a political independent in Ghana under Rawlings. I also met in my New York office with exiled dissidents from Haiti, Guyana, Congo-Brazzaville, and Ivory Coast.

In a talk to Paul, Weiss lawyers, I summarized my encounters with foreign leaders as follows:

Most impressive: Nelson Mandela of South Africa.

Most charismatic: Fidel Castro of Cuba.

Most corrupt: Mobutu Sese Seko of the Congo.

Most misjudged: Omar Torrijos of Panama.

Most secretive: Carlos Andres Perez of Venezuela.

Most intriguing: Anwar Sadat of Egypt.

Most ruthless: a three-way tie between Nicolae Ceauşescu of Romania, Sani Abacha of Nigeria, and Manuel Noriega of Panama.

Most visionary: David Ben-Gurion of Israel.

Most unlikely: Yasser Arafat of the Palestinian National Authority.

Most eloquent: Shimon Peres of Israel (at that time, foreign minister).

Most puzzling: Carlos Salinas of Mexico, whom I met both while he was in office and after he left under a cloud.

Best educated: President Festus Mogae of Botswana, an Oxford graduate.

Most royal: another tie—the president of Gabon, Omar Bongo, and the Emir of Fujairah.

Least royal: the president of Burundi and the president of Macedonia Kiro Gligorov.

Most flamboyant: President Niyazov of Turk-
   menistan, who offered to arrange a Turkmeni-
   stan wife for my happily married colleague. Also
   in this category was Prime Minister Charles
   Haughey of Ireland.

I did learn that not all dictators are visibly evil. At the
time I met Romania's Nicolae Ceauşescu, he had broken
with the Kremlin by recognizing Israel and professing
a desire for international relations with all; mild, soft-
spoken, he later proved to have been a monster. I was
less intimidated by the Latin American president who
hung a sign above his desk reading: "The greatest thief
is he who steals my time." When I met with the Congo's
Mobutu Sese Seko, who kept his pet leopard chained outside his front door (preparing, I remarked to a colleague,
for a local broadcast of *Eat the Press*), he was hailed by
the United States as the one man who could unify and
pacify that turbulent country, thereby keeping it out of
Moscow's orbit; but he later proved to be both a tyrant
and a thief on a grand scale.

When I was asked by President Mobutu, to persuade
World Bank president Robert McNamara to mediate the
government of Congo's dispute with the European mining giant whose assets it had expropriated, both parties
regretted my success. McNamara, whose recommended

settlement was not accepted by the Congolese government, never quite forgave me; and Mobutu called me in, curtly demanding to know under what authority I had "brought that man" to the Congo. When I reminded him that his minister of finance had relayed that message from Mobutu himself, the president shouted: "As our lawyer, you should have read our Constitution, and known that under the Constitution only I have authority here, not some minister!"

In 1983, when introducing Robert Mugabe of Zimbabwe at the Council on Foreign Relations, I expressed high hopes for his future; he was seen as the rising star of the new Africa; not now.

In Nigeria, in September 1995, I had begun advising General Sani Abacha, the last military dictator to rule that country, on a transition to civilian rule, when he asked me how to improve his relations with the United States. When I replied, "Free all political prisoners, and do not execute General Obasanjo," he responded with anger that this was none of America's business.

I told him that I was unwilling to lobby for his government in Washington but I proposed that I draft a memorandum to President Clinton's national security advisor setting forth my informal understanding of what positive steps the Nigerian head of state might take if assured the United States would reciprocate, enabling a limited dialogue to begin without loss of face on either side. What I "understood" would be forthcoming from Nigeria actually included more recommendations from me to the head of state than positions he had asked me to include; and my list of U.S. initiatives by way of reciprocity was similarly based more on my own recommendations to the Clinton White House than on any knowledge of U.S. flexibility.

First I had to get out of Nigeria. My Israeli client's plane flew me from Abuja to the Lagos International Airport. My KLM midnight flight to Europe was finally ready to depart, but I was blocked from boarding by two uniformed officials who led me back to the terminal. They interrogated me on "security grounds," and I discovered their concern—the private plane on which I'd arrived had been "parked" in the spot reserved for the president. I complimented them on their alertness, and rushed to make my plane. In any event, before my assignment could be implemented, General Abacha died in the arms of one or more female companions; civilian rule was reestablished; General Obasanjo came out of prison and became president.

On a consultation visit to Angola, the government facilitated my entry, but provided me with no Currency Declaration Form in the process. Upon leaving several days later, I found that I could not depart the country without that form, despite my assurance to an armed functionary that I had not had occasion during my brief stay to change any American dollars into Angolan currency. He asked to examine my wallet; and, as he did so, asked whether I would be coming back to his country. Hoping to sound gracious, I replied affirmatively. "Good, you can get this [wallet] back then," he replied. Fortunately a passing government official recognized me and intervened; I retrieved my wallet and left.

One of my most satisfying and largest projects was almost accidental. An American friend of the African National Congress, headed by Nelson Mandela, asked on behalf of the ANC if I would assist in negotiating ANC's contract with a Washington political fund-raiser to prepare for South Africa's first free election in 1994. I accepted, adding that, for such a good cause and brief assignment, our firm would provide its services pro bono—no fee, only expenses.

I found that neither the intended consultant nor anyone else saw any prospect of raising sufficient money in the U.S. for a South African election in the time that remained, inasmuch as U.S. law prohibited corporations from contributing to foreign elections in expectation of business. I recommended the establishment of a new

American foundation on South African voter education, the South Africa Free Elections Fund (SAFE) to
which contributions would be tax-deductible. Chaired
by two extraordinary individuals, Irish business executive Anthony O'Reilly and my Paul, Weiss partner, the
late Judge A. Leon Higginbotham, SAFE proved to be
a major factor in the South Africa election. It raised millions of dollars; used hundreds of thousands of dollars'
worth of free legal services from Paul, Weiss lawyers,
led by my associate Chris Merkling; and financed extensive voter and poll worker training that proved indispensable in South Africa's historic first free election.

When I first met O'Reilly, who had already contributed $100,000 to the cause, he asked me how successful
we had been raising money. Having been earlier advised by the ANC of another American business executive, Dwayne Andreas, willing to contribute the first
$100,000 if I would call him personally, which I had, I
answered O'Reilly truthfully: "It's coming along very
well—the average contribution so far is $100,000."

On July 1, 1993, Mandela came to Paul, Weiss for
SAFE's first formal board meeting, and held a press
conference when our meeting concluded. Consider his
answer to a softball question from a reporter: "Mr.
Mandela, how do you feel about Philadelphia making
you and South African President de Klerk co-awardees

of the Liberty Bell prize, when he was part of the regime that imprisoned you for twenty-seven years?" Mandela quietly replied: "I have no problem with that. The people in Philadelphia must make their own decision. Right now, President de Klerk and I need each other, and we will continue to be bound together until we go our separate ways."

The South African Free Election Fund started at Paul, Weiss with no office, no staff, and no funds less than one year before the election. By Election Day, a tremendous turnout and an extraordinarily low percentage of spoiled ballots proved that SAFE's mission had been accomplished. Few endeavors in my own career, in either the public or private sector, have made me more proud.

At O'Reilly's Bahamas estate the following New Year's Day 1994, I explained to Mandela why the tax-exempt SAFE funds could be used only for voter education and registration efforts and not for political campaigns and party activities. He immediately recognized that the ANC would be the indirect beneficiary of this, acknowledging that even he—an educated lawyer—did not know how to mark a ballot, having never voted. We later learned how great a challenge we faced when, in an early test ballot, most new South African voters thought that putting an "X" next to a candidate's name meant crossing him off the list.

On our flight back to New York on O'Reilly's private jet, Mandela and I had a long, wide-ranging conversation, discussing everything from Jackie Onassis and Elizabeth Taylor (both of whom impressed him), to the singer Michael Jackson (was he guilty of sex abuse charges? Mandela asked), to his twenty-seven years' imprisonment and his family life. He told me that his granddaughter had recently refused to go to college, as he had urged, because she insisted that she was the only one who knew his needs and could take care of him; and he confessed that, in his heart, he was ambivalent about her decision.

He told me of his love and admiration for his father, who died when Nelson was a child, and how he sought as a young man to imitate with powder or chalk the gray patch in his father's hair, but was not happy when his own hair whitened years later. He said it had been hard to break his childhood habit of two meals a day—a kind of cornmeal mush or stew in the evening, and leftover mush the following morning, when, depending on the weather, it might have begun to spoil. Yet he found most of the prison food even more inedible. Lean and fit at age seventy-five, he had given up jogging and tennis for long walks.

He mentioned the refusal of his cellmate Andimba

Toivo ya Toivo to face any white visitor, even sympa-
thizers, and was intrigued to learn from me that Toivo
ya Toivo had subsequently married a white American
civil rights lawyer who bore him twins.

He also told me of his fund-raising trips on behalf
of the ANC upon his release from prison, in which this
staunch devotee of democracy found that African dictators had one advantage—they could authorize and provide a substantial government contribution to the ANC
in a matter of minutes, while democracies required days
if not weeks of parliamentary debate.

For providing the PLO with a picture of him em-
bracing Arafat and a statement that South Africa was
a possible example of peaceful reconciliation that the
Israelis and Palestinians could follow, he told me, he
had been attacked by his longtime allies in the South
African Jewish community, including even his former
defense attorney, who said he was now sorry that he
had defended him. Mandela then insisted on meeting
all his Jewish South African critics as a group, explaining to them that the ANC needed to welcome support
from wherever it came; that he valued his longtime alliance with South Africa's Jews, who had been a key to
ANC success; but that he could not avoid noting that
Israel had supplied arms to the apartheid government

of South Africa. They were not wholly mollified, he said, in contrast with U.S. Jewish leaders with whom he had held a similar and more successful meeting in Geneva.

During his July 1993 visit to the United States, he told me, the Chicago police had found a man in an apartment overlooking the site of his talk, with a rifle and telescopic lens. He was grateful that South African president de Klerk always passed along to him South African government intelligence reports on assassination plots against him. He realized, he added, in words reminiscent of JFK, that he could not prevent all snipers because he must campaign in crowds, including in violent areas, but he hoped to get a special car with a bulletproof bubble top and bomb-resistant structure.

He regarded his relationship with de Klerk as both close and distant, and the man as both principled and artful. Mandela said he had been outraged when, at the constitutional talks with all party leaders, it was agreed that all would speak in alphabetical order, but that de Klerk could speak last as president. Mandela accepted and persuaded other ANC leaders to accept; then de Klerk used that rebuttal-free opportunity to attack the ANC.

He also told me how in Oslo, at the time they received

their joint Nobel Peace Prize, a pro-ANC crowd of Norwegians surged below their hotel window, and both he and the de Klerks greeted them; but when the crowd broke into the ANC national anthem, the de Klerks had ostentatiously chatted throughout, and Mandela had to mollify an outraged crowd ready to storm the hotel.

He liked George H. W. Bush, who he said was the first head of state to call him upon his release from prison; but he had no regard for Ronald Reagan, who had once alleged that there was no true believer in democracy in Africa, then later amended that to say he had met one—Zulu chief Mangosuthu G. Buthelezi, Mandela's principal rival, who, Mandela believed, sought guaranteed regional rule without being elected to the post and without cooperating with those who were elected.

My first trip to Cuba, in April 1977 (three months after my nomination to be director of central intelligence was withdrawn), was arranged through my friends in the government of Panama, which had close relations with Havana. I cleared it with the Carter White House, which gave me a list of possible U.S. objectives to secure, including the release of a particular political prisoner. The trip was undertaken on behalf of a variety of clients, including the Tempelsmans, who hoped to use the Cuban connection to make an arrangement on diamond sales in Angola, where Cuban troops were assisting the anti-Western-supported forces. I also explored the possibility that Soviet oil tankers on their way to Cuba might use my client Northville's transshipment port in Bonaire, but received no response to that inquiry. For his part, Cuban president Castro asked that U.S. agents not interfere with his ability to fish undisturbed at his favorite site.

At our first meeting, Castro told me that Cuban transmitters could steal signals from Florida television stations, enabling Cuban citizens to receive American movies, including *Jaws*. But that raised a high-level policy question, he said: Would showing the movie to the Cuban people reduce their enjoyment of the beaches that season, or was reduction of beach congestion a good thing? Such are the high-level decisions facing Communist dictators.

When I then announced my wish to present him with a copy of my book *Kennedy*, he beamed and said: "Why didn't you say so all this time?" Because, I explained, I could not get a word in.

When I lunched with Cuba's director of sports to discuss the possibility of Cuba's prizewinning heavyweight boxer making an appearance under the auspices of Paul, Weiss client Madison Square Garden, Fidel suddenly walked in and joined our table, joking with my host about the government basketball league rivalry between the teams from the Sports Authority and the president's office. The director replied good-naturedly that the president was not above using his official status—and his height—to intimidate the referee.

On my second trip, a few months later, I accompanied Continental Grain negotiators hoping to make a future arrangement on bartering Cuban sugar for U.S. corn, soybeans, and other agricultural commodities, provided a U.S. government license could be obtained. The U.S. Treasury Department would later raise questions of whether both my client and I had come dangerously close to violating the Cuban embargo and thus the Trading with the Enemy Act, by discussing potentially actual, not merely future, deals. But knowing the law, we had been careful.

On my second visit, I was invited to meet with Castro to discuss the book I'd given him at our first meeting. Wearing fatigues, cigar in hand (that cigar was no longer in evidence when I saw him in 2002, after his health had declined), occasionally correcting his translator's English, he discussed with me my book's account of the Cuban missile crisis. He was scornful of the Soviets for not publicly announcing the missile emplacement, for lying about it, for not informing him about U.S. U–2 spy plane flights over Cuba, for not firing at those planes from the outset, and for not insisting that Soviet removal of the missiles be conditioned on an end to the U.S. military base on Guantanamo Bay, an end to the U.S. economic embargo, and an end to the covert raids being sponsored by the CIA at that time—in short, an intriguing discussion of the crisis from two totally different perspectives. Our meeting began at midnight and continued until 4 A.M., whereupon Castro—partly for the irony of it all—sent me to a new hotel on the Bay of Pigs.

I next saw him when he came to the United States in 1995 for the United Nations' fiftieth anniversary commemoration. JFK Jr.—then the publisher of the new magazine *George*—asked me to seek an interview appointment for him, which I did. Fidel replied, "Why not?" and the interview took place in Cuba not long after.

Later, in talks with the Cuban ambassador to the United Nations and another Cuban diplomat in Washington, I discussed the possibility of an independent initiative to explore normalization of diplomatic, political, and economic relations between the two countries. The opposition to such talks in this country seemed largely emotional and political, generated by anti-Castro hard-liners, Cuban-Americans in Miami, who were increasingly outnumbered by members of the American business community who had an economic stake in opening new channels and markets. Even the Cuban exile community was beginning to include a younger generation less opposed to normalization; meanwhile more Cuban-American claimants of expropriated property were realizing that only through talks could any serious possibility of compensation materialize.

Another Latin American mission was my participation in an unofficial delegation, headed by Mayor Ed Koch of New York City, touring Central America to monitor or facilitate (it was never clear which) the implementation of Costa Rican President Oscar Arias's "Peace Plan," which was designed to end the externally guided civil conflict in the region. I was not surprised, but saddened to learn on that trip that both sides in the Sandinista-Contra struggle in Nicaragua had their own human rights "protection" organization, each funded by U.S. sources. One beleaguered Nicaraguan centrist asked me, "Why don't you and the Russians take your conflict to some desert island and leave us out?"

In Managua, Nicaragua, where our group attended a Sandinista stadium rally, Mayor Koch was invited to mount the stage where the Sandinista leader was about to speak. As a friend, I advised him not to do so, cautioning that he was certain to be embraced in Latino fashion, and a resulting photograph of that hug on the cover of the New York *Daily News* might harm his political career. I also advised him to avoid drinking the water or any drinks with ice; his subsequent reliance wholly on beer caused his New York doctor a week later to term him the only man who ever gained weight traveling in Latin America.

When Koch discovered, as we were about to leave Managua for Costa Rica, that his business shoes and socks were inaccessible in a suitcase loaded aboard our plane, I assured him that he could wear tennis sneakers with no socks for an informal visit in the office of President Arias. After that meeting, when he and all the other members of our delegation had left Costa Rica for Puerto Rico, President Arias kindly invited me to dinner, where he asked in all seriousness whether Mayor Koch's footwear in his office that morning had been a "deliberate sign of disrespect." I assured him it was not.

Ed Koch was an irrepressibly delightful traveling companion, but not a skilled diplomat. I told him that his diplomacy on that journey had included both high and low points: his high point came when he presented New York Yankee uniforms for the Sandinista president's sons in that baseball-crazed country, only to be asked by the president (who had led the crowd the previous night in an anti-USA chant) why the mayor had not brought a Yankee uniform for him, adding, "I'm a Yankee fan, too," to which the mayor deftly replied: "Last night you weren't."

When I first met General Omar Torrijos, the Panamanian leader, at a client meeting in 1971, and asked him about the prospects for a canal treaty, he replied: "Either the United States agrees to acceptable terms on a new treaty this year or else!" I asked: "Or else what?" He said: "Or else we start down the Ho Chi Minh Trail [i.e., guerrilla terrorism]." I said: "You have better options than that." When he asked what they were, I put on my lawyer's hat: "When I get back to my office, I'll write you a long letter with some options." I did, he was pleased, and that began a long friendship.

But my real adventures in Panama began five years later, in late November 1976, when the chairman of my petroleum storage and distribution client, Northville Industries, my good friend Harold Bernstein, called me to point out that day's newspaper report that the U.S. government would not permit the export of Alaska North Slope oil flowing through the Alaska Pipeline.

"So?" I replied. "That means that all that oil must go to the lower 48 states because they have no need for it in Alaska and cannot use it all on the West Coast," he said. "So?" I replied. "So," answered Harold, "that means supertankers unwilling to take the cost and risk of traveling around the Cape of Good Hope and back up to the U.S. East Coast will need a transshipment port on the Pacific coast of Panama to transfer oil into tankers able to traverse the Panama Canal." "That is a great idea," I said. "What are you doing about it?" "I'm calling you, that's what I'm doing," he said.

The previous day, at the request of General Torrijos, I had informally briefed his assistant, Señor Vellarde, on the leaders and leanings of the incoming Carter administration, so I told Harold I could help. I reached Vellarde in his Washington hotel room, asked him to come back to see me, and briefed him the next day on the opportunity for both Panama and Northville created by the export limitation on Alaskan oil.

Ten days later he reported that the major oil companies were "sniffing around," and that my client and I should come to Panama as soon as possible to secure our position. Harold's assistant and I were taken to a meeting with Panamanian minister of commerce Juan Sosa and others on the island of Contadora. Soon the rest of the group flew back to the Panamanian mainland, leaving me sitting alone on the back porch of a lovely island hacienda. As darkness fell, General Torrijos and his interpreter appeared, and we settled down for a long night of beer, shrimp, and talk. I related the tale of Northville's humble origins, with a horse and wagon from which the Bernstein brothers' father, Sam, had distributed ice in the summer and coal in the winter.

The general was intrigued by the proposed project, and even took out a map to show me possible sites for a deepwater port. I was wary when he specified by name the Panamanian lawyer we should retain; but attorney Jaime Arias turned out to be the finest lawyer in Panama. The general had been reputed to have an insatiable appetite for beautiful women and alcohol, and each round of Panamanian beer added to my apprehension, wholly unwarranted, about what other challenge I might face that night on behalf of my client.

When our initial round of negotiations with Panama concluded, we had effectively outmaneuvered giant oil companies and established what is still the principal facility transshipping Alaskan oil to destinations on the U.S. Atlantic coast.

Coincidentally, negotiations between the United States and Panama over the future of the Panama Canal were continuing with difficulty, under ferocious attacks from the American right, which was determined not to "give away" the canal, which, as one U.S. senator pointed out in all seriousness, "We stole . . . fair and square." My own successful negotiations for Northville were nearly concluded one day when a meeting in Panama City was interrupted by a summons to meet with General Torrijos immediately at his hideaway in a northern Panama military base, Farrejon. When I arrived, the general was planning an early press conference, to renounce the canal treaty negotiations and denounce the United States. He had been enraged by a White House background briefing in which Special Ambassador Sol Linowitz reportedly reassured Americans that the Panama Canal would be safe because the U.S. military, even under the pending new draft treaty, could always intervene in the event of any danger. Torrijos was especially infuriated by the use of the word "intervene," which Linowitz later swore he had not used. When I suggested that the U.S. government might be willing to retract the reported remark, Torrijos scoffed: "Empires never retract." When I suggested he protest to the American ambassador, he dismissed him as "a messenger boy." When I suggested he request a meeting with the White House, he insisted he would not "crawl on his knees," and that his students would be "in the streets with anger" upon returning from their vacation.

He welcomed my suggestion that I call the White House, and I accepted his offer to use the telephone next to his bed, even as he added: "Remember, more than two governments will be listening." I reached President Carter's national security advisor, Zbigniew Brzezinski, through the White House switchboard midday on Saturday, and carefully explained the situation to him. Speaking with equal care, he stated that he understood and would look into what could be done.

The general invited me to stay for lunch. The special phone at his side rang one or two hours later. The Panamanian ambassador to Washington, Gabriel Lewis—later foreign minister and my good friend—was calling to say that a bulletin had been posted in the White House press room stating that the previous day's briefing was speculation and did not represent official U.S. policy, a one-sentence statement that received no attention in the press. It was enough for Panama. The general flashed me a thumbs-up sign, gave telephone instructions calling off his press conference, and said to me: "Forget your other work, stay here and work with me." I gently explained why I was not prepared to move to Panama.

Neither then, previously, nor subsequently did I have any role in the Panama Canal treaty negotiations. Wholly unbeknownst to me, on that same weekend, the

U.S. intelligence community had obtained word of the proposed Panamanian press conference, its subject matter and cancellation, and the Senate Intelligence Committee had set out to discover an explanation, with those on the Republican right suspecting that some secret deal had been hatched, under which the United States, according to a UPI report, offered major concessions.

When these critics later learned of the Sorensen-Brzezinski telephone call, for which the White House tape had been accidentally discarded, they were certain that was the smoking gun proving their suspicions. Upon being interviewed by the Senate committee staff, both Brzezinski and I explained that our conversation and my presence in Panama had nothing to do with any such deal or with the treaty negotiations. Long before the committee interview, I received a telephone inquiry from my friend, the *New York Times* conservative columnist William Safire—who frequently received leaks from conservative senators—asking me about the phone call. I explained its circumstances to him, and he accepted my explanation.

When my role was explained on the floor of the Senate in a rare closed session, Republican Senator Malcolm Wallop of Wyoming grumbled that "the lack of sworn testimony went to the credibility of the substance . . ."

(i.e., Zbig or I could have lied); committee chairman Birch Bayh, one of my defenders during my earlier CIA nomination, replied: "I have no reason to believe that Ted Sorensen is trying to mislead us." In the weeks that followed, Brzezinski and I signed sworn affidavits. No secret deal was ever uncovered, the canal treaty was ratified by a one-vote margin, and I received a form letter from President Carter thanking me for my "participation in this deliberative process."

Graham Greene, an admirer of Torrijos, was certain that the plane crash that killed the general was no accident; but Panama today accepts the verdict of history that it was. Shortly before his death, I had gone to see Torrijos about a new enterprise for Northville, and he memorably replied: "No. Your present project is successful. If you're good at growing lemons, don't try anything new—not even lemonade."

I had started working with the general on that project in 1976 on behalf of Harold Bernstein, the president of Northville. Thirty years later, I accompanied Harold Bernstein's son, Jay, then president of Northville, to a meeting with Torrijos's son, Martin, then President of Panama. We met in the home of Gabriel Lewis's son, Samuel, then Vice President of Panama. Only my role was basically unchanged.

. . .

Early in July 1976, I received a call from the Egyptian ambassador in Washington saying that President Anwar Sadat wanted me to come immediately to Egypt. Later that month, I met with President Sadat in his grand villa in Alexandria, which he preferred, he said, to Cairo, because he did not like the stuffiness of the city and the easy access to him there by bureaucrats. I found him to be a man of enormous charisma, vitality, eloquence, and self-confidence. He had aspects to his personality that some might regard as vain, qualities akin to those of a flamboyant actor, and not totally unknown in presidents in my own country. Whatever the subject, he had comparatively little interest in details, preferring the big picture, and was given to dramatic statements and sometimes rather quick decisions—characteristics that can bring a chief executive difficulty but can also result in visionary accomplishments.

President Sadat had summoned me because he was engaged in writing his memoirs and wanted me to represent him in marketing the non-Arabic language rights. I agreed, insisting that I would seek the best publishers, regardless of religion. He asked whether I thought Jewish publishers would be willing to handle the book. I assured him they would if it looked like a successful book; my certainty was subsequently shaken when a Jewish Paul, Weiss associate felt that he might be uncomfortable working with me on the contract. Ultimately, one of the best publishers and editors in New York, Michael Bessie of Harper and Row, who also happened to be Jewish, made the winning bid, and traveled with me in November to Cairo to meet the president, with whom he got along famously. Jimmy Carter having just been elected president, Sadat commented to us somewhat caustically on the number of American travelers who all claimed to be representatives sent by Carter to find out what Sadat's attitude would be on pending issues.

On that first trip in July, as we sat talking in his beautiful home on the Mediterranean, served tea by a liveried butler, having explored the parameters of a publishing contract, Sadat's aide cleared his throat nervously: "There is the matter of Mr. Sorensen's fee." Sadat feigned surprise. Waving his hand grandly in those luxurious surroundings, he said to me: "Ah, but how can I pay you? I have no money." I assured him that our firm could arrange to deduct its fee from the large publisher's advance I hoped to get for him.

The following year, he made his historic trip to Jerusalem, adding that bold initiative as an epilogue to his book, which proved to be a success in the United States and thirteen other countries outside the Arab world. It was a best-seller in Egypt, but not in the rest of the Arab world, where one of his critics said it belonged on the fiction rather than nonfiction list. Sadat had told me early in our 1976 discussions that it was his intention to donate the lion's share of his book proceeds to the village in which he was born, Mit Abul Kum, and the rest to his wife's favorite charity for the rehabilitation of wounded Egyptian war veterans.

After the historic breakthrough in Jerusalem, and then another with Carter and Israeli Prime Minister Begin at Camp David, there was interest in the television and film rights to the book, which ultimately went to a somewhat flamboyant show business character, who assured Sadat's aide and me that he would take care not to have a Jewish actor portraying President Sadat. After Sadat's assassination, this same individual called me to say that he had not previously been able to sell the rights to the film, partly because it needed a dramatic ending—and now it had one. This gives you some idea of his sensitivity. I do not know what happened to either this man or his movie.

Sadat's aide and amanuensis, Dr. Rashad Rushdy,

was one of the most cultured men I ever met, a play-wright, author, and choreographer as well as head of the Egyptian Academy of the Arts and advisor and assistant to the president for cultural affairs. He told me one memorable anecdote—that he had submitted a play during the Nasser years, which the censor refused to approve. Finally, when Rushdy pressed him, the censor said the last six lines could be interpreted as lacking confidence in the future of Egypt. Rushdy said: "I'll change the last six lines." He did, the play was produced, and Rushdy instructed the actress who delivered those watered-down closing six lines to deliver them with great irony, and then to fall down dead. There was nothing the censor could do about that performance.

Having first retained me to represent him on his memoirs, President Sadat later asked me to formulate in practical terms a plan to realize his vision of a joint religious shrine on Mount Sinai to all three faiths that regarded it as sacred. I learned a lot about the laws and likelihood of fund-raising in many parts of the world, and presented to him at length the measures I thought he should authorize. He nodded, puffing on his pipe, and when I finished, sat quietly for a moment and said to Rushdy: "That's what is so wonderful about the

United States of America." "You mean American lawyers?" asked his aide. "No, no," said Sadat, "I mean their ability to organize these intricate matters." Getting the agreement of the three faiths was not easy. Getting agreement *within* each of their own ranks was impossible. At the time I talked with him, he thought that division within the ranks of Islam—primarily Sunni and Shia—would be the least problem; but that turned out to be the biggest.

When I saw him in Washington in September 1981, we talked about progress on his second book. The first had been called *In Search of Identity*, and the second was to be called *In Search of Peace*. The rights to that book had also been deeded by him as a gift to his village. That was the last time I saw him. Security was not one of Sadat's obsessions. It was a subject I once raised with him in a very indirect way. Again he gave me that easy, expansive wave: "I walked the streets of Cairo the entire length of the Shah's funeral procession. No other Arab leader could do anything of the kind."

In fact, my brother Tom, who was a Middle East expert and Arabist, had been cautioning me for some time that Sadat was not as popular or successful at home as he seemed abroad, and that he might not be president for very long.

. . .

In January 1995, after the Oslo Accords between the Israelis and the Palestinians had suggested the location of a "free trade industrial zone" on the border between Gaza and Israel, the United Nations Development Program asked me to travel to the area to jumpstart the project by drafting a concept paper or even a memorandum of understanding for the two parties to negotiate. The task was to develop an "industrial zone" that could provide jobs for the increasingly unemployed Palestinians, whose living standard was falling dangerously low, increasing restless resentment and violence, and at the same time provide less expensive labor for Israeli companies that did not want Palestinian workers coming into Israeli territory and had shut them out whenever tension rose.

Upon arriving, I was struck by the many contrasts— the ancient city of Jerusalem, still one of the most beautiful cities in the world, and the dilapidated condition of Gaza City, its streets flooded—presumably with sewage, because there had been no rain; reports of nightly shootings, and the constant sight of men bearing weapons. There were contrasts within Gaza itself. Across the street from the dingy homes of Palestinians were the

shining Israeli settlements, modern apartment buildings with greenery, guarded by Israeli forces, although
joint Israeli-Palestinian patrols moved about elsewhere.
The sight helped me understand something of the resentment that fueled the continuous violence there.

Despite warm respect on both sides for the skilled
UN emissary Terje Larsen of Norway, who accompanied me, the UN itself was not beloved or fully trusted.
I heard warnings that driving at night was dangerous,
even in UN-marked vehicles. I also heard rumors that
there would be "fireworks tonight." When a United
Nations car took me from Gaza back to Jerusalem that
night, a World Bank official warned me that displeasure
with the UN on both sides in the Palestinian-Israeli
dispute, then boiling up again, could make that car a
target of either side.

Traveling both to and from Jerusalem, we encountered numerous Israeli police checkpoints, reminding
me of my earlier passage through Checkpoint Charlie at the Berlin Wall. Although I learned in Israel of
a remarkable number of contacts, even cooperation,
between mid-level officials in Israel and their counterparts in the Palestinian Authority, that kind of cross-
border respect did not always extend to those at lower
levels. When standing at the entrance to the Temple
Mount mosque, one of the two holiest Islam landmarks,

I was dismayed to see an Israeli soldier, guarding the inner courtyard, casually toss his cigarette butt on holy ground.

During my visit to the region, I had productive meetings on both sides with intelligent and supportive officials, including the Palestinian minister of planning, a graduate of the Wharton School in Philadelphia, and Shimon Peres, always eloquent and determined, but more weary and gloomy than usual after another car bombing. He favored the UNDP project: "I don't want to be responsible for Palestinian poverty—we have enough of our own."

My mission required a long session with Palestinian leader Yasser Arafat. Because he was deemed to be in constant danger of assassination, his aides insisted that our discussion take place away from windows. "Should we sit on the floor?" Ambassador Larsen asked. When Gaza's unreliable electrical power system failed during our meeting, no one in the room spoke or moved from his chair for those few minutes of darkness.

Weary of repeated studies, missions, and proposals ultimately blocked by the Israelis anyway, Arafat was suspicious that I was representing the United States government, with whom he was then feuding over some perceived slight. At the time, his word was not trusted by either Western or Arab officials. He was also indignant over Israeli charges that the perpetrator of the latest car bombing was hiding in Gaza, whose police, Israelis alleged, had made no serious effort to find him. "Even I have on occasion hidden successfully in Gaza, where everybody knows me," Arafat said to me. Throughout our discussion, he kept one eye on his television set, which was showing reruns of the old American television series about a dolphin, *Flipper.* Ambassador Larsen later told me not to be offended, that he had been subjected to the same experience with children's cartoons.

At the end of my meeting with Arafat, I told him that his decision was important, and recited to him JFK's favorite poem about the bullfighter, not the bullfight critics, being the only one in the arena who "knows." He laughed, escorted me hand-in-hand through his outer offices to my car, where he gave me a close hug and kiss before I departed. Fortunately, there were no cameras present to record that embrace.

Identifying the correct form of address for Arafat was complicated. The Israelis would not call him "president," which might indicate he headed a "government," which might indicate a "state." So he was "chairman" of the Palestinian Liberation Organization, not the Palestinian National Authority. On such important points, my mission ultimately foundered, as did negotiations conducted after my departure, when the Israelis decided that one word in my concept paper implied the existence of a "state," and the Palestinians would not yield on that one word. Nor did it help that Arafat was skilled in playing his feuding ministers off against each other, making PLO approval of my paper more difficult—if one minister supported it, another automatically opposed it.

When I arrived at Tel Aviv Airport at the end of my stay to fly home on El Al Airlines, I was interviewed by an Israeli security officer, who asked with whom I had met during my trip. Knowing that the answer "Yasser Arafat" might delay my return trip for hours, I truthfully replied: "Most of my meetings here were held in the offices of the Israeli Foreign Ministry." I was waved aboard.

I have had my share of Middle Eastern intrigue. Upon mounting the platform to deliver a public lecture in Tel Aviv in 1966, I noticed on the lectern a plain white —envelope addressed to me. The letter read:

Dear Sir! I am from Russia, few weeks. The affairs I want to speak with you about is more important than Penkowsky [a Soviet officer spying for the U.S. and UK executed as a traitor in 1963]. *This* hour, *this* minute in your hands, maybe, is the key to the Kremlin. I am in a brown single-breasted suit, in brown spectacles, and with *Time* in my left hand.

After the lecture, I found him at the exit, and we went to my room to talk. He made an impassioned plea that I obtain U.S. government help in arranging for the departure from the Soviet Union of three friends who would bring with them a treasure trove of confidential documents from the files of a former Soviet foreign minister. Upon my return to New York, I arranged through Mac Bundy to relay the information and request to a high CIA official. I heard nothing more about it.

I have also had my share of Middle Eastern frustrations. On the evening of December 6, 1979, an individual of perhaps German or Austrian origin, allegedly with addresses in Tyrol, Sharjah, Switzerland, and Egypt, tried to reach Senator Ted Kennedy with the claim that he was an intermediary who could settle the then-raging dispute that had imprisoned a number of American diplomats as hostages in the American embassy in Teheran.

Senator Kennedy referred him to me, and he entered my office well after normal business hours, dressed in a flowing cloak. He introduced himself with an Arabic surname, Khalifa, and showed me a photograph of himself seated at the feet of the Iranian leader, the Ayatollah Khomeini, to whom, he asserted, he was an advisor. Khalifa wanted Senator Ted or his personal representative (me) to accompany him to the appropriate neutral international location, where "we will release" one hostage "to him personally"—a move that, he predicted, would assure Kennedy's election as president the following year. Saying that he would call later to see what I was able to arrange, he vanished into the night. The next day, I wrote to Mr. Khalifa emphasizing that Senator Kennedy, like all Americans, wanted all the hostages released—not just one. The hostages were finally released on January 20, 1981, as a result of intermediation by the Algerian government—the Iranians having refused to release them until Jimmy Carter was no longer president. Both the U.S. State Department and the White House had been frustrated by a number of false intermediaries and phantom proposals. I believe my visitor was one of them.

Not all clients prove in the end to be as honest as they initially portray themselves to be. For a friend acting as a business advisor to an influential Saudi princess, in administering her vast business empire, I provided a number of practical and legal services until, to his profound embarrassment, she proved to be neither Saudi nor a princess nor influential nor presiding over a vast business empire.

In 1967 I made the first of my many trips to Moscow, combining on that trip business meetings—with, among others, veteran Soviet Foreign Trade Minister Patolichev—and a vacation tour of Russia with my sons Eric, Steve, and Phil. We visited my maternal grandparents' hometown of Chernigov in the Ukraine, Yalta (the site of an historic World War II Allied conference), and the cultural capital, St. Petersburg (then called Leningrad).

In Moscow, we stayed in the historic National Hotel, across from Red Square. For an intercultural experience worth writing a magazine article about—as intended— my two older sons spent several days at a "Pioneers'" youth camp where they readily made friends with young Communists around the Ping-Pong table.

Near the end of our visit, a Soviet functionary, who had solicitously befriended us throughout the visit, invited us to go fishing on a lake near the dacha outside Moscow used (he said) by the Soviet foreign ministry.

His deputy came along and divided the group into two boats, the deputy and my three sons in one, and the two "seniors" in the other. It was a "fishing" trip, all right. Not long after our boat embarked, Viktor began to talk to me about the importance of our remaining in touch, for the sake of our friendship and better relations between the two superpowers. Soon he was suggesting that, by remaining in touch, we could improve understanding between our countries, and he could gain clearer insights into American policy. I finally and firmly said: "Viktor, I am sure you know I cannot give you any confidential information." The conversation drifted to other subjects.

The next day, as the boys and I packed for our trip home, he called and asked that we talk immediately. When he arrived, I wanted to continue packing as we talked, but he insisted that our conversation take place out in the hall, not in my room. I do not know whether the room was bugged, or whether he had been reprimanded by his superiors for approaching me so bluntly the day before. In the hall, he said: "You know that yesterday I was not asking you to do anything illegal in your country." "Viktor," I said with a smile, "I know you would never do such a thing," and returned to my room to pack.

. . .

Perhaps my proudest legacy is the number of young
men and women who worked closely with me at Paul,
Weiss before pursuing distinguished careers of their
own, in public service and private enterprise, in the
United Nations, the International Court System, multilateral banks, development funds, and the great foundations. I am proud of them all and am still in touch
with most of them. On May 7, 1995, I had a wonderful
surprise when Gillian invited many of those still in New
York to our apartment to celebrate my sixty-seventh
birthday.

My selection of a firm led by such giants of the law as
Simon Rifkind and Arthur Liman, a firm famed for its
pro bono and public interest representations, and for
the superb intellect of its lawyers, is another example of
my good luck. It was not a stuffy Wall Street firm. Not
every client was 100 percent pure, not every case was
won, not every long night of drudgery was filled with
fun. I made errors of judgment in both selecting and
advising clients. Nor was the commitment to the public interest uniform throughout the ranks of all part-

ners for all forty-two years. I have never pretended that the private practice of law was as exciting as my eleven years with Kennedy; but it was challenging, constantly changing, immensely satisfying, and, more importantly, fun, an unending adventure, full of tall tales and larger-than-life personalities.

On many trips abroad I was accompanied by Gillian, Juliet, my sons Eric, Steve, and Phil, or all of the above. A business trip to Peru included a side trip to Machu Picchu; a meeting in Cairo followed a vacation on the Upper Nile. A lecture tour in New Zealand—which the travel agent said could be reached on the other side of the world by flying in either direction from New York— turned into a round-the-world journey with my sons when they were teenagers. Negotiations in Panama were followed by a vacation on Contadora Island, where I had first met General Torrijos. Highlights of three African trips included visits to game parks, a wonderful family vacation comparable only to a later family adventure whitewater rafting in the western United States down the Salmon, Toulame, and Colorado Rivers. A business deal in Newfoundland was negotiated in the Premier's fishing cottage on the Gander River. Lots of fun—and, in Yogi Berra's words, it's not over until it's over.

It was not all work and no play.

Chapter 32

My Continuing
Involvement in Politics

Senator Robert F. Kennedy's
1968 Presidential Campaign

Not surprisingly, the possibility of Robert Kennedy running sometime soon for president arose immediately after President Kennedy was killed. Bobby knew it was impossible—indeed unthinkable—to challenge LBJ for the presidency in 1964, when Johnson had barely assumed the job after the death of the president. RFK ran instead for the Senate from New York; and, when asked, I interrupted my writing on Cape Cod to make several campaign appearances for him. When I moved to New York in January 1966, I became one of his constituents.

In July 1966, with Humphrey ensconced as LBJ's vice president, I prepared a memorandum for RFK outlining all the contingencies he should bear in mind for a future presidential bid, organized under three headings, exaggerating tongue-in-cheek the alliteration for which I was often teased. First, I wrote, "the futility of prophecy is in direct proportion to the multitude of possibilities (in other words, who knows?)." That paragraph listed all the possible contingencies that would affect President Johnson's and Vice President Humphrey's availability to run for president in 1968 and 1972, including their death or defeat. Second, I wrote, "the paucity of potential Presidential contenders presently prominent permits increased perspective." Under this heading, my objective review of Democratic senators, governors, and leaders revealed surprisingly few likely to be backed by LBJ as his successor. Third, "Nomination requires a majority, not merely a plurality." Under this heading, I noted that a 1968 front-runner, presumably LBJ, could not afford to have placed in nomination the names of a host of regional candidates and favorite sons, or to step aside from every binding primary he thinks they might win, or to be shut out in either the

South or the small and middle-sized states of the Farm Belt and West. To assure a majority, he would need them all.

But I did not expect Bobby to run in 1968. A year after I sent that memo, during a summer trip to Russia, I told Soviet journalists—and apparently an Associated Press reporter in the meeting who filed a story—that the chances of Senator Robert Kennedy's being elected president the following year were virtually zero. The *San Francisco Examiner* headlined, "Bobby a 'Zero'—JFK Aide." Shortly thereafter, I received a copy of the article, with a note at the bottom scrawled in Bobby's familiar handwriting: "Ted—headline writer a friend?—Or is this by chance a Repub. Paper? (!)"

Nonetheless, I kept providing memoranda to RFK— some at his request and some on my own initiative— analyzing what it would take to win a majority of convention delegates, and I continued to participate in strategy sessions to discuss the possibility of his entry. One such discussion took place on the afternoon of Sunday, October 8, 1967, in Pierre Salinger's room at the Regency Hotel in New York City. At a subsequent meeting nearly two months later at Bill vanden Heuvel's home, I expressed my concerns about RFK running in 1968. It would be futile for Bobby to enter the primaries hoping to win, I explained, and impossible for him to campaign enough on behalf of antiwar candidate Gene McCarthy without being implicated in Gene's likely failure. My comment prompted Ethel, Bobby's always candid wife, to say, according to Arthur Schlesinger's journal: "Why, Ted, after all those high-flown phrases you wrote for President Kennedy!"

But what she saw as pessimism, Senator Ted Kennedy, brother-in-law Steve Smith, and I saw as political realism. That is why all three of us opposed RFK running for president in 1968. We were concerned not only with the difficulty of denying a presidential nomination to the incumbent who controlled the convention, but also with an RFK-McCarthy split of the antiwar vote handing the nomination to LBJ, and with an RFK-LBJ split handing the fall election to the Republicans. Why run against his brother's designated successor in a divisive campaign that we doubted he could win, when he would have a much clearer path to both the nomination and the presidency in 1972?

On the other side of this debate, RFK's Senate staff, led by Peter Edelman, Adam Walinsky, and Tom Johnson, was urging him to run, emphasizing that it was the only way to secure an early end to the Vietnam War. This was a compelling argument to Bobby, who believed that LBJ had altered his brother's approach on Vietnam by committing combat troop divisions, abandoning all talk of withdrawal, and appearing less interested in a negotiated solution. As U.S. military involvement in Vietnam deepened under Johnson, and casualties mounted, it is hard to recall now which occurred first—RFK's leadership in the antiwar effort or his emergence as a possible presidential candidate.

When approached by leaders of the anti-Vietnam movement about becoming its candidate in a campaign to unseat Johnson, RFK initially demurred, though he was unhappy when that role then went to Senator Eugene McCarthy, a man whom the Kennedys had long regarded with little respect or affection.

He was also unhappy when a splinter Democratic faction in New Hampshire began, without his consent, to gain strength and raise funds by filing a slate for the primary under the "RFK for President" banner. Not wanting to be used—if there was to be any Kennedy campaign in New Hampshire, he wanted it to be directed by people of his own choosing—he asked me to visit the state to persuade the maverick leaders of this spontaneous movement to withdraw. I did.

When LBJ heard about that, he assumed that I had halted the Kennedy movement in New Hampshire on his (Johnson's) behalf, and asked me to come see him in the White House on March 11, 1968, the day before the New Hampshire primary. Apparently, except for

McNamara, I was an exception for Johnson—a close friend of RFK in whom he could nevertheless confide. En route to the White House, I visited with Bobby in his Senate office. His highest priority was to end the Vietnam War, he said, and he asked me to relay to Johnson, without identifying its source, the proposal—which he had recently received from Mayor Richard Daley of Chicago—for an independent blue-ribbon commission of wise men to evaluate America's role and prospects in the war.

After my arrival in the Oval Office, Johnson moved the site of our conversation to his small private study—perhaps to make it more intimate and informal, or perhaps to avoid its being recorded. Our frank and cordial two-hour meeting was wide-ranging. He gave me candid views on (1) Bundy's successor as national security advisor, Walt Rostow ("more of a coordinator or craftsman, much less of a policy maker than Mac Bundy"); (2) Dick Goodwin (he "disliked" him, saying Bill Moyers had "sold" Dick to him as someone "caught in an RFK-Shriver squeeze"; and he added that until the day Dick left he had never dissented from Johnson's Vietnam policies); and (3) Adlai Stevenson, who had asked for his help to become the New York Senate candidate in 1964 instead of RFK, and "after I refused, never said another kind word to me."

To me, the president sounded like a presidential candidate talking about the upcoming campaign. But he told me he did not want to run in the Massachusetts primary for fear of forcing Ted Kennedy to choose between LBJ and Eugene McCarthy, recalling a 1940 incident in which FDR had told him not to block a Texas delegation from going to Vice President Garner, because the resulting disunity might hurt FDR in the fall. He quoted FDR as saying, "Let them all go to Garner; if I can't win without those 25 votes, maybe I won't run at all." LBJ emphasized to me that last line—"maybe I won't run at all"—in his melodramatic way, implying if this year's convention was so close he couldn't give up one state, then maybe he wouldn't be a candidate.

Robert McNamara had earlier told RFK that Johnson had promised Lady Bird in the summer of 1967 that he would not run in 1968; but all the signs—he was organizing, hiring pollsters—indicated that he had changed his mind. But this reference to FDR in Texas was an indication that he might not run.

Getting to what I considered the purpose of our meeting, I suggested that he consider one or two steps (urged on me by RFK, but I did not disclose that) to demonstrate that he was not deaf to criticisms of his Vietnam policy—first, that he replace Secretary of State Rusk; and second, that he appoint a national commission on

Vietnam similar to his blue-ribbon commission on urban violence, composed of independent thinkers who
could evaluate all the information and recommend future
policy. I raised this without attributing it to either Chicago's Mayor Daley or RFK. LBJ replied that Daley had
made the same suggestion, with RFK as a commission
member. He thought the idea had some merit, provided
it did not look abroad as though we did not know what
we were doing, and was not cast as an insult to Rusk.
We talked at length about possible members for such a
commission, and he asked me to supply him with a list,
adding that I would make a good member.

Johnson then expressed his hope that I would return
to public service, saying that I had been more generous
to him in my public statements than he had a right to
expect, given my closeness to the Kennedys and my opposition to the war, that my comments had been very
constructive, but he had not called on me for any assignment for fear it would be misunderstood because of
my relationship with Bobby. He made other flattering
references to my work for President Kennedy, and the
brief time I served him in the White House, mentioning
more than once the time I had recast a State Department
letter to Khrushchev in language that was more condu-
cive to friendship without changing its substance.

The next day, McCarthy's surprisingly strong showing in the New Hampshire primary, where RFK had expected LBJ to fare well, totally changed the political dynamics, increasing RFK's interest in running, and increasing LBJ's interest in an independent commission. McCarthy and his followers now took the Minnesotan's supposedly token candidacy for the presidency more seriously, and were visibly—and justifiably—sour on the idea that RFK might take advantage of their effort by competing against their candidate after refusing to enter the race when Johnson looked unbeatable.

A day later, upon completing a college lecture in upstate New York, I received an urgent message to call the White House. The president, I was informed, would consider the Vietnam commission and wanted me to suggest names. When I was finally able to reach RFK at 1 A.M., he informed me that he had an appointment with Secretary of Defense Clark Clifford early the next morning and wanted me to join him. I slept for a few hours, and flew to Washington.

At the Pentagon, RFK and I urged Clifford to accept the Vietnam commission proposal as a way for Johnson to end America's involvement in an unjust, unpopular war without retreating or losing face. Asked for names, I read names I had hastily scrawled on a yellow pad en route to Washington. My list included thirty-nine people then or previously prominent in various categories: international affairs (Reischauer, Kennan, Ball, Gilpatric, Bundy, Kaysen, Goldberg, J. Johnson, S. Wright, Yost, Young), the military (Ridgeway, Norstadt), Congress (Senators Bayh, Mondale, Carlson, Anderson, Ervin, and Aiken, and Congressman Brad Morse), government and politics (Governors Hughes of Iowa and Chafee of Rhode Island, former Governor Thomas E. Dewey, David Bell), academia (K. Brewster, Kissinger, Fairbank, Barnett, Brzezinski), business (Heineman, Roosa, J. Irwin Miller, G. Hauge) and media (Cowles, Donovan), as well as all of the then-presidential aspirants (McCarthy, RFK, Nixon, and Rockefeller).

Bobby made clear that he would become a candidate for president committed to end the war in Vietnam if the president could not find a way to end it. Clifford replied that Bobby had no chance of winning the nomination, and that, even if he did, the split in the party would elect the Republicans in the fall—the same argument Senator Ted Kennedy, Steve Smith, and I had been making to Bobby for months.

The discussion ended with an understanding that Clifford would review the commission idea with the president. It had been—as was always the case with Clark—a genial conversation, but RFK and I left not knowing what the answer would be. As we drove to his Senate office, RFK said once again that this was the last chance to end the war—and in that sense, the last obstacle to his decision to run for president. Privately, I hoped the commission proposal would be accepted, not only to end the war, but also to avoid an RFK candidacy that year.

A few hours later, Secretary Clifford called me at RFK's Senate office, and said the answer was no—emphatically no—that President Johnson was not a man to delegate decisions to outsiders and was not going to permit anyone else to decide his course on Vietnam. We said good-bye. I have since learned that Johnson—who reportedly viewed the whole commission proposal as "a ploy" by Bobby to put Johnson "in a hole"—was listening in on Clifford's end. RFK, who had also been listening in on my end, immediately said he was going to run for president. It was his obligation, he said, because his candidacy was the only way that America could end its disastrous involvement in Vietnam. Promptly, he began making arrangements for a meeting that evening at his Northern Virginia home, Hickory Hill, with a trusted group to advise and assist him on entering the presidential race.

For months the same players had discussed the same

subject. But that night and the next day, in seemingly endless sessions at Hickory Hill, the question was no longer whether, but how. Senator Ted was dispatched on a secret mission to notify McCarthy, then campaigning in Wisconsin, and to discuss with him the possibility of a joint effort against Johnson. Not surprisingly, McCarthy was uninterested. He had the ground troops, the money, and the momentum. Using a private plane, Ted returned promptly, awaking me to report on his trip. A few hours later, Bobby, Ted, and I, with Bobby's dog in the backseat, drove to the Senate Office Building. Bobby told a large press conference of his candidacy.

It had all happened in one week: my meeting with LBJ on Monday; the New Hampshire primary on Tuesday; the meeting with Clifford on Thursday; then RFK's announcement on Saturday, March 16. On Sunday evening, RFK issued a statement setting forth his version of the commission proposal:

Mr. Sorensen did not get this idea from me, was not representing me, did not propose me as a member, and did not link the idea in any way to my prospective candidacy [actually, I did get the idea from Daley via RFK] . . . Two days later the White House called Mr. Sorensen to tell him that the President had decided to pursue the idea, and wanted a list of names . . . I made it clear that, if it were more than a public relations gimmick, if both the President's announcement of the commission and its membership should signal a clear-cut willingness to seek a wider path to peace in Vietnam, then my declaration of candidacy would no longer be necessary . . . Several hours later Mr. Clifford called to say the President had no intention of taking such action . . . It then became unmistakably clear to me that, so long as Lyndon B. Johnson was President, our Vietnam policy would consist of only more war, more troops, more killing, and more senseless destruction of the country . . . That night I decided to run for President.

After RFK's Saturday announcement, I flew back to New York City and collapsed in bed after a series of sleepless nights, only to be awakened in the middle of the night by a telephone call from Fred Dutton, then acting as a traveling aide to RFK, calling from Topeka, Kansas, RFK's first campaign stop. Fred relayed a message from RFK that Clifford was leaking to the press his own version of the commission meeting, which maintained that RFK was running for president only because he was "sulking" since his attempt to take over the government through this commission had failed. RFK, said Fred, wanted me to hold a press conference as soon as possible to set the record straight. I agreed, and promptly fell back to sleep. Only weeks later, when RFK, seated next to me at a strategy meeting, casually asked: "Whatever happened to that press conference?" did I remember Fred's call—a reminder of what excessive fatigue in a presidential campaign can do!

At a dinner in his home that same week, RFK asked me to move to Washington to join Senator Ted and Steve Smith in managing the national campaign. I did a few days later. The three of us—Ted, Steve, and I—worked well together, having collaborated in other campaigns. But a troika at the top typified the disorganization of that hastily formed campaign. Overlaps, differences of perspective, and resentments were unavoidable, including among speechwriters. Occasionally Bobby asked for my help or advice on speeches, even though he had his own gifted speechwriters. The particularly brilliant and liberal Adam Walinsky, it was reported to me, "thought he would be Bobby's 'Ted Sorensen'— and then the real one came along."

The dynamic of Kennedy administration veterans like me working with young RFK staffers like Adam prompted news articles referring to the Old Guard that had moved into the RFK campaign. Even my old friend Arthur Schlesinger, in an incisive memorandum on "the old politics and the new," emphasized that RFK "must not appear to be surrounded by figures from the past." For years I had been the youngest person in the room. Now suddenly I was part of the Old Guard? I was not yet forty!

My primary role in that tragically brief campaign was not speechwriting but advising, strategizing, analyzing delegate numbers, occasionally speaking on the candidate's behalf, and contacting Democratic leaders. On one occasion, a senior New York State Democratic Party chieftain whom I knew well from JFK days came to Washington to talk to me about the campaign. Kenny O'Donnell, who, to the best of my knowledge, had no official role in the campaign, learned of this. In a surprisingly obscene telephone call, he demanded that I cancel the appointment, leaving my visitor, who had already arrived, waiting in the reception area. I never understood the reason for Kenny's vitriolic call. Now, in retrospect, it seems another indication of his long-standing hostility toward me.

As I had for JFK, I helped prepare RFK for his press interviews and debates, including the list of questions that he should be ready to answer. I did not shrink from any I knew would annoy him:

> What accomplishments do you claim? Does that include wiretapping Martin Luther King? How do you explain your association with Senator Joe McCarthy? What is your position on population control in the Third World, in view of your own 11 children? Why did you not run for President until [Gene] McCarthy in New Hampshire cleared the way?

Similarly, deciphering my notes of advice to RFK for his campaign debate with McCarthy, I find the following: "In clothes and haircut, look old, distinguished, serious, dignified. . . . Make him look far out, unrealistic, making you more conservative . . . do not recite too many agonies—bloated bellies. . . ."

On the night of March 31, together with other friends and advisors gathered at Bobby's New York City apartment, I watched President Johnson's final televised address, expecting a speech focusing on a U.S. bombing pause in Vietnam. Astonished when, at the end of his remarks, LBJ announced his withdrawal from the presidential race, I urged RFK to have a friendly farewell meeting with the president—a reconciliation meeting seeking, at the very least, his neutrality in the campaign. RFK immediately liked the idea, and asked me to arrange it and attend.

At 10 A.M. on the morning of Wednesday, April 3, 1968, RFK and I were escorted to the Cabinet Room and told that the meeting would be held there. "Perhaps the Indian Treaty Room would be more appropriate," I whispered to Bobby.

The president, looking extremely fit, walked in carrying his grandson, then showed us that the baby could walk at eight months. For the next hour and forty minutes, we discussed Vietnam, the president showing us the latest dispatches on possible peace talks. Sitting across from the president, who had two aides present, NSC advisor Walt Rostow and presidential counsel Charles Murphy, the senator and I saluted his emphasis on peace in his withdrawal speech.

The entire conversation was frank but conciliatory. LBJ did 90 percent of the talking, referring to the ill feeling that had divided him and RFK for so long, and to RFK's attacks on his policy. Bobby expressed his regret that relations between them had deteriorated. "A lot of it was my fault," he said. "People try to divide us," LBJ responded, "and we both suffer from it."

When President Johnson seemed prepared to close the meeting with no further reference to politics, RFK requested a discussion on the president's role, asking bluntly, "Where do I stand in the campaign? Are you opposed to my effort and will you marshal forces against me?" "I want to keep the Presidency out of this campaign." LBJ replied. "I'm not that pure, but I am that scared . . . if I had thought I could get into the campaign and hold the country together, I would have run myself."

As the meeting wore on, the president seemed to mellow. He said he would try to conduct himself in the campaign in the same way he would wish Senator Kennedy to behave if their positions were reversed. "I feel toward [Hubert], the way perhaps that you, Ted, feel toward Bobby here . . . I want you to know, Senator Kennedy, that I do not hate you, I do not dislike you, and I still regard myself as carrying out the Kennedy-Johnson partnership." He began to reflect on the past few years, saying that he had tried to find some way to avoid running in 1964, but could not; that he had never wanted to be president, and had been counting the days to the end of his term since it began. Waxing sentimental, he stressed that he had done reasonably well in carrying on the Kennedy policies and programs, and that JFK, "looking down," would agree.

By the end of the discussion, the atmosphere had grown warm and friendly. The president restated that he had removed himself from the presidential campaign to prevent his bid for peace from becoming politically suspect by those whom he was unable to win over. In response, RFK cleared his throat and said, "You are a brave and dedicated man, Mr. President." But he choked on his words, and the president, not clearly hearing him—or perhaps wanting to hear it again—said he did not hear him—so RFK repeated it.

With possibly genuine expressions of appreciation and friendship on both sides, the meeting ended. As we left, the president turned to me and said, "None of this would have happened if you hadn't left." There are several possible interpretations of that, but I chose to regard it as a compliment. As we exited, Bobby and I learned from a friendly Secret Service agent that Vice President Humphrey was the next visitor.

With the exception of a brief talk in the car afterward—in which Bobby and I agreed the discussion had gone well, hopefully prolonging LBJ's neutrality sufficiently to prevent an early Humphrey entry—we had no other opportunity to discuss the meeting in depth. The next day, Dr. Martin Luther King Jr. was assassinated. Although Dr. King and I had a cordial telephone conversation when I was on the lecture circuit in Atlanta in 1965, I did not know this remarkable man, but had long admired him. His murder took both Bobby and me back to that terrible day in November 1963.

Addressing a shocked black gathering in Indianapolis, RFK gave extemporaneously the most moving and powerful speech of his life, pleading for domestic peace as well as justice. He then telephoned me at home in Washington and asked for my thoughts on a speech scheduled for the next day in Cleveland, saying he would call me back in an hour. When he hung up, I scribbled as quickly as I could on scraps of paper—with the assassination of King in my mind, but the assassination of John F. Kennedy in my heart:

[The] mindless menace of violence in America . . . is not an issue between the parties . . . The victims of violence are black and white, rich and poor, young and old, famous and unknown. They are, most important of all, human beings whom other human beings loved and needed. Because fate is capricious and life is troubled, no one can be certain who next will suffer from some senseless act of bloodshed, no matter where he lives or what he does. And yet it goes on and on and on. Why? What has violence ever accomplished? . . . Whenever any American's life is taken unnecessarily—whether in the name of the law or in defiance of the law, by one man or a gang, in cold blood or in passion, in an attack of violence or in response to violence—this whole nation is degraded . . . Yet this nation tolerates the rising level of violence that calls into question our claim to be a civilized society. . . .

We acccpt with equanimity in our daily newspapers the reports of civilian slaughter in far-off lands. We glorify killing on our movie and television screens and call it entertainment. We make it easy for convicts, lunatics, juveniles, and junkies to acquire whatever weapons and ammunition they seek. We permit—and some Americans even teach—racial and religious hatred in our communities, while refusing to end the desperate conditions of poverty and inequality that inevitably breed crime, frustration, and tension in the midst of our affluent cities.

Some Americans, who preach non-violence abroad, fail to practice it here at home. Some, who accuse others of inciting riots, have by their own conduct invited them. Some look for scapegoats, others look for conspiracies, but this much is clear: violence breeds violence, repression brings retaliation, and only a cleansing of our whole society can remove this sickness from our soul . . .

When Bobby called back, I read the above notes as he wrote them down. I don't know whether he was on his plane or in his hotel room. I remember only that it was a night of ineluctable sadness. My text was a portion of his moving address the next day. His team later that night inserted my language into a speech they had drafted. As his biographer, Jack Newfield, would write: "The speech can now be read as RFK's own epitaph." Nearly four decades later, the 2006 film *Bobby* closed with an audio clip of him delivering that speech. It carried my own deepest convictions then and now.

In the midst of the campaign, I wrote to my sons:

> *The campaign continues hot and heavy . . . It is going to be very tough at the convention against Humphrey . . . I am running as a candidate for delegate to the convention from New York. I am a 3–1 underdog. For that reason I have been doing some radio and television . . . as well as some campaigning in halls, homes, and on street corners in the district. But, generally, I'm here at national campaign headquarters day and night . . . This has been a beautiful Spring, sunny and crisp. Good softball weather, but I haven't had a chance yet to play . . .*

The RFK campaign fared well, getting off to a fast start, winning nearly every primary, including Nebraska, where my brother Phil played a key role. Two years earlier, Bobby had hosted a fund-raiser in his New York City apartment for Phil, who was running for governor of Nebraska. Opening his remarks, framed against a picturesque view of the Manhattan skyline, Phil quipped: "One photograph of this in the Nebraska papers and my campaign is over."

In June, having lost in Oregon, RFK knew he might lose in California and thus lose the nomination. The week before the California primary, I had, at his request, campaigned for him up and down the state, marveling at the growing support he was receiving from rich and poor, black and Latino and white, old and young, a campaign that was characterized by more idealism, energy, and enthusiasm than any campaign in either party perhaps before or since, until Obama in 2008.

That 1968 campaign was in many ways a turning point for the Democratic Party, a redefinition of its future, a campaign that reached beyond traditional party leaders and organizations into suburbs and inner cities, campuses and grassroots operations, as never before, a campaign that was unashamedly based on high moral principles.

After his California victory was clear, the scene in RFK's Los Angeles hotel suite was one of unrestrained jubilation. Even though Steve, Senator Ted, and I had planned an all-day meeting with the candidate for the next day before leaving California, Bobby asked me to chat briefly in the bathroom—the only quiet and private spot in his suite—before he went down to the Embassy Ballroom to address his supporters. In our chat, he reflected philosophically about his loss in Oregon the previous week, noting that he should have known things were awry there. We talked about the intense schedule he would face in the coming weeks, including the possibility of a trip to Romania; we spoke of establishing a delegate hospitality headquarters at Hyannis Port, inviting all the delegates from the East Coast, including those leaning to Humphrey, to meet the senator; we spoke of appearances at state conventions and state committee meetings all over the country.

After we finished our discussion, I stayed upstairs, watching on the television set in his virtually deserted suite, as he greeted and thanked his supporters downstairs, closing with the words, "And now it's on to Chicago, and let's win there!" As he left the ballroom through the kitchen, followed by cameras, I watched in horror and stunned disbelief as the awful nightmare recurred. How could it happen again? What kind of world was this? Amid all the tears of joy and congratulations, amid all the security precautions, amid all the celebrations that he was on his way to the presidency, tragedy had struck again.

With others, I made my way to the hospital, awaiting final word. President Johnson asked the White House switchboard to track me down there, and called with a heartfelt message of sympathy and grief. Ultimately I made my way back to Washington and then to New York, for RFK's solemn funeral Mass at St. Patrick's and the sad funeral train to Washington for his burial beside his brother.

The leaders of my law firm held a memorial service on Friday afternoon, the day before the funeral, to give everyone in the Paul, Weiss family an opportunity to mourn. They asked me to speak; I could barely get the words out. It was all too much to bear.

What a tragedy—for all of us who knew him, and for this country. Continuing his outspoken boldness, he no doubt would have been a controversial president. A Robert F. Kennedy administration offered the possibility of leading the country and healing it at the same time, and relieving the nation's grief and still aching sense of loss after JFK's death, moving it into an era of peace abroad in Vietnam, and moving ahead at home with civil rights—and in all these ways and possibly more, ushering in another golden age in Washington.

The death of Robert Kennedy made the nomination of Hubert Humphrey all but inevitable. A mutual friend had earlier compared Senator Humphrey to a bird released from its longtime cage that flies straight up, hovers, gains a view of his surroundings, and then takes off vigorously and cheerfully in one direction. When Vice President Humphrey invited me to meet with him in New York City a month before the convention, he was not the cheerful "happy warrior" I had always known him to be. He was full of complaints, and I was surprised that he sounded so defensive and bitter.

Senator Ted decided not to endorse any of the remaining contenders for the Democratic nomination, or to bargain with them for the vice presidency, or to seek the presidency for himself. His brother-in-law Steve Smith was not so certain that Ted should take himself out, nor was Mayor Daley of Chicago. Steve called me about talking with United Auto Workers president Walter Reuther, and others. Rumors of a "draft Ted Kennedy" movement spread.

In a phone call with Ted, I told him he could postpone his decision, but that he should let those of us in his corner know whether he wanted either the presidential or vice presidential nomination. Finally, the senator called Mayor Daley and told him that he could not accept. At that point, most of the Kennedy delegates, including me, rallied around Senator George McGovern, the former JFK aide. But McGovern—the nominee four years later—could not derail Humphrey.

A month earlier, while I was working for RFK, I had been falsely accused by Humphrey forces of telling the press that Humphrey was offering the vice presidency to every Southern senator he met. Humphrey, spotting me in a crowd one evening, called out: "Ted, I wish I had seen you before I went down South—how would you like to be vice president?" Everyone laughed, including the crowd, the vice president, and me. But after the Chicago convention was over, I was told that one Humphrey advisor, Bob Short, had privately indicated that my name was high on the final list of four vice presidential possibilities. Senator Ted told me that, before the distinguished Maine Senator Ed Muskie was nominated for vice president, Humphrey had called Ted to ask him whether he had any preference between Muskie and Oklahoma Senator Fred Harris. Ted told me he replied that a more dramatic choice might be necessary to solve Humphrey's problems within the Democratic Party, and that he would recommend me. Humphrey responded that, for a variety of reasons, the choice was down to Muskie or Harris. That was both the start and the end of the Sorensen for VP "boomlet"—so brief and quiet that no one, including me, knew it existed.

I was asked to do little in the 1968 campaign for Humphrey, and I did little. That was fine with me, inasmuch as I had fallen in love with Gillian and had higher, personal priorities that fall. Ultimately, Humphrey came within an eyelash of defeating Richard Nixon for the presidency. I have no doubt that Robert Kennedy, had he lived, would have been nominated, garnering all the McCarthy delegates after Gene's defeat in California, and many of the Humphrey delegates who wanted a winner in November. Bobby would have united the divided party, thereby winning the presidency. What a president he would have been.

My 1970 Senate Campaign

When I moved to New York in early 1966, Senator Robert F. Kennedy did not merely encourage me to take part in New York state politics, he practically pushed me into it. At his initiative, I was named to a commission preparing for a state constitutional convention, and then made chairman of a special committee to explore how the New York State Democratic Party could be revitalized. Our committee held meetings and hearings throughout the state, and those travels continued after RFK's death. In time, those contacts evolved into my candidacy for the United States Senate, encouraged by scores of new friends and well-wishers urging me to carry on the Kennedy legacy. I was sufficiently naive and self-centered to think they represented the voice of the people.

Soon after Bobby's death, a group of nine Nebraska Democrats wrote to New York's Republican Governor, Nelson Rockefeller, urging him to appoint me to RFK's vacant Senate seat; unsurprisingly, he paid no attention. But, while my fellow Nebraska Democrats could not get me an appointment from or even with the New York Republican governor, my future father-in-law, John Martin, Michigan's Republican national committeeman and a longtime friend and onetime college classmate of the governor, not only put in a kind word, at Gillian's request, but arranged a meeting. Also helpful as an intermediary was a mutual friend, Rockefeller's foreign policy advisor, Henry Kissinger.

On Saturday morning, July 13, 1968, I met with the governor in his Fifth Avenue apartment for breakfast. He said that the only other prospect for appointment to

RFK's Senate seat with whom he had talked was New York City Mayor John Lindsay, who, he said, badly wanted the job. But they did not like each other, and Rockefeller did not expect that Lindsay would be appointed. He said I was the only Democrat to whom he had given "active" consideration, adding that I could be helpful in "creating a climate" for his own nomination for president by the Republicans. Nevertheless he was concerned about the reaction of Republican leaders who did not like his being endorsed by Democrats "and would be extremely angry if [he] named a Democrat to the Senate seat."

I noted in the private memo of our conversation that I jotted down later:

> It seemed to boil down to his feeling that appointing me would make sense only if he receives the Republican nomination . . . with some enthusiasm. If his party were bitterly divided, he would have to nominate a Republican who could help heal those divisions . . . he did feel an obligation to name someone who would maintain the spirit and standard of the man (RFK) who previously occupied the seat . . .

Ultimately, the appointment went to Republican Charles Goodell.

This brief consideration gave me the political "bug." I wanted to do more in public life than give speeches and write. I wanted to act. Almost two years later, as Goodell's interim term expired, I decided to run for the United States Senate. In my declaration of candidacy, I noted that I was not running as the candidate of any one faction, section, or bloc (in hindsight, a weakness), and that "I am not a professional politician" (possibly another weakness).

It was an ill-considered move. I should have remembered the advice once voiced by my friend Senator Fritz Hollings of South Carolina: "The best way to run for office is strong, hard, and unopposed." I had three strong opponents in the June 1970 Democratic primary—each a veteran candidate and experienced fund-raiser—each with a political base: Congressman Richard Ottinger from the Westchester suburbs, Congressman Richard "Max" McCarthy from Buffalo, and former councilman Paul O'Dwyer from the New York City Democratic Reform movement. I discovered that my years of maintaining a low profile in government had given me no distinct public identity of my own.

The race was complicated by the fact that two of my law partners and friends—Arthur Goldberg, the former Kennedy secretary of labor and Supreme Court ap-

pointee, and Morris Abram, who had an early association with the Peace Corps—were also considered logical
contenders. On August 22, 1969, Judge Rifkind, the unofficial head of the firm, thought it necessary to call this
fact to the attention of all Paul, Weiss lawyers and staff:

> It is a source of great satisfaction to know that, if
> the contest does occur, whichever of them prevails,
> the Democratic candidate will be a citizen of excep-
> tional merit . . . It is our concern that it not generate
> such tensions in the firm as would adversely affect
> the morale of our office. No partner or staff will be
> recruited or solicited . . . Any partner or member of
> the staff may, if he so desires, volunteer his services
> to any candidate or abstain . . . His relations to the
> firm will be entirely unaffected . . . Anyone who
> does engage in political activity will be expected to
> do so in his or her own free time.

At that time, the party nomination in New York was
a two-step process. The Democratic State Committee
Convention selected a candidate for endorsement, but
other candidates were permitted to run in the primary.
From my 1956–1960 experience with JFK, I knew
something about obtaining convention endorsements,

and money was not the deciding factor. I crisscrossed the state, speaking to Democratic dinners and meetings in every locale, and appealing to party leaders and Democratic officials at every opportunity, all in the pattern pursued in the years leading up to JFK's 1960 presidential nomination. At the convention, I received the state committee endorsement on the first ballot. But in that turbulent year, that endorsement did not prove to be helpful, and may even have been harmful. The endorsement was regarded as a mark against me by reformers; the local regular party organizations failed to turn out rank-and-file voters for me in the primary, and neither the Democratic State Committee nor the local organizations financed my candidacy.

It was a new experience for me to cast off the role of advisor and make campaign decisions. I doubt that it was a role that suited me, but I tried. I talked in the campaign about Vietnam, narcotics, Israel, and the environment. Unable to make any sharp distinctions in my positions from those of the other candidates, I emphasized my experience and accomplishments with JFK, a strategy that only reinforced the charge that I was tying my candidacy to the Kennedy name, even as I recognized the need to develop my own political identity. One columnist said that the only advantage I had in the slogan

"John Kennedy trusted him" was that John Kennedy was not alive to contest the claim, and called this "Mausoleum Politics, or the politics of necrophilia."

I celebrated my forty-second birthday in the middle of the primary, and reflected on its tribulations in my usual doggerel:

> I feared the utmost
> From *The Times* and *The Post*,
> And can't make *The News*—any edition;
> And while I've traveled this far,
> With no dough or p.r.,
> I do face severe competition . . .
> So I have a tough fight,
> And must work day and night,
> Unless someone comes up with a million;
> But I cherish my team,
> More skilled than they seem,
> And I have a fantastic campaigner in Gillian.
> I hope we can all
> Celebrate in some hall
> When I finally reach age 43,
> And rather than hedge,
> I hereby do pledge
> To fly up for that night from D.C.

Gillian was indeed a tremendous campaigner. The *Binghamton Sun Bulletin* said she "crackles with energy and intense confidence." The *Buffalo Courier Express* called her "well-informed and articulate . . . radiating the kind of charm and enthusiasm that helps win elections." Oh, if only she had a better candidate.

For me, that campaign will always be summed up in my encounter with a middle-aged woman in a park in Queens as I was concluding a long and tiring day. "If you are elected," she demanded to know, "will you get rid of the nails in the boardwalk?" Not knowing which government agency had jurisdiction over the boardwalk and too weary to give a fuller answer, I tried to give her an interested smile and replied: "I'll do the very best I can." "That's not good enough for me!" she snapped, and stalked away.

One embarrassing incident took place when I asked a Bronx congressman to share a press conference I had scheduled to announce my anticrime program on television news. The congressman showed up, but the cameras did not. Similarly, an attempt to tape a radio commercial ended in failure when my hand-picked interrogator took too seriously his assignment to demonstrate my ability to handle tough questions. He continuously pressed me with questions so hostile that any listener would think ill of me whatever answer I gave; we threw away the tape.

The campaign generated a few column inches when Israeli Prime Minister Golda Meir commented to the press on a statement I had made in Moscow urging the Soviet government to permit the emigration of Jews to Israel. The prime minister said: "The Sorensen statement was extremely important. He should be admired for his courage in saying that on Russian soil . . . I don't know of anybody who publicly did that in Russia before." The *Jerusalem Post* was impressed, but its circulation was limited in New York.

Perhaps the most constructive feature of the campaign was a lawsuit I brought, with the assistance of my law partner and friend Mark Alcott, on behalf of Malcolm Berk, one of many U.S. soldiers about to be sent to Vietnam. Berk had called my campaign headquarters seeking legal representation after we issued a press statement highlighting an ancient New York statute prohibiting New York citizens from being sent to fight in foreign wars not authorized by the U.S. Constitution.

Supported by distinguished lawyers from the American Civil Liberties Union, we brought the lawsuit against the Department of Defense. Justice Byron White of the United States Supreme Court issued a temporary stay ordering the government not to deploy Berk anywhere outside the United States. I argued in the United States District Court for the Eastern District of New York that

President Nixon's decision to invade Cambodia, without explicit congressional authorization, was contrary to the U.S. Constitution, and that he therefore could not legally send abroad the young New York citizen I represented in the case. In part, I said:

> May it please the Court, it is now clear from this discussion today, as well as the briefs, that the key issue in this case is: Did Congress explicitly authorize the massive combat effort undertaken by this nation in Vietnam? . . . [The government] stated on page 13 of its brief [that] "Plaintiff apparently believes that Congress did not mean what it said."
>
> We have looked at what Congress said, and it appears that the Government would like this Court to believe that Congress meant *what it did not say.* [Emphasis added.]

Along with another case (Orlando), it was the first time any federal court had been willing to hear a constitutional challenge to the war in Vietnam. Unfortunately, the courts ultimately decided that congressional action in approving military appropriations constituted "sufficient action to ratify and approve" a war launched by the executive. We lost. But it was an important precedent on the right of judicial review of unconstitutional presidential wars. Berk later expressed his appreciation for our unsuccessful effort on his behalf—in a letter to Alcott—from Vietnam.

My campaign, buoyed by donations from a handful of supporters, labored to solicit contributions. I was unable to raise in toto an amount equal to the sum that my principal opponent, Congressman Richard Ottinger, raised from one donor, his mother. I disliked fundraising and was not good at it, two obviously related handicaps.

Nor did I seek, expect, or receive financial help from the Kennedy family. Senator Ted Kennedy delivered a helpful speech at the annual New York State Democratic dinner, and he hosted a postcampaign fund-raiser to reduce my campaign debts.

The whole endeavor was hubris on my part. I was still a newcomer to New York, with no political base of my own. My record of accomplishment as an advisor to JFK and author was primarily outside the state, as was my education and upbringing. One congressman, whom Robert Kennedy had thrust aside in his own race for the New York Senate seat, told the press "Ted Sorensen is Bobby Kennedy's anointed candidate to run for the Senate. Sorensen can't even vote yet in New York." His facts were wrong, but his spear was well aimed.

My campaign also provided an opportunity for a

younger generation of New York City liberal critics to accuse me of abandoning my liberal principles in my choice of clients and causes as a Paul, Weiss lawyer. They charged that I had decided, after leaving the White House, to make money rather than fight for my ideals; I was out of touch, they charged. "Sorensen stands as the man who has not seen what has happened in America," one wrote. I took some heat from my liberal friends for being retained in 1966 by General Motors, which was assailed for hiring a private detective to investigate auto safety critic Ralph Nader, even though I had advised GM president James Roche to apologize in public before a Senate committee. In truth, I had sought a prosperous private sector career, having never earned a significant salary in government; and I did not fully understand the radicalism of the young antiwar liberals in the late 1960s and early 1970s. Ironically, many liberal Democrats thought I was too establishment, and many establishment Democrats thought I was too liberal.

When it came time for newspaper endorsements, the *New York Times* editors called me "perhaps the most intellectual of the contenders, and one who could be counted on to contribute positively to Senatorial debate and to a thoughtful examination of public policies . . . [with] undoubted native ability to wrestle with

the largest of national and international issues . . ."
— then they endorsed Ottinger.

"Sorensen makes sense," my campaign fliers announced. Apparently not many people agreed, and I lost,
despite valiant efforts by my campaign manager, Glenn
Van Braemer and his small, overworked, but enthusiastic staff. The whole experience—from the endorsement of the state committee convention on April 2 to
the primary on June 23—lasted less than three months,
a forgettable bump in a long road of otherwise stirring
memories. My brother Tom served as my strategist and
sounding board, sometimes impersonating me in telephone interviews with the press. I remember tearfully
apologizing to him on primary night. The frustration
of my defeat was compounded by our sadness and grief
when we learned on the day before the primary that
our mother had died after a long illness.

Many of my White House colleagues were also running for—and losing—statewide office at about the
same time. Pierre Salinger lost his U.S. Senate race in
California. Kenny O'Donnell lost his gubenatorial race
in Massachusetts. Sarge Shriver aborted his campaign
for governor of Maryland. We all thought that, from
watching JFK, we knew how to do it; clearly that was
not enough.

I had earlier declined the invitation of Pat Cunningham, the Bronx County chairman, to accept his committee's designation to challenge the incumbent Congressman Jonathan Bingham, whose record in the House I admired. I was not willing to give up my Senate ambitions for a less powerful, two-year House seat. But however ill-considered my Senate race may have been, I did not—and do not now—regret my decision to try. I learned many hard lessons from that brief entry into electoral politics, all of which I should have known earlier, having observed both John and Robert Kennedy master those same lessons. I felt I would be wiser next time. But I recognized that I had no enthusiasm for constantly fudging or dodging controversial issues, that I was not comfortable writing and delivering the kind of shallow applause lines that help garner headlines and generate contributions. I knew there would not be a next time.

Three Decades of Advice to Potential Presidents

Following my failed race for the U.S. Senate, my continued participation in Democratic politics was almost entirely at the national level.

Although I have been involved in nearly every presidential race or convention since 1956, my post-RFK involvement in politics was not limited to campaigns.

The Nixon Watergate furor in 1973 stimulated another initiative on my part, more unique than controversial. When Nixon's Vice President Spiro Agnew resigned as the result of corruption charges, leaving the vice presidency temporarily vacant, there was widespread speculation that Nixon himself might be impeached or forced to resign. Democratic Speaker of the House Carl Albert of Bug Tussle, Oklahoma, could then have suddenly replaced the Republican president, automatically switching control of the entire executive branch from one party to the other without an election.

An intelligent, genial, moderate Democrat, Mr. Albert, who had no executive branch or national campaign experience, was widely if unfairly regarded as wholly unprepared. Having known and liked him from my attendance at President Kennedy's weekly White House breakfasts with congressional leaders more than a decade earlier, I wanted to help. Having participated in the successful Eisenhower-Kennedy transition of 1960–1961, as well as the traumatic Kennedy-Johnson transition of 1963, and having prepared a set of transition recommendations at the request of Democratic nominee George McGovern in early autumn, 1972, I felt that I could help.

Nine days after the "Saturday Night Massacre," in which Special Prosecutor Archie Cox (the same Archie

Cox who complained that his speech drafts weren't being used by JFK during the 1960 campaign) had been
fired by Nixon, and Attorney General Elliot Richardson and his deputy had resigned, generating almost two
dozen bills in Congress calling for an impeachment investigation, I sent Speaker Albert, on October 29, 1973,
a letter stating:

> *Whether you wish it or not, you could*
> *become President at any time. Given the unique*
> *unpredictability of both the times in which we live*
> *and the incumbent now in the White House, his*
> *sudden resignation . . . will always be a possibility . . .*
> *[He could be] impeached and convicted, before*
> *Congress could agree on either a Vice President or an*
> *alternative plan of succession . . . While all of these*
> *possibilities may seem remote, the contingency of*
> *your own unexpected elevation remains a fact of life*
> *about which you must never speak but often think.*
> *I suggest therefore a comprehensive "contingency*
> *plan," never to be discussed with others, its*
> *existence not even to be announced . . . to lie sealed*
> *in your desk for use if needed, and for destruction*
> *unopened if not . . . when a new Vice President is*
> *confirmed . . .*

In his reply three days later, Speaker Albert wrote: "It is perhaps the better part of wisdom that your suggestion be implemented. Will you give me a rough draft as a starter?" A week later, I sent him a nineteen-page first draft. My memorandum, dated November 8, 1973, advised:

> A new President . . . must smoothly . . . take charge of the instruments of office in fact as well as name . . . before other centers of power in the government, the nation, and the world start spinning off in different directions.

I included a warning based on my memories of the early Johnson days after JFK's assassination. "Beware of men and nations seeking to take advantage of the pressures to test you, to commit you, or to outmaneuver you; make no decisions or announcements at the request of others until necessary and until all . . . have been consulted."

Speaker Albert promptly replied with thanks, adding:

> With each passing day, the likelihood of my needing it is diminishing . . . I am going to keep it in my

safe as long as I am in the line of succession. The consequences of not acting swiftly and correctly, should catastrophe ever strike, are too great for one not to have some advance knowledge of what he should do . . . [in that event], I should within a matter of hours call on at least one man from the staff of President Kennedy and another from that of President Johnson—the two I have in mind are you and Joe Califano.

My memorandum was never needed. Gerald Ford was named vice president, and succeeded Nixon upon the latter's departure. The memorandum remained locked in Speaker Albert's safe for nine years. Secrecy was important.

My first letter to Albert said of the proposed memorandum, "Its existence, if discovered, might be misinterpreted as evidence of an improper motivation on your part for the President's ouster." Not surprisingly, Mr. Nixon, in retirement, upon learning of the memorandum, disclosed by retired Speaker Albert in a *Washington Post* interview, concluded that it confirmed his suspicion that his bipartisan removal from office was all a Democratic plot.

· · ·

Just as I had counseled Bobby in 1968 against challenging LBJ, in 1980 I counseled Ted Kennedy against trying to unseat an incumbent Democratic president. Ted rejected that advice and decided to run in an effort to unseat Jimmy Carter. I offered my help, and Ted asked me to serve as his representative on the Platform Committee. He lost, so did Carter, and Reagan won the presidency.

In early 1984 I was about to meet with Ohio senator, presidential prospect, and former astronaut John Glenn, when he called to say that a sudden blizzard had paralyzed Washington and he could not get out of his driveway. Whether that was divine intervention, I cannot be certain; but I ultimately was asked to introduce Gary Hart at a New York City meeting, and soon found myself the national cochairman of Hart's unsuccessful 1984 campaign for the Democratic nomination. Expecting to resume that effort in 1988, when Senator Hart decided to try again, I was scheduled to introduce him at a large fund-raising dinner in New York to celebrate his front-runner status, when news headlines heralded his fall from grace as a result of his long-rumored, and that day photographically confirmed, extramarital activities. The dinner proceeded, as did my introduction—urging the audience and the country to focus on the "real issues" of the time. But I sympathized with those dedicated Hart staff members who had moved to Denver to work for a campaign that his poor judgment had destroyed. When Senator Hart inquired by telephone months later about coming back into a lackluster Democratic nomination contest, I discouraged him from trying.

That same year, 1988, I served as executive vice chair of the Democratic National Convention Platform Committee, responsible for writing the initial draft. The Democratic National Committee chairman, Paul Kirk, and Platform Committee chairman, Michigan Governor James Blanchard, agreed with my goal of shortening the typical platform by omitting the usual laundry list of promises to every interest group, ethnic group, and party faction.

Invaluably assisted by David Goldwyn, a young law firm colleague, I prepared a two-thousand-word statement of the party's principles and goals. After more specifics were added by the Drafting Committee, the Platform Committee, and the convention itself, my two thousand words became nearly forty-nine hundred. But that length compared favorably with the platforms of 1980 and 1984, and was reportedly the shortest since World War II. Maybe it still is.

I had no major role in the 1992 presidential campaign. I had known Bill Clinton and admired his enormous political and communications skills ever since our first encounter at the 1984 convention. Early in 1992, when we appeared at a speaking engagement together, I told him that I was committed to support Nebraska's Bob Kerrey, who had asked for my help months earlier. I assured Clinton that, if Kerrey's campaign did not succeed, I would be happy to help him. Clinton responded warmly, saying that he would have thought less of me had I not told him that I was helping my fellow Nebraskan, and that he (Clinton) would look to me for help in the future. It was a heartfelt reassuring response, and I heard nothing further. After his election I was asked to help advise one of his transition teams, and he later asked me to serve on two presidential commissions— one selecting White House Fellows, a terrific program that I wish the Kennedy White House had conceived; and the other encouraging free enterprise in the newly independent former Soviet states of Central Asia.

For those future presidential candidates among my readers today who want my advice, the following is a condensed compilation of all the related memos I've written to would-be presidents who approached me for advice over the last several decades—including Ted Kennedy, George McGovern, Jimmy Carter, Gary Hart, Mario Cuomo, Bob Kerrey, John Kerry, and Barack Obama.

To: Presidential Hopeful
From: Theodore C. Sorensen
Subject: So You Want to Be President

WHETHER TO RUN

Make certain your family, doctor, and banker approve before you begin the long, tough road to becoming president. You must first think hard about why you want the job. You should run only if you want the unparalleled opportunity that office offers to make this a safer, happier, healthier world; only if you genuinely conclude that no other equally able candidate is likely to win; only if you and your family are ready to have your personal lives relentlessly scrutinized. If agonizing is required to produce affirmative answers, don't run—it would be an agonizing campaign.

If you answer yes, you may still be wondering, am I smart enough to be president? I suggest you review that question in three contexts: First, compare your intelligence, judgment, courage, and ability to lead with those of the others who have recently held, sought, or will be seeking the presidency. Neither Jefferson nor Lincoln is running this time. Experience is relative. No office provides meaningful preparation for the unique responsibilities of the presidency.

Consider the next crucial question: Can you win? The presidential race is not a single national campaign but many campaigns contested state by state. Your political advisors should periodically "war game" which states you can realistically hope to win for a convention and electoral majority. Consider whether the odds of nomination and election are sufficiently good to justify surrendering whatever seat or seniority you now possess. Ask yourself what substantial political base (regional, ethnic, or other) is yours alone.

INITIAL PREPARATIONS

No announcement now, even no decision now, does not mean no action now. By quietly building a base now, you preserve the options of running or not running, and inducing at least some important political friends not to commit themselves too early to other candidates.

Several years before the election, you should strengthen your national image; beef up your staff and mailing operations; and obtain the public opinion research and political intelligence required for sound decision making and action.

As soon as possible and occasionally thereafter: commission in-depth surveys ascertaining how registered voters feel about you now and in terms of the presidency; about your future, the presidency, liberals, conservatives; and about major national issues. Simultaneously arrange for a knowledgeable contact in each state to report regularly on rising stars; on the activity of other candidates; factionalism within the state party; and the most important meetings or groups for you to address. Study techniques used in the last campaign by candidates in both parties. Obtain whatever databases are available regarding Democratic donors.

In addition, compile a comprehensive list of every accusation, incident, and complaint, true or untrue, that has ever been raised against you (or could be raised), and set forth factual answers to each of them.

You must show maturity. This can be accomplished by soliciting advice from respected elders; Robert Kennedy had Maxwell Taylor, Averell Harriman, and Robert McNamara; you should have a similar group whose wisdom and experience you value. You should also show a sense of American history—certain American basics don't change, and anyone speaking in historical terms is a stabilizing force.

DEVELOPING A STRATEGY

Remember one unknown but energetic, enthusiastic worker is better than a whole committee of prominent citizens; fifty $100 contributors are better than one $10,000 contributor; and one hour at a barbecue in Dayton, Ohio, may be worth more than six hours with consultants in Washington, D.C. Keep in mind that no one's vote can be delivered except your own and your mother's—and make sure she's registered; a firm stand on an issue, even when it threatens to cost you votes, is better than a cheap headline.

Frequently remind your staff that bold, unorthodox, come-from-behind front-runners have too often been turned into cautious, orthodox losers. Dramatic, unexpected, imaginative, unconventional themes should be solicited, but you will not be nominated or elected if you are perceived as a far-out radical, or desperately engaged in campaign gimmicks.

In public, you should exude determination and confidence but not sound boastful, or extravagantly optimistic. Let your aides make public claims about your political progress and expectations, while you sound modest. Confidence is best expressed through quiet actions and manner, through humor that is more self-deprecating than sarcastic. Seek fewer news stories about your winning tactics, polls, and media advisors, and more about themes, ideals, ideas, and governing.

Regarding interviews, keep your answers brief, specific, and affirmative (even when the questioner tries to put you on the defensive). Do not attack other candidates. As for the drawbacks of being the front-runner—attacks from the media and your competitors—keep cool, they could be worse and soon will be, as you gain strength; confess error where appropriate; answer all attacks quickly and forcefully. Remember, your best friends in the press will betray you first and damage you most.

IF YOU BECOME THE NOMINEE

Determine which states will comprise your electoral majority, and then ruthlessly reject all pleas and pressures to spend precious time and money elsewhere. Because you have a real chance of winning the presidency, you must avoid the temptations and pressures to make campaign commitments that will handicap your flexibility and thus your effectiveness once you are in the White House. Governing is more important and difficult than campaigning. A leader free from specific obligations to any interest group is far more likely to be both a successful candidate and a successful president.

THE PRESIDENTIAL DEBATES

Be aggressive, positive, not strident or sarcastic. Use questions on a limited topic as a vehicle for declaring broader positions. Some long-range visions and inspiring eloquence are needed to rise above petty partisanship. Also consider selecting a specific question to which there is only one truthful answer—and politely ask that question of your opponent at the close of your answer on that topic, just before his time to comment begins.

DEVELOPING A MESSAGE

Focus at all times on the main events, the issues by which the country rises or falls. Do not waste your time and credibility on fringe issues or passing fads. You need to build the most difficult image to attain—that of the statesman (a president, not a vice president), the wise and eloquent leader who takes the long view of the national interest. This requires thoughtful and provocative speeches. The emphasis should be on foreign affairs. At times, there is diminished public enthusiasm for the subject; but its central importance to our role as a nation will endure. Be the first today to warn about back-page issues that may become headlines before November.

The best politics now is to be above politics. People are fed up with politicians, with "politics as usual," and have a bad impression of the Congress.

SELECTING A VICE PRESIDENT

Running mates rarely make a substantial difference to a presidential candidate's prospects for victory in November, and should therefore be selected primarily on the basis of which person is likely to hurt your chances least, inasmuch as the appeal of the presidential nominee, already the most popular man in his party, can only be diluted by adding to the ticket a less popular candidate. The criteria I would advise for selecting a vice president are:

- Credentials to serve as president in the event of your death.
- 100 percent assurance of the prospect's loyalty to the presidential nominee, both during the campaign and thereafter.
- 100 percent assurance of no embarrassing disclosures in his history that could surface, and of a disciplined approach to campaigning that will avoid gaffes.
- Ability to add the electoral votes of a specific sizable state or bloc of states that will otherwise be difficult for you to win . . .
- Strong compatibility in views on issues and approach to governance, including support for party platform during the campaign.
- Credentials to impress voters and pundits as your first cabinet member.
- Willingness to serve as "attack dog" or to deflect the opposition's main line of attacks on you . . .
- Despite all of the above, polls identifying the segment of the vote least attracted to you could be an important guide.

However you approach this topic, your choice will define your campaign. Good luck.

Chapter 33

My 1977 Nomination for Director of Central Intelligence

When Jimmy Carter first walked into my New York law office late one summer afternoon in 1975, I liked him immediately—and I believed this honest man had a good chance of winning the presidency after the Vietnam and Watergate debacles, though I did ask him whether he thought the country was ready for a president named Jimmy. Gillian and I hosted his first fundraising dinner in New York, after which he spent the night in our home. The next morning, our frightened two-and-a-half-year-old, Juliet, came running into our room to declare that a strange man was brushing his teeth in her bathroom.

In time, I contributed my thoughts on issues, political strategy, and speeches to the Carter campaign—and hoped, immodestly but not unreasonably, for an appointment in his administration, should he win.

Once the election results were in, the process of nominations for presidential appointees went forward without me. Of the group that had worked with me on the campaign in New York, several were named to State Department, Treasury Department, and White House positions. Even my Republican friend Elliot Richardson was named special ambassador for law-of-the-sea negotiations. Tongue in cheek, I wrote him that I had been certain that our debate on New England–wide public television, representing the two presidential nominees, guaranteed that one of us would receive a high-level appointment, whichever candidate won—and, sure enough, it did: The Democratic nominee won and Elliot was appointed.

As time went by and no appointment came my way, I assumed none would. Then, suddenly, I began hearing reports from friends that I was under consideration to be director of central intelligence (DCI). From the beginning, I was not convinced that it was the right place for me. I told Dick Neustadt, a Carter transition advisor (just as he had been Kennedy's in 1960), that the job was "full of snares and headaches," particularly after the Church Committee and Rockefeller Commission investigations had exposed the agency's wrongdoings over the years, leaving it in disrepute with Congress, the press, and the public.

"No, that's not the job for me," I told Jack Watson, originally secretary to Carter's Cabinet, later his White House chief of staff, and the man who, together with Neustadt, had suggested my nomination to Carter. (When the nomination later came under attack, I wondered whether, in view of the bitter rivalries within the Carter camp, the fact that my nomination had been suggested by Jack Watson worked against me.)

In a conversation with Senator Ted Kennedy, I told him I had grave doubts about my own suitability. But Ted had already been asked by Watson and Vice President–elect Walter Mondale about my fitness for the job, had recommended me, and urged me to take it as "one of the most important jobs in government."

The director of central intelligence headed not only the CIA but in theory the entire intelligence community, including the intelligence offices of the Defense Department, the individual military services, the State Department, and others, a group of rivals not easily led into consensus.

I wanted to be a policy maker, but this agency was rightfully excluded from policy making. Could I, as a lawyer, oversee employees constantly breaking the laws of other nations? Could I, as a moralist, direct operations widely condemned as immoral? With my insistence on candor and truthfulness, could I head the most secretive and deceptive agency in government? I was also concerned about my limited experience in the world of intelligence.

On December 15, after a newspaper article stated that I was being considered for the DCI post, I talked by telephone with the president-elect, who asked me to come to Plains, Georgia, to discuss a possible appointment. I do not recall whether he mentioned DCI as a possibility during that call, but I do remember that, after I hung up, I called my brother Tom, who, having covertly worked there, knew a great deal more than I about the agency. He urged me to accept the position, if offered.

When I visited President-elect Carter in Plains three days later, he asked me a few casual questions about conflicts of interest in my legal work and investments. When I assured him I could think of none, he abruptly asked me to serve as director of central intelligence. I was surprised that he had not taken more time to review my background and suitability for the job. But in a lightning calculation—considering my desire to return to government in a meaningful position, and my unwillingness to say no to a president-elect urging me to accept a key job, even with my own doubts about this particular post—I said yes. A few days later, on December 23, my designation was announced publicly.

Initially, everything seemed fine. I received a form letter from the president-elect, addressed to all his major appointees, advising us that we would be contacted by a specialist on his transition team; that news media requests could be referred to his press secretary, Jody Powell, "or use your own judgment"; that the new president, vice president, and cabinet would meet after Christmas; and that he hoped I would attend.

While awaiting confirmation, I was afforded an office at CIA headquarters in Langley, Virginia, where the staff treated me royally. Once the kitchen learned that I liked ice cream, it began arriving with every meal. The CIA's deputy director informed me that, for my protection, my official car would be a "lightly armored sedan," and headquarters would install in my bedroom at home a "panic button" that would summon security in the event of an intruder or some other dangerous development; that my mail would be screened for plastic bombs; and that my name would be substituted as the defendant in every lawsuit then pending against the agency. What an honor!

It was not long before the first warning flare appeared—a telephone call from Carter's top political aide, Hamilton Jordan, asking about a report he had received that I had been a conscientious objector thirty years earlier. I later learned that my own personal Inspector Javert, Kenny O'Donnell, had called a Carter aide to tell him that because I had been a conscientious objector, I would be in an untenable position dealing with military officers in the intelligence agencies. "They're not going to stand for it. . . . I don't want to see Carter get hurt by this." Apparently, Kenny's warning had reached Carter. As my father had learned before me, politics ain't beanbag—it's a contact sport.

I was surprised by Ham's call—surely they had looked closely at my background before making so sensitive an appointment. But I was not surprised that the issue caused concern on the Carter team. My father had warned me, before I was old enough to register for the draft, that any position I took out of the mainstream could damage my prospects for a future in politics. As always, he was right. Robert Kennedy, when reviewing a draft manuscript of my book *Kennedy*, had given me similar advice, suggesting that I delete a reference to my early draft status. But in my phone call with Ham, and thereafter in my conversations with senators and the press, I refused to renounce my views on nonviolence as a youthful folly—that would have been unworthy and insincere.

Still, I had initially expected opposition to my nomination to come only from a few right-wing activists and conservative senators. I heard that witnesses on the far right were planning to bring up charges of womanizing that had been leveled against John and Ted Kennedy, and somehow link that to my own marital history. Even two close Carter associates asked my friends whether my two failed marriages indicated that I was not sufficiently stable for the job.

Senator Barry Goldwater, who had criticized me on the Senate floor more than a decade earlier for my draft classification, said later that he would have supported me for almost any other job in government, but that I had "a basic dislike for the responsibilities that [the CIA] job entails." Similarly, Senator Jake Garn of Utah, the senior Republican member of the Senate Select Committee on Intelligence, told me that a right-wing extremist had visited him with allegations that my ulcer doctor in Boston had prescribed relaxation drugs, implying that I had some mental deficiencies. No such drugs had ever been prescribed. Senator Garn said he threw him out. Senator Bob Dole, after assessing the views of his fellow Republicans, urged that my nomination be withdrawn. I bore no grudge against Goldwater, Garn, Dole, or Howard Baker, who also opposed me. They were simply doing their partisan political duty, seizing an opportunity to embarrass the new president.

What began as a trickle of objections from the right swelled to a flood tide. Among the streams that flowed together to create that flood were anti-Kennedy, anti-Carter, and anti-Sorensen rivulets. I paid courtesy calls on each member of the Senate Select Committee on Intelligence, which planned to hold a hearing on my nomination on January 17. I also met with the bipartisan Senate leadership as well as the chairman of the House Intelligence Committee, the outgoing attorney general, and the outgoing CIA chief, George H. W. Bush, who kindly invited me to dinner at his home. Many of these visits—along with reports I was receiving from friends and the press—confirmed that my nomination was under fire. It took me totally by surprise. "It was like being blind-sided by a truck," I told one reporter.

Most unexpected—and most damaging—was criticism from my own party. Democratic Senator Robert Morgan of North Carolina opposed me because he did not believe my testimony years earlier to the Church Committee, when it was looking into assassination plots, in which I stated my belief that President Kennedy was unaware of any CIA plot to assassinate Fidel Castro.

During my courtesy call, Morgan also justified his reservations about me by saying that he "detested Bobby Kennedy" for incivility. What did that have to do with my nomination? I wondered.

The chairman of the Senate Intelligence Committee, Democrat Daniel Inouye, one of the men in politics I most admired, reacted negatively to my youthful conscientious objector status and consequently felt even more strongly that the Carter team had not properly consulted him before my selection, a complaint shared by others.

Another Democratic member of the committee bizarrely concluded that he could not confirm me because he was suspicious of the CIA's role in the Kennedy assassination.

Senator "Scoop" Jackson, my prospective employer in 1953, was also opposed to my nomination.

Some suspected that I had been involved in the alleged plots to assassinate Castro—suspicions unwittingly fueled by Carter, who had exaggerated my background during the press conference announcing my nomination, saying that I had "worked as a direct representative of President Kennedy in dealing with the CIA and other intelligence agencies." Never. All these charges, combined with attacks on my early draft status, meant that I was being denounced simultaneously for participating in assassination plots and for favoring nonviolence. But until the week before my Senate Intelligence Committee hearing, I thought I would garner enough votes to be confirmed. Then Senators Adlai Stevenson III and Joseph Biden entered the picture. A Democratic member of the Intelligence Committee, for whom I had campaigned in Illinois, Adlai told me I had "no qualifications for this job," and said he had advised Carter to appoint his friend Jim Schlesinger, "a man who really understands the Soviet menace." Adlai let it be known that he was also against me on grounds that, during my courtesy call to his office, I had "taken notes" on his views, which he interpreted as reflecting that I must have been woefully ill-prepared on his opinions. Though he claimed that I was not sufficiently "tough" to earn the respect of CIA agents, it was Stevenson who tearfully told me in his office that he was opposed to my nomination. He also criticized me for donating my papers, including classified documents, to the Kennedy Library and receiving a tax deduction for that gift, possibly not realizing that his father, former UN ambassador Adlai Stevenson, had done the same.

Meanwhile, Democratic Senator Joseph Biden of Delaware had his staff locate my affidavit in the trial of Daniel Ellsberg, one of the Pentagon Papers cases. Reportedly, Biden found my affidavit "very disturbing," and brought it to the attention of committee chairman Inouye, who urged that President-elect Carter be notified immediately. It was the beginning of the end, particularly after Adlai, alerted to my affidavit, circulated it widely on Capitol Hill.

My role in the Pentagon Papers cases began in 1971, when I was contacted by the *New York Times*. Nixon's Attorney General John Mitchell was seeking to enjoin or indict the *Times* for publishing, without the government's permission, a copy it had obtained through Daniel Ellsberg of the so-called Pentagon Papers. The latter was an authoritative account of U.S. involvement in Vietnam prepared by Pentagon historians under the direction of Leslie Gelb, at the time an assistant secretary of defense.

The project had been initiated in response to then-secretary of defense McNamara's request for an "encyclopedic" classified study answering difficult questions on the accuracy of executive branch statements over the years about the Vietnam conflict. McNamara's 1995 memoir, *In Retrospect*, received harsh criticism from those who blamed him for the escalation of the war and its tragically prolonged continuation. But I think that his acknowledgment of error—indeed, guilt—was better for the country and for future decision makers than no acknowledgment at all (which has been the pattern for most other mistaken warriors).

In response to Attorney General Mitchell's lawsuit, lawyers and editors for the *Times* had been soliciting testimony from former government officials, questioning whether U.S. national security would inevitably be harmed by the publication of these or other classified documents. I agreed to provide an affidavit, in which I stated my belief that while there was often a legitimate need for government secrecy, the executive branch routinely overclassified documents and kept them secret long after there was any legitimate secret to protect. I further noted that, in the early 1960s, it was common practice in Washington for government officials to take classified documents home to review, that it was not uncommon for some officials to leak classified information to the press, and that documents of far greater importance to national security than those in the Pentagon Papers had been leaked to the press without criminal prosecution.

In a letter thanking me for my affidavit, *Times* columnist Tom Wicker wrote that many others whom the *Times* had contacted did not have "the courage and the honesty to defend publication . . . It might shock you to know how many others refused even to write a letter to the editor in defense of the First Amendment. But you spoke up and put your name to it."

Managing editor Abe Rosenthal added, in another letter, that my affidavit "helped us in our presentation to the court . . . because you were willing to speak out publicly . . . Not many were . . . [in this] tense and critical time . . . No small reason for the good feeling we all have is the fact that people like you backed our decision to publish." A similar letter came that summer from publisher "Punch" Sulzberger.

Having given the *New York Times* an affidavit affirming the relative harmlessness of the Pentagon Papers in terms of national security, I did not see how I could do any less when subsequently approached by defense attorneys for Daniel Ellsberg and his codefendant, Anthony Russo Jr., who were charged with theft, conspiracy, and espionage for conveying these "secrets" to the press. In any event, if I declined, I was told, they were prepared to subpoena me to repeat my testimony in their trial.

Ironically, one of Ellsberg's defense attorneys was Charles Goodell, the Republican whom Governor Rockefeller had appointed to Robert Kennedy's Senate seat in 1968. Goodell and the other defense attorneys were trying to show that Ellsberg's indictment was an example of "selective prosecution." Hoping to prove that it was common practice for government officials to take classified material with them when they left government, and to use it for their own purposes, they asked me on the witness stand whether I had taken, upon leaving the White House, government documents that I had written and material that others had written. To those questions I answered yes.

In the introduction to my affidavit, I stated:

The public's right to be informed, and the Congress's right to be informed, have not to my knowledge been regarded as important criteria by those determining classifications. Nor is consideration given to the danger of irreparable injury to the national security interest if the public and Congress are denied facts necessary for an informed judgment, enlightened debate, the correction of mistakes, the discontinuation of invalid policies and strategies, and the prevention of a repetition of past errors . . .

All still true today.

At the close of my testimony, the U.S. attorney asked me no questions, instead seeking to discredit me by irrelevantly noting that I had never served in the military or spent any time in Vietnam. My testimony was delivered on March 15, 1973, and I left Los Angeles for New York at 10:30 P.M. that night, eager to return to Gillian, who gave birth to our daughter, Juliet, one week later. More than thirty years later, as a practicing lawyer researching a First Amendment case and discovering my small role, Juliet wrote me in a treasured e-mail: "Dad, I am very proud of you for having filed an affidavit in that historic case! Thank you on behalf of many."

In the end, the publication of the Pentagon Papers did no harm. No one has ever shown a secret thereby released that damaged national security. Both Judge Murray Gurfein in New York and Judge Gerhard Gesell in Washington invited the government to present to the court the strongest examples of sensitive material, and neither was impressed. The government eventually lost its cases against the *New York Times* and Ellsberg. The latter case was dismissed because of government misconduct.

Nonetheless, the merits of my Pentagon Papers affidavits did not matter when my CIA nomination became the center of controversy. Those pressing the Carter-Mondale team to withdraw my nomination, while not contesting the accuracy of my affidavits, implied that I could not be trusted to keep secrets (ironic, considering all the secrets I have kept—and continue to keep).

It was a devastating charge, considering the post for which I was nominated.

Resistance to my nomination came not only from the Hill. Unbeknownst to me at the time, a large bloc of opposition had formed among then-current and former members of the defense and intelligence communities. One retired intelligence officer spread word that I would be "about as well received at Langley," the CIA headquarters, "as Sherman was in Atlanta." Among those opposed to my nomination were supporters of larger Pentagon budgets who felt that, under my direction, the CIA would not be sufficiently alarmist to justify new weapons systems. Retired CIA covert action operatives feared that I would strengthen the ongoing trend to oppose covert operations (true); some old-time employees of the agency even opposed me because of JFK's negative statements about the CIA after the Bay of Pigs. Another remote possibility briefly crossed my mind—perhaps these operatives were acting to make certain I never got access to agency files on President Kennedy's assassination.

In May 2001, nearly a quarter century later, I was approached at the Council on Foreign Relations by a stranger who introduced himself as a former (was he?) CIA covert operations agent, who said that for years he had wanted to tell me that he and his colleagues had "made a big mistake" in undermining my nomination. What the agency needed at that time, he said, but only belatedly realized, was a leader who could persuasively articulate its role and indispensability, and that I "would have been the perfect person for the job." He acknowledged that some of the "dirty tricks" and other opposition to my nomination had come from within the agency.

I always wondered about the source of one paid newspaper column, written by a conservative representative of the AFL-CIO, which worked closely with the CIA overseas. The article reported my speaking in support of a dissident candidate at a Steelworkers Union meeting in Pittsburgh, implying that it demonstrated antiunion sentiments on my part. I had never heard of the dissident candidate, never attended the meeting, and never made the speech.

An old proverb proclaims, "Only in the winter can you tell which trees are evergreen." I found, throughout that experience, a few friends in the Senate who were truly evergreen: Democratic senators Birch Bayh of Indiana, Howard Metzenbaum of Ohio, George McGovern of South Dakota, and Gary Hart of Colorado (Bayh and Hart were also members of the committee). Republican senators Clifford Case of New Jersey and

Robert Stafford of Vermont supported me, as did Senator Mark Hatfield, Republican of Oregon, whom I had visited in his gubernatorial office nearly twenty years earlier to discuss JFK's entrance into the Oregon primary. Other friends held back. Senator Ted Kennedy was supportive, but decided not to urge my nomination publicly, fearful—perhaps correctly—that a prolonged fight might revive questions about my advice to him on the fatal automobile accident in which he was involved.

Support also came for unexpected reasons. One Republican senator told me his researcher had found a letter I had written in the White House declining free theater tickets, and that this show of honesty impressed him. A Southern Democratic senator, whose car was stuck in the snow, asked for assistance from a passerby, who happened to be my sister; she told him she wouldn't push unless he promised to vote for me—and he did!

Having never been a radical, and having in fact considered myself something of a conformist if not establishmentarian, I was astonished to find myself the most controversial of all of Carter's high-level appointees. At a breakfast meeting at CIA headquarters with Clark Clifford on the Saturday before my Monday committee hearing, Clark and I decided to ask Carter to fight for me. But when Carter did call four of the Democrats on the committee, he did not—as previously agreed—

dismiss the criticisms as unfounded, ask that his nominee be confirmed, or ask for assistance; he merely asked for an appraisal of my chances.

On Saturday night, I spoke with the president-elect by telephone. He assured me that he was "behind" me. It turned out he was way, way behind me. He also said he was too busy working on plans for his inauguration to intervene on my behalf. (It reminded me of an encounter Gillian and I had with Queen Elizabeth months earlier in 1976, when Carter was the Democratic presidential nominee. When Gillian asked the queen whether she had met Carter, I interjected: "She hasn't had time." "No," Her Majesty gently corrected me. "*He* hasn't had time.")

Time had little to do with his abandonment of my nomination. Carter did not want to use any of the political capital he was husbanding to get his longtime friend Griffin Bell confirmed as attorney general (Bell was under attack for alleged past racist activities). After it was all over, the *New York Times* speculated: "What would have happened in the Senate if President Carter had nominated Theodore Sorensen to be Attorney General and Griffin Bell as Director of Central Intelligence?" Good question. I also discovered that my friend Andrew Young, another early Carter backer, who was appointed to the job I wanted—ambassador to the United Nations—actually wanted to be head of CIA. Surely some hand of fate could have worked all that out in advance.

During our Saturday night call, Carter kept hinting to me that my withdrawal was the best solution. He suggested that I call Clark Clifford, whom he expected would urge me to bow out—but Clark, while acknowledging that Carter did not "have the stomach for a fight over the nomination," urged me to rebut the charges, whether I ultimately fought or withdrew.

Although I had considered withdrawing in a press conference Sunday afternoon, more defamatory leaks from the Senate only increased my determination to have a nationally televised hearing to air my response to these false accusations. On Sunday morning, Carter avoided the press outside church. When I told him by telephone that I was unwilling to withdraw without an opportunity to answer the scurrilous charges against me, he responded. "Well, it looks like you and I are working at cross purposes," adding that he wanted me to withdraw, and that Vice President–elect Mondale, who telephoned me moments later, would "arrange" it.

Accompanied by Gillian, Jack Watson, and my law partner Arthur Liman, who was assisting in my confirmation process, I went to Fritz Mondale's home on Sunday afternoon. When Hamilton Jordan arrived moments later, Mondale huddled privately with him and then began the meeting, memorialized in Liman's handwritten notes:

Mondale, with great emotion: "I have come closer to crying in the last two days than at any time in the eight years I have been in Washington . . . You brought to the Carter Administration something we needed . . . You have been attacked unfairly. In a fair forum, you would win confirmation. But the Senate plays dirty, and Governor Carter and I are convinced that withdrawal is the only course."

TCS—eloquently and emotionally, but with control: "Everyone in this room knows that I did not seek this position. When Jack Watson first mentioned that he was recommending me, I said, please no . . . But when Jimmy urged me to take the post and stressed the importance of the assignment to him, I accepted out of a sense of duty and principle, even though it meant a great personal sacrifice to my family and me. Now because I agreed to my selection, I am being irreparably damaged by vicious personal attacks. My reputation is my most precious asset, and I will not withdraw under fire without an opportunity to confront my brave anonymous accusers . . . I understand that the President does not want to face political defeat at the outset of his Administration, and that my reputation is a secondary consideration to him . . . I am a realist, but I must be vindicated on these charges to consent to a withdrawal."

Mondale: "The President is deeply disturbed by the unfair attacks on you . . . but the votes are not there."

TCS: "I don't share the opinion that the President did all he could for me. There is a marked contrast between the public support he gave to Bell and his silence on my nomination."

Jordan: "He stated that he was behind you. There was a foul-up when the Assistant Press Secretary said no comment."

Liman: "I saw [Carter] on CBS last night, with a microphone thrust in front of him, refuse to comment on the attack . . . the President-elect's silence, in contrast to his spirited defense of Bell, was deadly."

Jordan—belligerently to TCS: "Didn't you tell Jimmy that you had decided to withdraw?"

TCS: "I asked him to get an assessment of the attitudes of the Committee since I did not wish to cause him the embarrassment of a defeat . . . That was before these personal attacks stepped up."

Gillian—. . . to Mondale: "How could [the president-elect] be turned down by the Senate if he really pressed for an affirmative vote? He said he wanted Ted, and now he is sacrificing him."

Mondale: "I have been in the Senate for ten years—they are very independent."

The meeting closed with a consensus decision that my withdrawal would not be announced until the next day lest the committee hold no hearing at all, thereby preventing me from refuting, in front of my accusers, the accusations against me.

On the morning of my Senate nomination hearing, Monday, January 17, 1977, the *New York Times* front-page lead article was headlined: "Carter Stands Firm, Supports Sorensen as Director of CIA," a reference to a supportive statement issued by Carter Sunday afternoon, once he was alerted to my forthcoming withdrawal. It was the *Times*'s first supportive headline in a month.

The Senate Intelligence Committee opened its hearing, not by hearing first from the nominee but by giving each committee member an opportunity to denounce me, repeating all the false allegations that the senators and their staffs had leaked to the press. There was one notable absence: After circulating vicious attacks against me, Adlai III did not have the courage or decency to show up at my hearing and confront me in person.

When the issue of my views on nonviolence was raised, New York Senator Pat Moynihan, who had accompanied me to the hearing, came to my defense: "Surely, we are not about to impose religious qualifications for public service at this late date, when persons of convictions have become so few as to make the issue increasingly moot."

Soon after the hearing began, Pat leaned over and whispered in my ear: "Good God, this is a hanging jury!" George McGovern would call it "a shameful moment in the recent history of the Senate."

My statement to the committee under oath began:

I'm grateful for this opportunity . . . to answer the scurrilous and unfounded personal attacks which have been circulated against me, largely on an anonymous basis. I did not seek or lightly accept this assignment, and some of my friends have suggested that anyone agreeing to take the job lacks either the sanity or the judgment necessary to fulfill it . . . I do not intend to be intimidated . . . I prize both my country and my honor too greatly to desert this post under that kind of cloud; and despite the prejudgments already voiced by some members of the Committee before I have been heard, I am here to appeal to [your] sense of fairness.

I proceeded to demonstrate that each of the charges against me was totally false. My rebuttals were not challenged by a single member of the committee. I also stated those subjects on which my views obviously clashed with those of my detractors. Having read the portion of my testimony distributed to the committee and press, I turned to a new page:

But it is now clear that a substantial portion of the United States Senate and many members of the intelligence community are not yet ready to accept as Director of Central Intelligence an outsider who believes as I believe . . . [For me] to continue fighting for this post, which would be my natural inclination, would only handicap the new Administration if I am rejected, or handicap my effectiveness as Director if

I am confirmed. It is therefore with deep regret that I am asking Governor Carter to withdraw my designation . . . I return to private life with a clear conscience. When my nomination was announced on Christmas Eve, my youngest son said to me: "Now you will have to do some things you don't want to do." I replied: "I never will." I have never compromised my conscience, and I am unwilling to do so now in order to assure my nomination.

When I concluded my statement, Chairman Inouye said: "I know that this has been a difficult time for you . . . but knowing Theodore Sorensen, I am certain that this painful episode will not in any way dampen his interest and concern in the well being of this country . . . If it is of any consolation, this Committee has received a report from an agency of the intelligence community, the FBI, which has given you a four-star rating." At which point my law partner Mark Alcott whispered in my ear: "Out of a possible 10."

I never lost my admiration for Inouye. On the other hand, the prize for political hypocrisy in a town noted for political hypocrisy went to Joe Biden. On my first courtesy call to his office, he could not have been more enthusiastic, supportive, and gracious, calling me "the best appointment Carter has made!" At the opening of the hearing, he changed both his tune and his tone, stating: "Quite honestly, I'm not sure whether or not Mr. Sorensen could be indicted or convicted under the espionage statutes . . . whether Mr. Sorensen intentionally took advantage of ambiguities in the law or carelessly ignored the law." After listening to my statement of defense and withdrawal, he said: "Ted, you are one of the classiest men I have ever run across in my whole life."

Less than an hour and a half after it convened, the committee recessed. A lively impromptu press conference followed outside the hearing room:

Q: "At what point this morning did you decide to withdraw?"

A: "This is a decision that has been evolving over the weekend . . . I knew prior to my entrance . . . At approximately two minutes to 10 this morning, I spoke to Governor Carter on the telephone in the booth downstairs as I entered the building. . . ."

Q: "What made you wait until this morning?"

A: "I wanted to answer the personal charges that had been made against me before I withdrew. . . ."

Q: "Why save your withdrawal until the end rather than announcing it at the beginning and then answering the charges against you?"

A: "Possibly because none of you would have been listening when I answered the charges."

Q: "Who did circulate the charges against you, what kind of people?"

A: "Take a look at the organizations who have asked [for time] to testify against me: the American Conservative Union, the Liberty Lobby, spokesmen for the John Birch Society. . . . You might also talk to those reporters who have talked to Senators who have been putting out this information."

Q: "What Senators?"

A: "I assume the press knows that, since those Senators always refuse to be quoted by name."

Q: "You believe there were Senators circulating some of those allegations?"

A: "According to the press—and I believe a little bit of what I read in the newspapers. . . ."

Q: "Do you agree or disagree with Senator McGovern's saying that the ghost of Joe McCarthy stalks the land?"

A: "I believe it is more appropriate for me to talk about my statement, and Senator McGovern to talk about his statement. . . ."

Q: "Did the President-elect or his staff know prior to your designation about the Ellsberg affidavit and *New York Times* affidavit?"

A: "I haven't the slightest idea how thorough their investigation of my background was . . . this is all on the public record . . ."

Q: "Do you agree with Senator Baker's analysis that the designated head of the CIA should be above controversy, above reproach?"

A: "He certainly should be above reproach, but to say that he should be above controversy invites a repetition of what happened here, whereby those who are opposed to an individual for his views will start circulating totally unfounded charges against him and then say he is controversial and therefore must be rejected."

Q: "Given this experience . . . what would you recommend to Mr. Carter about a successor?"

A: "I think it's clear from the statements by the mourners after the deceased had been laid down that, in their consideration of the next director, they could do worse—and they probably will."

Gillian, our toddler Juliet, and I left for a "rest and recovery" vacation in the U.S. Virgin Islands, skipping the inaugural festivities. When I returned, I found the following handwritten letter from the new president on White House stationery, dated January 22:

I know that you and Gillian have been through a very difficult time, while only offering to do well for our country. Your withdrawing [he continued to insist that it was my decision, which he had nothing to do with] is a loss for all of us . . . I'll always wonder if it would have been better to fight it out . . . Sincerely, Jimmy.

In my reply on February 4, I thanked him

for the confidence placed in me last December . . . and for your willingness last month to stand behind my nomination until we both recognized that it was no longer viable . . . I shall always believe that I would have made a difference as DCI, that you selected me for that reason and that I was blocked for that reason . . . none of this has diminished in the slightest the immense respect . . . with which I have long regarded you.

Okay, so we both fudged the truth a little.

A front-page *New York Times* article recapitulated the reasons for the "collapse of the effort to install [me] as Director of Central Intelligence . . . a rare defeat for an incoming President," citing many factors, including "timidity among Senate liberals and Democrats and, above all, misjudgments and an apparent failure of nerve by the new administration." The *Times* identified my opposition as consisting of "15 unnamed CIA employees . . . conservative circles in the Senate . . . [and Republicans] still smarting from Watergate." A *Boston Globe* editorial, "Savaging Sorensen," read:

> The real reasons for the destruction of the nomination can only be divined out of a witches' brew of old animosities, fears and contentions dating back to the Kennedy era when Sorensen was a force to be reckoned with in the White House. Never a well-loved man with his icy brilliance and his hard eye for competence, Sorensen was, and evidently remains, a man anathema to the legions of Kennedy haters on the right in both parties.

Columnist Murray Kempton in the *New York Post* wrote that I had played my "part in the ceremony of immolation as the Carter administration's first martyr with considerable dignity. . . . He went manfully to the stake without inflicting the embarrassment of being carried there."

My favorite commentaries on the entire episode,

however, were two cartoons: one, by Douglas Marlette of the *Charlotte Observer*, depicted me being interviewed by an unidentified official asking: "Could you describe your experience with the CIA, Mr. Sorensen?" as I sat there with an assortment of knives, daggers, swords, and similar weapons protruding from my back. The other, by the incomparable Herblock of the *Washington Post*, depicted a huge crocodile, labeled "Senatorial Attacks," finishing off a lunch with scraps labeled "Sorensen Nomination," as the creature, weeping "crocodile tears," says: "Alas—burp—this splendid fellow!" I asked Herb for the original, and it hung in my law office for years.

Had Jimmy Carter fought for my nomination, I believe I would have obtained a majority of that committee, including up to four Republicans. Years later, when Carter's memoirs, *Keeping Faith*, were published, few reviews were more critical than that of *Washington Post* editor Robert Kaiser, who began:

Modern Presidential memoirs . . . understandably cast [their authors] in a favorable light . . . by omitting embarrassments . . . The name of Theodore Sorensen does not appear in *Keeping Faith*. But it was Carter's decision—under pressure from the Senate—to withdraw Sorensen's nomination as Director of the Central Intelligence Agency in the early days of his Presidency that first established him as a weak figure that the Congress could push around.

The whole experience was brief but bruising, and I welcomed a return to private life, jokingly telling a luncheon of Paul, Weiss lawyers that my withdrawal and return to the law firm were part of a "deep cover" plot, and that I was in fact secretly the real CIA director. The transition from public to private life in America is, as Ben Franklin once said, a promotion from servant to master. In the end, the experience did not sour me on public service. But it again confirmed Harry Truman's familiar quip: "If you want a friend in Washington, buy a dog."

Chapter 34

Family and Health

Just as my brief flirtation with the DCI nomination in January 1977 left little scar tissue, in hindsight, my defeat in the 1970 Senate race was a blessing. It marked the beginning of a new, more predictable life, enabling me to rediscover the joys of family that I had too often overlooked in the previous two decades. Having married just a year before my time-consuming, energy-draining Senate campaign, Gillian and I at last had time for ourselves.

Juliet's arrival in 1973 was eagerly awaited, and she filled our days with delight. She inherited her mother's enthusiasm and talent for dance, foreign languages, and horseback riding. Juliet thrived on life in New York, but eagerly accompanied me on business trips to Spain,

Italy, England, Ireland, Puerto Rico, and Panama—all in the tradition of C.A. taking me with him on his automobile trips around Nebraska—just as my sons, when they were in their teens, joined me for summer trips to New Zealand, Tunisia, Kenya, Newfoundland, Moscow, and Chernigov.

Eric, Steve, and Phil continued to join us for holidays in New York, and we sometimes traveled to Wisconsin. As they pursued their education, married, and began their own families in northern Wisconsin, we kept in touch with long letters, phone calls, and visits.

Until driven out of business by the large chains and the Internet, my son Steve and his wife, Julie, owned and operated an independent bookstore, while homeschooling my grandson Rory and granddaughter Hannah. My son Eric, a social worker and family counselor, performs and teaches music, playing stringed instruments at gigs ranging from local fairs to weddings. My youngest son, Phil, and our daughter, Juliet, made me proud by following in the family footsteps to become lawyers. Phil is a small-town solo practitioner, handling cases ranging from murder to dog complaints. Juliet is now an assistant United States attorney in Chicago, having spent two years in the Peace Corps in Morocco before attending Columbia Law School.

When Juliet married Ben Jones in 2000, two of my

grandsons, Phil's sons Lincoln and Trey, were ring bearers. I cherish all my grandchildren and enjoy every minute I spend with them. My grandson Olaf, Eric's son, who suffers from severe autism and mental retardation, is a lovable young man, healthy in all other respects. His annual visit is a special time for me, even though it leaves me filled with sadness over what might have been.

When I celebrated my seventieth birthday, accompanied by Gillian, my four children, and their spouses or partners, and my oldest grandson, Rory, on a white-water rafting trip down the Colorado River in the Grand Canyon, it was a time for "grand reflections" on how fortunate I was to be surrounded by my wonderful family.

Despite widespread geographic dispersal, all the Sorensens—my siblings and I and our spouses and descendants—try to gather for occasional family reunions. It is a large family, multicultural and multiethnic—a diverse family that mirrors the diversity of this country. We work a variety of jobs, have attained a variety of educational levels, and hail from rural as well as urban areas. Some are foreign-born, others have never left America's shores. But we all wholeheartedly embrace the ideals of peace and justice that C.A. and Annis taught to me and my siblings on Park Avenue in Lincoln, Nebraska, so many decades ago.

. . .

I do not come from a particularly long-lived family. I never knew either of my grandfathers and have lived more years than my father and my brother Tom, who died in 1997. But until 2001 I had experienced few serious medical problems, recovering quickly from two bouts with ulcers, a bad back, and various other minor ailments. Throughout the years, I tried to stay fit by walking everywhere, and swimming, and playing tennis year-round. At age fifty-five, I completed the New York City Marathon in just under four hours.

In the White House I organized a softball team that included Lee White, Mike Feldman, Walter Heller, and Jim Tobin. In games against the Washington press corps, my positions alternated between pitcher and first base. In my early days at Paul, Weiss, I also pitched in a New York lawyers' softball league, a role for which I am remembered fondly by former opponents who hit home runs off me. Despite being a lifelong baseball fan (changing my team with my city—from the Cubs to the Senators to the Mets), my favorite participatory sport has long been tennis. At a charity event in Pound Ridge— the northern Westchester town where Gillian and I have spent weekends, holidays and summers for decades—I had the thrill of playing in an exhibition doubles game with Arthur Ashe, the world tennis champion and civil rights activist whom I had long admired. He did not admire my unorthodox tennis stroke, which sliced and spun virtually every shot; and called to me across the net after a brief exchange: "Who was your pro?"

I had every reason to hope that I might be spared the usual frailties of aging and enjoy an active twenty-first century if I continued to eat wisely, drink sparingly, and exercise regularly.

On July 20, 2001, I addressed our law firm's summer associates on a favorite topic: "My Transition from Public Service to Private Practice." I told them the reasons why, after my service in Washington, and writing on Cape Cod, I had selected Paul, Weiss. I spoke of having represented both U.S. and foreign corporations, of having advised a number of heads of government—and I spoke of some interesting new matters on the horizon that summer, involving, among others, the implementation of the United Nations resolution on "conflict diamonds" (stones sold through corrupt, warmongering governments or individuals), the opposition to the continuing U.S. Navy bombing target practice on Puerto Rico's offshore island of Vieques, the organization of a new global foundation to protect sacred sites in all parts of the world, and an effort to seek the negotiated release of thirteen Jews arrested for alleged espionage in Iran. I touched briefly on my writing, speaking, and political activities.

The question and answer session following the speech revealed a number of young associates eager to help on these projects, one asking how I had time and energy for it all. As I left the lunch to return to my office, I felt I was running out of both time and energy. Inadvertently exiting the elevator one floor before we intended, my partner Jeh Johnson and I decided to climb the remaining two flights of stairs. When I reached my desk, sitting down to review a document, I found to my astonishment that I had a headache so severe I could not read. What I did not know was that all hell was breaking loose inside my skull—and that the productive life I had just described to those young summer associates was about to change.

Foolishly insisting that I just had a headache, I protested when a young lawyer, Diane Knox, and her secretary, Cathy Fuller, decided to call Gillian, my doctor, and an ambulance. Even as the ambulance team wheeled me out of the office, I was still protesting that it was "just a headache." As I later learned, the immediate intervention by Diane and Cathy saved me from far more severe brain damage or death. Many years earlier, I had vowed to a fellow senior partner that "I will never retire—they will have to carry me out of here feet first." That day they did.

Upon my arrival in the emergency room of New York Cornell Hospital, the triage nurse immediately diagnosed a cerebral hemorrhage, or stroke; and a young resident began a post–head trauma interview, telling me "These questions are to help us make you feel better."

Q: "Do you know where you are?"

A: "New York City."

Q: "What year is this?"

A: "2001."

Q: "Who was elected president last year?"

A: "Neither I nor anyone else knows the technically correct answer to that question; and that question is not making me feel better." [I do not think George W. Bush was "elected." He lost, then took office by means of a wholly partisan Supreme Court decision that had no basis in law.]

Q: "Your chart says you are a lawyer. What kind, a tax lawyer?"

A: "No, malpractice [I joked]. Better be careful."

At that point, I was wheeled into surgery for an operation to drain the pool of blood accumulating in my brain. The chief of neurology at New York Cornell Medical Center told Gillian to "cancel everything for the next three months."

When I awoke the next morning, not certain what day it was, I tried to call my office, discovering that I could not read the telephone dial, that every part of my body hurt to move, and that I was hooked up to too many tubes and tanks to walk to the bathroom. I called for help to no avail. Trying to get out of bed set off an alarm, and an attendant rushed in and literally wrestled me back into bed. Any previous illusions of indestructibility vanished.

The neurosurgeon gave me a quick briefing on what had happened, and asked whether I had any questions, I replied only half in jest: "One: why me?" He said there was no medical answer that would satisfy me; that I was luckier than most stroke victims because I could still walk. I asked whether it had been a waste of time for me to walk so many miles, swim so many laps, and eat so much tasteless low-fat food; and he calmly replied: "It was not a waste—that is why you are still here talking to me."

There was no apparent cause of my stroke. I had no history of hypertension, high cholesterol, diabetes, blood clots. An atrial fibrillation had been treated and reversed years earlier. I never smoked. I was not overweight, and I exercised regularly. It just happened. Apparently, fragile blood vessels leaked. But one thing was clear: July 2001 was payback time. Years earlier, when both my youth and my health seemed limitless, I abused my body through years of sleep deprivation, especially during the presidential campaign and White House years, in several other campaigns from 1968 onward, and in decades of international business travel, perhaps foolishly punishing my body by flying to Tokyo the day after I ran the 1983 NYC Marathon. During the first six months of 2001 I had flown to seven countries overnight from New York, often flying back the next night.

In the middle of that miserable first week in the hospital, I developed a high fever, and my doctors decided to perform a spinal tap to determine the cause. Recalling my history of lower back problems, I knew that a spinal tap can be very painful; I pleaded with them not to do one. While they weighed my objections, my fever subsided. The headaches continued, worsening with the slightest movement. I was fed intravenously, I developed nausea and lost substantial weight. Woozy, weary, and weak, I was little more than a grumpy old bag of bones crumpled on a hospital bed. I am told that two doctor friends, after looking in on me, pretty much gave up hope. But my loving wife was always at my bedside. She was thrust into the dual role of decision maker and caregiver for her critically ill yet incredibly cranky spouse. I was more accustomed to giving advice than receiving it. The whole ordeal was difficult for Gillian.

She coped, in part, by philosophically taking the long view, e-mailing our daughter, Juliet, that we had "been so unbelievably lucky to have had health, energy, opportunity and a . . . partnership for 32 years, more than most."

Despite my discomfort, I was patient and respectful when visited in the hospital by a clergyman, who wanted to pray with me. I told the good reverend, as my siblings sat by wondering how I would handle this one, that Unitarians believe in silent prayer. He approved.

My transfer to Mount Sinai Hospital for therapy started badly when the ambulance attendants dropped the stretcher on which I was being carried. Then I discovered to my dismay the hospital's new communications system, which enabled a central operator to reach every hospital employee in every room at every hour of the day. The loudspeaker was positioned just above my head. I also discovered that highly touted group therapy sessions did little for me. When the group leader cheerily asked, "What are we all planning for tomorrow? We must all plan for the next day," I responded: "Getting out of here—do any of you want to go with me?" One therapist told me that the purpose of my time in rehab was to enable me to "live an ordinary life." Having enjoyed more than half a century of an extraordinary life, I was not overly inspired by that goal.

A decade earlier, before the technological advances of brain scanning equipment and the development of new drugs, I probably would have died that day. Had I not received immediate treatment from some of the finest medical professionals in the world, I certainly would have incurred far more damage to my brain. But the most enduring impact of the stroke was on my vision. When my doctors told me that I would never regain my full sight I remembered, all too well, Carlyle's words: "Never! O reader, knowest thou that hard word?" They say that my eyes have all the normal components necessary for sight, but that the "control room" behind the eyes will never again be normal. I try to take a philosophical approach. My father wrote to his friend Walter Locke, when the latter's eyesight was failing: "So long as you continue to retain your sharp sensitivity to life in all its phases, and stay on fire with visions and dreams of what life on this planet can be made to be, your real eyes will remain undimmed, be your physical age 80, 90, or 105." When I hear audiences murmuring about my condition as I am helped to a podium, I sometimes admonish them: "Don't worry about my eyesight, folks. I have more vision than the president of the United States."

At first, I was in denial of the permanence of my vision loss and its consequences. Now I simply accept the fact that my world of limited sight is a different world:

every day is foggy, every room is dimly lit, every daylight hour is twilight, every TV and movie screen is unclear. In biblical terms, I now see through a glass, darkly. I previously prided myself on being able to accomplish much with comparatively little time and effort. After the stroke, I discovered that even little things take more time and more effort. Getting up each morning and dressing required more vision and dexterity than I could at first muster—buttoning my shirt, shaving, tying my shoelaces, walking unassisted. I am frustrated every time I accidentally knock something to the floor, every time I pour water or juice on the wrong side of the glass and onto the table. I try to laugh at the absurdity of it all when I put an article of clothing on backward, or do not see a spoon or straw protruding from the glass I put to my mouth. I have become reacquainted with books on tape and was proud when reminded that my book *Kennedy* had been recorded by the American Foundation for the Blind for the Library of Congress National Reading Program.

Occasionally I think about my 1961 trip to Paris with JFK. Now I remember more clearly and sympathetically watching President de Gaulle, in full military regalia with a braided cap, but too proud to wear his thick-lensed glasses, climbing the steps of the government guest house to greet President Kennedy and escort him to the ceremonial wreath laying at the Arc de Triomphe, stumbling almost imperceptibly as his foot missed one step. For one fleeting moment, before he regained his balance and composure, the general's stern, imperious visage was replaced by that of a puzzled old man who could not find his footing. I have experienced that same discomfort many times.

The stroke's damage to the right frontal lobe of my brain apparently produced a condition called visual agnosia, in which I see objects in their elemental forms but cannot always put them together—failing to recognize familiar faces even when I am able to make out details like lips, eyes, and ears. The distinguished psychiatrist Oliver Sacks wrote a book about this condition, titled *The Man Who Mistook His Wife for a Hat*. I have never made that mistake, but have made some equally troubling ones, mistaking a glass door for an opening, a rural mailbox for a deer, and a shadow for a step. When my eyes see only the end of a word, my brain often makes an incorrect assumption about the whole word. Is that restroom door marked "men" or "women"? I see "presented" and think I am reading "represented." I read "progress" when the word is "Congress." I saw "contender" where the article read "bartender." Was the president "furious" or merely "curious"? Upon leaving the hospital with my left field of vision still fully blocked,

I saw only the back half of automobiles driving along the street, a truly weird sight.

In those first months after the stroke, attempting to avoid excessive self-pity, I tried to focus on what I could still accomplish and how much worse the stroke's consequences might have been. But, after a few months, each day's discovery that there had been no improvement in my vision brought a new realization of all that I was no longer able to do. "A stroke knocks the stuffing out of you," my doctor told me. It certainly does—initiative, ambition, hope, interest in world events, energy, endurance, equanimity, even empathy—I barely noticed the turmoil inflicted on New York City and our country just two months later on September 11. For a long time it also impaired my optimism, my patience, my determination, joy, even occasionally my rationality.

My temperament changed. I had gloomy thoughts about my mother's illness, JFK's death, and the fate of other stroke victims I had known, including JFK's father. I recalled my 1968 visit to Hyannis Port with Bobby to have lunch with his parents, and how sad it was to see tears of frustration in Ambassador Kennedy's eyes when he could not talk to his son.

I disconsolately identified with Cyrano in my favorite Rostand play, when, in the final act, he limps with bandaged head toward his beloved Roxanne, muttering how, after all the blows he had survived over the years, he had been "Struck from behind, and by a lackey's hand!" The whole experience was a memento mori, another reminder of what November 22, 1963, had already taught me—that life is completely unpredictable.

I knew I had to control my anger and grief, and to resist any signs or thoughts of depression, which doctors say can easily result from a diminished blood flow to the brain. I don't believe I ever waded into the depths of true clinical depression. But I confess to feeling overwhelmed during those first weeks by a chronic sense of melancholy and exhaustion. Unable to see or walk normally, unable to move my head without pain, I found the dividing line between helplessness and hopelessness dangerously thin. Gillian had already endured the first stressful weeks of my critical stage in the hospital, where others were responsible for my care and comfort. Now she faced new challenges. I was unhappy, irritable, and unpleasant; and I appreciate all the more her unfailing patience, and her efforts to mollify this stranger for whose well-being she was suddenly solely responsible. During that first year, I often had the odd sensation that I was walking through life performing a part in a play, peering out at a new world stage. I saw myself differently: inhabiting Ted Sorensen's body, playing his role, meeting his schedule, keeping his commitments, voicing his views—and yet somehow feeling strangely detached.

At times the old United Auto Workers song that I supplied to JFK for a 1960 campaign speech in Detroit ran through my mind:

> Who will take care of me?
> How'll I get by
> When I'm too old to work
> And I'm too young to die?

Life was not all gloom. In those early weeks, I could still laugh. Earlier that year, when Gillian and I visited philanthropist Arthur Ross, an avid golfer at ninety-two, at his Jamaica estate, Arthur and I had a putting contest. To his chagrin and my amazement (I am not a golfer), I edged out a victory. Many months later, when he phoned after my stroke, I asked him whether, at his advanced age, he had ever suffered a stroke. He replied that he had not. "Arthur," I said with feigned glee, "in life as in golf, I am one stroke up on you."

At the hospital and later at home, Gillian read to me all the letters and telephone messages of hope and cheer—from family, friends, colleagues in the law firm, and from my Washington years, and from others, including Bill and Hillary Clinton, Al Gore, and former Nebraska senator Bob Kerrey, no stranger to hospital confinement, who wrote to me: "You are the lead Nebraska dog in New York, and we need you back on your feet." What would historians say about the nice letter that came from Khrushchev's Americanized granddaughter? My brother Robert sent me a headline from the morning sports page about a former Danish cycling champion: "Sorensen Still Pedaling After All These Years." The support of family and friends made all the difference.

It strengthened me to remember the autumn of 1954 when JFK, in pain, on crutches, far from giving up and taking life easy, was willing to undergo major spinal surgery that he knew—in view of his other health problems—could kill him. While I was confronting the consequences of my stroke, I had family and close friends battling potentially fatal cases of cancer, not one of them giving in to despair—on the contrary, remaining full of hope and good cheer.

Knowing that hope was the most important medicine, Gillian promised me a convalescent stay in our Pound Ridge home upon my discharge from the hospital. There, I began to walk briefly, at first slowly, carefully, then to swim, and then to receive visits from my friends and their families. I also visited my courageous neighbor, *Superman* actor Christopher Reeve, whose spinal injury from a riding accident had left him virtually immobilized in a huge wheelchair. Despite his condition, his spirits were so high, his interest in stem cell and other medical research so deep, and even his daily exercise regimen so inspiring, that I made up my mind not to permit my own far less severe physical limitations to dominate the final chapter of my life.

After our return to New York City from Pound Ridge, progress came slowly. The days passed into weeks and I was still in pain; I was still homebound; 2001 passed into 2002 and I still could not see fully. I felt increasing self-pity. Decades earlier, my friend Howard Samuels, a defeated Democratic politician, seated next to me at a political dinner where he was not even introduced, remarked glumly that the parade had passed him by. I felt the same way. But finally I made up my mind that I was not going to remain a homebound patient. There were many parades in which I could still march. I began to venture out for walks, to my office, to my doctors' offices. I walked home two and a half miles from my periodic therapy visits to Mount Sinai, despite protests from my home health care aide, who said she was not permitted to let me out of her sight but that she could not walk that distance. Her aching feet were no doubt a contributing factor in her early transfer to another patient. Soon I resumed my longtime practice of walking to all my appointments and meetings.

In recent years, I have been narrowly missed by automobiles and cyclists, and occasionally I bump into pedestrians. I am, like Tennessee Williams's Blanche DuBois, "dependent upon the kindness of strangers," relying as well upon the familiarity of my routes and such order as I encounter in this often disorderly world. I have learned which stoplights are hard for me to find, which curbs are deeper than others, and which sidewalks are likely to be blocked by construction, crowds, or baby strollers. Reminding my law partners of the Prudent Man Doctrine that we all learned in law school, I told them, "You haven't seen a really prudent man until you watch me cross the streets of New York."

There was no single moment when I suddenly emerged from the dark tunnel of affliction into the bright sunlight of recovery, no dramatic awakening, no magic pill or moment of arrival. It was a long, gradual process. I did not recognize many of those tiny steps at the time, even as I remained skeptical about some therapy procedures; but they all helped.

As I write this, I am chagrined that I am devoting so much space to my personal illness in a book about truly momentous events like the Cuban missile crisis. But, sadly, the stroke has shaped the course of this last half decade; and I classify much of my recent past in terms of whether it preceded or followed that one event. For me, each new July 20, another year alive and well, seems like an accomplishment, particularly when I recall how that high, poststroke fever had, at the time, made six more days look doubtful, much less six more years—for which my loving family and friends, and a superb team of doctors, deserve credit.

After the stroke, most people assumed my productive days were over. During the 1960–1961 presidential transition I advised JFK that he should not become involved in White House decision making until January 20, that Eisenhower, even as a "lame-duck" president, was still president and entitled to exercise all the powers of that office until the day he left it. So long as I still have the powers of life, I told myself, I intend to exercise them.

Three years before the stroke, in 1998, when I reached the firm-established retirement age of seventy, I felt that my health and practice were both strong enough to continue; and I negotiated an agreement with the firm to remain a practicing partner for a few years more. After the stroke, I formalized my retirement. In accordance with firm procedures, I continued my association on an "of counsel" basis with the firm that had been my professional home for almost forty years, retaining an office and secretarial services, as do other retired partners.

After those first few poststroke months, when my thoughts were lethargic and lachrymose, I decided to write again, first attempting some doggerel for Max, the little son of my friends Meg and Dick Leone.

Six months after my stroke, I spoke publicly for the first time when I delivered a eulogy for my friend Cyrus Vance, a Kennedy administration colleague and Carter's secretary of state. Guided to the church pulpit, with only one misstep on the stairs, I had to keep my eyes fixed on my large-print text, lest I lose my place if I glanced up. Receiving a warm response from Cy's colleagues, family, and friends that day was the most encouraging welcome back to the public arena I could have wanted.

When Gillian's boss, UN Secretary-General Kofi Annan, invited us to attend the ceremony in Oslo where he was awarded his richly deserved Nobel Peace Prize, I obtained the permission of my doctors to make that trip, undoubtedly because my wife was accompanying me.

It was the first of many international flights that I was to make in the immediate poststroke years—to London, Paris, Copenhagen, Berlin, Wiesbaden, Havana, Stockholm, Vienna, Rome, Beijing, Singapore, Panama, and Honolulu, usually assisted by a traveling companion. It is much easier to cross an ocean than an airport, I learned. Four years after the stroke, as I continued to write, lecture, and travel around both the city and the world, two of my doctors used the same word to describe my recovery: "miraculous." "Doctor, with all due respect," I replied, "I would rather have my recovery depend on medicine than on miracles."

Because the stroke came out of the blue, without visible cause or warning, at a time when I was feeling healthy, I knew that it could happen again at any time, no matter how complete my recovery seemed, and this realization hung over my head like the sword of Damocles, suspended by a single strand of hair. Roughly three years after my stroke, I had another, this time a mini-stroke that caused me to faint briefly, falling to the ground on a walk home from the hospital through Central Park. I promptly sat up, embarrassed, continued walking to my home, and consulted my doctors the next day. A brain scan showed that this one had been caused by a blood vessel collapsing inward rather than leaking out. Meanwhile, I had been diagnosed with prostate cancer, a leaky heart valve, another melanoma, Lyme disease, and a variety of other ailments, calling to mind the line from Shakespeare's *Hamlet*: "when misfortune comes, it comes not as solitary spy but in legions."

When visiting my oncologist about my prostate cancer, I learned that I would be treated with external radiation beams, a relatively new life-saving technique made possible through research conducted on linear electron accelerators. That sounded familiar. Sure enough, forty-three years earlier, I had included in Kennedy's 1961 budget message, after due inquiry, $114 million for a new scientific breakthrough called the "linear electron accelerator" for high-energy research. You never know when a little bread cast upon the water will come back and feed you.

Long before my stroke, I had contemplated writing my life story. While still in the hospital, when I found that despite the stroke, my memory was intact, I began to think seriously about this book as a project on which to focus my time and efforts. I knew that President Ulysses S. Grant, suffering from cancer as he wrote his marvelous autobiography with the help of Mark Twain, raced to complete his manuscript before his death. This project has occupied my time and energy in a constructive and creative way, giving me more motivation to get up and go on.

I am writing this note to myself on July 20, 2007, the sixth anniversary of the stroke that changed my life. After nearly six years of work, my book is nearing completion. My schedule is full—writing or preparing for articles, speeches, and lectures; travel; too many doctors' appointments; and lots of talk and visits with friends, including some wonderful new friends, and with members of my family. Weather permitting, I try to swim a mile, or half a mile, each day. Yesterday a friend called me "a survivor who has coped." Surviving is not enough. I am deeply grateful that I have been given six more years since that day most doctors would not have given me six months. But, more importantly, I have put those six years to good use—to tell others, especially young Americans, about John Kennedy, to inspire others to public service, to use my remaining abilities to write and speak, to keep on learning, laughing, aspiring to new goals. I want to keep on surviving, coping, laughing, writing, speaking, serving—maybe another six years, maybe sixteen—watching my grandchildren and their children grow.

For fifty years, I had written everything with a pen—all my memos, speech drafts, books, and articles. Now, though I can read large print in a strong light, I cannot read handwriting, mine or anyone else's. That is why organizing and writing this book has taken six years—and helped keep me alive six years. Not a bad trade-off. It has also produced another reward: Drawing on the memories and files of my years with John Kennedy has helped bring a kind of closure after all this time—I have completed my service to him.

Epilogue:
Reflections, Regrets,
and Reconsiderations

Do you ever tire of talking about John F. Kennedy?" I am sometimes asked. "No," I reply, "not as long as you do not tire of asking."

My eleven years with JFK were unquestionably the cornerstone of my professional life; and the cornerstone of our relationship was mutual trust. JFK brought me into his inner circle, confiding in me secrets that—had I discussed them with others—might have done serious harm to his political career, his public image, or perhaps his marriage. Noting my role and relationship with him, some have sought to replicate it. Decades after I left the White House, President Clinton's indefatigable press secretary Mike McCurry told me: "Everyone who comes to Washington wants to be you." I have heard such sentiments more than once. It is flattering, but what they really want is to work for John F. Kennedy.

Jackie once told a reporter that I was like "a little boy in so many ways . . . he hero worships Jack." She was right; he was my hero. My loyalty was often called single-minded, and the most frequently quoted quip in the press was "When Jack's injured, Ted bleeds." To a considerable extent I often judged others, including journalists and biographers, based not on what they said about me, but on whether they fully, favorably, and accurately reported JFK's role, his accomplishments, and his contributions.

I do not take seriously those scholars who cite me as an example of an over-powerful presidential aide who had unaccountable influence. I made no decisions and wielded no dangerous power of any kind, less probably than Harry Hopkins, Sherman Adams, or Karl Rove. Moreover, my views were wholly compatible with those principles for which John F. Kennedy was elected and revered, especially peace around the world and justice here at home. To the extent that my suggestions, advice, and opinions influenced his decisions, I am proud as well as grateful. The world needs not only inspired leaders, but people to advise and assist them. I never confused which of us was the elected leader and which was the assistant. I understood the difference: advisors advise; assistants assist; counselors counsel; but ultimately, decisions are choices that only a president can and should make.

Some say that the age of giants is over, that the likes of Franklin Roosevelt and Winston Churchill and their peers are gone. It is true that Sarkozy is no de Gaulle, Mubarak is no Sadat, and George W. Bush is no John F. Kennedy. But knowing something of what it takes to reach the top, particularly in a democracy, I do not underestimate any man or woman who leads a nation, large or small.

In the decades since President Kennedy's death, some observers have said that my loyalty is excessive, still keeping his secrets, and still denying my full role. I do not think so. John F. Kennedy honed my political skills, judgment, and humor. The experience I gained by his side established my credentials for all of my post–White House endeavors. If he could see all that has happened since his death, I believe he would be pleased, but not surprised, by my continued dedication to his ideals.

In my early years with JFK, I learned not only loyalty but deference, reticence, becoming almost anonymous, never asserting, assuming, or bragging, for fear of antagonizing not only him, but also his father or his brother Robert, both of whom were fiercely protective of Jack's image and career. This reinforced traits of circumspection that had already been part of my upbringing, and they remain today central to my personal ethics, limiting what I assert or disclose even in this book—about JFK's personal life and mine.

Each of us helped shape the other's career to some extent. Over the years, noting his increasing leftward shift in the Senate and White House, many writers have speculated that I was the cause, reinforcing, perhaps even accelerating, his move to a more consistently idealistic liberalism. A *Washington Post* editorial, upon my departure from the White House, asserted, "Friends of Mr. Kennedy felt it no accident that the Senator moved steadily in a more liberal direction after the lean Nebraskan joined his staff." Perhaps.

At the time we met, he was wary of liberals, many of whom had been wary of him, his conservative father, and the family's friendship with Senator Joe McCarthy. "I'm not a liberal at all," JFK was quoted as saying shortly after I arrived. "I never joined the Americans for Democratic Action," an organization in which I had long participated. "I'm not comfortable with those people."

Yet even when it became apparent to him—as it must have early on—that I was a liberal who wanted far-reaching change, he became increasingly comfortable with me. Gradually, in the Senate, I crafted a more liberal perspective into some of his speeches, justifying liberal answers as best for the country and consistent with the principles of the national Democratic Party. Even then, his naturally cautious instincts kept him initially in a balanced, middle-of-the-road position that failed to satisfy many liberals, but did represent a change from his days in the House of Representatives.

In time, our views converged. When I first met his father in 1953, the Ambassador promptly said: "You could never write for me—you're too liberal. But you're fine for Jack." Jack's own political philosophy expanded with his political growth. He started from his father's house as a conservative, whose exposure, through nationwide travel and politics, to new problems, perspectives, and people, including me, gradually revised his priorities and principles, accommodating the more liberal positions I was urging upon him. I started from my father's house as a liberal idealist, who learned from Kennedy—and from my exposure to practical politics in the Senate and national campaign—that philosophical purity can be so unrealistic as to deny the incremental success necessary to implement my ideals. The point at which our philosophies converged was pragmatic "idealism without illusion," the art of the possible, the ability to compromise on tactics without compromising principles.

I left Washington a long time ago. Not a single day

has passed that I have not thought about JFK. For well over forty-five years, when I have referred in a conversation to "the president," I have meant only one person. Each November I am flooded with contrasting memories of Novembers gone by—his election in 1960, his peaceful resolution of the Cuban missile crisis in 1962, his murder in 1963.

Gillian has arranged in our home my cherished keepsakes from those special years: the engraved silver napkin ring that once sat on my table in the White House mess; the framed photograph that depicts the president and me departing the West Wing to a waiting limousine, a photograph that Jackie inscribed a few months after his death: "To Ted, who walked with the President so much of the way and who helped him climb to greatness." Most of all, I treasure the silver calendar of the month of October 1962, specially crafted for the president by Tiffany & Co. to highlight the thirteen days of the Cuban missile crisis, inscribed with both his initials and mine. He presented this same gift, individually inscribed with the recipient's initials, to each member of the ExComm.

Sometimes I am amused to imagine how he and Jackie would react to the absurdly large sums people pay at auctions for mementos from Kennedy lives. Mine are not for sale.

JFK's presidency was a time of high ideals; and those who remember it well still mourn its loss. After I saw Ethel at the Robert F. Kennedy Book Awards ceremony in 1991, she wrote me a lovely note: "Ted, I loved looking over at you and remembering your friendship with Jack and all the vitality, creativity and dreams of the New Frontier." More than one stranger has approached me on the streets of New York over the years, saying: "You bring back memories of wonderful times."

But sadly, in little more than forty years, the message from Washington has completely changed. It was all summed up in one of Garry Trudeau's *Doonesbury* cartoons. The strip's first panel showed the two lead characters joking in a bar, one saying, "Remember 'Ask not what your country can do for you, ask what you can do for your country.'" In the second panel, they laugh at this loudly, the whole box filled with "Ha Ha Ha." In the third, they have serious, downcast expressions, one asking, "What's so funny about that?" In the last panel, they both bury their faces and sob.

These days, I am weary of hearing commentators and would-be historians recite the cliché that JFK was all style, not substance. Overcoming the religious bigotry and other obstacles that seemed certain to make it impossible for him to be nominated, much less elected, required more than style. Peacefully obtaining the withdrawal of Soviet nuclear missiles from Cuba required more than style. Launching the Peace Corps, and the successful voyage of mankind to the moon, required more than style. Blazing the trail for equal rights after centuries of racial discrimination required more than style.

Less than fifty years later may be too early to say that John F. Kennedy was one of our greatest presidents. But I believe posterity will note that three of the most significant events in American history were the Cuban missile crisis, when he peacefully resolved the world's first nuclear confrontation, his reversal of this country's centuries-old subjugation of blacks, and his establishment of a robust space program enabling the human race to travel beyond the limits of Earth. That is the Kennedy legacy having an impact on all today.

What has happened to JFK's standards for dedication and innovation? The luster of public service has been tarnished by the increasing role of incompetent presidential cronies and corrupt lobbyists. Affirmative action has been reduced to patronizing photo opportunities for company brochures. His emphasis on the power of diplomacy and economic assistance has been replaced by a foreign policy increasingly reliant on the power of guns and threats.

A week after JFK's death, his widow wrote to Chairman Khrushchev:

> *You and he were adversaries, but [were] allied in determination that the world not be blown up. . . . While big men know the need for restraint, little men will sometimes be moved more by fear and pride.*

How sad that less than fifty years after Jackie wrote this, little men have mired this country in a mindless war.

Nor have JFK's standards of presidential oratory—and the standards of speech and English usage in the White House—been maintained. That's serious. The less often that Americans hear thoughtful public rhetoric, the more likely they are to be vulnerable to deceptive demagoguery. Kennedy's eloquence is deemed old-fashioned today. His style, say some, is too lofty in this hectic age of cynical sophistication.

Today presidential themes and drafts are edited by committee. Stirring phrases have been replaced by sound bites and applause lines. Majestic understatement has lost out to hyperbole. Presidents announce but do not inspire. Politicians are obsessed with making the nightly news instead of making history.

The trend away from Kennedy's core standards and ideals seems irreversible. But I still have faith in the ability of the American people to reverse those trends, just as JFK reversed a century of federal inattention to civil rights, reversed the increasing dangers of the nuclear arms race, reversed the long record of American failures in space exploration. Even his contest for the presidency in 1960 challenged what appeared to be irreversible prejudices against a Catholic in the White House. I still have faith in the American people to do the right thing.

It is because there are so few inspiring voices today that Kennedy's words continue to be quoted—and distorted. Immediately preceding the Iraq war, as the Bush neoconservatives sought historical precedents for their unprecedented invasion, President Bush quoted a line from Kennedy's televised address to the nation on the Cuban missile crisis. Secretary of Defense Donald Rumsfeld asserted that Kennedy's conduct of that crisis was "certainly preventative and pre-emptive." It was nothing of the kind. Kennedy specifically rejected the option of launching a preemptive strike against Cuba, a step, he knew, that would lead to tragic escalation.

President Kennedy urged American citizens to ask what they could do for their country. Later presidents demeaned the public sector and exalted private interest. Kennedy wanted to explore outer space for peaceful uses; Reagan and Bush have sought to militarize it. Kennedy asked young Americans to serve in an independent Peace Corps, now compromised by the infiltration of representatives from the military.

John Kennedy's administration was a golden era. Nevertheless, like James Madison writing at age seventy about his "more full and matured view" of his decades-earlier participation at the Constitutional Convention, I see the past more clearly now. It was not Camelot. President Kennedy made errors, like the Bay of Pigs. He suffered setbacks, like his failure to obtain passage of such key legislation as Medicare. He dismissed too few mediocre officials, placed too much emphasis on civil defense in his first year and too little on civil rights, had a blind spot on Cuba and a deaf ear on China. In his first eighteen months, he gave Vietnam too many military advisors and too little of his attention. His determination to build a missile force so powerful that it would never be challenged or used may well have exceeded that standard, allocating to those obscenely expensive but idle weapons systems countless billions that could better have been used in rebuilding our schools, hospitals, and cities. In retrospect, his belief in a strong executive, and his invocation of America's obligation to world freedom, may have set a dangerous precedent for successors less able to lead with reason and restraint.

Near the end of his first year, he quickly corrected some personnel errors. But his biggest personnel error, which he never corrected or publicly regretted, was to continue in office the tyrannical director of the Federal Bureau of Investigation, J. Edgar Hoover. Arbitrary and undemocratic, Hoover became too powerful and difficult for either President Kennedy or Attorney General Robert Kennedy to manage fully. Reportedly JFK later justified his retention of Hoover with the statement: "You don't fire God." Mr. Hoover may have thought he was God, but I was never under that illusion.

Some years ago I obtained my FBI file under the Freedom of Information Act, indicating, among other things, that "in 1948 [I was 20 years old then] he was exempted from military service" and "had indicated he would take a non-combatant job" . . . "described as 'very liberal.'" It contained reports on my pre–White House position, including my years in JFK's Senate office, my prior government employment, and my "liberal" activities in college and law school and my good character. None was inaccurate or unverified, contradicting popular opinion that the FBI files are full of misinformation.

Clearly my post–government service life continued to be of interest to the FBI. Political activities within the Democratic Party were recounted, as was a private visit with my wife and children to leftist businessman Cyrus Eaton's summer home in Nova Scotia; my attendance at a China conference at a university in Montreal, characterizing a Chinese professor at the university as "an unofficial spokesman for Peking," adding that I had urged the conference to approve a resolution favoring "efforts to arrange private meetings between Mainland China and the United States." It was obvious that some mail from abroad addressed to me at my law office was intercepted and reviewed before it reached my desk.

My file also contained a letter from a private citizen to Hoover expressing, at great length, his concern that I might be "using the President and his dignity to destroy the grass-roots anti-Communist tide"—a useful reminder of the many different winds that blew across the country in those days.

Sometimes I ponder the "what ifs" in my story, of my repeated good luck. Like Benjamin Franklin, I often reflect on "the constant felicity of my life."

I have said from the start that my best luck was the genes with which I was endowed—the genes of Grandmother Sorensen who taught those neighbor women around a candlelit table in that little sod house on the prairie, the genes of Grandfather Chaikin who took off to India in search of his brothers and the world. Had my father not made his bold speech at Grand Island Baptist College and been invited by Walter Locke to come to Lincoln's University of Nebraska and Unitarian Church, he might never have become a reform attorney general or produced a son interested in public service. Had my mother not been willing to "leave Main Street," marry my father, and accept a life of domesticity, I would not have inherited those wonderful Russian Jewish genes that mixed so well with my father's Danish heritage, and I would not have grown up with my four supportive, inspiring siblings. I am lucky now to have four wonderful children of my own, and to have shared almost four decades with my loving wife, Gillian.

Certainly the fact that as a much younger man from a distant plain, I had a chance to join John F. Kennedy during his tragically brief rise to fame, and share in that moment of history, can only be characterized as extraordinary good luck. I am lucky to have then pursued my law career in New York at Paul, Weiss. I am lucky to be an American. Yes, I am the luckiest man in the world.

But, like most Americans, I have also surmounted my share of sorrows—as a teenager, my mother's illness; the cruel loss of JFK, my mentor, best friend, and leader in 1963; and the loss, less than five years later, of his brother; and much later the loss of full use of my eyes in a stroke. All were hard blows. I persevere because I believe that the cause of a more peaceful and equitable world must be pursued, against all obstacles and setbacks. I am, I suppose, an inveterate optimist, holding fast to the belief that the good ultimately offsets the bad, and that success often follows failure. I have faith in the essential goodness of human beings, their willingness to use reason in negotiating with their enemies, and their ability to exercise wisdom in guiding a democracy.

Most of the events in my life that in hindsight appear to have been major turning points seemed natural at the time, some even routine. But what about those potential turning points that, in the words of historian A. J. P. Taylor, failed to turn? Had President Kennedy proceeded with his State Department reshuffle in the winter of 1962–1963, and made me his national security advisor, would I have succeeded or would I have been swallowed up by the recriminations over Vietnam? I like to think I would have succeeded had I been confirmed as President Carter's director of central intelligence; but perhaps I too would have been tarnished by that agency's continuing record of wrong predictions and wrongful conduct.

As the twentieth century drew to its close at the end of calendar year 2000, I reflected on my blessings. Just five months earlier, at a celebration exquisitely planned and executed by Gillian, surrounded by our family and friends, our daughter, Juliet, took my arm, and I escorted her down our garden path to exchange her wedding vows with Ben Jones. It was a beautiful August day.

As the new century dawned, I was healthy at age seventy-two. My law practice was busy, fascinating, and making a positive contribution to the world. I lived in a safe, harmonious, and prosperous country that was respected abroad, governed by the wisest of constitutions and a bipartisan foreign policy emphasizing multilateral diplomacy, collective security, and international law. Within less than one year, all that changed. A stroke had impaired my eyesight and endurance, effectively ending my law practice, and a new president disregarded the Constitution, international law, and world opinion, promulgating a foreign policy based primarily on military might, not right. Islamic extremist terrorists successfully bombed the two cities in which I had spent most of my adult life, creating a new atmosphere of fear and suspicion. How suddenly my world and my life changed!

In September 2005, one month after Hurricane Katrina devastated one of the great cities of the American South, with minimal response from Washington, I received an eloquent letter from my son Phil:

> *I can hear the depth of disappointment in your voice on the phone when you mention, however briefly, today's political landscape . . . How sad it must be for you to have played such a major role in what appeared to be a new direction—The New Frontier—with a mind that the ideas so engendered would bring forth expanded ideas and programs to build upon and never look back, only to see liars and cheats . . . slash and eliminate advances made by a formerly great society and . . . squander the goodwill and despoil the shining light of freedom for which our nation was known the world over.*

Nevertheless, surveying my many decades, I realize how fortunate I was that the years in which I became politically aware and involved were a time of civility, decency, and integrity.

The shift in this country away from JFK's ideals is not a recent phenomenon. As early as the 1970s it was all summed up by an encounter with my old friend, Senator Pat Moynihan, on the streets of New York one evening. When I mildly suggested how he might modify some of his neoconservative positions, he responded, "Why, Ted, you sound just like a 1960s liberal!" I still am a 1960s liberal, and I am saddened to find my idealism—and Kennedy's idealism—considered by many to be a relic from some bygone, irretrievable past. More and more Americans seem to be losing hope for better government, growing more cynical with each new disappointment.

Those who governed America in the first half of the twentieth century left to their successors a country more respected and secure abroad, and less racially, religiously, and economically divided at home than the country they had inherited from their predecessors. The current generation of American decision makers is the first to break the tradition of leaving to its heirs a better society than it had inherited. It will be delivering to the next generation a country, once almost universally respected, that is now deeply resented and feared; a country weakened by a widening gap between rich and poor; a world of growing terrorist violence, proliferating weapons of mass destruction, and increasing environmental degradation. Our current executive branch is dominated by people who do not believe in government, too many of whom consequently show no competence at governing, except for granting privileges and patronage to their cronies. It truly is time to pass the torch to a new generation of leaders.

In May 2004 an antiwar commencement address I delivered in upstate New York met with unrestrained hostility, not from students or faculty, but from parents and townspeople in the audience determined to drown out my comparison of President Bush's disastrous response to terrorism with President Kennedy's measured response to the Cuban missile crisis. They booed, hissed, and stomped their feet, demanding that I leave the stage or shut up. I neither left the stage nor stopped speaking, but instead held the microphone closer and delivered more loudly the facts I thought each new graduate ought to hear. The important question that day was not what happened to me—but what had happened to our country?

Later that same month, asked by my friend and fellow Nebraskan Bob Kerrey to deliver the commencement address at the New School University, where he is president, I tried to answer that question.

"There is a time to laugh," the Bible tells us, "and a time to weep." Today I weep for the country I love, the country I proudly served, the country to which my four grandparents sailed over a century ago with hopes for a new land of peace and freedom. I cannot remain silent when that country is in the deepest trouble of my lifetime.

The damage done to this country by its own misconduct in the last few months and years, to its very heart and soul, is far greater and longer lasting than any damage that any terrorist could possibly inflict upon us.

Last week, a family friend of an accused American guard in Iraq recited the atrocities inflicted by our enemies on Americans, and asked: "Must we be held to a different standard?" My answer is yes.

Our greatest strength has long been not merely our military might but our moral authority. Our surest protection against assault from abroad has been not all our guards, gates and guns, or even our two oceans, but our essential goodness as a people. Our richest asset has been not our material wealth but our values. . . . A European host recently asked me to "Tell us about the good America, the America when Kennedy was in the White House." "It is still

*a good America," I replied. "The American people
still believe in peace, human rights and justice;
they are still a generous, fair minded, open-minded
people."*

I do not want either my life or my story to conclude in
the shadow of despair generated by our current national
leadership; by our president's failures in leadership,
competence, and integrity; by the failures of the courts
and Congress to hold him constitutionally accountable
and the failure of my own party in opposition to meet
its obligations to oppose. But a one-man aberration,
however disastrous, is not permanent. A democracy is
by definition self-correcting. Here, the people are sov-
ereign. Inept political leaders can be replaced. Foolish
policies can be changed. *We the People* have learned
from our mistakes and misfortunes. A new leader and a
new era are on the way, and I will continue to fight, to
write, and to hope.

Less than half a century ago, John F. Kennedy
showed in fewer than a thousand days how quickly
our country's role in the world can be changed for the
better. Ultimately, I predict, the American people will
grow sick of cynically corrupt political hypocrisy and

turn on those who permit our security and international standing to erode, our environment to be despoiled, our fiscal problems to worsen, and our energy independence to wither. In time, they will return once again to the idealism of the New Frontier.

I'm still an optimist. I still believe that extraordinary leaders can be found and elected, that future dangers can be confronted and resolved, that people are essentially good and ultimately right in their judgments. I still believe that a world of law is waiting to emerge, enshrining peace and freedom throughout the world. I still believe that the mildest and most obscure of Americans can be rescued from oblivion by good luck, sudden changes in fortune, sudden encounters with heroes.

I believe it because I lived it.

Acknowledgments

Given the limitations of my eyesight in recent years, producing this book required a lot of help. I am indebted to my loving wife, Gillian, for her devoted support, unfailing encouragement, and patient endurance throughout this long journey. I am also grateful to many others: Marge Hornblower, my associate for more than forty years, for her friendship, wisdom, and invaluable research and editing assistance; Maria Gorecki, who kept the chapters moving with her flawless organizational and technical talents; my siblings, Robert, Ruth, and Phil; my friend and law partner, Jack O'Neil; Laurie Morris, my secretary at Paul, Weiss; my agent and friend, Mort Janklow; Tim Duggan, my patiently persuasive editor at HarperCollins, and assistant editor Allison Lorentzen; my friends Bob Bernstein, Mike Bessie, Jim Blight, Ralph Buultjens, Chris Jochnick, Carl Kaysen, Dick Leone, Bill Miller, and Jeff Shesol for generously giving their time and comments; and Caroline Kennedy, for graciously permitting me to quote my treasured letters from her mother. I also want to acknowledge my debt to my late friends Arthur Schlesinger and Mike Feldman for their good counsel; and to express my gratitude to those who undertook special research and other help when the need arose: Richard Baker, the historian of the U.S. Senate; Barbara Burbach; John Cavanaugh; Bob Ellis; Max Frankel; Chuck Googe; Norman Liss and Brian Andersson of the Ellis Island Restoration Commission; Ralph G. Martin; Associate Professor Elizabeth Nattale; Charles Niles at Boston University; Alicia Kolar Prevost; Don Walton; Lee White; Laura Olson and David Rubenstein, who assisted me with research thanks to the generosity of Northwestern University; Sharon Kelly, Megan Desnoyers, Maryrose Grossman, and Stephen Plotkin at the John F. Kennedy Presidential Library; Barbara Constable at the Lyndon B. Johnson Library; the Franklin D. Roosevelt Presidential Library; and the helpful staff of the University of Nebraska and the Nebraska Historical Society.

T.C.S.

Except as noted below, photographs are from the author's collection, family albums, and courtesy of the John F. Kennedy Presidential Library and Museum.

Insert: Page 3, bottom, photograph by and courtesy of Josiah C. Hornblower; page 4, top, photograph by F. Clyde Wilkinson; page 4, bottom, photograph by Paul Schutzer; page 6, bottom, photograph by Ollie Atkins; Page 7, bottom, photograph by Abbie Rowe; page 8, top, photograph by Art Rickerby, courtesy of Getty Images for *Life* magazine; page 9, top, photograph by George Silk, courtesy of Getty Images for *Life* magazine; page 10, top, photograph by Larry Norwalk; page 10, bottom, photograph by and courtesy of Josiah C. Hornblower; page 12, bottom, photograph by Joan Vitale Strong; page 13, top, photograph by and courtesy of Lisl Steiner; page 14, top, courtesy of Redux for the *New York Times*, photograph by Angel Franco; page 15, top, photograph by Joe Menahem; page 15, bottom, photograph by and courtesy of Lisl Steiner; page 16, top, courtesy of the *Lincoln Star Journal*, photograph by Eric Gregory; page 16, bottom, courtesy of AP Wide World Photos, photograph by Charles Rex Arbogast.

HARPER LUXE

THE NEW LUXURY IN READING

We hope you enjoyed reading
our new, comfortable print size and found it
an experience you would like to repeat.

Well — you're in luck!

HarperLuxe offers the finest in fiction and
nonfiction books in this same larger print size and
paperback format. Light and easy to read, HarperLuxe
paperbacks are for book lovers who want to see
what they are reading without the strain.

For a full listing of titles and
new releases to come, please visit our website:

www.HarperLuxe.com

HARPER LUXE